EDITORIAL EXCELLENCE IN BUSINESS PRESS PUBLISHING

The Neal Awards

The New York University Business Magazine Publishing Series

Business Journalism: Management Notes and Cases
Albert N. Greco

The Business Press Editor
Edgar A. Grunwald

Editorial Excellence in Business Press Publishing
The Neal Awards

EDITED BY FRANK C. TAYLOR AND ALBERT N. GRECO

NEW YORK UNIVERSITY
New York and London

Copyright © 1990 by New York University
All rights reserved
Manufactured in the United States of America

LIBRARY OF CONGRESS
Library of Congress Cataloging-in-Publication Data

Editorial excellence in business press publishing : the Neal
awards / edited by Frank C. Taylor and Albert N. Greco.
p. cm. — (The New York University business magazine
publishing series)
Includes index.
ISBN 0-8147-5762-6   ISBN 0-8147-8187-x pbk.
1. Business. 2. Business writing—Awards. I. Taylor, Frank C.,
1941–   . II. Greco, Albert N., 1941–   . III. Series.
HF5351.E27 1990
650—dc19   88-22481
                                                          CIP

New York University Press books are printed on acid-free paper,
and their binding materials are chosen for strength and durability.

Contents

Jesse H. Neal	vii
The Association of Business Press Publishers and the 1987 Neal Awards	xi
The Awards	xii
The Certificates of Merit	xv
The Chair of the 1987 Neal Board of Judges	xviii
The Board of Judges	xix
Foreword by Albert N. Greco	xxi
Introduction	xxiii

Classification A—Gross Advertising Revenues up to $2,000,000

Best in-depth analysis article or subject-related series: Raoul D. Edwards, Editor; Herbert Swartz, Contributing Editor; James H. Hyde II, Managing Editor; Laura M. Christiana, Managing Editor; *United States Banker,* for "Lender Liability"   1

Best staff-written editorial or subject-related series: Joseph C. Thompson, Editor; *Modern Jeweler,* for "Diamonds, Gold & Apartheid"   19

Best article or subject-related series of articles demonstrating excellence in reporting: Shelle S. Jensen, Associate Editor; David Federman, Executive Editor; Joseph C. Thompson, Editor; Claude Zajakowski, Art Director; *Modern Jeweler,* for "The Refashioning of Zale"   25

Best regularly featured department, section or column: Ronald B. Mack, M.D., Department Editor; Jeffrey H. Forster, Editor; A. Michael Velthaus, Art Director; Karen J. Ward, Copy Editor; Ingrid A. Lang, Editorial Assistant; *Contemporary Pediatrics,* for "Poison Pen"   55

Best how-to article or subject-related series: Vince Zortman, Associate Editor; Carol Gunther, Graphic Art Director; *Pork '86,* for "Hands-on Options Strategies"   71

Classification B—Gross Advertising Revenues $2,000,000 to $4,000,000

Best in-depth analysis article or subject-related series: Murray Forseter, Editor; Steve Malanga, Executive Editor; Faye Brookman, Senior Editor; Rick Gallagher, Associate Editor; Nanci Brickman, Associate Editor; Michael Hartnett, Associate Editor; *Chain Store Age General Merchandise Trends,* for "Sears: The Family Store"   81

Best staff-written editorial or subject-related series: Derek Cassels, Editor; *The Medical Post,* for "The Curious Case of Dr. William Jory"   107

Best article or subject-related series of articles demonstrating excellence in reporting: Charles Haberstroh, Editor in Chief; Kevin Hannigan, Features Editor; Ann Przybyla, Technical Editor; Charles Morris, Midwest Editor; Dianne Taylor, Contributing Editor; Scott Stephens, Art Director; *Food Engineering,* for "State of the Food Industry"   117

Best regularly featured department, section or column: Sigrid Nagle, Associate Editor; Jean Arbeiter, Departmental Editor; Marianne Dekker Mattera, Managing Editor; James A. Reynolds, Editor; *RN,* for "Patient's Advocate"   139

Best how-to article or subject-related series: Rosemarie Kitchin, Editor; Philip Katcher, Research Editor; John Wirebach, Senior News & Feature Editor; Gail Krueger-Nicholson, Senior Editor; *Automotive Marketing,* for "Retail Sales Training"   147

Classification C—Gross Advertising Revenues More Than $4,000,000

Best in-depth analysis article or subject-related series: Ethelyn N. Fuller, Senior Editor; Lucy H. Labson, Executive Editor; Robert L. Edsall, Deputy Editor; Clayton Raker Hasser, Editor; Judith A. Cash, Managing Editor; Elizabeth R. Pollack, Art Director; *Patient Care,* for "Nutrition and Primary Care"   169

Best staff-written editorial or subject-related series: D. P. Eigo, Editor; Scott E. Henjum, Managing Editor; Steven C. Taylor, Art Director; Peggy S. Navarre, Associate Art Director; Marcie Tibbling, Copy Editor; *Fleet Owner,* for "What the Hell, I Can Always Drive a Truck!"   187

Best article or subject-related series of articles demonstrating excellence in reporting: Marcia Ruff, Managing Editor; *Motor,* for "Toxic Waste"   193
and
Beverly Russell, Editor in Chief; Karin Tetlow, Business Roundup Editor; Wolfgang Hoyt, Photographer; Colin Forbes, Art Director; Maryann Levesque, Art Director; *Interiors,* for "American Express Headquarters"   213

Best regularly featured department, section or column: Ralph Emmett Carlyle, Senior Writer; Willie Schatz, Washington Bureau Manager; David R. Brousell, News Editor; Parker Hodges, Managing Editor; Karen Gullo, Assistant News Editor; Kenneth Surabian, Art Director; *Datamation,* for "Behind the News"   225

Best how-to article or subject-related series: Lucy H. Labson, Executive Editor; Clayton Raker Hasser, Editor; Robert L. Edsall, Deputy Editor; Judith A. Cash, Managing Editor; Elizabeth R. Pollack, Art Director; Diann Peterson, Senior Copy Editor; *Patient Care,* for "Emergency Handbook '86"   243

Jesse H. Neal

Jesse H. Neal (1874–1958) was a dedicated man who served the common good of business publishing and left an extra-large imprint on it.

He spent his early professional years in advertising agency work in Ohio. As chairman of the Cleveland Advertising Club's Vigilance Committee, he led Ohio to be the first state to enact the Printers' Ink Model Statute into law. In 1916, while engaged on a special assignment for the United Publishers Corporation (forerunner of Chilton Company), he was chosen to head the embryo organization, Associated Business Publications, the precursor of today's Association of Business Publishers. This group, whose roots reached back to 1906 as the loosely knit Federation of Trade Press Associations, was being transformed into a unified body and needed an experienced and courageous man as its first managing executive. Jesse Neal proved to be that man, in abundant measure. He served as the new organization's managing director from 1916 to 1926, when he resigned with the belief that his mission had been achieved.

He started at less than scratch—without office, staff, program, or roadmap—and with a treasury boasting $112.73. From his own resources he financed a month's rent on a hole-in-the-wall office, a typewriter, and letterheads. He breathed life and vigor into a proud and productive cooperative organization. Today's members of ABP who knew Jesse Neal remember him as a forceful and colorful personality, a man of ideals and integrity, a man to respect. The association he brought through adolescence honored him most appropriately by giving his name to its prized Jesse H. Neal Editorial Achievement Awards, given annually since 1955. The growth in the number of entries for these awards from 22 in 1955 to a record-breaking 774 in 1989, testifies to the growth of the industry, the prestige of the awards, and the long-lasting memory of the man for whom they were named.

WILLIAM K. BEARD
ABP President (1950–1964)

The Association of Business Publishers and the 1987 Neal Awards

Specialized business publications have been an expanding force in the history of the United States for over three hundred years. During their development, they have established the tradition of providing service to the business community on two levels. First, they are the unique and primary source of highly specialized technical, professional and economic information for every kind of business audience. Beyond that, they strive to act as the conscience of the field they serve.

One of the main functions of the business press is to enlighten, stimulate and, in many instances, to move the reader to action. Throughout the years its influence has shaped the paths of countless individuals and companies; it has stimulated them to make things happen, to accelerate change, to help or hinder, to make or break. It is to acknowledge these contributions on the part of business press editors that the Association of Business Publishers (ABP) established the Jesse H. Neal Awards thirty-three years ago.

The Neal Competition, supervised by the association's Editorial Committee, is held annually to reward editorial excellence in audited, independent business publications. The purpose of the competition is to further the high standards of editorial achievement championed by Jesse H. Neal, the association's first managing director.

In most cases, the recipients of the Neal Awards have spent many months and many thousands of dollars to research and write these stories, which represent achievement of the highest goal of the business press: to educate and inform the business, professional and industrial community. In every issue of every business publication, editors are attempting to keep readers abreast of the changes, trends and problems in their industry. The Association of Business Publishers extends appreciation to its member editors, who make the business press the powerful medium that it is today.

The entries were submitted in one of three classifications, based upon the publication's gross advertising revenue. All material was published in English in an issue bearing the cover date of November 1, 1985, through October 31, 1986.

The judging was conducted on two levels. All entries were first submitted to a peer screening board composed of ABP member editors. Their selections were then judged by a panel consisting of media experts and journalism educators. The Board of Judges labored a day and a half to select the award and certificate winners listed herein from the 676 entries submitted in the 1987 competition. Judging was based on the following criteria: journalistic enterprise, extent of service to the field and editorial craftsmanship.

The Awards

Classification A

Gross advertising revenues up to $2,000,000

CATEGORY 1

Best in-depth analysis article or subject-related series
Raoul D. Edwards
Herbert Swartz
James H. Hyde II
Laura M. Christiana
United States Banker
Lender Liability

CATEGORY 2

Best staff-written editorial or subject-related series
Joseph C. Thompson
Modern Jeweler
Diamonds, Gold & Apartheid

CATEGORY 3

Best article or subject-related series of articles demonstrating excellence in reporting
Shelle S. Jensen
David Federman
Joseph C. Thompson
Claude Zajakowski
Modern Jeweler
The Refashioning of Zale

CATEGORY 4

Best regularly featured department, section or column
Ronald B. Mack, M.D.
Jeffrey H. Forster
A. Michael Velthaus
Karen J. Ward
Ingrid A. Lang
Contemporary Pediatrics
Poison Pen

CATEGORY 5

Best how-to article or subject-related series
Vince Zortman
Carol Gunther
Pork '86
Hands-on Options Strategies

Classification B

Gross advertising revenues $2,000,000 to $4,000,000

CATEGORY 1

Best in-depth analysis article or subject-related series
Murray Forseter
Steve Malanga
Faye Brookman
Rick Gallagher
Nanci Brickman
Michael Hartnett
Chain Store Age GMT
Sears: The Family Store

CATEGORY 2

Best staff-written editorial or subject-related series
Derek Cassels
The Medical Post
The Curious Case of Dr. William Jory

CATEGORY 3

Best article or subject-related series of articles demonstrating excellence in reporting
Charles Haberstroh
Kevin Hannigan
Ann Przybyla
Charles Morris
Dianne Taylor
Scott Stephens
Food Engineering
State of the Food Industry

CATEGORY 4

Best regularly featured department, section or column
Sigrid Nagle
Jean Arbeiter
Marianne Dekker Mattera
James A. Reynolds
RN
Patient's Advocate

CATEGORY 5

Best how-to article or subject-related series
Rosemarie Kitchin
Philip Katcher
John Wirebach
Gail Krueger-Nicholson
Automotive Marketing
Retail Sales Training

Classification C

Gross advertising revenues more than $4,000,000

CATEGORY 1

Best in-depth analysis article or subject-related series
Ethelyn N. Fuller
Lucy H. Labson
Robert L. Edsall
Clayton Raker Hasser
Judith A. Cash
Elizabeth R. Pollack
Patient Care
Nutrition and Primary Care

CATEGORY 2

Best staff-written editorial or subject-related series
D. P. Eigo
Scott E. Henjum
Steven C. Taylor
Peggy S. Navarre
Marcie Tibbling
Fleet Owner
What the Hell, I Can Always Drive a Truck!

CATEGORY 3

Best article or subject-related series of articles demonstrating excellence in reporting
Marcia Ruff
Motor
Toxic Waste

and

Beverly Russell
Karin Tetlow
Wolfgang Hoyt
Colin Forbes
Maryann Levesque
Interiors
American Express Headquarters

CATEGORY 4

Best regularly featured department, section or column
Ralph Emmett Carlyle
Willie Schatz
David R. Brousell
Parker Hodges
Karen Gullo
Kenneth Surabian
Datamation
Behind the News

CATEGORY 5

Best how-to article or subject-related series
Lucy H. Labson
Clayton Raker Hasser
Robert L. Edsall
Judith A. Cash
Elizabeth R. Pollack
Diann Peterson
Patient Care
Emergency Handbook '86

The Certificates of Merit

Classification A

Gross advertising revenues up to $2,000,000

CATEGORY 1

Best in-depth analysis article or subject-related series
Tom Quaife
Carol Gunther
Pork '86
Drug Residues: The Real Issue

CATEGORY 2

Best staff-written editorial or subject-related series
David R. Stone
Mark L. Dlugoss
Molly Reeves
American Automatic Merchandiser
Do Vendors Need Tamper Resistant Packaging?

CATEGORY 3

Best article or subject-related series of articles demonstrating excellence in reporting
Steve Hull
William Demers
James Kitfield
Madeleine Carroll
Military Logistics Forum
What's Wrong with the Army?

CATEGORY 4

Best regularly featured department, section or column
Richard Hefter
Mike Thompson
Kerry Lydon
Susan Whitehurst
Joan Ducey
Glen Luensman
Security
Equipment Focus

CATEGORY 5

Best how-to article or subject-related series
Patricia Dwyer Schull, RN, MSN
Tony DeCrosta
Maryanne Wagner
Maureen N. Pross
Jake Smith
Gretchen H. Tara
NursingLife
Special "How-to" Issue

Classification B

Gross advertising revenues $2,000,000 to $4,000,000

CATEGORY 1

Best in-depth analysis article or subject-related series
David Rowe
Tom Adams
Jack Schember
David Allen Shaw
Mary Hughes
Video Store
Freedom of Choice?

CATEGORY 2

Best staff-written editorial or subject-related series
Jerry Whitaker
Brad Dick

Carl Bentz
Dan Torchia
Paula Janicke
Dawn Hightower
Broadcast Engineering
Same Song, Umpteenth Verse

CATEGORY 3

Best article or subject-related series of articles demonstrating excellence in reporting
Larry Jabbonsky
Jeanne Lukasick
Robert J. Smith
Ian C. Blair
Dean L. Holstein
Andrew Patapis
Beverage World
True Grit

CATEGORY 4

Best regularly featured department, section or column
Jean Arbeiter
Marianne Dekker Mattera
James A. Reynolds
RN
Legally Speaking

CATEGORY 5

Best how-to article or subject-related series
E. J. Muller
Jay Gordon
Distribution
Wanted/Found: Tomorrow's Logistics Pro

and

Jim Cory
Richard L. Carter
Hardware Age
Retail Insurance Guide

Classification C

Gross advertising revenues more than $4,000,000

CATEGORY 1

Best in-depth analysis article or subject-related series
Larry Frederick
Arthur Owens
Merian Kirchner
Nancy J. Wall
Polly Miller
Roger Dowd
Medical Economics
Private Practice in 1995

CATEGORY 2

Best staff-written editorial or subject-related series
Jim Winsor
Heavy Duty Trucking
National Truck Driver License: It's Long Overdue

CATEGORY 3

Best article or subject-related series of articles demonstrating excellence in reporting
Russell Shor
William George Shuster
Jewelers' Circular-Keystone
Diamond Misgrading: Problems, Solutions, Retribution

CATEGORY 4

Best regularly featured department, section or column
Thomas R. Fisher
Richelle J. Huff
Samuel G. Shelton
Virginia Chatfield
David A. Morton
John Morris Dixon

Progressive Architecture
Technics Department

CATEGORY 5

Best how-to article or subject-related series

Jane Victoria Smith
Deborah Holmes
Sally Maurer
Jewelers' Circular-Keystone
Gem Synthetics: Options & Outlook

The Chair of the 1987 Neal Board of Judges

Professor Henry F. Schulte
S. I. Newhouse School of Public Communications
Syracuse University

The Board of Judges

Caroline Dow, Ph.D.: assistant professor, Indiana University School of Journalism; head, Magazine Division of Association for Education in Journalism and Mass Communication; former magazine and newspaper reporter.

Derry Eynon: associate professor, Department of Technical Journalism, Colorado State University; former business magazine writer and editor.

James K. Gentry: chairman of Editorial Department and director of Business Journalism Program, University of Missouri School of Journalism; former newspaper editor and reporter.

Albert N. Greco, Ed.D.: director of Business Press Publishing Studies at New York University's Gallatin Division.

George Harmon: associate professor, Medill School of Journalism, Northwestern University; former assistant managing editor and financial editor, *Chicago Daily News*.

Walter A. Kleinschrod: editorial consultant, author, journalist; past chair, ABP Editorial Committee; former business press editor, Geyer-McAllister Publications, for thirty-two years.

Susan E. Meyer; president and publisher, Roundtable Press, Inc.; writer and editor; former editorial director of art and design publishing group, Billboard Publications.

Kathryn Klassen News: adjunct assistant professor and head, magazine sequence, Temple University; former managing editor, *Holiday, Réalités, Spring*.

Fred K. Paine, Ph.D.: former head, Drake University Magazine Journalism Program; former professor of journalism, Kent State University; writer, editor.

Byron T. Scott: Meredith professor of magazine journalism, director of Service Journalism Program, University of Missouri-Columbia; former magazine writer and editor, New York and Chicago.

James Irwin Smith: senior coordinator, Journalism Program at Humber College of Applied Arts and Technology, Toronto; former business press editor for twenty years.

Frank C. Taylor, Ed.D.: executive director, Business Press Educational Foundation; writer; former bureau chief, South America, McGraw-Hill World News.

John Tebbel: professor emeritus, Department of Journalism, New York University; writer and editor; member, Publishing Hall of Fame.

Elizabeth S. Yamashita, Ph.D.: director, School of Journalism and Mass Communications, University of Oklahoma; editorial consultant; former business writer and editor.

Foreword

In January 1987 I was asked by the Association of Business Publishers to be a judge for its annual Jesse H. Neal Editorial Achievement Award. The Neal Awards have long been viewed by industry leaders and journalism professors in the United States and Canada as the most coveted prize that could be bestowed on a business press editor or reporter, this industry's equivalent of the Pulitzer Prize.

The first article I read and evaluated was "The Refashioning of Zale," and I was struck immediately with the fact that this "case" was better than any study I ever read in graduate school. As I continued to go through over ninety submissions, I came to believe that, from the point of view of style and content, these were first-rate articles covering a multitude of business, professional, and academic areas, from trenchant feature articles to acerbic, finely tuned editorials.

At the conclusion of the two-day judging, I asked William O'Donnell, the president of the Association of Business Publishers and one of the key leaders in this diverse, dynamic industry, if the Gallatin Division could publish the Neal Award–winning articles in a book. I felt that such a book would be an invaluable resource for editors and reporters seeking to improve their skills. In addition, journalism professors could use such a book as a supplemental reader in a variety of feature article, editing, and reporting classes.

Editorial Excellence in Business Press Publishing is the result of months of discussion and work on the part of Bill O'Donnell and his associates at ABP. This book contains slightly edited versions of the 1987 Neal winners. Due to various production restrictions, we were unable to duplicate the four-color photographs, drawings, and so forth, that originally appeared in the articles, and, accordingly, editorial references to these illustrations had to be deleted in this book.

These articles cover an impressive array of subject areas, from detailed medical and health care topics to toxic wastes to options strategies. I believe that general readers and specialists alike will find this book to be a rich source of stimulating ideas and opinions. I hope you enjoy these articles as much as I did.

ALBERT N. GRECO
New York University

Introduction

In the old days when journalism professors wanted to show their students what excellence in magazine writing was all about, they'd point only to consumer magazines. Now, increasingly, they come to class with articles from specialized business publications and say, "Here, look at that!"

Business press editors place great emphasis on editorial quality. They have to. They write for a select group of knowledgeable professionals and business decision-makers who depend on them for critical information and in-depth analysis of the news. Every word counts to them. Fluff won't do; neither will boring writing. They want what they read to be snappy, creative, and interesting.

Journalists working for the specialized business press work hard. Few of them start as experts in the fields they cover, so they have to be expert learners. They keep at it throughout their careers to keep abreast of the fast-moving developments affecting their readers.

Their diligence has its rewards. Their ability to identify new trends and explain technological advances and problems often makes them important news sources for the general media. Their objectivity, professionalism, and ethics establish them as the conscience of the sectors they cover. Most importantly, unlike most other journalists, they have the satisfaction of knowing that their work truly makes a positive contribution to their readers' careers and businesses and to the health of the nation's economy.

The Association of Business Publishers created the Jesse H. Neal Editorial Achievement Awards in 1955 to recognize the most outstanding examples of enterprise, craftsmanship, and service in reporting and writing of the editorial staffs of its more than seven hundred member publications. This book is a compilation of the sixteen articles that a panel of top journalism educators and writing experts judged worthy of receiving the award in 1987. Its purpose is to honor the achievements of the individual and teams of writers who won this highest distinction in the business press and to share their excellent work with their colleagues and the next generation of business journalists.

FRANK C. TAYLOR

Lender Liability

Raoul D. Edwards
EDITOR

Herbert Swartz
CONTRIBUTING EDITOR

James H. Hyde II
MANAGING EDITOR

Laura M. Christiana
MANAGING EDITOR

"Lender Liability" was the first in-depth analysis of a serious new threat to the banking industry: borrower lawsuits against lenders. The article explained how lender liability can affect the lending policies and practices of financial institutions and interpreted the new risks involved. For the first time, senior management had a single source for advice on how to protect themselves and their institutions against litigation by borrowers.

United States Banker serves senior management in the field of finance and banking. "Lender Liability" first appeared in the May 1986 issue of *United States Banker,* published by Kalo Communications, Inc. © 1986. Reprinted with permission.

No bank should be more aware of how painful the sting of lender liability can be than Bank of America. The nation's second largest bank, BofA currently faces a number of lawsuits brought by borrowers and other interested parties. In just four of these cases, plaintiffs are seeking damages totaling an astounding 20 percent of the bank's $2.56 billion market value (or 10 percent of its estimated net worth).

THE FOUR CASES IN POINT

For decades, Bank of America had been lending to the Jewell family, owners of an apple orchard in Sonoma County, California. In a series of convoluted events starting in 1976, certain of the borrowed funds were invested by the Jewells in the O'Connell Company, a local apple-drying plant. Then, in 1980, BofA shut off the credit tap. The Jewells went out of business and later sued the bank. Since that time, the following events have occurred:

■ In 1985, the Jewell family and the O'Connell shareholder won a jury award of $47 million (for which the bank has no outside insurance coverage). Of that, $26 million was in punitive damages. The trial judge refused to set aside the verdict or to order a new trial. He did, however, reduce the punitive damages to $6 million (which, if upheld on appeal, would still be the largest such award in the history of the state). Appeals have been filed by both sides (the plaintiffs are seeking restoration of the original punitive damages), but no decision is expected before 1987. In the meantime, BofA has been hit by a real estate lien and is incurring interest costs of $6,000 per day.

■ The O'Connell Company has brought a separate antitrust action in federal court against the bank—even though O'Connell never did business with the bank during the time in question. If successful, treble damages are possible and the judgment could reach a staggering $200 million.

■ Attorney Barry Cappello of Capello & Foley of Santa Barbara, counsel to the Jewells, has initiated another related suit against BofA seeking $100 million in damages. Brought on behalf of an apple cooperative (which included the Jewells) in Sonoma County, the suit involves many of the same issues pondered in the Jewell case.

■ No doubt spurred by his earlier successes, Cappello has brought an unrelated $100 million suit against the bank on behalf of McNamara & Peepe, a lumber company in northern California.

Such is the magnitude of the threat of lender liability to Bank of America in particular. But BofA is not alone. "Cases are coming in from all over the country," says Cappello. "I only accept about one case in 10—just the horror stories—so I'm deadly serious when I sue and for the amount I put on a case." Adds attorney Tom Thomas of Kolodey & Thomas in Dallas: "I get at least two calls a day from everywhere." (Thomas won the first big lender-liability case.)

In fact, so quickly spreading is the stain of lender liability that unless checked or prevented by a change in lending practices (see "An Action Checklist for the Lender" on page 12), it could shake the very foundation of banking. After all, the business of banking is the business of lending money. As such, it can be fraught with hazards: if loans aren't repaid, banks are the losers. Now, add to that the new dangers posed by lender liability.

Practitioners rightly describe bank lending

as an art. In the words of Peter Magnani, spokesman for Bank of America, the art of lending involves "having that sixth sense to know who is creditworthy." Lending, therefore, must be inherently selective. Unlike straight selling, in which vendors don't really know many of their customers, and the transaction is complete when the buyer pays, lending involves the borrower's fulfillment of the bank's faith in him: He must repay. He must comply with the bank's expectancy under the terms of the loan.

Lending used to appear so simple. The borrower was screened, then granted credit if worthy. If the loan soured, the bank decided whether to call it, reschedule it or work out

Anatomy of a Lender-Liability Case

For many years, Knoxville-based K.M.C. operated a wholesale and retail grocery business throughout Tennessee. In 1979, the company needed new financing and approached the Irving Trust Company.

A deal was hammered out and a $3 million line of credit was issued to the company. In return, the bank took a security interest in K.M.C.'s accounts receivables. In 1980, the line of credit was increased to $3.5 million.

Then, on March 1, 1982, K.M.C. requested $800,000 from the bank. Irving refused, notwithstanding that the new funding would still have left the company's total borrowings below the $3.5 million approved line of credit. Shortly thereafter, K.M.C. collapsed.

Knoxville attorney William Vines III, of Butler, Vines, Babb & Threadgill, brought suit in federal court on behalf of K.M.C. He contended that the bank should have given his client notice it was about to cut off credit; that such action by the bank was a breach of good faith; that good faith was part of the credit arrangement, even though the exact words did not appear in the loan agreement; and, finally, that the bank's breach of good faith caused the company to fail.

Irving Trust admitted the requirement of good faith — despite the absence of that term in the documents. But it contended it had exercised good faith. It further maintained that its conduct was reasonable, since K.M.C. was about to collapse regardless of what the bank did. As a result, the bank argued, it could not be responsible for the failure.

The jury, however, sided with K.M.C. and awarded damages of $7.5 million. The U.S. Sixth Circuit Court affirmed the award. In her opinion, Judge Cornelia G. Kennedy stated:

"There is ample evidence belying Irving's characterization that on March 1 [it] . . . was faced with a sudden crisis of unprecedented proportions. On this basis alone, the jury could have found [was right in finding] that Irving did not fulfill its obligation of good faith performance to K.M.C. when it cut off financing without prior notice.

"Whether or not the $800,000 requested would have been sufficient to cover all of K.M.C.'s outstanding checks, Sarokin's [Irving's loan officer] abrupt refusal to advance funds to K.M.C. on March 1, amounted to a unilateral decision on his part to wind up the company . . . from which the jury could have concluded that . . . his action was arbitrary and capricious.

"If Irving had given K.M.C. 30 days, 7 days, even 48 hours notice, we would be facing a different case."

Thus, the doctrine of lender liability was recognized and sanctioned by a federal circuit court.

What Some Judges Have Said

State National Bank of El Paso v. Farah Manufacturing Company was the case that first brought lender-liability headline status. Some excerpts from the opinion of the Texas Eighth Court of Appeals follow:

"[The attorney for the bank] admitted that the parties to the loan agreement were legally obligated to deal in good faith with one another.

"Economic duress [business coercion] may be evidenced by forcing a victim to choose between distasteful and costly situations, i.e., bow to duress or face bankruptcy, loss of credit rating, or loss of profits from a venture.

"There is evidence that the loan to FMC [Farah] was not in default at the time the warnings were given to the lenders. . . .

"However, there was no circumstance to authorize the manner in which the warnings to declare default were made. This is particularly true when given the evidence that the lenders previously had either decided not to declare a default which would result in FMC's bankruptcy or reached no decision on the matter.

"The lenders accrued an unjust benefit merely by their efforts to insure that FMC would be managed by those who had been 'previously approved'. They had the power to injure the business and property interests of FMC upon the issuance of their warnings. The evidence is sufficient that injury was sustained by virtue of the lender's pressure to have . . . others manage FMC and to have Farah excluded from active management.

"As admitted by the lenders, legitimate options were at their disposal. Such options, however, were not pursued. The very nature of their warnings constitutes duress. It caused Farah and other board members to do what they would not have otherwise done. . . . Thus, the evidence establishes that the elements of an actionable claim of duress have been met.

". . . The evidence is legally sufficient that the lender interfered with FMC's business relations, its election of directors and officers and its protected rights.

" 'It is true that the evidence does not establish to a mathematical certainty the exact amount of damages caused by appellant alone, nor does it separate with exact accuracy the damage caused by appellant from that caused by others . . . ; but the law does not require such exactness. Where the evidence establishes that a plaintiff has suffered substantial damages, he is not to be denied a recovery merely because others than the defendant contributed to bring about his loss and he is unable to show distinctly the amount of damages contributed by each tortfeasor. All that the law requires is that the best evidence of which a case is susceptible be produced, and if from such evidence the amount of damages caused by the defendant

---

another solution. But over the last two years, this so-called art form has evolved from a simplistic perspective—minimalism—into one far more complex. The perils are becoming ever greater, as borrowers' lawyers across the land begin to explore lender liability frontiers.

The parameters of these new frontiers to date encompass six major common-law grounds for litigation against banks:

- Fraud/Duress
- Breach of Fiduciary Duty
- Breach of Contract
- Breach of Good Faith/Fair Dealing

can be inferred or estimated by the jury with reasonable certainty, then the amount of such damages is for the jury.'"

In the case that has been a major thorn in Bank of America's side, the Jewells and the O'Connell shareholder against the bank, Judge Laurence K. Sawyer said in his "Order Denying Judgement Notwithstanding Verdict and conditional Order Granting New Trial":

"The wrongful conduct of the Bank arose out of a series of complicated financial transactions which occurred over the period of almost a decade. In the handling of these financial transactions, the Bank . . . exhibited a conscious disregard for the rights of the parties [though] . . . there is also ample evidence that some bank officials, especially at the local level, continued to support the business activities of the parties and advanced money through hard economic times.

"The defendant . . . deceived the parties with respect to the making of a long-term loan. . . .

"The evidence shows . . . . the wrongful conduct of the defendant [Bank]. . . .

"The court has considered the deterrent effect of the reduced amount of punitive damages in light of the defendant's financial condition. The Court is of the opinion that a total punitive award of $6,000,000 will not be absorbed by the Bank with little or no discomfort. Although the punitive award is only about one-tenth of 1 percent of the bank's net worth, the award is approximately 1¾ percent of the net income of the Bank. Given the nature of the conduct described above, the Court is of the opinion that the award as modified herein will properly punish and deter the defendant."

In her opinion in *K.M.C. Co., Inc. v. Irving Trust Company,* United States Court of Appeals for the Sixth Circuit Judge Cornelia G. Kennedy ruled:

"The essence of the Magistrate's instruction to the jury was that there is implied in every contract an obligation of good faith; that this obligation may have imposed on Irving a duty to give notice to K.M.C. before refusing to advance funds under the agreement up to the $3.5 million limit; and that such proper notice would be required if necessary to the proper execution of the contract, unless Irving's decision to refuse to advance funds without prior notice was made in good faith and in the reasonable exercise of its discretion. . . .

". . . . We find that the Magistrate's instructions were an accurate statement of the applicable law. . . . 'If a notice was requisite to its proper execution, a covenant to give such notice will be inferred, for any other construction would make the contract unreasonable, and place one of the parties entirely at the mercy of the other.' [Then citing UCC #2-309 comment 8] ('The application of principles of good faith and sound commercial practice normally call for such notification of the termination of a going contract relation-

- Breach of Joint-Venture Agreement
- Indemnity.

Fraud/Duress

The charge of fraud—beyond what could be termed outright cheating—is a major thrust in lender-liability suits. Questions emerging from it strike at the very heart of lending: Did the bank fully reveal to the borrower why it was continuing to lend? Or why it refused to lend? Was the bank really trying to better protect its security—or gain more security? Did the bank tell the borrower about dealings it had with competing borrowers? Did the bank make

ship as will give the other party reasonable time to seek a substitute arrangement.')

"We agree with the Magistrate that just as Irving's discretion whether or not to advance funds is limited by an obligation of good faith performance, so too would be its power to demand repayment. The demand provision is a kind of acceleration clause, upon which the Uniform Commercial Code and the courts have imposed limitations of reasonablenes and fairness.

". . . [Irving] suggests . . . that before liability can be imposed, the proof must establish not only abuse of discretion but also bad faith, which it defines as synonymous with dishonesty. . . . We do not understand . . . bad faith as well as abuse of discretion, . . . as a general statement of law. We conclude that the abuse of discretion standard upon which the issue of liability was decided in the trial below was the correct one to apply in this instance.

". . . There must at least be some subjective basis upon which a reasonable loan officer in the exercise of his discretion would have acted in that manner. . . . There is ample evidence in the record to support a jury finding that no reasonable loan officer in the same situation would have refused to advance funds to K.M.C. as Sarokin [Irving's loan officer] did on March 1, 1982.

"Counsel for Irving conceded . . . that the bank was adequately secured. . . . He argued, however, that what is important is not the amount of the security, but the capacity of the debtor to pay back the loan. The jury was entitled to find that a reasonable notice period would not change the ability of K.M.C. to pay the loan. . . .

". . . [The appraiser's] valuation was based . . . on its [K.M.C.'s] projected performance following acquisition by a larger company. Upon this premise he built into his various projections certain assumptions with respect to the advantages enjoyed by larger over midsize companies. . . . The jury reasonably could have concluded that K.M.C. would be valued by larger companies based on such projections. . . .

"We are not insensitive to Irving's complaint that K.M.C.'s value on March 1, 1982, was less than the jury's award of $7,500,000. It is plain from the record that the company was heavily leveraged, its heavy losses in 1981 had eroded stockholder equity, and it had a substantial amount of uncollectible receivables in excess of its bad debt reserve. Nevertheless, the Magistrate concluded that the damage award was not outside the limits of reasonable range, and we are constrained to agree."

full disclosure about interest charges and other conditions of the loan?

Borrowers are alleging that a "no" to any of these queries constitutes fraud on the part of the lender.

Duress, as defined in *Ballantine's Law Dictionary*, is: "Any wrongful act of one person that compels a manifestation of apparent assent by another to a transaction without his volition. Compulsion or restraint by which a person is illegally forced to do, or forbear from doing, some act."

Some Cases That Bear Watching

Because New York is the country's financial capital, civil court rulings in the state are closely monitored across the nation. That being the case, as rules New York's Court of Appeals (the state's highest court), so rule many other states. New York judges and attorneys, therefore, are especially sensitive to the need for certainty and clarity in commercial law.

So, where does New York stand thus far on lender liability? It's one of those "good news-bad news" situations. The facts of the most important case are as follows:

United Department Stores (UDS) of New Jersey was a holding company for a number of department-store subsidiaries in the greater New York area. In June 1980, UDS bought the retail assets of Outlet Company and sought financing. As lead bank in the deal, Citibank agreed to a $15.2 million revolving line of credit. Shortly thereafter, UDS allegedly ran into trouble and requested a new round of financing.

Citibank agreed, and the $15.2 million credit was rewritten as a term loan, guaranteed by the four stockholder/officers of UDS. According to the guarantors, Citibank also promised an additional $8 million line of credit. No part of this $8 million line of credit, the guarantors claim, was ever advanced.

Unable to purchase Christmas merchandise, UDS declared voluntary bankruptcy. Citibank sued the four guarantors.

At trial, Citibank filed a motion for summary judgment — which means that unless the defendant contests the plaintiff's allegations (the UDS guarantors did disclaim, admitting their obligation) and can provide solid proof of its contentions, the plaintiff wins and the amount sought is placed in bond or surrendered to the court. The court granted the motion. The defense appealed, and this is where the first lender-liability cracks began to appear. The decision was upheld despite a strong dissent from the presiding judge of the Supreme Court Appellate Division. Last fall, the case reached the Court of Appeals, the state's highest court, and the lower court's decision was affirmed. The four guarantors owe Citibank and the other lenders $20 million.

Throughout, the guarantors have claimed a defense of fraud in the inducement. In an affidavit (which was not contradicted by Citibank), they charged that they wouldn't have signed unless the additional funding was advanced, and that Citibank promised "UDS had the line." But the guaranty they had signed was "absolute and unconditional."

Because of the incontrovertible nature of the guaranty, the Court of Appeals said that the defendants could not introduce oral evi-

Breach of Fiduciary Duty

Establishing that the bank, as a fiduciary, breached its duty of care is appearing more frequently as a major cause of legal action. Breach of fiduciary duty (far worse than simple negligence) is a standard under which the interests of the borrower—not the bank—come first. Fiduciary duty on the part of the bank can arise from a number of bank-borrower relationships: For example, the bank gives the borrower business advice, or it acts as the borrower's personal financial advisor.

Says William Vines III, of Butler, Vines, Babb & Threadgill of Knoxville: "It is inconceivable to me that the bank isn't a fiduciary,

dence of fraud as a matter of law: "The substance of defendants' guarantee forecloses their reliance on the claim that they were fraudulently induced to sign the guarantee by the bank's oral promise of an additional line of credit. To permit that would in effect condone defendants' own fraud in 'deliberately misrepresenting [their] true intention'."

The good news is the victory in the Court of Appeals.

But the narrowness of the holding is less than reassuring. Summary judgment would have been improper, the Court of Appeals was careful to note — evidence of the claimed oral fraudulent misrepresentations could have been introduced — if the guarantors had not disclaimed.

Another body, the Bankruptcy Court, has already authorized a suit against Citibank on behalf of UDS. New York could be looking at its first big lender-liability case. If the alleged fraud can be proven, says one of the authors of the *Business Workouts Manual:* "Look at the $15 million loan, the fact of a multimillion-dollar company, and punitive damages, and you could have telephone numbers in this case."

But the other legal issues the case will explore — such as the definition of a default — are what make some attorneys nervous. UDS claims that it never defaulted in the first place. And the case will also question the role played by "sophisticated businessmen" (a phrase that comes straight out of the ruling of the Court of Appeals) in guaranty and borrower suits.

Also of considerable concern is that the Bankruptcy Court has now authorized a lender-liability suit. This gives banks a new borrower's advocate to worry about.

And then there's RICO (the Racketeer Influenced & Corrupt Organizations Act). While lawyers for borrowers prefer to sue in state courts, RICO can be used only in federal courts — but it permits a treble-damages penalty, and it is a bankruptcy court's duty to win all it can for people or firms under its jurisdiction.

AND IN CALIFORNIA . . .

California courts are virtually as influential on case law in other states as New York. In no other jurisdiction is lender-liability proliferating more. In fact, new twists on this doctrine are churned out of California almost every day.

A few recent cases are worthy of note.

■ Williams, a San Diego car dealer, won cancellation of his $1 million debt to Security Pacific National Bank, plus damages of $5.7

when it blocks funds and ties up everything the borrower has. He can't even write a check. He's totally dependent."

Breach of Contract

Some borrowers are claiming banks breach contracts when they cut off further funding because of a nonperforming loan. Beyond the actual loan agreement, borrowers assert, the relationship between bank and borrower rises to the legal level of an implied contract. In other words, the bank is obligated by its course of conduct to continue lending funds necessary for the borrower to maintain his business through good times and bad.

million (including punitive damages of $2.5 million) in a case decided by a judge — no jury. Judge G. Dennis Adams found that the bank's lending practice amounted to a fiduciary relationship. As a result, Security Pacific faces the uncomfortable prospect of other suits filed by car dealers in the area.

The bank did get some good news, however. In appealing a suit brought by an asphalt contractor named Conley — the outcome of which was a jury award against the bank of $2 million in damages — the bank won a new trial. The appellate court overturned the lower court, but on a legal issue unrelated to lender liability.

■ An intermediate appellate court has ordered a new trial for a man named Barrett, overturning a victory for Bank of America. Barrett is a vendor of electronic parts and burglar alarms. More important than the vendor's victory, however, is that the court added a new stinger to lender liability for the retrial: constructive fraud. Since the bank is a fiduciary, the court said, it is liable for its misrepresentations, notwithstanding that they were unintentional or not even negligent, just so long as the bank benefited from the misrepresentations.

According to Jerry Cluff of Pain, Cluff & Olson of San Diego, representing Barrett, "This makes for a very big difference as a matter of law. The bank can be liable even if it didn't do anything wrong."

Why such phenomenal succcess for borrowers? "Banks have only themselves to blame," says attorney Patrick Frega of San Diego, who represented Williams. "People simply don't like the way banks do business."

Cluff concurs: "There is a wellspring of dissatisfaction with banks. People think worse of banks than they do of lawyers. We're finding on *voir dire* [a procedure by which potential jurors are questioned to determine any prejudices] that 85 percent of people say they have had bad experiences with banks."

But there are champions for the banker's cause. Perhaps none works harder than Willim Burke, of Shearman & Sterling in Los Angeles. He represented Security Pacific in the successful appeal against Conley. Burke races around the country at a dizzying pace, speaking at seminars to keep bankers informed.

In addition, to keep him on top of the situation, he has set up a network of attorneys nationwide, who send him copies of lender-liability pleadings. From this central file, Burke has formulated a comprehensive checklist for banks. (See "For More Information . . ." on page 17.)

Breach of Good Faith/Fair Dealing

The accusation that the bank breached its duty of good faith and fair dealing (the terms are actually interchangeable) is still the most open-ended possibility for liability. The Uniform Commercial Code (UCC) requires good faith and fair dealing in all commercial transactions. With roots dating from the 1950s and '60s, the UCC is now law in all states except Louisiana. Yet, just what is good faith? As defined in UCC Section 1-201(19), " 'Good Faith' means honesty in fact in the conduct of transaction concerned."

Attorney John Marshall of Powell, Goldstein, Frazer and Murphy of Atlanta, counsel for banks throughout the South, stresses that "good faith and fair dealing are the easiest concepts for a jury to understand." This may give impetus to a rise in cases claiming breach of good faith. "All the emotional factors are on the side of the borrower," Marshall adds. "Even if good faith and fair dealing aren't part of the credit agreements, once the jury is told they are to be considered part of the transaction, the bank is in trouble."

Breach of a Joint-Venture Agreement

As soon as the bank becomes involved in the borrower's business, which commonly occurs when a loan goes bad, a joint venture is created, claim attorneys for borrowers. The bank's involvement may take the form of a seat on the board of the borrower's company, a workout, or some other method of control over the company. Regardless of the type of intercession, as soon as the joint venture is established, the bank's concern for the joint venture (the borrower's business) must be paramount.

Indemnity

Finally, attorneys for borrowers maintain that in many cases, they have a cause of action to obtain indemnity. Indemnity? Bank to borrower? Yes, many attorneys allege, because the bank's exercise of control over the borrower's business makes the bank the principal and the borrower the agent. Agents, if they are damaged or held liable while conducting the affairs of the principal, are entitled to indemnity from their principal—something every first-year law student knows.

"A bank is damned if it does and damned if it doesn't," says attorney David Slavkin of Bryan, Cove, McPheeters & McRoberts of St. Louis, which represents a number of banks in Missouri. "If a bank doesn't come in and help the borrower," he says, "it will be sued for not acting. And if it does come in, it will be sued for not exercising control properly."

Another possible cause of action could be maladministration or malpractice.

Atrio Consolidated Industries of Hialeah, Florida, sued Southeast Bank of Miami. Besides fraud and breach of contract, attorney Sheldon Rosenberg, of Ress, Gomez, Rosenberg, Howland & Mintz, also claimed maladministration. The judge and jury agreed, and a verdict of $12 million ($9 million of that in punitive damages) was returned.

Besides borrowers, third parties (other than guarantors) are also becoming lender-liability litigants. A business that dealt only with the borrower may be able to bring suit against a bank, claiming the bank-to-borrower credit policy caused harm to the borrower and, as a result, to the third party.

"The Jewell case establishes that a bank can be liable to a third party for interference with a contractual relationship, interference with a business relationship, or fraud," says William Lukens of Lukens, St. Peter & Cooper of San Francisco, counsel for the O'Connell shareholder.

Banks are asking why they're being held accountable. Presumably a bank is a free agent, fully in control of to whom, and how and when it will lend money. Meticulous agreements spell out a bank's right to recoup, with interest, any funds it lends. It's the defaulting borrower who has failed to perform under the terms of the agreement. Ergo, when a borrower's note becomes delinquent, what's wrong with a bank opting to exercise its legal right to collect?

Plenty, respond plaintiffs' attorneys, and judges and juries are agreeing with alarming frequency. It will no longer be enough, Marshall points out, "for a bank to do the correct thing in terms of the loan agreement or in the interests of the bank. The issue is: Has the bank done the right things in the eyes of the jury?"

It All Began with Farah

Lender liability, as a multimillion-dollar threat, first gained headlines in a Texas courtroom. Farah Manufacturing Company, an apparel firm, sued the State National Bank of El Paso, claiming fraud and duress when the bank demanded the company replace its directors. The

An Action Checklist for the Lender

Bankers have a number of options that can reduce the likelihood of a lender-liability lawsuit or increase the odds of winning if one is lodged.

All banks should create their own action checklist. And there are other aids available in the field (see "For More Information . . ." box on page 17).

Meanwhile, here is a checklist developed by *U.S. Banker:*

THE BASICS

1. Use committees to decide whether to terminate a loan. No one officer should have the authority to terminate a line of credit or call a loan. There is always a potential for clashes of personalities between an officer and a borrower. Committees will help to prevent any one person from touching off a lender-liability suit. "In today's world, it is foolish to think any loan officer will have the necessary emotional control that is required," says attorney Raymond Shapiro of Blank, Rome, Comisky & McCauley of Philadelphia, who wrote Chapter 8 in the *Business Workouts Manual.*

2. Keep the files clean. Banks have a tendency to put everything in writing — to stuff files with a variety of documents. It must be assumed that every file could be subpoenaed at any time. One negative memo could provoke a libel or slander suit.

3. Simplify loan documents. Onerous boilerplate terminology that serves no real purpose for the bank should be eliminated. While it may sound impressive, a borrower's attorney could hold it up as proof of the bank's insensitivity.

4. Make certain that legal documents clearly reflect the understandings between the parties. Telling a borrower that provisions of the agreement "aren't really enforced," or "are just there for the lawyers" is a big mistake. Also, if a legal agreement seeks too much — that the borrower waive his constitutional rights, for example — "the bank is digging its own grave," warns attorney William Vines III, of Butler, Vines & Threadgill in Knoxville. When a disputed contract goes before the court, judges invariably are tougher on the party that drafted it.

5. Use consultants. Both the bank and the borrower would be well advised to contract consultants. "They serve as a valuable buffer," notes Shapiro.

6. Have a well-founded reason for terminating (or legally trying to collect) a loan. Make sure you can prove there has been a substantial change in the borrower's position. Further, the bank must be able to show it has exhaustively investigated and can verify the changes. When a bank reaches a sud-

---

case resulted in a jury award of $19 million to Farah.

In August 1984, The Eighth Circuit Court of Appeals of Texas affirmed the award won for Farah by attorney Tom Thomas. In its decision the court said: "The central theme of FMC's [Farah's] case is that the lenders interfered with FMC's own business relations and protected rights. Although the lenders may have been acting to exercise legitimate legal rights or to protect justifiable business interests, their conduct failed to comport with the

den determination that the borrower is unable to pay, it's admitting that the initial decision to lend was erroneous.

7. Don't suddenly terminate or try to collect. "Telegraph what you are going to do," says Shapiro. Good faith demands timely notification of the borrower by the bank.

8. Have the borrower provide warranties and representations of his creditworthiness and the condition of his business. This will allow the bank to show how the borrower's status has changed, and could prove he deluded the bank. It may help, too, to blunt charges that the bank acted in haste and without proper consideration when it terminated an agreement.

9. Be careful about how credit inquiries are handled. Statements made about credit policies should be consistent. Disparities offered by different sources invite charges of misunderstanding.

Also, responses to credit inquiries about a borrower from a third party must be accurate, up-to-date and complete. Not telling the whole truth could constitute misrepresentation. Make sure the borrower has approved the release of such information. And stick to the facts — avoid subjective opinions about the character of the borrower or his business.

10. Establish a solid training program for lending officers. This is critical. Absent such training, a borrower can assert a lack of fair dealing, claiming there was no attempt by the bank to monitor lending officers.

11. Have management policies in place for terminating or collecting loans. Without these, the bank is admitting its lack of proper guidance and supervision.

Also, continually update manuals and policy statements to reflect any changes. And make sure policy provisions aren't oppressive. If they are, they could be used to show a lack of good faith.

12. Develop a full understanding and knowledge of the borrower's business. By doing this, a bank will be better able to justify its claim that a borrower is no longer creditworthy, or that he can't repay. Expertise in the borrower's company also helps justify the need for a workout.

13. Don't become intractible. What is best for the borrower can change frequently, Shapiro points out. "So don't get locked in. No course [of action] is written in stone."

14. Avoid oral commitments. These are as important as a written agreement in the eyes of the jury. Any variations could prove costly.

15. Make good faith a course of conduct. Good faith and fair dealing have to be a way of life. "The days of intimidation and threats by bank officers are past," Shapiro stresses. Good faith has to start the minute the borrower sets foot in the bank and continue until the loan is repaid. It should be required in

standards of fair play. . . . Upon consideration of the private interests of the parties and the social utility thereof, the social benefits derived from permitting the lenders' interference are clearly outweighed by the harm to be expected therefrom."

Then, in March 1985, lender liability was expanded by the United States Court of Appeals for the Sixth Circuit (Kentucky, Michigan, Ohio and Tennessee). In *K.M.C. Co., Inc. v. Irving Trust Company,* Judge Cornelia Kennedy, affirming a $7.5 million award for

everything said, every document signed and every action taken.

16. Avoid suing for a small delinquency. A lender-liability suit almost always arises as a counterclaim to a collection suit filed by the bank. If the delinquent balance is small, it may not be worth a lawsuit.

17. Don't overreach and take all possible collateral simply because it's available. Overreaching is something plaintiffs' attorneys consider preeminent. When trouble arises, the last thing the bank should do is jump in and tie up everything the borrower has. "The bank looks like a vulture," says William Lukens, counsel for the O'Connell shareholder in its case against Bank of America. "What a better posture if it forgoes some collateral," he adds. Other attorneys recommend that as the relationship goes on, some collateral should be released. They also point out that a fiduciary duty may be created when collateral is frozen. If the borrower is left some room to maneuver, the bank will have an easier time convincing a jury it acted in good faith.

And don't call a loan simply because you "think" the collateral is eroding — unless you can prove outright fraud.

18. Make workouts symbiotic. Commercial borrowers aren't deadbeats. Their businesses can be adversely affected by myriad economic considerations. If the workout can benefit both sides, it's better to resolve the situation in good faith.

19. Listen to the borrower. "These [lender-liability cases] aren't consumer cases," claims Cappello, the attorney who handled the Jewell case against BofA. "The bank judged the borrower an expert in his business once, so what has changed? More than likely it is the economy — or maybe actions by the bank — and not the borrower's stupidity that has caused the grief. The borrower doesn't want to sue, unlike the consumer. He wants to secure his business, and so should the bank." If a free exchange of ideas is facilitated, a way to avoid a real problem may emerge.

20. Beware of overzealous workout people. Traditionally, the special-assets officers, the "workout boys," have been the heavies. "It has been my experience," says Cappello, "that it is these people who finally drive the borrower to sue. A bank has a lot to fear from its own workout people."

21. Recognize that there are two types of problem loans. There are loans that can be repaid with patience and help, and loans that can't be repaid at all. "If there is absolutely no chance for the borrower to repay, then the bank is entitled to pursue all legal remedies and there won't be any [lender liability] suit," Lukens points out. "But, if the borrower can repay, or can make a claim that he can, that's when the bank can hurt him. That's when the bank can run into liability." He

K.M.C., a grocery chain, wrote: "Just as Irving's discretion whether or not to advance funds is limited by an obligation of good faith performance, so too would be its power to demand repayment...."

In spite of all the recent attention, however, lender liability is not new doctrine per se. "The principles we're applying all stem from common law, or have been on the books for years," Thomas points out. "All that is new is the willingness of plaintiffs' attorneys to assert rights that borrowers have always had."

In the Sixth Circuit Court's opinion in K.M.C., for example, cases from the 19th

continues, "That's why senior management should be brought in, to classify which type of problem loan the bank has. And if the loan might be repaid, the bank has to do everything it can to help the borrower repay."

22. Allow the borrower to play the leading role in a workout plan. As written in the *Business Workouts Manual:* "The development of a sound plan is a collective effort. While creditors can develop and sponsor a plan, it is more usual, and generally preferable, for the debtor's management to do so . . . Management's commitment and enthusiasm for the plan are critical for its successful implementation. This commitment and enthusiasm will be significantly greater if management has played the central role in developing and sponsoring the plan. This is true even when the plan proposes some changes in management personnel."

SOME IDEAS ON AVOIDING THIRD-PARTY LIABILITY

23. When lending is based on a guaranty, don't inhibit the primary borrower's ability to pay the loan. A bank's duty of good faith extends to a third party who is guaranteeing the loan, Lukens notes. "A bank can lose this obligation if it does anything to inhibit the primary borrower's ability to repay. So the bank is better off if it deals directly with the guarantor."

24. Treat the third-party recipient of the borrowings with good faith, just as if he were the primary borrower. The Jewell case against Bank of America establishes this duty, so long as the bank is aware of the party for whom the proceeds of the loan are intended. This entails full disclosure by the bank of any competing borrowers, to both the borrower and to the eventual recipient of the funds.

25. When in doubt, assume there is a third-party recipient of the funds. If a third party sues a bank for lack of good faith, full disclosure, or antitrust, it will do the bank little good to claim that it was not aware of the third party. If a jury has a chance to determine that the bank did know or should have known about a third party, assume it will. This caveat can prevent the kind of huge damage awards to a third party now faced by the Bank of America. "Any amount of caution, or going the extra mile, has to be cheaper than a lender-liability suit," offers Cappello. It isn't enough for the bank to review its own relationship to the third party; it should check as well what the third party claims the borrower said to him.

Finally, warns Lukens, "When a bank is lending to someone who is in competition with the third party, there is no limit to how careful the bank must be."

---

century were cited. And proper notification of the borrower by the bank, the court declared, can be found right in the UCC: "The application of principles of good faith and sound commercial practice normally call for such notification of the termination of a going contract relationship as well as give the other party reasonable time to seek a subsequent arrangement."

Thus, considering that as a matter of legal technicality, lender liability has been around a while, the expectancy that plaintiffs' attorneys will continue to tackle only the "horror-story" cases is myopic. They may be just the tip of the iceberg. Lawyers will probe the doctrine, looking for new ways to expand its applications, and in so doing, can be expected to press more routine cases. For example, should O'Connell prevail in its antitrust suit, antitrust claims will be yet one more way to put bankers up against the wall.

For the moment, as might be expected, banks are trying to play down the extent of the danger posed by lender liability. They emphasize that they are still winning the majority of cases brought. It is just that the "victories by borrowers get the headlines," says bank attorney Helen Davis Chaitman of Wilentz, Goldman & Spitzer of Woodbridge, New Jersey.

BofA's Magnani considers lender liability an anomaly, "attributable to farming failures and a downward economy." However, lender liability is manifestly sparking more than just farming cases. Attorneys for borrowers speak of cases involving real estate, clothing, and accounts-receivable financing across the board. Farah was in the apparel business; K.M.C. was in the grocery business. And "energy is the next big area," says Cappello.

Additionally, not all lender-liability cases can be attributed to a "downward economy." In good economic times and bad, borrowers borrow, lenders lend, lenders try to collect, and borrowers go broke.

Further, because of the headlines, these cases are attracting a number of lawyers. And they're not just stars, such as Cappello, Thomas, and William Vines III (Vines won the *K.M.C.* case). (See box on page 6.)

"It would be a mistake for banks to underestimate the skills of the plaintiffs' bar [attorneys] in general, and how the publicity is going to bring them to lender-liability cases," Marshall says. "Banks are such easy targets," confided another attorney who requested anonymity. "We could be talking the motor-vehicle torts of the eighties."

Events are beginning to suggest a trend, and the blind belief that banks "will succeed on the law" seems far too optimistic. The Sword of Damocles is real, and banks should be prepared. And even if they adapt their lending conduct in the future, banks will still have to worry about alleged past transgressions. Depending on the jurisdiction, the statute of limitations runs anywhere from one to six years.

Then there is the matter of damages. Banks are losing far more than just the borrower's obligation. They are also being hit with multimillion-dollar damage judgments—sometimes even when the plaintiff hasn't pressed for these awards. "All we were looking for was zero," says attorney James Wirken of Spradley & Wirken in Kansas City, Missouri. "We would have won if just the indebtedness was canceled. But the jury came back and gave us $7.5 million." (The damage judgment in *Centerre Banks* v. *Distributors* has since been reversed on appeal. The case will be retried on the issue of canceling the plaintiff's $500,000 indebtedness. At the retrial, Wirken will also pursue damages (including "intentional infliction of emotional distress") against individual officers of the bank.

As the Texas court noted in *Farah:* "Where the evidence establishes that a plaintiff has suffered substantial damages, he is not to be denied recovery merely because others than the defendants contributed to bring about his loss and he is unable to show distinctly the amount of damages contributed by each tortfeasor."

MEETING THE CHALLENGE

With the law offering a shrinking refuge, how can banks meet the challenge of lender liability in the future? "By changing their historical ways," answers Lukens. Everyone —and that includes attorneys for borrowers —believes that banks control their destinies and that the challenge can be met. But how?

To prevent lender liability, banks are going to have to change their lending philosophies. Attorneys have several suggestions: "Be more sensitive," advises Marshall; "more reliance

For More Information....

There is a growing body of reference material for bankers who want to learn more about lender liability. We offer a few here.

- *The Business Workouts Manual*, edited and co-written by attorney Donald Lee Rome of Robinson & Cole, Hartford, Connecticut, can be purchased for $85.50. It is published by Warren, Gorham & Lamont, 210 South Street, Boston, MA 02111.

Of particular interest to bankers is Chapter Eight, "Problems Resulting From Improper Lender Conduct During the Workout." It was written by attorney Raymond Shapiro of Blank, Rome, Comisky & McCauley of Philadelphia.

- A 200-page outline on "Emerging Theories of Lender Liability" has been prepared by attorney William Burke of Shearman & Sterling, 725 South Figueroa, Los Angeles, CA 90017-5430, telephone: (213)239-0311.

- A three-volume, 2,500-page opus from the American Bar Association (ABA — not to be confused with the American Bankers Association), also entitled *Emerging Theories of Lender Liability* is available for $150. It comprises various papers presented at a series of seminars on lender liability held last year by the ABA. To order, contact the American Bar Association, 750 North Lake Shore Drive, Chicago, IL 60611, or call Ernestine Murphy at (312)988-6204.

- Two seminars are scheduled for May and June: The first, "Representing the Lender in Litigation," is sponsored by the Practising Law Institute (PLI). It will be held on May 12 and 13 at the Doral Inn in New York. It will be offered again on June 12 and 13 at the Beverly Hilton in Los Angeles. A course handbook is also available for $390. For more information, contact PLI at 810 Seventh Avenue, New York, NY 10019, telephone; (212)765-5700.

The second seminar, entitled "Lender Liability," is to be held on May 29 and 30 [1987] at the Marriott Marquis Hotel in New York. It will be held again on June 2 and 3 [1987] at Le Bel Age Hotel in Los Angeles. The course is being run by Law & Business, the publisher and sponsor of a number of legal-education programs. Those wishing to attend can contact Jeffrey Jacobs at Law & Business, 855 Valley Road, Clifton, NJ 07013, telephone: (201)472-7400.

- Finally, for those who want a greater number of bank employees to learn about lender liability, at the behest of the American Bar Association, Banc-Video has developed a 40-minute film entitled "Sue the Lender." Sold for $395, or available for 30-day rental, it comes with a 32-page handbook citing a number of lender-liability cases. To order a videotape, contact Banc-Video, 1895 South Brentwood Boulevard, Suite 206, St. Louis, MO 63144, or call (314)968-0220.

---

by loan officers on the bank's attorneys," suggests Slavkin; eschew "the traditional rigidity that besets all banks," suggests Lukens; and of course, more training of loan officers, all observers agree. If banks will but "make fair dealing and good faith commonplace," Chaitman urges, "they have nothing to worry about." Once banks establish standards of good faith and fair dealing, says Marshall, "I am confident we can persuade juries to treat us with good faith and fair dealing in return."

Off the record, however, attorneys don't think banks have as yet fully learned the lesson. And if their handling of the current spate of lender-liability litigation is any indication, the prognosis for change is not favorable.

"Banks spend years accruing all these documents saying what a great guy the borrower is," offers Cappello, "and then they come into court and tell the jury what a rogue he is. The banks make the case for us."

"There has been a tradition of arrogance attached to lending money," says Lukens, "but that day is over." Warns Cappello, "Most banks still aren't getting the message. They still think people are supposed to come in and kiss the ring when they want to borrow. If banks keep thinking like that, they're going to keep getting killed in court." Wirken adds, "Look at any of these cases and you'll find some guy for the bank who comes in and testifies and who looks and sounds and talks like Captain Bligh. What can the bank expect the jury to do?"

Because of the emotional factors and the prevailing negative perceptions, juries may continue to hand down big awards for borrowers unless banks take the necessary precautions. But can they learn what these are and put them in place in time? Or will they fall victim to "arrogance," self-righteousness and complacency? ■

Does Lender Liability Now Include Banker Malpractice?

Doctors can be sued for malpractice, as can attorneys and a host of other professionals.

But bankers?

Yes, answers a Florida court.

A case recently tried in that state has in theory added banker malpractice, or maladministration, to the growing list of grounds for a lender-liability lawsuit.

Atrio Consolidated Industries, a maker of lamps, small tables and wall units in Hialeah, Fla., was persuaded by Southeast Bank of Miami to switch banks, and become a borrower at Southeast's new asset-based lending division.

Trouble followed, however, and on behalf of Atrio, attorney Sheldon Rosenberg, of Ress, Gomez, Rosenberg, Howland & Mintz in North Miami, brought suit against Southeast in circuit court. The borrower charged fraud and breach of contract, and the jury agreed.

But attorney Rosenberg also charged maladministration. And the judge put the question to the jury: Did the bank owe the borrower any duty of care beyond the written loan agreements?

"Yes," responded the jury—and the judge did not overrule the point. The jury then returned a verdict of $12 million ($9 million of that in punitive damages). The case was settled ("for a significant amount," says Rosenberg) before the appeal was heard.

During the trial, Rosenberg used testimony from a bank expert to show that Southeast's asset-based lending practices were improper. The jury was apparently impressed, and found the bank negligent on the issue.

Commenting on the central issue of the case, attorney Edward Waller Jr., of Fowler, White, Gillen, Boggs, Villareal & Banker in Tampa, affirms that in theory, banking malpractice has now been recognized by a Florida judge and jury. And when *U.S. Banker* asked: "Is banker malpractice now part of the emerging theories of lender liability?" he answered: "Yes, banker malpractice now exists in theory." ■

Diamonds, Gold & Apartheid

Joseph C. Thompson
EDITOR

In 1986 diamonds and gold were drawn into the national debate over the American response to apartheid. These two editorials urge jewelers to acknowledge their industry's clear —if uncomfortable—connections with South Africa. It puts forth the view that jewelers must inform themselves about apartheid and be open and honest in response to consumers' questions; to aid them, the editorials contain a detailed primer on the issues involved.

Modern Jeweler is circulated to retail jewelers in the United States and their suppliers. "Diamonds, Gold & Apartheid" first appeared in the August and September 1986 issues of *Modern Jeweler,* published by Vance Publishing Corp. © 1986. Reprinted with permission.

Diamonds, Gold & Apartheid, I

The remark was spectacularly stupid. Last month, White House Chief of Staff Donald Regan, in defending Reagan Administration opposition to economic sanctions against South Africa, rhetorically asked reporters, "Are the women of America prepared to give up all their jewelry? Are the Israelis, the Belgians, the Netherlands' people prepared not to engage in any more diamond trade?"

Besides being tasteless and insensitive, the remark was inaccurate. Even in the stiff sanctions bill recently passed by the House of Representatives became law, it would not affect trade in diamonds and jewelry since diamonds are not imported to the U.S. directly from South Africa. Nor do the sanctions now under consideration by the European Economic Community involve diamonds. There was wincing all around—from the Administration, which was embarrassed, to womens' and black groups, which were offended.

No doubt there was a good deal of wincing at De Beers too, where they have been taking great pains of late to point out the "international" character of the diamond—mined in 20 countries, polished in cutting centers on three continents and retailed throughout the world. The idea is to avoid any identification of the diamond as a "South African mineral" so as to spare the diamond trade any political fallout such as killed the Krugerrand last year.

For two years, while the horrors of South African apartheid dominated American headlines, diamonds were never mentioned, neither in the context of the unrest there nor sanctions here. Then suddenly last month, all that changed, there and here. In South Africa, black miners struck De Beers' diamond mines for the first time in the current unrest. Here, overnight, Regan's remark had the press and politicians buzzing about the connection between South African diamonds and American jewelry.

The shadow of South African apartheid is long and ugly and, like it or not, it is falling on the jewelry business. The connections between the industry are clear, and in the current political climate, uncomfortable. Gold and diamonds are the bread and butter of this industry. South Africa is the largest free world producer of gold and the second largest supplier of gem-quality diamonds. Of the men who mine these precious materials, eight of every 10 are black.

What do these connections mean for the jewelry trade? They do not mean that jewelry will become targets of anti-apartheid activity —although such a scenario is not totally out of the question. More likely, though, is that as the South African crisis worsens, the country's gold and diamond riches will be drawn deeper into the growing debate about how to respond to the urgent need of South African blacks to end the crime of apartheid. Regan's remark should alert every jeweler that he or she must be prepared to discuss this industry's South African connections. Inevitably, as consumers hear more about South Africa and sanctions, they will have questions. Do gold and diamond mining firms support apartheid? How are black miners treated? Are these diamonds from South Africa?

There are answers to these and a dozen other legitimate questions consumers may have. Jewelers must be prepared to answer them, openly and accurately. That's why we've reprinted in this issue a recent article from the *Financial Times* of London reviewing how the apartheid crisis has affected black gold miners and the gold mining houses. The article points out that some, but not all, of the gold mining

Diamonds, Gold & Apartheid, II

"Diamonds could be anti-apartheid's second best friend."

So stated *The Economist*, a prominent British weekly, recently in calling for a free world boycott of all South African gold (anti-apartheid's first best friend) and diamonds. Closer to home, the Senate Foreign Relations Committee last month passed a bill which lists diamonds as one key South African export which would be banned from the U.S. should the South African government fail to take significant steps toward ending apartheid within a year.

As we indicated here last month, diamonds have quickly become a hot topic in the international debate over what to do about South Africa. The opinion here is that hot topic will get hotter. As South Africa burns and Western politicians and media simmer over sanctions and as students return to college campuses, the diamond's South African connections will become an increasingly sensitive subject.

What's a jeweler to do? Be open and honest and informed in the face of consumers' questions and concerns. What follows are a few questions jewelers can be expected to hear this fall and a few answers.

Is South Africa the world's major source of diamonds?

No. South Africa ranks fourth among world diamond producers after Zaire, Botswana, and the Soviet Union. South Africa's 9.9 million carats mined last year amount to less than 15% of the 66.5 million mined worldwide. Of that total, about 20% is gem-quality diamond; South Africa is a major source of gem diamonds.

How reliant is the diamond industry on black labor?

---

houses have championed the cause of black rights in South Africa. Anglo American Corp., the largest gold mining company, controlled by Harry F. Oppenheimer, has led the liberal forces in the South African business community in their fight against the government's oppression of blacks.

De Beers' record is equally strong in favor of black rights. The series of strikes that hit five De Beers mines between July 4 and July 10 were not directed at the company but at the government. They were called by the National Union of Mineworkers (NUM) to urge mining firms to pressure the government to release 900 black trade union leaders who were summarily jailed in June. Police rounded up the union officials along with black community, church and political leaders in the early hours of June 12 after State President P. W. Botha declared yet another "state of emergency" in South Africa just prior to the 10th anniversary of the Soweto revolt. In all, 18,000 gold, diamond and coal miners staged job actions to protest the detention of their leaders.

The De Beers' strikes involved 2,000 black workers at the four mines in Kimberley and 1,200 workers at the huge Finsch mine located about 60 miles northwest of Kimberley. In response, De Beers' Chairman Julian Ogilvie Thompson sent a telegram to South Africa's Minister for Law and Order calling for the release of the detained union officials. De Beers reportedly made several appeals on behalf of the black union officials, after which the striking workers returned to work. As of this writing, the officials are still in detention.

Keeping abreast of developments in South Africa is not easy. We are half a world away and events in that tortured country are often hard to fathom. Nevertheless, we will continue to do our best to keep jewelers informed about how events there impact the gold and diamond industries. American jewelers are more than innocent bystanders. The more informed the industry is, the better able it is to understand and explain the fire we watch from afar. ∎

Very reliant. Approximately 80% of the 20,000 people De Beers employs in its mines in South Africa, Namibia and Botswana are black. That 80–20 ratio corresponds roughly to the percentage of non-white vs. white population in South Africa.

What do black diamond workers earn?

The average monthly wage of De Beers' black mineworkers, including overtime and other payments, was 706 South African rand last year. That's equivalent to $270 per month at the current rate of exchange. That dollar figure is deceptive, though, since the rand has fallen sharply against the dollar in the past three years due to South African unrest. In 1983, the same R706 was equivalent to $635. The minimum starting rate for an unskilled worker was R340 per month ($130). By South African standards, those wages are good, amounting to 2½ times the average monthly incomes of blacks generally. A black gold miner, by comparison, earns only R285 ($138) per month.

In general, white miners earn significantly more than blacks, partly because they hold supervisory positions which blacks are forbidden by law to hold. The average monthly pay of a white miner is five times that of blacks, according to the National Union of Mineworkers, which represents black gold, coal and diamond workers.

What is De Beers' position on apartheid?

De Beers, along with its sister company, Anglo American Corp., South Africa's largest gold producer, has actively opposed apartheid since the South African government installed the system in 1948. Harry F. Oppenheimer, long-time chairman of Anglo and De Beers, has long been identified with anti-apartheid forces in South Africa. Anglo American Chairman Gavin Relly has followed in Oppenheimer's footsteps, taking a leading role in the fight against apartheid. Relly has repeatedly denounced the government's repressive policies and urged it to free Nelson Mandela, end all forms of apartheid, and begin negotiations with black leaders on a new constitution which would grant equal rights to blacks. Last fall, in defiance of South African law, Relly led a delegation of business leaders to Lusaka, Zambia, to meet with leaders of the African National Congress, the black activist group banned by the South African government.

Is it true that the gold and diamond industries keep South Africa's racist government in power?

That's oversimplification, but indirectly they do. Gold and diamonds represent 52% of South Africa's total exports last year, 46% and 6% respectively. They brought R19 billion ($9.2 billion) into the country. That's why some anti-apartheid forces want sanctions against South African gold and diamond products.

What is the mining companies position on sanctions?

Officials at Anglo American, De Beers and the South African Chamber of Mines oppose sanctions. They argue that sanctions will hurt the single greatest force for black advancement in South Africa, the growth of the South African economy.

What is the position of black miners on sanctions?

Leaders of the NUM, which represents 300,000 black miners, have called for sanctions against South Africa. ■

The Refashioning of Zale

Shelle S. Jensen
ASSOCIATE EDITOR

David Federman
EXECUTIVE EDITOR

Joseph C. Thompson
EDITOR

Claude Zajakowski
ART DIRECTOR

Zale Corporation, the world's largest jeweler, had been plagued for two years by lackluster earnings, several waves of executive firings and hirings, and a hostile takeover bid. This special report contains a detailed account of what was actually happening: the most radical market repositioning in the history of the jewelry industry.

Modern Jeweler is read by retail jewelers in the United States and their suppliers. "The Refashioning of Zale" first appeared in the July 1986 issue of *Modern Jeweler,* published by Vance Publishing Corp. © 1986. Reprinted with permission.

For more than two years, even before the highly publicized bids by Peoples Jewellers of Canada to take over the company, the jewelry trade has watched and wondered, "What is going on at Zale?"

For more than two years, Zale Corp., whose 1,600 stores in 49 states, two territories and four foreign countries make it the world's only billion dollar jewelry retailer, has been undergoing enormous changes. Outsiders have had glimpses of the changes. Familiar faces have left Zale's executive suites. Unfamiliar faces have appeared and with them new directions and new programs.

Few people outside the company, however, realize how long Zale Corp. has been planning its changes or how deep those changes go. In April, *Modern Jeweler* editors Shelle S. Jensen, David Federman and Joe Thompson spent a week at Zale headquarters in Irving, Texas. They interviewed more than a dozen top Zale executives about Zale's past, present, and future. Subsequently, they talked to informed Zale watchers, including former Zale executives, jewelry suppliers and retailers and retail stock analysts.

What is going on at Zale is a massive modernization unlike anything seen before in jewelry retailing. After years of market study and sometimes painful self-scrutiny, Zale has set out an ambitious plan to radically redefine, restructure and reposition itself in the jewelry marketplace. New economic realities, new consumer attitudes, and new competition meant that the "House that M.B. Built" had to change.

How the family-run, tradition-bound Zale came to that decision, how it has changed and is changing and how those changes will affect jewelry retailing is the subject of this 27-page special report, "The Refashioning of Zale." It is a complex story. Our report is written in seven parts. It outlines Zale's new corporate strategy and identifies the new breed of Zale executive who is executing it. It explains what that strategy means for Zales Jewelers and the new Bailey Banks & Biddle division. There are also interviews with Zale Chairman Donald Zale and President Bruce Lipshy, whose decision it was to refashion the firm their fathers formed. Plus there is a detailed account of the still unfolding drama of the Peoples bid to take over Zale Corp. ■

Corporate Strategy: "Making What We Can Sell, Not Selling What We Can Make"

The news was enough to make De Beers executives turn whiter than a D/flawless diamond. In late 1984, Zale Corporation, the world's largest retail jewelry chain and a buyer of De Beers rough diamonds since 1957, stopped advertising its 750 non-guild outlets as "diamond stores" and started referring to them as "Zales Jewelers . . . Leading with Style" To find out why, De Beers invited the company's top officers to London.

What De Beers' marketers learned hardly restored their color. The move marked the launch of what is probably the most radical repositioning campaign in the annals of jewelry retailing. With one slogan change, Zale was altering its market niche as the world's top seller of bridal diamonds in favor of a broader fashion image derived largely from department stores.

Although the identity shift seemed both abrupt and extreme, it had actually been incubating since the late 1970s when Zale Chairman Donald Zale first began to modernize company operations. The process accelerated in the 1980s when dramatic changes in the marketplace convinced Zale of his company's urgent need to change its hallowed ways. In March 1980, the first wave of diamond price deflation rocked the jewelry market. Eventually that deflation was to smash to bits the inventory profits-based underpinnings of diamond wholesaling and retailing. At the same time, traditional jewelers like Zale were fighting furiously to hold their own against a horde of catalog showrooms, department stores, and discounters which was moving aggressively and successfully into the multibillion-dollar U.S. jewelry market.

For Zale, the result was slow-to-no-growth and shrinking profits. Between 1980 and 1984, Zale's share of the precious jewelry and watch market slipped slightly from an estimated 6.4% to 6.3%. Although net sales generally increased during the 1980s, rising from $721 million in fiscal 1980 to $1.0 billion in fiscal '85, profits from Zale operations during that time went from $47.5 million to $38.8 million (see chart). Return on sales dropped from 6.5% in 1980 to 3.5% in '85, reflecting the changes in the economics of the industry.

During this period, Zale Corp. was taking a cold, hard look at itself and its market. That scrutiny was conducted by Zale veterans like Donald Zale and President Bruce Lipshy and by a group of newcomers Zale had recruited for specialized skills from such major outfits as Sears and Xerox. The inescapable conclusion was that to maintain its traditional leadership in jewelry retailing, Zale Corp. would have to radically restructure itself. To do it, Donald Zale would have to turn outside his company and the jewelry industry again, this time to department stores and other mass merchandisers to find the talent he needed to take the company where he wanted it to go. "Our traditional concept of skills development no longer worked," he says. "In the past, we, and I suppose others, just kept promoting the good salesperson from manager to supervisor to vice president. It hadn't dawned on us that in a firm of our size, specialized merchandising and marketing skills were required."

But in going outside the industry to get those skills, Zale was setting the stage for as painful a culture clash as any that ever gripped an American company. Himself the product of a "paternalistic" corporate culture, one whose values reflected the decades of domination by his father, Morris B. Zale, who founded the firm in 1924, Zale found it hard to break himself and his company of its old autocratic management style. Yet there was no other way to begin the momentous transition toward modern systems-based operations. Division chiefs needed more autonomy and accountability.

Letting go of old ways took two turbulent years, during which many Zale veterans who could not adjust resigned, retired or were fired.

The shift from "the diamond store" to "Leading with Style" summarizes Zale Corporation's new internal philosophy as well as the new external image it wishes to project. Zale no longer sees itself as the highly diversified conglomerate that it was a decade ago. To the contrary, it sees itself as first and foremost a jewelry retailer, the *leading* jewelry retailer. Toward that end, it sold off its sporting goods, footwear, and drug store businesses in 1980, and its direct-mail division in 1985. In May, it sold its Aeroplex newsstand division (1985 sales: $50.7 million) to Greyhound Corp. and is in the process of divesting its O. G. Wilson catalog and showroom division (1985 sales: $47.3 million). Now there is even talk that the company will shed its European jewelry retailing operations (Zales Jewellers Ltd. in England and Christ Jewellers in Europe), leaving it with three divisions: Zales Jewelers (incorporating Mission Jewelers, its 50-store, low-end chain), Bailey Banks & Biddle and Diamond Park Fine Jewelers (its group of 152 leased departments).

The new Zale strategy involves a series of

major repositionings in its corporate philosophy and practice. Among them:

- Repositioning Zale Corp. from a manufacturing-driven to a marketing-driven company, more attuned to the modern consumer, with increased focus on "differentiating" itself in the marketplace.
- Repositioning Zale executive management style from its traditional entrepreneurial model to that of a corporate team.
- Repositioning the Zale retail division as retailers of fashionable gold, colored stone and pearl jewelry, and not strictly bridal diamond jewelry.
- Repositioning the 325-stone Fine Jewelers Guild into a cohesive, centralized division under the name of the guild's flagship store Bailey Banks & Biddle. Eventually, the guild's 36 different trade names will be reduced to about 10, all of them identified as "A Bailey Banks & Biddle Jeweler."

Zale 1985 Sales by Division (in million $)

Division	Sales
Zales Jewelers	$435.7
Fine Jewelers Guild*	$326.3
Diamond Park Fine Jewelers	$61.2
Aeroplex**	$50.7
Catalog Showrooms	$47.3
Christ Jewellers, Europe	$45.8
Zale Jewellers Ltd., U.K.	$32.9
Mission Jewelers	$24.8
Willoughby & Taylor***	$8.0

(*renamed the Bailey Banks & Biddle division)
(**sold in 1986) (***sold in 1985)
Source: Zale Corporation

GOODBYE TO GOOD BUYS

Ask any Zale executive to tell you the single most important change at the company in the last few years and he or she will invariably respond: the switch from a "manufacturing-driven" to a "marketing-driven" orientation. That means, as one top executive puts it, "Decisions will be made with the customer in mind."

The switch is not just of consequence at Zale. To the contrary, Zale's new orientation is a critique of the basic modus operandi of the retail jewelry industry. From De Beers on down, say Zale executives, most jewelry industry firms are not really attuned to their customer base. At least, not to the degree that department stores are. Lack of market attunement is a grave charge to level at an industry which likes to think it excels in customer service and satisfaction. Nevertheless, Zale executives feel more than justified in making the charge. Here's why.

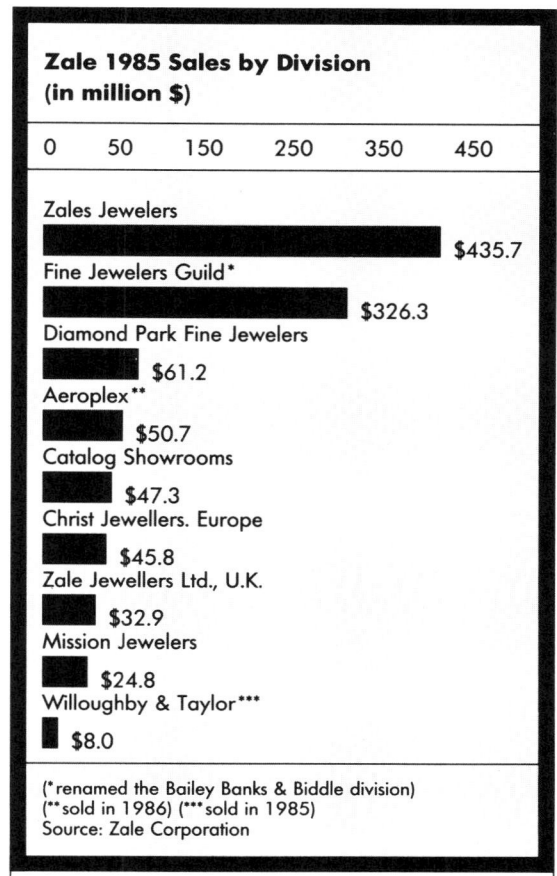

Put simply, "manufacturing-driven" means a company's merchandising and advertising reflect its strength at the buying more than the selling end of the spectrum. In an industry that concentrates heavily on diamonds, this is a very easy approach to take, especially if you are a firm of Zale's size and clout. "If the company could make a good buy on say, jade, it did so, whether or not it was actually needed. It was just assumed you could always use jade," explains David Gan, chairman of Zale's manufacturing division. "There was no idea of fine-tuning buying to actual consumer wants."

Zale can be excused for its "good buys"

merchandising philosophy, still a standby of jewelry retailing. If you don't think so, just look at a local newspaper. You're almost sure to find at least one jewelry store ad that boasts of making a killing on diamonds in Antwerp or Israel in order to give the public great cost savings. Such ads are textbook examples of "manufacturing-driven" selling and are to be expected in an industry dominated by De Beers Consolidated Mines Ltd., the ultimate "manufacturing-driven" company.

As diamond miners and distributors, the company's marketing programs are usually geared to surpluses and imbalances in its stockpiles. In the 1970s, for instance, prompted in part by the steady rise in use of synthetics, De Beers realized there was a fortune to be made in terms of added value by converting as much as possible of its vast industrial stockpile to jewelry stones. So it launched an all-out campaign for small diamonds, one so successful that it helped India attain its present preeminence as a cutting center.

More recently, however, De Beers has not been able to work the same kind of marketing magic that it did in the 1970s. Its 4Cs campaign (carat-weight, color, clarity, cut), designed to stimulate sagging sales of larger finer quality diamonds, has not budged the American market from its seemingly intractable preference for steadily lower grades. Zale executives point out that manufacturing-driven companies can quickly lose their clout in the marketplace when their objectives and the market's needs diverge. Suddenly, the company's greatest strength can become its biggest weakness.

"De Beers probably has no choice but to do what it does. After all, it's a mining company," says Michael Barlerin, Zale's senior vice president of corporate marketing. "But a firm like Zale does. Being manufacturer-driven, however, robbed us of a certain responsiveness to the marketplace."

Today, by contrast, Zale is seeking to use its size and the fact that it is vertically integrated (meaning it buys rough gems loose and makes most of the jewelry in which they are set) to greater advantage. Toward that end, it has centralized merchandising, which used to be largely in the hands of store managers, and made it responsible for telling Zale's manufacturing division what to buy and make.

Those decisions are based on very precise computer tracking of merchandise, reduced in recent years to five basic product categories: diamond, gold, diamond and precious, pearl and semi-precious jewelry, plus watches. The narrower product mix has actually meant greater inventory depth than before in the kinds of jewelry Zale thinks important, something essential if the company is to successfully project a fashion image. In addition, central planning, and more efficient inventory control, allows Zale to make more, not less, of the jewelry it sells. Already, Zale's manufacturing division produces 60% of the jewelry in its Zale division stores, bad news for outside vendors who rely on Zale orders.

Until recently, however, when Zale merchandising was more a matter of strength than strategy, it reflected sheer buying might, especially in diamonds. The company prided itself on its buying prowess. Zale was the first retailer to attend regular sights (sales of rough diamonds) at De Beers' Central Selling Organization in London, and at one time it was the single biggest importer of Indian diamonds to America.

Indeed, its New York buying organization was the envy of its peers. But all the buying power in the world couldn't buffer it from the ravaging decrease of inventory values and simultaneous increase of financing costs in the early 1980s.

"When we called ourselves the diamond store, we were seeking to capitalize on our strength in diamonds, principally bridal diamonds," Barlerin says. "Unfortunately, that made us little more than diamond distributors. We weren't really retailers. But as long as money was cheap and diamond values increased year after year, it was easy to pretend we were."

EAR TO THE GROUND

When Zale executives say the firm wasn't really a retailer, it means, in Barlerin's words, "we didn't have our ears to the ground." It wasn't easy to put one's ear to the ground at a company like Zale where all ears—and eyes—were fixed at the top.

For most of its 62-year history, Zale, like most entrepreneurial firms, was driven and dominated by the vision of its founder, the legendary M.B. Even when he passed the chairmanship to his trusted brother-in-law Ben Lipshy in 1971, M.B. continued to oversee and influence policy. In the 1980s, as the next Zale/Lipshy generation attempted to deal with a changing marketplace, M.B.'s resistance to change became a problem. Even as late as 1982, company insiders admit, M.B. was using his power to influence emerging policy. The problem is symbolized by M.B.'s presence in a tiny, windowless office just across the corridor from Donald Zale's along Executive Row in Zale's Irving, Texas, headquarters. When Zale's new headquarters was built in 1984, luxurious offices were designed for the emeritus officers (M.B., Ben Lipshy, and former vice-chairman Leo Fields) in an annex building across the street from the main headquarters. Nevertheless, when the company moved into the new building, M.B. scorned his spacious annex office and set himself up in the small room near Don's. Donald had to override his father, paving the way for restructuring to begin in earnest.

Restructuring started, as it frequently does nowadays, with corporate introspection. Out of this long, often traumatic process came a radically new definition of company strategy, one that clearly showed the influence of Zale's new recruits from general merchandising and their philosophy. Richard Mitchell, Zale's vice chairman and chief administrative officer, summed up this philosophy in a speech given to the Dallas Retail Financial Executives Association last year:

"Today retailing *is* marketing. It takes its lead from the consumer. Profitable retailing must turn its attention to market share and return on investment. More traditional performance goals, such as sales volume, gross margin and inventory turnover, are important but too short term to be positioned as 'the corporate gospel' for retailing."

Once long-term (or strategic) planning, as

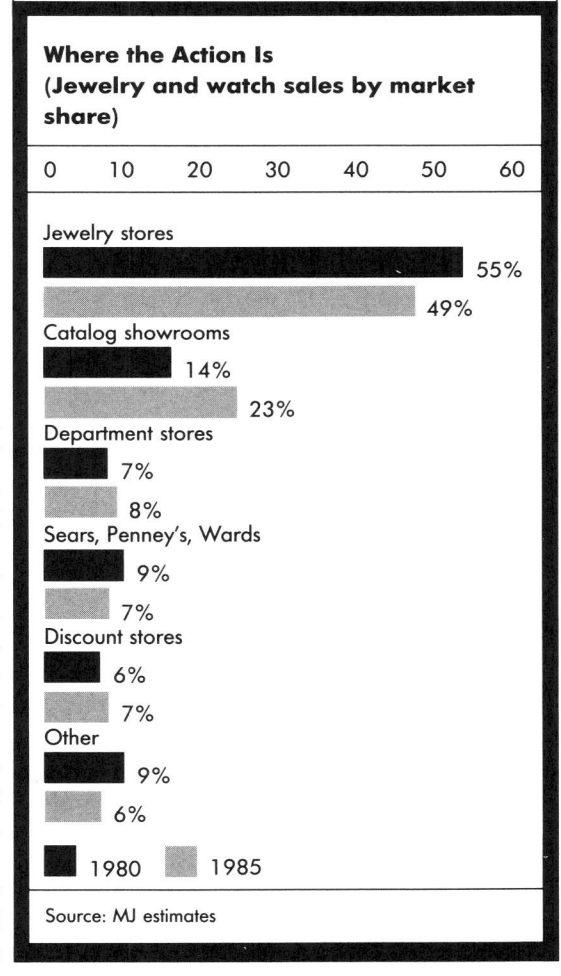

Where the Action Is
(Jewelry and watch sales by market share)

Category	1980	1985
Jewelry stores	55%	49%
Catalog showrooms	14%	23%
Department stores	7%	8%
Sears, Penney's, Wards	9%	7%
Discount stores	6%	7%
Other	9%	6%

Source: MJ estimates

opposed to short-term (tactical) planning became the basis of decision-making inside Zale, the firm set about redefining its presence in the outside world. Its corporate strategists knew, as did its counterparts elsewhere, that jewelers were faced with persistent problems like threshold resistance. They also knew that the market was oversaturated with jewelry stores, especially in malls where consumers had as many as a dozen jewelry stores to shop —not to mention department stores and catalog showrooms.

The main job as Zale executives saw it, was "differentiation," a business school buzzword for standing out in a crowded environment. Being one of 12 diamond stores (albeit the best known) in a mall didn't mean much when, as Zale's own illuminating market surveys showed, store loyalty was an eroding market factor. Jewelry store customers, 80% of whom were women (a growing number of them working women with college educations keen on accessorizing themselves) were far more loyal to product than people. Further, Zale's market research was demonstrating over and over that traditional jewelry retailing with its emphasis on value (the 4Cs) over fashion was sorely out of touch with market reality. The upshot: a shift to a consumer-responsive fashion orientation.

THERE GO THE BRIDES

Zale's shift in orientation should not be interpreted as an abdication of the firm's leadership in diamonds. Far from it. Zale's fashion emphasis means that diamond jewelry will have less space in Zale division stores and hold a smaller percentage of division total sales. They accounted for 62% of sales in 1984; the target for 1987 is 54%. Nevertheless, total diamond jewelry sales are projected to increase. Despite the smaller space, diamond jewelry inventories have doubled in small stores and tripled in larger ones as Zale makes more economical use of store space. Diamond assortments have changed with more emphasis on styles and prices consumers prefer.

To underscore the fashion image, there will be increased emphasis on 14k gold jewelry. By 1987, the typical Zale division store will have 50% more linear feet of fashion jewelry than it did last year. Store inventories of gold jewelry will triple by 1987 to help meet an ambitious jump in that category's sales from 10% in 1984 to 23%.

Hand-in-hand with the fashion emphasis is a new approach to store design. By 1990, every Zale division store will feature a uniform "fashion salon" look and layout to go with a much more homogeneous merchandise mix, the product of central planning and buying. In fact, inventory from store to store will be nearly 80% identical, a far cry from the old days when hundreds of district managers came to the New York office to select a sizeable share of their inventory. Store design will buttress the "Leading with Style" concept, and also help reduce threshold resistance. Zale intends to invite store browsing—and hopefully, impulse buying—with affordable gold merchandise tailored to the fashion-conscious female shopper Zale wants most to reach.

To get that shopper inside, redesigned stores will open directly with karat gold jewelry, averaging almost 30 feet of display space, instead of the traditional diamond counter with its intimidating big-ticket sparklers. In short, stores will project relevance to wardrobe-conscious women with money to spend on themselves. As important, they will be readily differentiated from other mall stores which tend to lead with expensive staples rather than affordable styles.

Some of the same thinking is also strongly evident in Zale's fine jewelers guild division, renamed the Bailey Banks and Biddle division last month. Although more merchandise variation will be permitted between its 325 stores, centralized merchandising will mean formulaic inventories there too that are roughly 60% identical. ■

The Peoples Takeover: Sorry Wrong Numbers

With his takeover bid of Zale Corporation, Irving Gerstein, head of 300-store Peoples Jewellers Ltd. in Canada, becomes the jewelry industry's first corporate raider, a small-scale version of Rupert Murdoch and T. Boone Pickens. Like these masters of merger mania, he's using a Chinese menu of cash and "junk" (scoffers call them "box top") securities to get Zale stockholders to swallow the idea of takeover.

Only they're not biting, at least not the ones who count. Gerstein's latest offer at $484 million, made last month—previous ones for $420 million and $470 million came in February and March respectively—equals roughly $46 per share (only $42 of it in cash). That was nowhere near appetizing enough, despite the fact that the offer price was more than Zale stock's book value of $38 and significantly above its recent selling price. Nonetheless, some stockholders feel entitled to more. One big-bloc holder notes that it is now routine to offer 1½ to 3 times book value in takeover deals. Given such high expectations, Gerstein has got a lot of sweetening to do to make takeover tasty.

Zale executives think it's highly doubtful that Gerstein can up the ante much further. Because Peoples Jewellers is only one-fifth the size of Zale, they contend that Gerstein doesn't have the asset base to raise more cash without substantial outside help. Gerstein, on the other hand, says he's not about to give up, although he refuses comment on when he'll make his next move or what it will be.

Meanwhile, Zale is doing its own share of counterpunching to take some of the spin off its stock which has risen from $28 before Gerstein's bid to $36 at *Modern Jeweler*'s press time. (Most of the lift comes from arbitrage buying by Wall Street takeover specialists who are betting the deal will go through.) Such maneuvering, say brokers, may be behind the company's $71 million inventory writedown, a move that will cut Zale stock's book value and, perhaps, its attractiveness.

FRAGILE FEALTY?

Although some Wall Street speculators are gambling that Gerstein will become the new owner of the Zale Corporation, Zale executives feel confident that he won't. To see that he doesn't, the Zale and Lipshy families are making a formidable show of unity. They've registered their resistance to the takeover by jointly filing a 13D statement with the SEC that flat-out rejects the offer as unacceptable. As long as the families feel this way, the Peoples' takeover is no deal, even if every Wall Street analyst were to agree with the advice to Zale shareholders of E. F. Hutton's retail specialist Arthur Lichtendorf: "Take the money and run."

Zale has one thing beside family solidarity going for it: Texas law, which requires 66.7% of a company's shareholders to consent to a merger. With 33.4% of Zale stock in family hands, Gerstein can't get the numbers he needs for a go-ahead—at least not as long as the Zale and Lipshy families stand united in opposition.

Just how strong is that opposition? The question must be raised since *Forbes* hinted that Zale's united front may be mostly a front. In its June article on the Peoples' takeover bid, it implied that Leo Fields, a Zale director and former vice chairman who controls 10% of the company's stock, will defect from the family ranks should the firm's founder, M. B. Zale, now 85 and the victim of several recent strokes, die. Fields denies any intention of deserting the cause and says he was quoted out of context.

"Their reporter asked me if M.B.'s death would change things and I answered yes," he explains. "But my yes was never intended to mean I'd sell my stock to Gerstein nor did the question, as I understood it, have anything to do with the offer. The question was far broader. Obviously, M.B.'s death would have an impact on the company."

However, another former Zale executive with sizeable holdings is less skittish about the possibility of selling out. "There comes a point where money talks," he says. "I think someone would be crazy to refuse an offer for, say, $50 per share."

RAIDER VERSUS RETAILER

Right now, the takeover bid is stalemated. Although Peoples is the largest single Zale shareholder with a stake of 15%, a 1981 standstill agreement prevents it from accumulating more than 21% without Zale board approval. Given such an agreement, and the Zale family's domination of the board, why is Gerstein persisting in his attempt to buy Zale?

Opinions vary widely on the motives for Gersten's bid. Some say he may be thinking more like a raider than a retailer. If so, that could possibly mean he's up to "greenmail," Wall Street's way of saying he's trying to force the Zale family to buy out his stock at a handsome price or, perhaps, even his company (which Zale executives insist they have no interest in acquiring).

More likely, as one Prudential-Bache broker puts it, "Gerstein is driven by dreams of empire. By merging Peoples and Zale he'd have the largest retail jewelry chain in history —overnight. That would certainly give his ego a boost. But it would also make good business sense."

As the Bache broker sees things, "The jewelry industry is the farm belt of retailing. Only the biggest and best will survive. Consolidation is the wave of the future and Gerstein is practicing it on the grandest scale jewelry retailing has ever known."

To a firm like Peoples, the logic of consolidation is compelling, indeed. First, Zale and Peoples combined would have extraordinary buying power that could make for major economies of scale, an important advantage in today's cutthroat marketplace. Second, merging operations could bring greater efficiency to them by eliminating overlapping white-collar jobs. The bottom line: sufficiently improved cash flow to pay the hefty finance costs of the takeover.

Gerstein, for his part, refuses to discuss any aspect of his takeover bid. When asked about claims by Zale officials that he's approved of every change in corporate strategy, he ducks the question. "I sit on 10 boards," he answers. "It's hard to remember everything these companies are doing." When pressed further, he backs off altogether. "Once outside the boardroom," he says, "only the chairman of a company should make statements about it."

So now Zale and Wall Street wait for Gerstein's next move. Zale officials are hoping there won't be one. But judging from activity in Zale stock, Wall Street expects another offer. If there is another bid, and it's tempting, will it weaken Zale family unity? Officials at Zale say Gerstein's numbers are far from seriously testing family resolve. But even Zale chairman Donald Zale knows there is a point where family pride would be pointless. "My feeling on the takeover business is that the group with the most money wins," he says.

Many observers applaud the changes now underway at Zale. "I like where they're going with the company," says one long-time Zale vendor. "It took a lot of guts to face up to where this market is headed."

Others aren't so sure. Some say Zale's new merchandising strategy, which Zale execs freely admit is borrowed from department stores, is more of a blunder than a brainstorm, based, some think, on overreaction to declining market share." Just because the fox stole a few more chickens than usual is no reason to switch to rabbits, especially when you're No. 1 in chickens," says the head of jewelry operations at a major department store. For its strategy to work, critics say, Zale will have to dramatically increase the number of customers and the frequency with which they buy jewelry. That's a mountainous uphill battle for a retail jeweler, critics contend, since jewelers are identified in the consumer's mind with either once-in-a-lifetime events like weddings or once-a-year events like anniversaries. Naysayers charge that the traffic patterns Zale is trying to build run so much against the grain for jewelry stores that they will be nearly impossible to achieve.

Zale corporate planners are well aware of the difficulties in repositioning a firm that is primarily known for special event and gift jewelry as a fashion center that should be visited every couple of weeks for self-gratification.

Early returns are favorable. In eight of the past nine months, Zale division sales have been ahead of the previous year's. Sales for fiscal 1986 ended in March were up 5% to $1.1 billion. However, the company posted a $61.1 million loss for the year due to an $84.6 million writedown. Most of that came from disposing of dated merchandise and losses on the disposal of the airport newsstand, catalog showroom and international retail businesses. "Our restructuring actions had a significant impact on fiscal 1986 results," says Donald Zale. "We fully expect, however, that the positive effects of these actions will be realized over the next several years as the realignment and concentration of our focus produces growth in market share and margin expansion." That conviction is practically a matter of religious conviction at Zale today.

DON'T CALL US, WE'LL CALL YOU

That wasn't always the case, though. One of the most difficult aspects of the refashioning of Zale was redefining the role of its manufacturing division, centered in New York City. For the new strategy to work, Richard Mitchell explains, Zale had to "reposition the manufacturing procurement arm on the company away from the role of profit center and into the mode of providing a competitive advantage to the retail operations." In short, manufacturing was made subservient to merchandising. Instead of selling what it could make, as it had in the past, Zale now would make what it could sell.

Suddenly, Zale manufacturing people were no longer calling the shots as to what merchandise the retail divisions would sell. Instead, they were taking orders from a new breed of merchandiser, new to Zale, who in certain cases knew lots about retailing but little about jewelry. The transition was tough.

At that time, and to some extent now, Zale merchandisers sought to imitate the Japanese manufacturing system whereby components are acquired as near to actual time of need as possible. From a cost-savings standpoint, this "just in time" system, as it is called, is admirable. But, in the jewelry world, it remains mostly an unattainable ideal, something Zale procurement pros tried, at first with no success, to point out.

"Try the 'just in time' approach when you're buying 150,000-plus carats of Indian diamonds a year averaging 40 stones to the carat," says Marvin Zale, the New York–based vice chairman of Zale. "You're talking about at least six million diamonds, all which have to be assorted. So you've got to buy these goods on a fairly steady basis and not just when you need them."

If attempting to accommodate "just in time" thinking created headaches, they were aggravated by rigidly specific buying plans. Zale diamond buyers, used to bulk purchasing and the price leverage it gives, had a hard time adjusting to merchandisers who insisted on certain sizes—and would brook no substitutions. Such inflexibility forced impatient merchandisers to buy on the open market, sometimes paying, according to former employees, 30%–40% premiums for strict selectivity and, occasionally, sacrificing in-house quality control on finished jewelry.

As a result, the manufacturing division, which had been responsible for as much as 75% of the company's diamond and precious stone jewelry (Zale's major products), made only 50% of the same category merchandise in 1984. Some veterans saw this as an unfair and unnecessary slap in the face, more punishment than policy. Those who could not or would not adjust to manufacturing's new role left or were asked to leave the company. Says a former procurement bigwig, "Suddenly, 'vertical integration' was a dirty word at Zale. But it was really one of our greatest strengths."

MAKING BIG BEAUTIFUL AGAIN

Today Zale management feels a lot more positive about the power of vertical integration, that is, its ability to buy raw materials for much of its jewelry and make the finished pieces in house. "The company overshot the mark," admits Zale director and former vice chairman Leo Fields. "But the pendulum has swung back. Once again, they're emphasizing in-house manufacturing and its value to the company." This year Zale expects to produce 75% of its diamond and precious stone jewelry in-house as well as the lion's share of its pearl jewelry.

Only now there's a big difference. Manufacturing is producing based on sophisticated market data and inventory control systems. The end result, say Zale executives: the greatest coordination between merchandising and manufacturing in Zale history. "There was a time," says Marvin Zale, "when manufacturing didn't keep its promise dates for goods and no one was terribly upset. Today, failure to keep promise dates is a serious crime around here." The new cooperation gives Zale new leverage, the ability to capitalize on its size.

Outsiders are beginning to pick up on the fact that Zale has adjusted to momentous changes inside and outside the company. In fact, every retail stock analyst *MJ* talked to for this story was aware of Zale's new corporate strategy and the merchandising philosophy that has resulted from it. "Zale is on to the right trends," says Arthur Lichtendorf, a retail stock specialist at E.F. Hutton. "Consumers don't consider jewelry an investment but, rather, something more of a fashion statement. So it follows that Zale doesn't want to be identified with diamonds."

Having said this, Lichtendorf still questions whether Zale can bring off its bold shift from diamond store to fashion center. "They've invaded department store turf," he says. "That's a very hard thing to do. Success will depend on just how good the company's merchandisers really are." ■

The New Breed: No Jewelry Experience Required

Listening to Randy Lively is like listening to a football coach psyching up his players for a big game. Lively even looks like a football coach. His large, thick hands move rapidly as he talks, while his hunched shoulders suggest he's about to put a secret strategy in play. He smiles broadly, with a conviction that could be mistaken for cockiness.

Lively, chairman and chief executive officer of Zale's upscale Bailey Banks & Biddle division, is symbolic of the new breed in power at Zale Corp. these days. He was a credit executive at Sears, Roebuck & Co. when he was recruited in 1981 to update Zale's unwieldy and antiquated credit operation. He presided over the creation of Jewelers Financial Services, Zale's computerized, centralized, state-of-the-art credit department. Before long, Lively's administrative skills had propelled him to the post of corporate executive vice president, one of the top five officers in the company. Earlier this year, when top management was looking for someone to reorganize the Fine Jewelers Guild into a new centralized division, they tapped Lively, even though he has had virtually no experience in jewelry retailing. Lively makes no apologies: "I feel no guilt because I don't know how to use a loupe," he says.

Not long ago, the rise of Randy Lively would have been unthinkable at Zale, a company famous for home-grown management. "Our concept of personnel promotion," says Zale Chairman Donald Zale, "was, if you hired a person and he developed into a good salesper-

Crediting Zale

Zale Corporation's credit operation has changed dramatically since the 1920s when M.B. Zale advertised "$1 down and 10 cents a week." Today, through Jewelers Financial Services, Zale's computerized, centralized credit division, the company's 1,600 retail jewelry outlets can advertise $1,500 of credit in 15 minutes. Says John Skinner, JFS president and a former credit executive with Sears, "Zale has the most state-of-the-art credit operation in any retail company."

Prior to the founding of JFS in 1981, credit was being extended and approved by each individual store manager. Says Bruce Lipshy, president and chief operating officer of Zale, "The cost of our credit was exorbitant."

Credit sales, which account for almost 50% of the company's entire sales, were costing 11% of total sales, or $37.7 million in fical 1982. By fiscal 1985, thanks to JFS, those losses were cut to a mere 1.1% of total sales, or $4.1 million. The number of Zale employees in credit operations was also cut as a result of centralization. Between 1982 and 1985, the number was cut from 1,800 to 600.

Other changes impacting on the cost-savings include the consolidation of credit centers. During the last several years, JFS consolidated its location to five regional centers — Tempe, Ariz.; Richardson, Texas (JFS headquarters); Houston, Texas; Tampa, Fla.; and San Juan, Puerto Rico.

In addition to cost-savings, JFS created other efficiencies as well. With the use of electronic technology, credit approval now takes an average 8–10 minutes, compared to several hours or days as in the past. When a customer applies for credit in the store, the form is sent via computer to one of the five regional credit centers. At the center, a credit operator checks the application and sends it to the local credit bureau. The credit bureau then sends it back to the center along with the customer's credit history. The application is rated and sent back to the individual store. For those customers with a good credit rating, credit cards are in hand within 5–10 days.

son, he's got to be a good manager. And if he's the best manager, he'll be a great supervisor. And the best supervisor is going to be vice president and eventually president, because he was the best salesman in the beginning."

Such through-the-ranks executive training, long the norm in retail jewelry companies, no longer applies at Zale. In the past two years, for example, Zale has replaced the top executives in its two key divisions, Zales Jewelers and Bailey Banks & Biddle (formerly the Fine Jewelers Guild). Of the four new division heads, only one (Zales Jewelers Chairman Kenneth Cort) had prior jewelry retailing experience and only one (Lively) has been with Zale more than two years.

The arrival of a new breed of executive was a crucial step in the refashioning of Zale Corp. The new breed brought the expertise and energy the company needed to chart the new course Donald Zale had set. However, the presence of this proud new breed in this proud old company precipitated a bone-crunching clash of corporate cultures. Out of that clash came casualties, then consensus.

NEW ARRIVALS

The new breed arrived at Zale essentially in two waves. The first lasted from 1978 to 1981, a time when Donald Zale felt the company needed to improve its internal systems. "Executives were brought in to upgrade staff services in areas of financial control, planning, marketing and management information systems," explains Gary Kastel, vice president of corporate communications. A number of people who would figure prominently in the repositioning were recruited at that time. One was David Gan, currently chairman of Zale's manufacturing division, who came from Xerox in 1978. In 1980, Gene Morphis, senior vice president for corporate development, arrived from Holiday Inns; Michael Barlerin, senior vice president of Zale's newly formed corporate marketing department, arrived from IM International, a fashion forecasting company; and Jerold Grubstein, senior vice president for finance, arrived from Petrie, a large discount retailer. In 1981, Lively joined Zale from Sears.

"The second wave of new executives came in 1984," Kastel continues, "as a result of the new strategic direction for the company." That new direction, the result of two years of analysis of the company and its role in a changing marketplace, was dramatic and, for many managers, traumatic. Essentially Zale decided that to stand out in the marketplace it had to position itself as more of a fashion center than a diamond center. To do that, it had to select product based on customer demand, making what it could sell, as it were, rather than selling what it could make. Hence, its corporate philosophy had to shift from being manufacturing-driven to marketing-driven. It wasn't easy.

"When we wanted to make those changes, we didn't have the people on board to do it," says President Bruce Lipshy. "Our managers kept coming in and asking us what to do. They were very reactive and you just can't have reactive managers in this business. You've got to be pro-active."

NEW LOYALTIES

Zale found its "pro-active" people in the department store ranks. Kenneth Cort, chairman of the Zale division, came from the Finlay Jewelry division of Seligman & Latz, with prior retailing experience at Abraham & Straus. Melvin Wilmore, president of the Zale division came from Abraham & Straus where he worked with Cort. William Roberti, newly appointed president of the Bailey Banks & Biddle division came from Mervyn's. Those retailers, Lipshy says, "were light years ahead of us. They were paying attention to marketing. They had done a great job and they had systems we didn't have, and they were fashion-oriented."

For many veterans at Zale, the substance and style of the newcomers took some getting used to. Most of the recruits cut their teeth as marketers and merchandisers in giant retail outfits. They see themselves as *retail* executives, not *jewelry* executives. They have pragmatic, go-with-the-flow attitudes about jewelry retailing. Whatever the Lolas of this world want, the Lolas get. And if consumer surveys (the new breed is big on market research) show that the Lolas, who are by far the biggest block of customers in jewelry stores, are swayed more by style than product knowledge, so be it. The new breed is beholden to market research, not market tradition. And when that research showed that women don't much care about a diamond's 4Cs, then Zale shifted its focus to diamond fashion.

Zale newcomers take a similarly pragmatic approach to other so-called "industry issues." Hot topics like discounting, gray market watches, and gem treatment disclosure, which infuriate many jewelers, don't upset the new Zale people. They consider them "gravity issues," realities of the modern marketplace that one factors into the marketing plan.

Buzzwords—"gravity issue" is one—are popular with the new breed. In *MJ* interviews with a dozen top Zale executives, expressions like "positioning," "leverage," "differentiate," "power curve," and "clarity of offer" recurred, each referring to some aspect of the company's new marketing direction. They also talk a lot about "corporate culture," those values, attitudes and behaviors that distinguish one company from another.

HARD TIMES

When Donald Zale set out to change some of those attitudes and behaviors by inviting outsiders into Zale's executive suites, he knew full well there would be conflicts. What he did not realize was how explosive those conflicts would be. "It was the neutron bomb," he says somberly. "It destroyed the people and left the company standing."

As the new men went about refashioning Zale in an image and likeness more suited to the '80s, they clashed with the old guard loyal to the tried and true policies which had made the company great. Those who didn't agree with the new philosophies resigned or were fired. "There was probably more bloodshed than we would have wanted," concedes Bruce Lipshy. Particularly painful was the departure in 1985 of long-time associates Allen Ginsberg and Willis Cowlishaw, both directors of the company. Ginsberg was president of Zale's International Diamond Division; Cowlishaw, president of the Fine Jewelers Guild.

Says one former executive, critical of the brashness of some new breeders, "I'm not saying we didn't make mistakes. But we were treated as if all our years of experience counted for nothing. There is no way anyone can tell me M.B.'s knowledge no longer mattered. You can't say that about a man who went from owning one store to running a billion-dollar company. It could have been a beautiful marriage if only the new guys had listened a little more."

The transition from Zale's traditional entrepreneurial corporate culture to today's corporate team concept was painful, particularly for Donald Zale. "We made plenty of mistakes," he says. "I've spent many a sleepless night thinking about all the changes we've put this company through."

Out of Zale's corporate culture clash, however, came the current consensus on Zale's new vision and direction. Today, Zale management is convinced that the new people and new ideas have become integrated in a newly defined corporate culture. The company defined its new management philosophy in a chapter on "Corporate Culture" in its 1985 Annual Report: "The management team will be cohesive in all respects. Open discussion and criticism will be considered healthy and welcome. Once a decision has been reached, management will support that decision in every respect."

It remains to be seen just how Zale's turn to outside executives will affect its profit performance. Certainly the improvements and controls the new breed has brought to Zale's internal financial, credit, planning, management information and other systems can only help the firm operate more professionally in an increasingly competitive and complicated marketplace. The test will be how well its new department store–styled merchandising and marketing programs work in the specialized world of fine jewelry retailing.

The Zale team is confident. They believe they foresee the future of jewelry retailing and they are prepared to take advantage of it. They believe they have the right people in the right places with the right plans and systems. Says Bruce Lipshy, "Zale Corporation used to have a mentality of 'ready-fire-aim'. Now we're 'ready-aim-fire'." ∎

Donald Zale: "We've Got to Be in the Fashion Business"

Donald Zale, 53, has been chairman of Zale Corp. since 1980 and chief executive officer since 1971. Son of M.B. Zale, he literally grew up in the jewelry business and his father's company. In April *MJ* editors David Federman, Shelle Jensen and Joe Thompson met with Zale in his office at the firm's Irving, Texas, headquarters. What follows are highlights of that interview.

MJ: Can you give us a bit of the background to the changes now underway in the company?
DZ: In the late '70s, we began to look at our business and decided that to grow we would have to do a better job of differentiating our merchandising in each of the divisions. It was no longer effective for us to take our traditional concept of skills development and utilize it.
MJ: What was your traditional concept of skills development?
DZ: Our concept of personnel promotion was if you hired a person and he developed into a good salesperson, he's got to be a good manager. And if he's the best manager, he'll be a great supervisor. And the best supervisor is going to be vice president and eventually president, because he was the best salesman in the beginning. When we really looked at that, it didn't make a lot of good sense because each of our divisions was getting so big that it required specialized skills. Our Zale division does $450 million and our guild division does about $300 million. Those are big businesses. If you're going to differentiate your merchandising, you have to differentiate your marketing. And you've got to have people who understand.

We decided to put merchants who had good marketing backgrounds into our divisions. At the same time, we were realizing that jewelry is an infrequent purchase and 8 times out of 10 is bought by females. And how do you appeal to females? You've got to be in the fashion business. How? You can't be in the fashion business without the right people buying the right merchandise. You've got to have fashion merchants, people who think that way.
MJ: Who decided to hire these outside people? Was it difficult for those already with the company?
DZ: It was my decision. I'll take the blame or responsibility. You bet it was difficult for those inside. It was a neutron bomb. It destroyed the people and left the company standing. It certainly wasn't anything I was happy to be a part of.
MJ: How long did this sorting out of management take? What was it like for you?
DZ: It took two or three years at least. And we made plenty of mistakes, let me tell you.

In the guild division, we put some management in there that we thought could do the job and they didn't. One of the things I learned from Ben Lipshy is don't grow on your mistakes. If you make one, admit it, change it and go ahead and do something different. I really strive hard not to let my ego affect a tough decision. I'd rather say I made a mistake—and I did.

I've spent many a sleepless night thinking about all these changes we've put this company through. If my name were not Zale, and if I were not a big stockholder, I probably would have been fired on the basis that I was just making too darned many changes in this company. You know, "If it ain't broke, why fix it?" A lot of my folks didn't think it was broke.

MJ: There's a new attitude in the company now, new people, new systems that weren't here before, more centralization. How did that evolve?

DZ: Listen, when M.B. Zale was involved in the day-to-day activities of this business, he could open the mail that came into the office from every store, and could talk to every manager—we knew them all by first name because we only had 100 guys. When you've got 1,500 store managers and intense competition, the problems are different and you have to have different concepts of how to solve those problems. You used to be able to put hot shots out there, put them in charge, say do it, and they did it. You can't do that today. In the first place, we're sitting on an inventory that would make a grown man cry, and to have all those guys out there buying is just financially impossible. You can't control it that way.

MJ: What happened in the late '70s or early '80s, besides the need for new management, that heightened the difficulties?

DZ: The whole bloody economics of the industry changed. Traditionally during the '60s and '70s, money was cheap. Gold was rock steady up to the early '70s and diamonds never went down. Although you owed a little bit more money at the end of the year, you had a bigger inventory, so you were a hero. Inflation was bailing you out and you really didn't know it. Come 1980, all those little lines on the graphs reversed.

MJ: What else was happening in the market?

DZ: The competition was getting a lot more aggressive and I think the customer had changed by this point. The customer is loyal only to the merchandise. The old business of having a family jeweler is also fading to a great extent. The customer is very, very fickle. When you recognize that and lay it all out, what you have to do becomes obvious. You have to be realistic about your business. We're against some tough competition for the consumer's disposable income and it's not just Macy's, Gordon's, Kay's and Service Merchandise. It's American Airlines, and Honda motor scooters and TV sets.

MJ: Where do you want to take the company? What do you want to achieve?

DZ: I would like for us to be the preeminent jeweler in the customer's mind. From the customer's perspective, I would like us to be their jeweler of choice, so they know if they go to Zales, they will get the best value and most fashion-current jewelry. I want Zales to be associated with good value, reliability, trustworthiness. And obviously, I'd like us to be profitable with reasonable returns.

MJ: What constitutes a reasonable return?

DZ: Our return on equity probably averaged 9% in the last four to five years and at its best, was probably 14 to 15%. That's our target again. I believe we can do it by virtue of the programs we've put in place. I'd also like to see us get back to a 5% net after-tax on sales, whereas it has been at about 3%.

MJ: What other goals do you have for Zale Corporation?

DZ: I would like to see us regain our A-credit rating which we lost. I'd also like to see our business simplified. We probably have one of the most darn complex businesses around. The accounting we have is very efficient and very timely, but it is very complex. We're on the retail method of accounting and we've used LIFO, but we can't use a standard LIFO index. We have to build our own. We're manufacturers, we have our own insurance company, and we're on the installment method of accounting. You put all these things together, and it is a very complex reporting system. I don't know how in the world to simplify it, but it's one of the things we're trying to do. If we can accomplish these things over the next three or four years, along with having seasoned merchants who are responsible for operating the divisions, I'll probably trade in my sailboat and get a bigger one.

MJ: How has your role changed?

DZ: I have to bite my lip an awful lot. Sometimes I have to watch our people do a lot of things I consider to be mistakes. I'm talking about buying mistakes, merchandising mistakes, but I let them do it. I have tremendous confidence in our organization. I'm in a role that I find much different today than five years ago. As for my time, I spend a lot of time traveling internationally, and the recent situation with Peoples Jewellers has been all-consuming.

MJ: How did the Peoples Jewellers relationship evolve?

DZ: We have been friendly with the Gersteins in Canada for 25 years or so. Bert Gerstein, Peoples' chairman, and my father were good buddies, and I've known Irving, Peoples' president, for probably 20 years. We've seen each other socially, we visited them in Canada and they visited us here. In the late '70s, Peoples bought the Schubach stores in Utah, which eventually built up to a pretty good sized chain of stores. Peoples kept those stores for a few years and later decided to sell them. But they still wanted to maintain a position in the American jewelry market.

According to Bert Gerstein, it was at that time that Peoples told their financial bankers to take proceeds from the disposition of the Schubach stores and buy stock in Zale Corporation. Gerstein also says the bankers advised him to buy enough stock to do equity accounting. With equity accounting, Peoples could take into their Canadian income that portion of Zale Corporation's earnings that were attributable to the stock Peoples owned. That's a rather complex and technical accounting concept, but generally speaking, if you own 20% of another company and have met certain other criteria, you can take 20% of their earnings into your income statements. At this point, Peoples began buying stock in Zale Corporation, and in December 1980, we were advised that Peoples had acquired 5%.

We had just sold off all our nonjewelry business and were working on acquisitions in Europe. When we heard that Peoples had acquired 5% of Zale we decided it was not a healthy situation, primarily because we didn't think they could afford it and to have that much Zale stock in hands that weren't financially able to own it was perhaps detrimental to Zale Corporation.

We went through a period of time when we had lawsuits against each other and finally agreed to limit the amount of shares they could buy. In 1981, we signed what's called a standstill agreement which provided that Peoples could only own 20 or 21% of Zale, that they would have representatives on our board of directors, and they could not sell our Zale stock without offering it to us first. We kind of kissed and made up and quit suing each other. They assured us at the time that they were buying the stock only for investment, and stated so in the contract. The contract goes to the year 2000.

MJ: When did Peoples make its first hint of a possible buyout?

DZ: With three directors on our board, up until last year at this time, Peoples had been very supportive. Each of us had lived up to our contractual obligations. We had a stockholders meeting in August 1985, and I saw Irving a lot. We spoke together frequently. Then in December, before our stockholders meeting, we were visited by Irving Gerstein and one of his representatives. They proposed to enter into some kind of transaction to go private. We told them we weren't interested, and Gerstein said they wouldn't do anything unfriendly. I also told Irving that as a public company in America, and since I am only one stockholder, I had to take this proposal to our board. After all, I've got to keep my legal skirts clean as well. That was essentially when this whole thing kicked off.

They made their proposal bid on Valentine's Day. I had anticipated it was coming. The silence was deafening—you could just feel it—but we were prepared for them, as the records will show. They made their first pass at us and we turned it down as being inappropriate to consider. More than one-third of our shareholders said they wouldn't vote for any kind of a merger with Peoples.

They made their second pass several weeks later and increased their offering from $35 and $5 in preferred stock to $38 and $7 preferred stock. Somebody likened that offer to $38 in cash and box tops, because $7 worth of stock is really worthless. Essentially we turned down the second pass as inadequate. I don't know what they're up to. The stock is not for sale. My feeling on the takeover business is that the group with the most money wins. There have been many companies that had family ownership substantially greater than the Zale family that have had to sell.

MJ: In your opinion, does Peoples think Zale is about to take a leap forward? Is that why they are making the merger attempt?

DZ: Probably so. They were never critical of Zale's merchandising and marketing changes, and on certain decisions, they were vocally supportive.

MJ: Is Peoples in a position to buy out Zale, in your opinion?

DZ: I don't think they are. You know, my dad and I were walking down Fifth Avenue in New York when I was just a kid. It was in the late '40s and he was taking me to his office. We were walking by Rockefeller Center, and I'll never forget what he said to me. He said, "I'd love to own that (Rockefeller Center) one day, but you know, I can't afford it." I've often thought of that. There's a whole lot of things I'd like to own, but I can't afford them. ■

The Zale Division: Whatever Lola Wants . . .

Zales Jewelers is out to become, as one top executive puts it, "the golden arches of the jewelry industry." "Like McDonalds," explains Zale division senior vice president William Harris, "Zales should have a strong appeal to the middle market and be recognized immediately as the premier jeweler for the masses of America."

Zale Corp., of course, knows more than a little about the American masses. Morris B. Zale built his stores into the world's largest and best-known jewelry chain through his uncanny ability to appeal to those masses. Those masses, however, are changing. It was in response to those changes that Donald Zale undertook the major repositioning now underway in the Zale division, whose 750 stores accounted for $486.1 million in sales in the fiscal year ended last March.

In the early 1980s, Zale consumer research revealed its customer base was growing older, richer, smarter and more demanding. It was also becoming dominated by the emerging "new American woman" who is having a profound impact on the U.S. jewelry market. She is working more outside the home, earning more, dressing up more and buying more jewelry—a staggering 80% of all purchases. Moreover, research showed she is interested in stylish jewelry. She is less interested in a diamond's cut or clarity than how it looks set in gold jewelry. She wants jewelry that is affordable and gives the most effective look for the money. Moreover, Zale executives learned, to their chagrin, she and other consumers find very little difference ("differentiation") among jewelry stores and have little loyalty to a store when making jewelry purchases.

Such response from consumer studies convinced Zales to adopt an entirely new marketing position flagged by a new theme. So, in the fall of 1984, "Zales, the diamond store" became "Zales Jewelers . . . Leading with Style."

"The new slogan not only reinforces the fashion orientation, but helps get customers into the store more often, unlike 'Zales, the diamond store' which implied a once-in-a-lifetime purchase for that wedding or engagement ring," says Michael Barlerin, senior vice president of corporate marketing. In fact, since the Zale division's repositioning, the frequency of purchase by current credit customers has increased 34%.

Heading the division are two executives recruited from the department store ranks in 1984. Chairman and Chief Executive Officer Kenneth Cort was president of the Finlay Jewelry Division of Seligman & Latz. Prior to that, he worked for Abraham & Strauss. Division President Melvin Wilmore was senior vice president at Abraham & Straus, where he worked with Cort.

With the fashion orientation, Zale executives believe the division is more in tune with its targeted customer. Says William Harris, "It's basically the same customer we're talking to out there. We're just talking to them about different things—about jewelry as a fashion accessory." The target customer still falls into the $25,000–$40,000 income range, and often involves the working woman who makes her own jewelry purchases. "There is a jewelry junkie out there," Barlerin explains. "What we've done is identified that person and fine-tuned our merchandising and marketing strategies accordingly."

Zales' advertising program has also been revamped to match its new marketing position. Two years ago, Zales' advertisements positioned it as the diamond store with ads that were institutional in nature—promoting quality, confidence, reputation and trust, Harris says. Today, merchandise is at the center of every ad with price points, selection, style and value emphasized. "The ads are more straightforward, more contemporary in style and have more flair than in the past," Harris says.

Moreover, participation in different advertising media has changed dramatically. In the last two years, television network advertising has doubled, network radio has increased 50%, while newspaper has decreased considerably, Harris says. "With newspaper advertising, there's no color, and it's difficult to show merchandise dramatically," he explains. Also, since Zales was not a day-in, day-out advertiser, it would often get poor positioning.

With the shift from a manufacturing-driven to a marketing-driven company, Zale made a commitment to know and supply what the customer wants. "The Zale division has a merchandising responsibility it didn't have before," Barlerin explains. "Merchandising decisions are now based on what the customer wants, not what the manufacturing division makes."

GLITTER WITH GOLD

The marketing shift towards style and fashion ushered in an entirely new merchandising concept for Zales. The overall strategy: "To be in stock with targeted assortments of customer-preferred merchandise." That customer-preferred merchandise, as studies revealed, is fashion-oriented jewelry, jewelry that makes a statement to the customer, says Ken Cort.

"Gold jewelry, for example, is essentially a fashion accessory," Cort says. "Women today think no more of buying themselves a pair of gold earrings than they do about buying a silk blouse, a shetland sweater or a pair of shoes. It's not a purchase that requires male compliance, and it's generally not of high dollar value."

In the past, however, gold jewelry sales have been dominated by department stores and chains, Cort says. Therefore, Zales is attempting to dominate with a better assortment of gold jewelry at competitive price points. "Our gold chain starts at $30 and gold earrings start at $19," Cort says. "Although that's a competitive price point, our average sale on gold jewelry is still considerably higher than the department stores," he says. For example, Zales' average sale on gold earrings is a little over $60, which is about $20 higher than the department stores.

In addition to a better assortment, gold jewelry display space has been increased from 12–15 linear feet in the old stores to 45 linear feet today. Gold fashion earrings, chains and bracelets at affordable prices have been moved to the front of the store to catch the eye of the style-conscious customer as she shops. A new category of gold jewelry which capitalizes on Zales' previous diamond orientation has been added to the inventory—diamond accent jewelry, gold jewelry with small diamond accents. By 1987, Zales hopes to shift its sales of gold jewelry to 23% of total sales, compared to 10% in 1984.

"Diamonds are still the heart and soul of our business," Cort explains. "We've done nothing except enhance that business with gold. Gold is an additive, a supplement. It's not replacing diamonds."

Other classifications of merchandise in the Zale division include: diamond jewelry, diamond and precious color, pearls, watches, and South American and semi-precious color. As with gold, Zales plans to attack the competition with dominance and assortment in these categories as well.

Although Zales' diamond bridal business has always contributed the most in sales, the division plans to even out that business by offering a stronger assortment of diamond fashion and diamond and precious stone jewelry. Diamond bridal jewelry space has been cut by 40%; while display space for diamond fashion jewelry has increased 50%. In addition, each Zales store now carries no less than 72 pieces of diamond and precious jewelry ranging in price from $175–$500. Diamond and semi-precious jewelry ranges from $140–$300 with approximately 80–110 pieces in each store. As a percentage of total sales, Zales hopes to shift its diamond sales to 54% by 1987, compared to 62% in 1984.

As for precious colored stones, Zales hopes to shift its sales target from 3% in 1984 to 5% in 1987. Pearls and South American colored stones sales target will move from 4% in 1984 to 6% in 1987.

Display space for pearl, precious and South American colored stone jewelry has been doubled as a result of the boosted sales targets. Together with diamond jewelry, that display space accounts for approximately 45 linear feet per store. Pearl earrings start at $19 with pearl strands at $1,500. In addition, Zale has eliminated all costume jewelry, gold-filled jewelry, class rings, accessories and gifts from the stores.

Watches, a heavily branded item and often discounted by other retailers, have been streamlined in the Zale division. Store space displaying watches has been reduced by half to approximately 18 linear feet per store. In addition, watches have been moved to secondary space—in the back of the store. "Watches as a percentage of our total had dropped in the past two years and brought us the lowest margin of all classifications," Cort says. "So we've narrowed our resources to basically three brands—Citizen, Seiko and Pulsar." Zales' sales target for the watch classification has shifted from 13% of total sales in 1984 to 10% in 1987.

As a result of the new merchandise mix, merchandise sources have changed as well.

Zale's manufacturing division has stepped up production to supply the Zale division with 87% of its diamond and colored stone jewelry — about a 13–14% increase over last year, Cort says. Combined with watches and gold and pearl jewelry (categories which Zale does not manufacture), about 60% of Zales' merchandise will be internally manufactured this year.

Customers should be noticing the changes in Zales' merchandise by now, Cort says. "The new merchandise assortment came into the stores visibly in October 1985," he says, "and since that time the Zale division has been in double digit sales increases."

BREAKING THE BARRIER

When Zales queried customers about store environment, the nearly unanimous opinion was that stores not be intimidating. "High apprehension is a major threshold barrier for our stores," says Gene Morphis, senior vice president, corporate planning and development, Zale Corp. "We want people to feel as comfortable buying jewelry as they are buying pantyhose."

With that thought, a year and a half ago, the Zale division initiated a store redesign plan that would reflect the merchandising and marketing changes already in motion. Headed by Melvin Wilmore, president and chief operating officer of the Zale division, and three people from Zale Corporation's store design department, the store design group made decisions concerning what the stores should look and feel like. "We wanted to surround the people and the goods with a warm and exciting physical environment so that our stores could more easily be browsed," Wilmore says.

Today, Zales' stores are being redecorated in soft tones of mauve and gray. The stores have been downsized from approximately 2,300–3,000 square feet to an ideal size ranging from 1,000–1,500 square feet. While square footage has decreased, in some stores jewelry showcase space has increased as much as 40–50%, Cort says. "We used to sell off the backs of the walls," he says. "We'd take chains and hang them on the back of the wall like pasta drying in the sun. Jewelry is a tiny commodity with great detail and we were distancing the customer."

Today those same walls are used for graphic and logo treatment with oversized mirrors enhancing the quality of the merchandise.

Although all 750 Zales stores have been re-merchandised, not all have been redesigned or refurbished. Stores are being refurbished by markets at a time so that area customers experience the same feeling in any store they visit, Wilmore says. If the redesign plan holds firm, by the end of fiscal 1987, 25% of the Zales' stores will be refurbished or remodeled.

"We think that Zales Jewelers should be the magnet attraction over any jewelry store in a mall," Wilmore says. And apparently that magnet is working. The stores that have been redesigned have posted dramatic increases in sales, Wilmore says.

MANAGING METHODS

Ten years ago, a Zales store manager was expected to be the top salesman. Today, that same person is a sales manager rather than the lead salesman, says Jerry Daws, senior vice president of corporate human resources. "Today's store manager is an executive and manager and is expected to plan, train and capitalize on good salesmen."

Zales is currently testing a new management training program in the Dallas area for store managers. Called the Executive Development program, the training offers actual hands-on management skills training with seminars and paper and pencil tests. In the past, the training program was called Career Development and focused primarily on how to increase sales with minimal management skills provided.

"Products and sales are important," Daws says, "but we also need to develop our store managers as planners, schedulers and motivators, so that we can leverage their abilities through other people."

As a result, Zales has devised new training programs over the last several years. Sales associates in the stores now have interactive video training programs available on subjects such as gemology. One such video features a jeweler modeled after Indiana Jones in the movie "The Raiders of the Lost Ark." The jeweler relates the exciting history and lore of gemology to his grandson. The video features a test with questions and answers on different gem facts.

Other management changes include the restructuring of Zales' buying staff. Previously, product ordering was done in almost every individual Zales' store. That buying has been centralized in the last two years, and now all ordering is done by a ten-person staff in Dallas, consisting of seven buyers, the executive vice president, and two senior vice presidents. "It's a lot easier to put ten people together and understand what the business is about than it is 800," Cort says. ■

Bailey Banks & Biddle: Curing the Guild Complex

Try to imagine running 325 jewelry stores with 36 different trade names, 15 regional vice presidents and 53 district managers. Now, imagine those stores all making their own advertising and merchandising decisions, while at the same time calling themselves a division. That's what Zale's Fine Jewelers Guild division did for years.

Contributing almost 40% of the entire company's sales, the guild was one of the glories of Zale Corporation. The loose collection of upscale stores capitalized on their prestigious trade names, not on the fact that they were owned and operated by the world's largest jewelry retailer. Between 1980 and 1985, sales increased 34% from $243.7 million to $326.3 million before slipping to $317.5 million in the year ended last March.

Yet despite increasing sales, problems existed. "The guild was not a division," says Michael Barlerin, senior vice president of corporate marketing. "It was a decentralized environment with no positioning strategy and sales as the only objective. And there was confusion as to where profits came from."

To make the guild more competitive and profitable, Zale top management devised a strategy to take advantage of its size and strength by giving it a strong national identity. This spring, they changed the name from the Fine Jewelers Guild to the Bailey Banks & Biddle division, linking all 325 guild stores with the name of the oldest and largest store in the division, Philadelphia's prestigious BB&B. All stores in the division, whether Corrigan's in Houston, Hausmann's in New Orleans or Granat's in San Francisco, are now referred to as "A Bailey Banks & Biddle Jeweler."

The key element in the change is centralization. "A centralized merchandising department will be the heart of our new organization," says Randy Lively, BB&B's chairman and chief executive officer. "For the first time in the division's history, we can defray marketing and merchandising costs across the entire division. Although the trade names had been loosely connected through the Fine Jewelers Guild, there was no strong central entity to provide an umbrella for effective advertising and special merchandising opportunities."

The centralization of the division brings the following advantages:

■ Centralized merchandising. A national merchandising staff will centrally direct all buying for the division. Previously the bulk of the buying was done in each store. National buying will enable the division to negotiate better prices for its merchandise.

- National advertising campaign. The division will be able to purchase national advertising with all stores gaining the benefits. As of July 1, all advertising for stores in the division carries the Bailey Banks & Biddle tagline. A national advertising campaign is scheduled to break Oct. 1.
- National credit card. Customers holding credit cards for any of the 36 trade names will now have credit approval at more than 300 jewelry stores nationwide. Until the new Bailey Banks & Biddle cards are issued in October 1986, cards from any of the trade stores will be honored.

Centralized buying will not only create cost efficiencies, but product efficiencies as well. "For the first time in our history we'll be able to participate in national branding," Lively explains. Currently the division is exploring a Bailey Banks & Biddle watch bearing either the name or the division's new double unicorn logo. In addition, pearl strands with the logo on the clasp are another possibility being considered.

WHAT'S IN A NAME?

When Joseph T. Bailey and Andrew B. Kitchen founded Bailey and Kitchen Jewelers in 1832, they had no idea that would create a historic jewelry operation that would someday be linked with more than 300 jewelry stores nationwide. But it was that historic past, exclusivity, and reputation of the Bailey Banks & Biddle name that led to the linkage.

When the top guild trade names were compared in terms of sales, profits and number of stores, Bailey Banks & Biddle emerged as the trade name that most enhanced the division's other prestigious identities. "The Bailey Banks & Biddle name had the most historic and equitable name," says Lively.

In addition to manufacturing and selling jewelry, silver and stationery, for years Bailey Banks & Biddle served as the official designer and manufacturer of medals, ribbons and honor awards for the U.S. government and its military and naval academies. The current version of the Great Seal of the United States was designed by a Bailey Banks & Biddle artist in 1904. While manufacturing operations of both BB&B's silver and stationery departments were phased out long ago, the firm's insignia department continues to serve many clients, including societies and universities.

"Bailey Banks & Biddle has the trade name and history representing a unique, significant value no other jeweler can point to," Lively says. "And that's the image we want to reflect to our customers."

Bailey Banks & Biddle joined Zale's Fine Jewelers Guild division in 1961 and since that time 55 additional stores with that name are now scattered throughout 11 states in the Northeast. That number will grow. Some of the BB&B division stores will change names completely to Bailey Banks & Biddle. For example, the 15-store Jacobs Jewelers chain in Florida will be changed to Bailey Banks & Biddle by Oct. 1. "Trade name equity will be measured and stores that have weaker names in their markets will be changed," Lively says. By 1991, the division expects to have the 36 trade names whittled down to about 10.

MORE FASHION CONSCIOUS

The BB&B division is about one year behind the Zale division in overhauling its marketing and merchandising strategies, executives say. "We're going to do things in months that would usually take years," Lively says.

As for the division's product orientation, as in the Zale division, fashion will be at the forefront. "We're still aiming for that customer in the $40,000–$80,000 and up income range, but with a different orientation," says William Roberti, president and chief operating officer of the division. "Our price points and quality of merchandise will still be higher than in the Zale division, but we'll be a little more fashion conscious, offering more gold jewelry assortments in 18k, as well as diamond accent jewelry." Better quality pearls and higher-priced watches such as Rolex, Baume & Mercier and Ebel will be carried in the BB&B division stores.

Centralized operations also called for a realignment of divisional employees. During the last year, the chain of command has been streamlined to accommodate those changes. Whereas there used to be 15 regional vice presidents of stores reporting to two senior vice presidents, there are now only nine. Reporting to those nine regional vice president now are 29 directors of stores (new title), compared to 53 district managers in the past. As for the buying office, although the numbers have not changed, the decisions are more centralized with the nine buyers corresponding to the nine regional vice presidents.

VISUAL THEATER

The BB&B division will use drama to add excitement and life to its stores. "We're going to bring real theater to our fine jewelry stores," Lively says. "And the customer will notice that theater and enjoy shopping in our stores."

On October 1, that theater will come in the form of interactive user-friendly video kiosks. These kiosks will be introduced in certain test market stores. They will tell the Bailey Banks & Biddle story and provide product information, such as the 4Cs of a diamond and the cut of crystal. "We want the customer to gain comfort from shopping in our stores," Lively says, "and the video tube is something the customer has learned to trust. One of the greatest barriers to our industry is consumer anxiety about 'what I'm buying . . . is it worth what I'm paying for it?' The video will explain *everything* to customers."

The kiosks will be evaluated after six months and depending on their success, will be rolled out to the other stores. Lively identifies three phases of video kiosk usage: First, as simple informational devices for the customer; second, as support for the store salespeople; and third, as a direct order device whereby customers could order directly from the video screen. "Ours will be the carriage stores for the jet-age consumer," Lively says.

In addition, stores will promote the BB&B linkage to customers visually when the division's new double unicorn logo is introduced on packaging, gift boxes and shopping bags in the next few months. The double unicorn is an updated version of the Bailey Banks & Biddle symbol that has been used since the early 19th century. Other visual changes in the BB&B division include future refurbishing of stores.

Despite centralizing marketing, management and merchandising operations in the division, Zale executives point out they are not positioning the division as a national chain of high-scale stores.

"The linkage is not being promoted as a chain orientation," Barlerin says. "It's a value-added enhancement to an already established name." But, Barlerin admits, the key challenge remains how to maximize on size, yet still retain the "specialness" of each store. Lively sums it up best.

"Ours is a personal selling business," he says. "The key is to not lose the Bailey Banks & Biddle touch, and that comes with how well we train our people. If they believe in the culture, history and tradition of Bailey Banks & Biddle, then the customer will believe. And we will be a success." ∎

Bruce Lipshy: "We Couldn't Do Business on the Back of an Envelope Any More"

Bruce Lipshy, 45, has been president of Zale Corp. since 1978. He is the son of the late Ben Lipshy, Zale's second chairman, and a nephew of Zale founder M. B. Zale. *MJ* editors David Federman and Shelle Jensen interviewed Lipshy in his office at Zale's Irving, Texas, headquarters in April.

MJ What happened in the market during the last decade that forced Zale corporation to change its strategy?

BL: Lots of things. Our commodities—gold and diamonds—started to fluctuate in price. Try to manage your business during that kind of fluctuation and it's almost impossible. If you're in the oil business and your prices go through extreme inflation or deflation, it's bad but at least you're turning your inventory ten times a year. In the jewelry business, you're turning your inventory once a year. In the late '70s, we never worried about the size of our inventory because we always knew it would be worth more at the end of the year than it was at the beginning. Diamond prices continued to go up and gold was fairly steady. We woke up one day and that wasn't true anymore. We were stuck with a lot of overpriced merchandise and while we were bringing in new merchandise that was fairly priced, we had a layer of inventory that was getting older and older. We tried to manage around that and finally decided to write it off and get rid of it. We'd never had to do that before.

MJ: At this point, what did you need to do that you hadn't done before?

BL: We had to start worrying about turning our inventory. We had to start worrying about what was in stock, what was selling and what wasn't. We had to decide what to start marking down and determining what was selling in one part of the country and not another. We couldn't do business on the back of an envelope anymore. The environment, the customer, the economy wouldn't let us do that anymore if we wanted to survive.

MJ: What changes did you have to make to survive?

BL: We had to bring in people with a new mentality. We found when we wanted to change we didn't have the people on board to do it. Zale Corporation was and is a great company. It was built by hard-working people who were very loyal and devoted, but they were used to doing business a certain way and it was very difficult for them to change.

MJ: What strategies did you want to take and why couldn't the "old mentality" provide that?

BL: We wanted to start being fashion-oriented. We wanted to know what the customer was thinking. We wanted to start making merchandising decisions close to the customer instead of only making the merchandise that *we* wanted to. We wanted our stores to be jewelry retailers, not merely jewelry distributors. When we were saying all these things, our managers kept coming in and asking us what to do. They were very reactive and you just can't have reactive managers in this business. You've got to be pro-active. And that's what we did. We went out and found ourselves proactive people who were into the new way of doing business.

MJ: What was the "old" way of doing business?

BL: We had a real dichotomy. When you're vertically integrated, you always have the retail side fighting and arguing with the manufacturing side. The manufacturers will tell you what they want you to make and the retailers say no, this is what the customer wants. There was a lot of fighting for turf. That's all gone now. Today we have a team and everybody is working together.

MJ: Who are these pro-active people you brought in?

BL: The guys who were the sharpest were the department store people. They were light years ahead of us. They were paying attention to marketing. You could go into a department store and see how they boutiqued all their various floors to compete with specialty stores out in the mall. They had done a great job, they had systems which we didn't have and they were fashion-driven.

MJ: What was it like to bring in all these new people who may not have been as "seasoned" in the jewelry business as yourself, Donald Zale and the other corporate executives?

BL: It was hard because of things we knew that had been instilled in us since we were kids. Many new folks who came in knew a better way of doing something. They showed us and proved it to us, although sometimes we didn't give them an easy time. We second-guessed a lot of decisions.

MJ: What about the decision to become fashion-oriented? What was behind that decision?

BL: Being a jewelry store is more than just selling diamonds. We were spending an enormous amount of our asset base on diamonds and the customer would walk into our store and want other things. We didn't know for sure if the customer, for instance the working woman, was interested in the 4Cs. We spend lots and lots of money training our people on the 4Cs. After we did some consumer research, we found out that's not what the customer wants. What she wants is something pretty, something fashionable and affordable.

MJ: With the shift from a diamond orientation to a fashion orientation, have you abandoned consumer education about gems? Where do the 4Cs fit into the strategy?

BL: I think we have to be prepared to talk about the 4Cs if the customer wants to talk about them. Don't misunderstand me. I just don't think on every sale we need to get into that. If a woman comes in and wants to buy a diamond cluster ring for herself, which is very likely, she may want to talk about the 4Cs and we'll be happy to do that. In most cases, however, she would rather talk about what is fashionable, what is pretty, and what she can afford. No two customers are alike. One reason we train our people in the 4Cs is so they'll be prepared to answer it. We used to *always* talk about the 4Cs. The 4Cs normally come up when you're buying a solitaire. When you buy a diamond cluster ring, do you really care about the 4Cs? My case rests.

MJ: What if the customer is unaware of the 4Cs and doesn't know enough to even ask about it? How can that customer be assured of getting quality and value?

BL: I think you're talking about credibility. Zale Corporation, in all our advertising, always stresses credibility. We stress the fact that we've always taken care of our customers, that we're 62 years old and we've been around for a long time. It's unfortunate that the industry has the ripoff artists that impact everyone. That gets back to what the trade should be. That's not really a burning issue to me. I know a lot of retailers talk about the gray market and how it's killing them, but I think it's a gravity issue. I can't do anything about it just like I can't do anything about gravity. I have to learn to live with it. So as for the guys out there taking advantage of the gravity issues, there's not a whole lot we can do about it. What we need to do is take care of our business and our customers.

MJ: What other things did your consumer research tell you about your customers?

BL: Several years ago, we made the decision to take windows out of all our stores because it was less expensive to build a store with no windows and we thought it looked nicer. We did some consumer research and found out the consumer likes to window shop. Another thing we learned during consumer research is that when a customer goes into a mall, she's going to go to several, if not all the stores, looking for the item. About 80% of the purchases are preshopped by the woman.

MJ: How did you change your strategy after you learned these things about the consumer?

BL: Well, when you go into a mall you've got seven, eight or nine jewelry stores plus each of the department stores have their own counters, well-stocked, I might add. That's what you're competing with.

You've also got the fact that when a customer goes into a store to buy jewelry, it is a scary, intimidating purchase. Heck, *I'm* intimidated walking into some of the upscale jewelry stores. The front door looks like a vault and the guard is standing there holding a .357 magnum. Can you tell me that company is serving the customer? Maybe they're going for an entirely different customer, but I doubt it because they're in a lot of the malls we're in.

We took all that research and decided to differentiate ourselves from the competition. We decided to differentiate ourselves on the basis of assortment and service. When a customer comes into our store, we want him or her to say, "My God, this is exactly what I'm looking for and this is exactly the person I want to deal with."

MJ: What about the mass-merchandisers and the discounters? What do you have that they don't have?

BL: Our business is not a self-service business. It's a people-selling business. We can compete with the mass merchandisers because the person behind their diamond counter was probably selling lawn mowers last week. But don't get me wrong, the competition is getting better. They are tough, tough competition and I'm talking about retailers like J.C. Penney.

MJ: How has the customer base changed in the Bailey Banks & Biddle division and the Zale division?

BL: Prior to the change in the demographics of our customer base, the guild customer was the carriage trade. But what is the carriage trade today? You try to define that and it's very difficult to do. A lot of the up-scale competition is trying to go for the top 10%. Take the entire customer base, say it's 100%, and 10% of that wants to buy cubic zirconia. Then you've got another 20% above that is very price-driven. Then you've got middle America which is probably 50–60%, and of that probably half are Zale customers and half are Bailey Banks & Biddle customers. Then at the top, you've got the 5–10% who are the carriage trade and really want to shop at the Tiffany's, the Cartier's and so on. You can't live on that 5 to 10% anymore. You just can't do it.

With our Bailey Banks & Biddle stores we've done a very good job of selling 200 to 300 customers in a town. But you're really not going to be profitable doing that. If you're going to grow your business, you had better grow your customer base.

MJ: Are you saying that the difference between a Zales store and a Bailey Banks & Biddle store is very slight and that there's more overlap now than before?

BL: The difference is much hazier than it was before. There's a lot of blending of the two, but there's no question in my mind that Bailey Banks & Biddle is still going higher up. In both stores, we've gone in and decided to stand for what we're in, and that's bridal, diamond fashion jewelry, diamond and color, pearls, gold jewelry and watches. Although the overall strategies are the same in each division, the Bailey Banks & Biddle division will be aimed at the more affluent customer with higher quality merchandise at higher price points.

MJ: What is your response to stock analysts and others who say that Zale Corporation is not performing well and future growth is questionable?

BL: I want everyone to remember that we have 1,600 stores and it's like trying to turn a battleship or an aircraft carrier around in a bathtub. Change is not easy to do. It takes time.

What nobody seems to understand is how costly it is to make the change. We had to blot out a lot of inventory, change a lot of stores and a lot of people. We made a lot of mistakes. For example, when we started reassorting the Zales stores, we pulled out a lot of merchandise and didn't replace it right away. Our sales fell off because we were giving up sales before we were replacing it with new goods. Our timing wasn't just right.

We made a lot of mistakes like that. But go look at our stores today and see what we've done. We've done it and our numbers are starting to reflect it. We had a hell of a Christmas. The Bailey Banks & Biddle division is a little bit further behind, but it's going to be there; it's already on its way. Plain and simple, Zale Corporation used to have a mentality of "ready-fire-aim." Today we're "ready-aim-fire." ∎

Poison Pen

Ronald B. Mack, M.D.
DEPARTMENT EDITOR

Jeffrey H. Forster
EDITOR

A. Michael Velthaus
ART DIRECTOR

Karen J. Ward
COPY EDITOR

Ingrid A. Lang
EDITORIAL ASSISTANT

Accidental poisoning is a leading cause of death and emergency hospitalization in children. Time is precious; a rapid and accurate diagnosis and effective treatment are essential. This section keeps pediatricians informed on relevant matters, such as the best therapies and information on new sources of poisoning.

Contemporary Pediatrics serves pediatricians and other health professionals involved in the care of children. "Poison Pen" first appeared in the February 1986, August 1986, and October 1986 issues of *Contemporary Pediatrics,* published by Medical Economics Company, Inc. © 1986. Reprinted with permission.

Poisonous Mushrooms— Nature's Iscariot

The words we use to communicate with fellow medical professionals must be clear, succinct, and directed toward the cognitive. There are times, however, when we really need a poet. No one, for example, has captured the essence of the mushroom better than Emily Dickinson: "Had nature any outcast face, could she a son contemn, had nature an Iscariot, that mushroom—it is him."[1]

This outcast fungus exacts its revenge on the unwary. Children are the most frequent victims of mushroom poisoning, accounting for about 70% of all cases. The preschool child in particular is a forager who explores the environment freely with hands and mouth. At the other end of the spectrum are teenagers who get into trouble by seeking and ingesting fungi that can produce a mind-altering experience. Other victims may mistake a poisonous mushroom for an edible one while searching for new and different food experiences. Most edible mushrooms, in fact, have one or more poisonous look-alikes.

There are so many varieties of toxic mushrooms—100 in the United States alone—that the pediatrician who does not acquire training or experience with them literally can be lost in the woods. The first step is to attempt to identify the mushroom. Many cities have qualified experts in mushroom identification. They are known as mycologists, and they are often found on the faculties of colleges or high schools. If the mushroom itself is not available, a mycologist may be able to determine the species by examining the spore. The spore is obtained from the victim's emesis, gastric lavage contents, or stool.

The general approach to most ingested toxins applies as well to poisonous mushrooms: Give ipecac if the patient is alert or try lavage if the reflexes are obtunded. If the patient has not had a catharsis from the ingestion, follow with activated charcoal and a cathartic.

MUSHROOMS THAT POISON QUICKLY, BUT NOT LETHALLY

A more specific approach to mushroom poisoning is needed, however, because the effects are nearly as varied as the species. A straightforward way to sort out the problem is to divide toxic mushrooms into two groups based on the incubation period, the time from ingestion to the onset of abnormal clinical features (Table 1). The short-incubation varieties do their damage within 15 minutes to two hours; fatalities are rare. The long-incubation mushrooms have delayed clinical toxicity—about three to 24 hours after ingestion—and can kill. Some authors divide poisonous mushrooms into seven clinical types, five of the rapid-onset and two of the delayed-onset variety.[2-3] The five rapid actors are those that produce:

Gastrointestinal irritation. The most common and probably the most benign toxic mushrooms are those that cause gastrointestinal adversities only. The category encompasses many genera and species. Nausea, vomiting, diarrhea, and abdominal cramps are the usual symptoms, appearing 30 minutes to two hours after ingestion. Treatment is symptomatic and primarily involves maintaining proper fluid and electrolyte balances. With such management, the outcome should be good.

Ibotenic acid. Mushrooms that produce ibo-

TABLE 1. Mushroom Poisons—the Deleterious and the Deadly

Toxin	Onset of Symptoms	Effects
Five fast actors		
GI irritants	30 min–2 h	Nausea, vomiting, diarrhea, abdominal cramps
Ibotenic acid	30 min–2 h	CNS effects—"inebriation-like state," staggering, incoordination, muscle spasms, hyperactivity, "visions," deep sleep
Psilocybin/ psilocin	30 min–1 hr	CNS effects, including vivid hallucinations, distortions of senses (colors are "felt," etc.), poor performance ability, compulsive hyperkinetic movements, vertigo, ataxia, muscle weakness, mydriasis, paresthesias, sleep. May be a "bad trip" with paranoia, panic, inability to distinguish real from unreal. Hypertension, tachycardia, fever, diaphoresis, chills, nausea, vomiting, cramps. Hyperpyrexia and seizures in very young children
Coprine	20 min–5 days when combined with alcohol consumption	Similar to those of taking Antabuse and alcohol. Metallic taste, flushing, swelling and tingling of hands, tachycardia, hypotension
Muscarine	30 min–2 h	Similar to anticholinesterase poisoning: salivation, lacrimation, urination, defecation, GI pain and cramping, emesis. Possibly miosis, diaphoresis, bradycardia, hypotension, bronchospasm
Two delayed-action killers		
Gyromitrin	6–8 h	Cellular destruction—painful bloating, severe headache, nausea, vomiting, diarrhea. Followed by liver enlargement and tenderness, jaundice, hemolysis, methemoglobinemia, possible liver or renal failure. Possible fever, incoordination, seizures, coma
Amatoxins (cyclopeptides)	10–14 h	Cellular destruction. Three stages: **1.** 24–36 h. Nausea, vomiting, severe abdominal cramps, profuse watery diarrhea. Can lead to circulatory collapse. **2.** 24–36 h. Latent period in which patient feels better if fluids and electrolytes are replaced and homeostasis is maintained. Lab results show abnormal liver enzymes, rising BUN, increasing creatinine. **3.** Renal failure (typically day 3), liver failure (typically day 4) with jaundice, hypoglycemia, convulsions, coma, possibly death (in 4–7 days)

*For the five rapid-acting mushrooms, give ipecac initially to alert patients or try lavage otherwise. If ingestion hasn't produced catharsis, follow with activated charcoal and a cathartic.

tenic acid adversely affect the central nervous system (CNS). Signs and symptoms appear within 30 minutes to two hours. The patient has an inebriation-like experience with staggering gait, incoordination, muscle spasms, hyperactive behavior, "visions," and a very deep sleep. Ibotenic acid metabolizes in the body to muscimol, a gamma-aminobutyric acid antagonist. Fortunately, the event lasts only a few hours and is self-limited, usually producing no sequelae. The treatment is supportive.

Psilocybin/psilocin. Mushrooms containing

Treatment*	Typical Outcome
Symptomatic; maintain fluid and electrolyte balances	Recovery
Supportive	Self-limited with no sequelae
Diazepam for seizures; antipyretic measures if needed. "Talking down" the teenager	Dysphoric state lasts 2–3 h or longer
None usually. Propranolol if tachycardia is a problem	Recovery in 2–4 h
Atropine 0.05 mg/kg IM or IV. Note: atropine efficacy in mushroom poisoning limited to muscarinic group	Recovery with atropine; dosage may be repeated at 15–20-min intervals until child cannot expectorate
Pyridoxine 25 mg/kg IV titrating according to patient's condition. Monitor fluids, electrolytes and glucose levels. Diazepam for seizures	If patient survives 5–7 days, recovery is quite rapid. Death reported in 4%–40% of cases
No proved therapy. Treat as for acute overwhelming hepatitis. Maintain fluids and electrolytes, blood sugar, give vitamin K when indicated, prescribe low protein diet	Most survivors have no sequelae although some may have chronic active hepatitis

psilocybin and psilocin also affect the CNS. These "magic mushrooms" produce vivid hallucinatory experiences as well as synthesthesias—paradoxical distortions of the senses whereby sounds can be "seen" and colors "felt." This dysphoric state begins within 30 to 60 minutes and lasts two to three hours or more.

The victim also experiences poor performance ability, hyperkinetic compulsive movements, vertigo, ataxia, muscle weakness, mydriasis, paresthesias, and sleep. Some have a very bad voyage, with feelings of nonexistence or self-disintegration, paranoia, panic, and inability to distinguish the real from the unreal. If such a patient ends up in your care, expect hypertension, tachycardia, fever, diaphoresis, chills, nausea, vomiting, and cramps. Very young children who accidentally ingest psilocybin mushrooms may experience hyperpyrexia and tonic-clonic seizures; diazepam should help the child (and quite possibly the parents). The treatment for a teenager who freaks out after eating such a fungus is nothing more than "talking him down" to relieve apprehension and restore contact with reality.

Coprine. Coprine-containing mushrooms produce a strange clinical picture only when combined with alcohol ingestion. The result is similar to the reaction seen when a patient on disulfiram (Antabuse) consumes alcohol. Coprine is an amino acid with biochemical properties similar to disulfiram; it blocks the metabolism of ethanol at the acetaldehyde stage. The reaction consists of a metallic taste in the mouth, flushing of the face and neck, swelling and tingling of the hands, tachycardia, and hypotension. It may occur as soon as 20 minutes after drinking alcohol and as long as five days after eating the mushroom (apart from the alcohol-guzzling teenager, let's not forget that young children may receive over-the-counter and prescription medications containing alcohol). The reaction resolves spontaneously in two to four hours, and treatment is usually not necessary. If tachycardia gets to be a problem, propranolol (Inderal, Inderide, etc.) may be of help.

Muscarine. Mushrooms with muscarine and muscarinic compounds begin to do their damage about 30 minutes to two hours after ingestion. The result looks for all the world like a poisoning with organic phosphates or carbamate insecticides. The patient experiences the S-L-U-D-G-E reaction—*S*alivation, *L*acrimation, Urination, Defecation, Gastrointestinal pain and cramping, and Emesis.* Other symptoms such as miosis, diaphoresis, bradycardia, hypotension, and bronchospasm may also be present. The clinical picture is one of cholinesterase inhibition.

This poisonous encounter can be treated with the same antidote used for carbamate poisoning—intramuscular or intravenous atropine. The dosage for children is 0.05 mg/kg as needed to relieve excess salivation. The dose may have to be repeated at 15- to 20-minute intervals until the child cannot expectorate. Most affected children do very well with atropine therapy. Earlier in this century, atropine was considered the antidote for all types of mushroom poisoning, but today its use is limited to ingestions of the muscarinic group.

THE DEADLY MUSHROOMS

The typical phone call I get about toxic mushrooms is from a physician who is somewhat concerned but not terribly worried because several hours have elapsed and the child does not appear sick. This, in fact, is the patient to worry about. If symptoms do not begin to appear until several hours after ingestion, a lethal variety may be at work. There are only two main groups in this category, but that is more than enough—they cause cellular destruction.

Gyromitrin. With these mushrooms, the toxin gyromitrin hydrolyzes in the body to monomethylhydrazine, which is a rocket propellant. The extent of the poisoning depends in part on the individual's ability to acetylate the hydrazine, an ability that varies significantly from patient to patient. Symptoms typically begin six to eight hours after ingestion with a painful bloated feeling, severe headaches, nausea, vomiting, diarrhea. this is followed by liver enlargement and tenderness, jaundice, hemo-

*See "Poison Pen: Carbamate poisoning: A Kafkaesque nightmare," *Contemporary Pediatrics,* October 1985.

lysis, methemoglobinemia, and possibly renal and liver failure. The patient may also experience fever, incoordination, seizures, and coma. Death has been reported to occur in 4% to 40% of cases.

The good news is that an antagonist is available. Monomethylhydrazine produces effects similar to those seen in acute isoniazid overdose by interfering with pyridoxine metabolism. Thus, reversing the toxicity requires administering pyridoxine 25 mg/kg IV, titrating the frequency according to the patient's clinical condition. Careful attention should be paid to maintaining electrolyte balances and proper fluid and glucose levels. Diazepam can help to control seizures. If the patient survives five to seven days, recovery is usually quite rapid. Recovery from renal impairment, however, may take longer.

Amatoxins. The ultimate incredible inedible mushrooms produce extremely virulent, thermostable toxins known as amatoxins or cyclopeptides. These toxins, particularly amanitin, inhibit nuclear RNA polymerase II, leading to cellular destruction. They are probably responsible for 95% of mushroom-eating fatalities.

The most lethal species is *Amanita phalloides,* also known as the "death cap." True to its name, one cap is enough to kill an adult; smaller amounts are deadly for a child. The onset of clinical abnormalities usually does not occur for ten to 14 hours. Cells affected by the amatoxin die and do not reproduce because the transcription of RNA and DNA has been disrupted. Cells with rapid turnover rates are especially wounded, including GI tract mucosal cells, hepatocytes, and renal tubular cells.

There are three stages in a "death cap" poisoning. In stage I, which can last 24 to 36 hours, the patient experiences nausea, vomiting, severe abdominal cramps, and incredibly profuse water diarrhea (as they say in North Carolina, "the bowels are locked in the open position"). The cholera-like fluid loss can lead to circulatory collapse. In stage II, if you have properly replaced fluids and electrolytes and maintained homeostasis, the patient usually feels better. This latent period of apparent clinical improvement is deceptive; the lab results are not promising and typically show abnormal liver enzymes, rising blood urea nitrogen, and increasing creatinine. Stage II can last 24 to 36 hours; do not send the patient home as yet. In stage III, the patient undergoes massive hepatic necrosis and acute renal failure with remarkable metabolic derangements, jaundice, hypoglycemia, convulsions, coma, and possibly death. In a typical fatality, renal dysfunction occurs on the third day and liver failure by the fourth. Death usually occurs within four to seven days and is secondary to hepatic and renal failure and their effects on the CNS and cardiovascular system. Most survivors recover without sequelae, although chronic active hepatitis may occur in a significant number.[4]

There is no magic bullet for *Amanita phalloides* poisonings. Many therapeutic modalities have been employed, all aimed at reducing the amount of toxin entering the cells, especially the hepatic cells. The approaches include penicillin, repeated doses of activated charcoal, steroids, and cytochrome *c;* none has been shown to make a significant difference. Extracorporeal removal has also been tried but does not seem to be the answer either. The most debated therapy in recent years is the use of thioctic acid. This Krebs cycle coenzyme was first used in amanitin poisoning in 1968, but no well-designed clinical trials are available to support its use. When faced with a death cap poisoning, you probably will not be amiss if you carefully maintain fluid balances and treat the patient as you would for acute overwhelming hepatitis—maintain the blood sugar, give vitamin K when indicated, and prescribe a low protein diet.

In approaching mushroom poisoning, keep in mind the unmagnificent seven groups. Mnemonics, often helpful in stirring the medical memory, can be used to remember them. To recall *I*botenic acid, *M*uscarine, *C*oprine, *Gy*romitrin, *A*manitin, *P*silocybin, and *G*astrointestinal irritants, consider that Indiscriminate Mushroom-eating Can Give All Patients Grief. Discriminating care, on the other hand, can give them needed relief. ■

REFERENCES

1. *Complete Poems of Emily Dickinson, 1830–1886.* New York, Avenel Books, 1982, p 132
2. Beware the wild mushroom, Emergency Medicine, October 30, 1985, pp 76–101
3. Hanrahan JP, Gordon MA: Mushroom poisoning: Case reports and a review of therapy. JAMA 1984;251:1057.
4. St. Omer FB, Giannini A, Botti P, et al: *Amanita* poisoning: A clinical-histopathological study of 64 cases. Hepatogastroenterology 1985;32:229

Carbon Monoxide: A Colorless Executioner

Do you feel sad after reading Albert Camus? That is like asking if you feel run-down after you are hit by a car. To Camus, life was absurd—brief, painful, and final. In *The Plague,* Camus uses an epidemic of bubonic plague as a metaphor for any form of pain or suffering that can afflict modern man.[1] If he were to write the book today, he might well choose a plague of carbon monoxide (CO) poisoning. This colorless, odorless, tasteless gas brings many children to the end of their earthly existence prematurely. This is absurd, and pediatricians need to help combat this gaseous plague.

It is very difficult if not impossible in the 20th century to avoid exposure to CO. It is the most abundant pollutant in our atmosphere; whenever there is incomplete combustion of organic material, CO is produced.

If your mother was a cigarette smoker, you received more of this toxin in utero than you cared to. Carbon monoxide rather easily diffuses across the placenta into fetal blood. The concentration of carboxyhemoglobin (HbCO) as a percentage of total hemoglobin reaches higher levels in the fetus than in the mother.[2]

On the ride home from the hospital, you probably had some more contact with CO. Automobile exhaust is the greatest source of it in our environment, and the amount is frightening. One automobile driven at 25 mph produces about 0.37 kg of CO per mile.[3] Just imagine what the freeway concentration must be at rush hour. Carbon monoxide in motor vehicle exhaust is the most prominent single agent among all accidental poisoning deaths and suicides. Most accidental deaths occur when cars are parked with the engine running to provide warmth.[4] Faulty exhaust systems are another common cause of CO intoxication.

You are not safe in your home, either: Cigarette smoking in the home produces CO concentrations ranging from 20,000 to 60,000 ppm. Carbon monoxide is also a common by-product of hot-water heaters, furnaces, and fireplaces. And don't overlook the increasing use of kerosene space heaters as alternative heat sources (not to mention the danger that young children may ingest the fuel). Parents may not think twice about bringing the charcoal grill onto the porch or even into the house when inclement weather ruins the cookout or the stove ceases to function. The use of methylene chloride as a paint remover can be another infraction of rational thinking if precautions are not taken; it is readily absorbed by bystanders and metabolized to CO in the body. The HbCO produced by methylene chloride has a half-life twice as long as that resulting from direct exposure to CO.

HOW CO ACTS ON THE SYSTEM

When inhaled, CO sneaks across the alveolocapillary membrane and binds with hemoglobin to produce HbCO, an unfortunately stable union. It is scandalous how much CO loves hemoglobin; CO has 250 times the affinity for hemoglobin that oxygen does. Just another example of the dangers of binding to the wrong mate—advice our parents were always eager to give us. Carboxyhemoglobin blocks the normal transfer of carbon dioxide and oxygen in the blood. To compound the problem, the presence of HbCO shifts the oxygen dissociation curve to the left; as a result, less oxygen goes to the tissues. Red blood cell 2, 3-diphosphoglycerate is also reduced, thus accentuating the left shift. A recent discovery suggests that CO binds with cytochrome *a* as well as to hemoglobin. This mitochondrial cytochrome oxidase system is responsible for the final release of energy. Carbon monoxide therefore not only disrupts oxygen transport in the blood but blocks its utilization in the cells.

SIGNS OF POISONING

With a good history of exposure, the diagnosis of CO poisoning is not difficult. Without a good history, you have to be a detective in order to discern the subtle manifestations. The onset can be quite nonspecific, especially if several people are involved simultaneously. The patient or patients may complain of headache, nausea, vomiting, dizziness, and weakness. It may appear to be a case of flu, food poisoning, or mass hysteria.

The clinical features of CO toxicity depend on the chronicity and the concentration of the exposure. Because toxicity results from hypoxia, the two organs that normally have the greatest oxygen consumption are especially vulnerable—the brain and myocardium. Thus, most patients with CO poisoning suffer from headache (often severe), dizziness, hyperventilation, obtundation, coma, chest pain, or tachycardia. Headache is an especially important clue—it is thought to be the most sensitive early indicator of exposure to low concentrations of CO.

Carbon monoxide can cause problems in

many organ systems. The skin and mucous membranes are usually pale or cyanotic. The myth of cherry-red skin and mucous membranes must be dispelled; it is uncommon in CO poisoning and probably seen only in cases of imminent death. What does occur commonly is redness and edema of the skin in association with vesicles and bullae, especially in pressure areas where the patient has been sitting or lying after being poisoned. Pressure necrosis of muscles can lead to rhabdomyolysis and renal failure, but muscle tissue dissolution and myoglobinuria have been reported without pressure necrosis.

The eyes can be involved; disturbances include decreased visual acuity or even temporary or permanent blindness. Retinal venous engorgement can occur as well, but the presence of retinal hemorrhages is quite important when the diagnosis is not clearcut. A retinal hemorrhage is not pathognomonic of CO poisoning but is a consistent finding in subacute cases.

While the effects of CO on the skin, muscles, kidneys, and eyes are damaging, the effects on the heart can be fatal. Because myocardial tissue is thought to be the most sensitive to CO's hypoxic effects, the cause of immediate death is usually cardiac. Cardiac dysfunction generally precedes central nervous system (CNS) disturbances. Severe intoxication can result in profound hypotension and deadly arrhythmias. When CO poisoning is suspected, obtain an electrocardiogram.

Clinical features that result from CNS involvement can be as mild as headache, dizziness, and blurred vision or as severe as seizures, pyramidal or extrapyramidal signs, deafness, blindness, coma, and death. These neurologic findings can be permanent or transient and may appear immediately or be delayed for several days. The most insidious effect is the delayed development of neuropsychiatric dysfunction. Within a few weeks after the poisoning, a fair percentage of patients manifest impaired judgment, poor concentration, memory loss, retardation, and personality changes.

These may result from damage to the globus pallidus, white matter, and the commissural surfaces of the hemispheres.

CONFIRMING THE DIAGNOSIS

Despite the variety of clinical signs, the physical examination probably will not be of much help in confirming a diagnosis of CO poisoning unless retinal hemorrhages are noted. A blood gas determination typically reveals that the partial pressure of oxygen remains near normal, but oxygen saturation is reduced. The current method of choice for laboratory confirmation of CO poisoning is determination of the HbCO concentration. The level of concentration is a function of inspired concentration of CO and the duration of exposure.

The classic correlation of HbCO concentrations with clinical features is as follows:

When the HbCO concentration is 10% to 20%, the features include headache, fatigue, and dilatation of cutaneous blood vessels. At 20% to 30%, the headache is severe and accompanies by dimness of vision, weakness, dizziness, syncope, nausea, and decreased motor dexterity. At 30% to 40%, the symptoms include syncope, nausea, vomiting, confusion, and increased respiratory and heart rates. The increased respiratory and heart rates persist at concentrations of 40% to 50%; other features include confusion, seizures, and coma. At 50% to 60%, the seizures and coma are still present, but now the patient has decreased respiration (often Cheyne-Stokes) and a depressed cardiovascular system. Similar symptoms are characteristic at levels of 60% to 70%, along with bradycardia and hypotension. At 70% to 80%, respiratory failure and death occur. Table 2 summarizes the correlation.

The bad news is that these signs and symptoms do not always correlate with the HbCO level. The passage of time following exposure to CO and any treatment instituted prior to

TABLE 2. Signs of Carbon Monoxide Toxicity

% of Carboxyhemoglobin	Clinical Features
10–20%	Headache, fatigue, dilatation of cutaneous blood vessels
20–30%	Severe headache, dimness of vision, weakness, dizziness, syncope, nausea, decreased motor dexterity
30–40%	Syncope, nausea, vomiting, confusion, increased respiratory and heart rates
40–50%	Increased respiratory and heart rates, confusion, seizures, coma
50–60%	Seizures, coma, decreased respiration (often Cheyne-Stokes), depressed cardiovascular system
60–70%	Same as at 50–60% plus bradycardia and hypotension
70–80%	Respiratory failure and death

Near-normal carboxyhemoglobin (HbCO) does *not* rule out significant CO poisoning; the HbCO level may be reduced by the passage of time following exposure or the administration of oxygen before measurement of HbCO.

the HbCO measurement (especially administration of oxygen) can remarkably lower the level. For example, the half-life of HbCO is five to six hours in room air but only 60 to 90 minutes in 100% oxygen. A hyperbaric oxygen chamber, if you are fortunate enough to have one, cuts the half-life to 20 minutes. Therefore, you need to find out if the emergency medical technicians or police administered oxygen before the HbCO measurement was obtained. It is fair to conclude that a near-normal HbCO level does *not* rule out significant CO poisoning.[5]

TREATMENT AND FOLLOW-UP

The treatment of acute CO poisoning is rather basic: Maintain respiration and administer 100% oxygen in the most efficient manner available in your emergency facility. Elevation of alveolar oxygen pressure accelerates the dissociation of CO from hemoglobin and the intracellular binding sites, restoring oxygen to the poisoned cells. Hyperbaric oxygen administration decreases the half-life of HbCO to about 20 minutes. If immediately available, it should be used when the HbCO level exceeds 25%. A recent addition to the treatment armamentarium is a hyperbaric oxygen administration system that involves placing the patient in an acrylic jacket. This eliminates the expense of the usual hyperbaric chamber.

It is probably best not to administer sodium bicarbonate to correct the acidosis that invariably results from CO poisoning until the pH of the blood is 7.3 or below. Mild acidosis shifts the oxyhemoglobin dissociation curve to the right; this is an advantage to the patient and does not need to be corrected. The patient should be maintained on oxygen until the HbCO level is below 10%.

The long-term follow-up of children with CO poisoning is a critical element. Long-term neuropsychiatric problems are only too common and need to be monitored. The electroencephalogram is abnormal in more than 90% of patients with acute CO poisoning, often returning to normal two to four weeks after exposure. Serial psychometric examination is one method for assessing damage, but careful observation by the parents and pediatrician as well as school personnel can provide further evidence of subtle damage.

Camus says man must succeed or fail on his own strength or weakness and not rely on a superior force. He is telling us who labor in the vineyards of the young to do the work ourselves that people have previously assigned to God. God knows we try. ∎

REFERENCES

1. Camus A: *The Plague.* New York, Vintage Books, 1948
2. Bureau MA, Monette J, Shapcott D, et al: Carboxyhemoglobin concentration in fetal cord blood and in blood of mothers who smoked during labor. Pediatrics 1982;69:371
3. Jackson DL, Menges H: Accidental CO poisoning. JAMA 1980;243:772
4. Baker S, O'Neill B, Karpf R: *The Injury Fact Book*, Lexington, Mass, Lexington Books, DC Health & Co, 1984
5. American Academy of Pediatrics, Committee on Accident and Poison Prevention, Aronou R (ed): *Handbook of Common Poisonings in Children,* ed 2, 1983, pp 50–51

Treating Cyanide Poisonings: Grace Under Pressure

When you are young, it helps to have some idea of what life is all about and what, if anything, you can do about it. You need guidance from those who are older, more objective, and have come to terms with reality. For me, part of this need was filled by Ernest Hemingway's novels. In Hemingway's heroic code, you were expected to do any job that you undertook well and completely, to do something useful rather than just sit around talking about it, to act stoically in the face of life's stresses—in short, to show grace under pressure. A patient who has been poisoned by cyanide (CN), one of the most rapid acting and lethal poisons, calls on physicians to exhibit unusual grace under pressure. It is a challenge scary enough to make you question why you are in this business in the first place.

The newspaper reports of deaths, near-deaths, and death threats from CN contamination of medicines and foods have become disturbingly familiar. You could not pick a better way to terrorize your fellow citizens than to allege that you have put CN in the food chain, unless you claim that you have slipped some plutonium into breakfast cereal. Cyanide, in fact, has long been a popular tool of death, from the judicial executions of the ancient Greeks to the mass suicides of the Jonestown religious cult.

Surprisingly, it is not too difficult for the average citizen to obtain CN. It is found in most chemical laboratories as either potassium CN or sodium CN (Table 3). Cyanide is widely used in industry in the manufacture of plastics and synthetic rubber; the electroplating of gold, silver, and copper; the coating, polishing, and extraction of metals; and the processing of photographic material.[1] In agriculture, CN is found in rodent fumigants, insecticides, and soil sterilizers. Do you have any in your home? You probably do if you have silver polish or certain rodenticides. A house fire may produce lots of CN from the burning

TABLE 3. Sources of Cyanide Poisoning

Chemical laboratories
Potassium CN or sodium CN

Industry
Plastics, synthetic rubber, electroplating, processing of photographic material, and metal coating, polishing, extraction

Agriculture
Rodent fumigants, insecticides, soil sterilizers

Drugs
Sodium nitroprusside
Phencyclidine (PCP)
Laetrile (amygdalin)

Household
Silver polish
Rodenticides
Seeds of almonds, pits of apricots, peaches, chokecherries, apples, pears (amygdalin)
House fires
  Burning of polyurethane, polyacrylonitrile, wool, silk, nylon

Tampering with foods, medicines

of polyurethane, polyacrylonitrile, wool, silk, and nylon.

The antihypertensive agent sodium nitroprusside has the potential to cause CN poisoning. This product is rapidly metabolized to CN in the body and converted to thiocyanate through the mediation of rhodanase, a hepatic enzyme. Thiocyanate is not toxic, but if there is insufficient availability of sulfur, especially thiosulfate, CN poisoning can occur. In addition, illegal drugs may contain CN or have cyanogenic potential. Cyanide is often used, for example, in the manufacture of phencyclidine (PCP), also known as "angel dust."

Several plant sources contain amygdalin, a cyanogenic glycoside, including the seeds of almonds and the pits of apricots, pears, apples, peaches, and chokecherries.[2] Amygdalin is also found in laetrile; a case of near-death involving a 4-year-old who ingested laetrile was reported recently.[3] When amygdalin is ingested, the release of CN occurs through mild acid hydrolysis or the action of such enzymes as β-glucosidase or emulsin. The microflora of the human intestine have these or similar enzymes capable of causing CN release.

HOW CN ACTS ON THE BODY

Cyanide is absorbed extensively and rapidly from all of the body's surfaces, primarily the lungs, mucous membranes, gastrointestinal tract, and skin. This does not leave much time to attempt to reverse the process. The volume of distribution of CN is 1.5 L/kg, and the chemical is found more in red blood cells than in plasma. Cyanide products are protoplasmic poisons; they severely disrupt the respiration of body cells by reversibly inhibiting enzymes that control the oxidative processes. The cells become anoxic by the inhibition of enzymes that contain the ferric (+3) ion. The one enzyme that is severely incapacitated by CN is cytochrome oxidase.[4] When CN inhibits cellular respiration, a shutdown in aerobic metabolism takes place. The medullary respiratory center becomes dysfunctional because its nerve cells can no longer obtain oxygen.

Although hemoglobin represents the body's largest store of iron, it is usually in the ferrous (+2) state and generally does not react with CN. A small fraction of hemoglobin does react to produce cyanhemoglobin, but this compound is stable, not oxygen-bearing, and does not kill.

RECOGNIZING A CN POISONING

The signs and symptoms of CN intoxication depend on the mode of entry, the form of CN that is doing the foul deed, and the amount. When *inhalation* or *intravenous* (IV) administration is involved, the process from life to death can be measured in seconds to minutes; you probably won't have the opportunity to do much except pronounce the patient dead. The victim experiences a sudden feeling of dryness and burning in the throat and a desperate hunger for air, not surprising in view of the cellular anoxia. A classic, somewhat frightening gasp is emitted; it is caused by the stimulation of the carotid body and respiratory center by tachypnea and hyperpnea. These symptoms are followed by apnea, seizures, and fatal cardiovascular collapse.

With *ingestions* of high dose CN compounds, the course is similar though not quite as rapid: Symptoms occur within several minutes and death within minutes to three or four hours. The more common examples of CN ingestions do not involve such high doses but nevertheless may be fatal unless treated quickly. In most cases, the patient becomes light-headed and confused and experiences nausea, vomiting, and epigastric pain. A burning, tightening sensation is felt in the neck along with a feeling of suffocation. The body makes an attempt to overcome these effects, and tachypnea and hyperpnea develop. The patient progresses from restlessness to stupor to coma and finally to convulsions with dilated and fixed pupils. Initial tachycardia and hypertension give way to bradycardia and hypotension. The picture is not a pretty one; it is difficult for anyone involved to display equanimity.

When amygdalin is swallowed, you have a bit more time to treat the problem; about 30 to 120 minutes may elapse before symptoms arise.

It is certainly possible to rescue a patient with CN poisoning who reaches a medical facility alive. It is important here to remember one of the first principles of toxicology: Treat the patient, not the poison. In most cases you will not have enough time to obtain specific diagnostic criteria. If there is no clear-cut history of CN exposure, clinical diagnosis is extremely difficult. Here are some guidelines:

Consider CN intoxication, in the early stages, in a patient with altered mental status and tachypnea without cyanosis and with bright red blood. Also consider acute CN poisoning in any patient with coma, seizures, and metabolic acidosis associated with bradycardia and hypotension. The physical exam is usually not much help, but if the retinal arteries and veins are of equal redness, think about a diagnosis of CN intoxication. Much has been made of the significance of bitter almond odor emitted by patients with CN poisoning. The odor is probably diagnostic, but unfortunately 20% to 40% of us cannot detect it. This sensory inability is believed to be three times more common in males.

TREATMENT: TIME IS OF THE ESSENCE

When faced with an extremely ill patient who may or may not have been poisoned and may or may not have CN intoxication, what do you do? Obtain stat CN blood levels? Even if your hospital does them, results take so long that they will not be of any help in an acute case. You might have time to get a few laboratory determinations that are helpful to diagnosis. Metabolic acidosis, for example, is usually detected by measurement of blood gases because normal aerobic metabolism has been disrupted. You can expect to find normal and equivalent values for arterial and venous pO_2, a high anion gap, a normal calculated oxygen saturation, and a decrease in the measured percentage oxygen saturation.[5] The calculated oxygen saturation is usually normal because the total amount of hemoglobin has not changed. As long as the patient is breathing, the pO_2 typically remains normal. There is no interference with normal oxygenation of the blood (although the cells can't use the oxygen), and the cyanhemoglobin level is not high. Measuring the percentage oxygen saturation with a cooximeter shows a lower level because some of the hemoglobin isn't carrying oxygen.

A bedside test for CN ingestion can be performed in five to ten minutes.[6] To 5 to 10 mL of gastric aspirate add a few crystals of ferrous sulfate and four to five drops of 20% sodium hydroxide. Boil the mixture, cool, and add eight to ten drops of 10% hydrochloric acid. If CN is present, a bluish-green precipitate or color forms and intensifies on standing.

Before getting to specific therapy, remember that symptomatic, supportive care is essential. It consists of administering 100% oxygen, control of the airway, maintenance of pulse and blood pressure, administration of anticonvulsants if needed, and correction of the acidosis by the judicious use of sodium bicarbonate.

The preferred method of treating CN poisoning in the United States involves inducing yet another disease, methemoglobinemia. This approach is based on the principle that methemoglobin has a greater affinity for CN than does cytochrome oxidase. The result is a disruption of the CN-cytochrome complex, allowing oxidative metabolism to resume.

The conversion to methemoglobin is accomplished with the Lilly CN antidote kit. Call your emergency room and ask if this kit is immediately available; in the case of the 4-year-old mentioned earlier, it had to be obtained from other hospitals. The kit should be renewed at least once a year.

The first phase of treatment involves the use of amyl nitrite inhalant. Crush two pearls of amyl nitrite in a gauze pad and hold them under the victim's nose for 30 seconds out of each minute. The pearls are used only until sodium nitrite can be given IV. Inject a solution of 3% sodium nitrite at 0.33 mL/kg in children, not to exceed 10 mL, at a rate of not more than 2.5 to 5 mL/min. Be *very* careful in administering sodium nitrite to children; it can produce a fatal degree of methemoglobinemia. Nitrites may produce severe hypotension as well. The lower the patient's hemoglobin, the less sodium nitrite you give.

After administering sodium nitrite, immediately give sodium thiosulfate in a 25% IV solution. For children, the initial dose is 1.65 mL/kg slowly over ten minutes. Sodium thiosulfate combines with the available CN to form the nontoxic thiocyanate, which is readily excreted in the urine. Oxygen should be continued during this treatment since it enhances the effects of the nitrites and the thiosulfate. If you are not completely successful the first time around, you may repeat the sodium nitrite and sodium thiosulfate once with half of the above doses. The approach to treatment is summarized in Table 4.

Other therapies are available for CN poisoning, but they are not approved for use in this country. The most intriguing is dicobalt edetate (Kelocyanor), the medication used in Europe. This substance chelates the CN to form cobalticyanide, a stable, harmless substance excreted in the urine. Another potential antidote is hydroxocobalamin, a vitamin B_{12} precursor available in Europe but with only investigational status in the United States. It binds with CN to form cyanocobalamin, also excreted in the urine. A few authorities recommend hyperbaric oxygen for CN poisoning along with antidotal therapy.[7] It is believed that hyperbaric oxygen can enhance the beneficial effects of the antidotes, but this approach is controversial.

Hemingway wrote, "There's no rule on how it is to write. Sometimes it comes easily and perfectly. Sometimes it is like drilling rock and blasting it out with charges." It is also not easy to diagnose and treat CN poisoning. It truly requires clinical grace under pressure. ■

TABLE 4. Treatment of CN Poisoning

Supportive treatment
100% oxygen
Control of the airway
Maintenance of pulse and blood pressure
Anticonvulsants if needed
Correction of acidosis with sodium bicarbonate

Therapy (Lilly kit)
Amyl nitrite
  Crush two pearls in a gauze pad and hold under the nose for 30 seconds per minute until IV sodium nitrite is given
Sodium nitrite
  Inject 3% IV solution, 0.33 mL/kg in children, not to exceed 10 mL, at a rate of not more than 2.5 to 5 mL/min. The lower the hemoglobin, the less sodium nitrite given
Sodium thiosulfate
  Inject 25% IV solution, 1.65 mL/kg in children, slowly over ten minutes.
Continue oxygen to enhance the effect of the nitrites and the thiosulfate.
If not completely successful, repeat the sodium nitrite and sodium thiosulfate once with half of the above doses.

REFERENCES

1. Goldfrank LR, Kirstein R (eds): *Toxicologic Emergencies: A Comprehensive Handbook in Problem Solving*, ed 2. New York, Appleton Century Crofts, 1982
2. Holzbecher MO, Moss MA, et al: The cyanide content of laetrile preparations, apricot, peach, and apple seeds. J Toxicol Clin Toxicol 1984;22:341

3. Hall AH, Linden CH, Kulig KW, Rumack BH: Cyanide poisoning from laetrile ingestion: Role of nitrite therapy. Pediatrics 1986;78:269

4. Arena J: Cyanide, in Haddad LM, Winchester JF (eds): *Clinical Management of Poisoning & Drug Overdose*. Philadelphia, WB Saunders Co, 1983

5. Hall AH: Cyanide poisoning. Rocky Mountain Poison Symposium, Cooper Mountain, Colo, 1985

6. Cyanide, sometimes not so sudden. Emergency Medicine, January 1978, p 233

7. The uses of O_2 under pressure. Emergency Medicine, March 15, 1986, p 32

Hands-on Options Strategies

Vince Zortman
ASSOCIATE EDITOR

Carol Gunther
GRAPHIC ART DIRECTOR

When agricultural futures options were introduced several years ago, hog producers and farmers were generally indifferent. This article is the first of its kind: It explains how to go beyond the Wall Street jargon and tells its readers, in their own language, how to use options, one of their most valuable marketing tools.

Pork '86 is edited for hog producers in the United States. "Hands-on Option Strategies" first appeared in the August 1986 issue of *Pork '86,* published by Vance Publishing Corp. © 1986. Reprinted with permission.

Hands-on Strategies That Use the Most Flexible Hog Marketing Tool Available to Producers

We're not going to drown you in another scholarly discussion of hog options, so put away your lifejacket. Neither will we try to shame you into using them by detailing how one producer made a mint a few months back using options one time.

What we'd rather do is show how hog options might be put to work to make your marketing more flexible, something you may not think is possible. We promise not to ask you to duplicate someone else's success, because when it comes to marketing, hindsight is 20/20. It also doesn't make you any money.

Different situations call for different approaches. This story looks at four different price risk-management strategies that can be employed with options, the most versatile and flexible hedging instrument available to hog producers.

Hold it. You might ask: If they're so wonderful how come so few producers use them? The biggest reason is that even though they've been trading for one and a half years now, they are still not widely understood by the industry.

"Even among my producer clients who regularly hedge, 95 percent still use straight futures hedges instead of options because they still feel more comfortable with futures," says Illinois ag lender Bruce Strom. "But," he adds, "the conversation has turned, and there's definitely more talk about options."

What those marketers may be finding out is that options are not dangerous, and they don't bite. "I don't completely understand them yet," says one hog marketer, "but I know enough about them that I use them, and they definitely make some marketing decisions a lot easier."

The hog market does not make you money, your marketing strategy does. The following sections contain practical, real-world strategic applications for using options to price hogs. We promise to explain the strategies ranging from conservative to aggressive, using plain English. Whether you're comfortable with options or still a little fuzzy on them, we hope you'll be able to see how they can sometimes take the work and worry out of marketing hogs.

STRATEGY 1: CONSTRUCTING A PRICE FLOOR

Among those hog producers who are using options to hedge, this is the most popular strategy. It is also the most simple and conservative. "It's the best way to get your feet wet using options, too," comments one hog marketer.

What's constructing a floor all about? Quite simply, you pick the lowest market price you want to live with and you protect it with the purchase of options—without locking yourself to that price if the market rises.

Nebraska feed salesman Dave De Jong did just that. Back in late May and early June he thought building a price floor at $40 for some last-half 1986 market hogs would be a good

Try This Definition

Forget you ever heard the words "put," "call," "strike price" and "premium."

Now let's talk about options. What is an option?

An option is a choice, a simple chance to say yes or no. To what? The right to asume a position in the futures market.

Who would want to get tangled up with futures? You, that's who. If market conditions favor you, you can say yes to assuming a futures position. If they don't, you have the choice to say no.

Let's say in September you buy the right to say yes or no to selling hogs for $45 dollars per hundredweight in December. You pay 50 cents per hundredweight for the privilege of having that choice. As December approaches, it's time to make a choice, to say yes or no to the $45 price.

If hogs are bringing $50, common sense says to say no to the chance to sell for $45. You paid 50 cents for peace of mind back in September, knowing you would take no less than $45. But prices are $5 above that level. The key is, you're not obligated to sell at $45, so you don't. You say no and sell for $50 like everybody else. You're out the 50 cents per hundredweight you paid for peace of mind. The person who sold you that option pockets your money.

But, if hogs are bringing $40 when December rolls around, you happily seize your opportunity to say yes to selling for $45. You're saying yes to an extra $5 per hundredweight. You still have a choice to say no, but why pass up five bucks. You spent 50 cents and gained $5; the person who sold you the option loses.

So where did the words strike price, put, call and premium go?

They're just nouns that can be applied in the place of words and phrases above. If you feel compelled to use those words, what was described above was the purchase of a $45 put option. You paid for the right, but not the obligation, to sell December futures at $45. The 50 cents that right cost was the premium; $45 was the strike price.

Had you bought the right in September to say yes or no to buying futures in December instead of selling, you would have owned a call option.

That's it. If you understand what you just read, you understand options.

You don't need to be a Harvard-educated economist to understand and use them.

---

idea. He was nervous the June *Hogs and Pigs Report* would project increasing hog numbers through the end of the year and into 1987.

To build his price floor, he bought options that gave him the choice of saying yes or no to selling October futures at $40. In the language of the trade, these are called "put" options. As a hedger, they are the planks in your price floor.

The time frame in which De Jong could say yes or no to selling October hogs at $40 will last until Sept. 19. That date is simply the option expiration date set by the Chicago Mercantile Exchange for options on October futures.

The $40 level was chosen by De Jong because it represented a small profit on last-half 1986 hogs.

It cost him 70 cents per hundredweight (approximately $1.50 per hog) to construct his price floor. Did that mean he could net no better than $40 per hundredweight? No. But it did mean he would take no less than that if the market did indeed go into a freefall.

As it turned out, the *Hogs and Pigs Report* projected dramatic cuts in hog numbers. October futures soared $6 in the week after the report's release. That made the choice to sell at $40 less and less attractive. With the market rallying, De Jong will likely say no to his chance to sell futures at those lower levels. The value of the options that gave him that choice dropped to 30 cents per hundredweight vs. his 70-cent purchase price.

Did he feel like a sucker who needlessly spent money for the options to construct an apparently useless price floor?

"No, the price floor made it easier to sleep at night going into the report," he says. To De Jong, the fact that even a chance existed that hog prices would dip below those levels made possession of some kind of backstop crucial.

Fine, you say, the options may have provided peace of mind, but they still represented a cost.

Options specialist and broker Phil Wagenknecht, of Linnco Futures Inc. in Chicago, has advised several producers hedging with options. Through that experience he has developed some rules of thumb regarding how much to spend for protection using a price floor strategy.

Wagenknecht (pronounced Wagonekt) says that, generally speaking, it's not a good idea to spend more than $1 per hundredweight ($2.20 per hog) to construct a price floor that protects your cost of production.

In summary, constructing a price floor works well in a depressed market. It prepares you for a worst-case scenario you hope never materializes.

STRATEGY 2: THE FLOATING FLOOR

A rising market puts a smile on most hog marketers' faces. But it also raises their blood pressure a notch or two because most know high prices don't last forever.

A rising market provides a good opportunity to put the floating floor strategy to work.

Humboldt, Iowa, hog marketer Dave Dodgen was ready to look at using a floating price floor in the aftermath of the bullish June *Hogs and Pigs Report*.

With deferred futures prices pushing higher, the question for him became: At what point do I lock in some of the attractive price levels?

To simply sell futures in a rising market invites margin call pressure. That's fine, if you can handle the cash flow requirements.

The beauty of the floating floor strategy is it allows you to lay back and follow the market higher. You ratchet up with the trend instead of fighting it. There's much less emotional stress compared to a futures sale or cash forward contract. And, since the floating price floor strategy involves the purchase of options (a one-time cost) you are dealing with nicely predictable cash flow requirements.

The first step of the strategy is to construct a price floor similar to the one detailed in the first strategy. You would buy an option that would provide the choice to say yes or no to selling futures at a given price.

After choosing your initial price floor, you would then have the luxury of waiting to see what the market would do. Suppose it kept pushing higher. To use a floating price floor you would sell back your first option (at a loss no doubt) and move to higher ground by choosing another price and constructing a new floor there. To construct your new price floor you would purchase another option or options that would once again give you the choice of saying yes or no to selling futures, only this time at a higher price.

Yes, it would require another cost. But since the decision is yours, you make the choice how much you want to spend.

Says Dave Dodgen, "If I spent 70 cents, or roughly $1.50 per hog, to build the first floor, I wouldn't hesitate to spend a like amount to build another one a few dollars higher in a rising market."

As far as Dodgen is concerned, the fact the

market has risen has changed the rules of the game, so to speak. That means a new expenditure is not that traumatic. "Spending more money to lock in a still higher price is very much worth it," he says.

Why not just construct the price floor at the higher level to begin with? Well for one reason, you would pay dearly to do that. When you are building a floor below where the market is, it is much more economical. Traders call options on price levels below the market "out-of-the-money." Out-of-the-money planks can be bought cheaper.

"Besides," says Dodgen, "if I laid out that money all at once for a higher-level floor, there would be an opportunity cost: Once you've spent money for an option you're not earning interest on it. It's better to spoon feed cash into a marketing strategy than to dump it in all at once."

The floating floor strategy can be used in a downtrending market as well. The difference is if you build the first floor and prices fall below it, you sell the options (your planks) at a profit, then move to lower ground, buy cheaper planks and build a new floor.

STRATEGY 3: HEDGING A HEDGE

Say you are a hog marketer and are very near to pulling the trigger on some kind of forward sale. Prices have rallied to a satisfactory level and you would like to lock in profits either through the use of a cash forward contract or a futures sale.

The strategy of hedging a hedge combines these forward-pricing tools with an option. The first step in this strategy is to pick your selling point and then pull the trigger with either the forward contract or the futures market.

Having done this, you have defined your highest selling price for those hogs and shut yourself away from further participation in any ensuing rally. If you sell futures at $45 and the market rallies to $50, you have $5 worth of margin calls. (You hope these will be offset by $5 worth of appreciation in cash hog prices.) If you cash forward contract for $45 and the cash market rallies to $50, you have passed up $5 in profit opportunity.

When hedging a hedge, you allow yourself a chance to participate in a market rally following your decision to lock in a selling price. How? Through purchase of an option.

Note that this option is a different type from the one used to build price floors. The option used to hedge a hedge needs to be the kind that provides the choice to say yes or no to buying futures at a given price, rather than selling them as in the previous examples. Traders call options that offer the choice to buy futures "call" options.

Why would a marketer—a seller of hogs—want to have the choice to buy futures? Only when he has made the mistake of selling too soon.

Using the benefit of 20/20 hindsight, here's an example of when hedging a hedge could have been an appropriate strategy:

Don and Jane (not their real names, by their request) raise hogs in central Illinois. In June, they hedged heavily in July futures at $50—a profit for their operation. Having seen the July contract rally $9 through the spring and early summer, they jumped into the market because of strong feelings the party may have been close to being over for the hog market.

At the same time they sold July futures for $50, Don and Jane considered buying an option for 50 cents per hundredweight that would allow them the chance to say yes or no to buying August futures at $50. (They looked at August options because options on July futures had already expired.) The reason for looking at that kind of August option was it would appreciate in value if the market kept going higher and thus allow them to participate in any further rally by offsetting margin call requirements from the July futures position.

As it turned out, Don and Jane did not hedge their hedges. The market kept rallying, taking July futures as high as $60. During the same time period, the August option they didn't buy appreciated in value from 50 cents to $6 per hundredweight—a $5.50 profit that could have been put against the $10 in margin calls.

"We should have used the hedged hedge strategy, but our concern was the cost might have been a waste of money," says Jane. "We also have to keep perspective: The $50 sale was a good one from our point of view no matter what happened." Don and Jane say the next time they're faced with a similar set of circumstances, they would consider hedging a hedge. "But, cost would be a consideration again and we probably wouldn't be interested in paying more than roughly $1.75 per hog (70 cents per hundredweight) to do it," says Jane.

As mentioned above, the "hedging a hedge" strategy works equally well with a cash forward sale as it does with a futures sale.

In fact, the purchase of the option that allows the choice to say yes or no to buying futures at a later date can remove much of the pressure associated with cash contracting of hogs. It does that by offering new flexibility to the strictly cash marketer.

Since, unlike a futures sale, a cash forward contract is irreversible, it puts that much more pressure on a selling decision—so much pressure, in fact, that many cash marketers end up making no forward pricing decisions at all, fearing they will sell too low.

Ownership of the option above represents nothing more than an insurance policy against selling too soon. With the insurance policy in hand, the cash seller can be more at ease when pulling the trigger on a forward sale.

If the cash market moves higher after his sale, the value of the option will also rise. If prices fall he loses the cost of his insurance but has made a wise selling decision.

STRATEGY 4: FENCING IN A PRICE

This is undoubtedly the most aggressive of the four strategies, also the most complex. It is definitely not the way to cut your teeth using options. The intent of the strategy is to choose a selling price, lock it in, and then dare the market to tell you you're wrong.

Fencing in a price requires you be both an options buyer and an options seller.

As the options buyer in this particular strategy, you again are interested in building a price floor. Just as in strategy No. 1, you are looking to buy an option that locks in the lowest price you want to live with.

The other half of the fencing strategy involves selling an option. The type of option you sell is the kind used in strategy No. 3. You are selling someone else the choice to say yes or no to buying futures at a given price. You are being paid by that buyer for that privilege.

If this all sounds silly, think about it for a second. What you as an options seller are doing in this case is selling an option you hope will never be exercised. You say, in effect, "The market will never get this high, and I'm going to make some money off an over-optimistic speculator who thinks it will."

So what if the over-optimistic speculator is right and the market rises? Then you as an options seller have to meet margin calls unless and until you buy the option back. But remember, those margin calls are being offset for you as a producer by a corresponding rise in the price of cash hogs.

Hold it. Margin calls, top selling price, corresponding rise in cash hogs . . . it all sounds strangely similar to simply selling futures. Well it is, but with one important difference. Unlike futures, you are being paid for making the sale. Picking up the extra money for making the options sale enhances your selling price.

Linnco's Wagenknecht has used the fencing strategy for his hog hedger clients, with mixed results. Generally speaking, he says, this is a strategy that works best after a strong rally because speculators who think the market is going even higher are willing to pay well for options to buy into that rise.

Wagenknecht points out that the fence-

Where the Market Is May Determine What You Use

Different options strategies are more appropriate given the market's position within one of the three historical hog price ranges.

A particularly effective strategy near the historical highs at the upper end of the green zone would be the fencing strategy (strategy four). The lofty prices there represent the best the market has historically offered. Therefore, an aggressive selling strategy like number four becomes a good idea because you are playing some strong percentages.

The lower end of the green zone and the upper end of the grey zone represent good profit levels. With prices there, strategy three (hedging a hedge) becomes attractive. Why? Because it enables you to lock in good profits via a futures sale or cash forward contract, yet protect against margin calls or lost opportunity should prices zoom to the upper reaches of the green zone.

In the red zone, strategy one (building a floor) is effective. History argues for improvement in prices at that point, yet building a floor there protects against further disaster.

Strategy two (the floating price floor) works well just about anywhere. Used in the green zone, it allows you to follow the market lower and take profits on the way down. Used in the red zone, it allows building of successive price floors as the market rallies.

building strategy would have worked particularly in the immediate aftermath of the bullish June *Hogs and Pigs Report*. The dramatic rise in futures also dramatically increased the price of options that allowed the choice to say yes or no to buying those futures. Sellers of that choice could ask good prices, because of demand from speculators and because those sellers had to face the risk of margin calls if the market went on up.

"The increase in the price of those options created an opportunity for hedgers," says Wagenknecht. He points out that at one point a hedger could have sold someone else the choice to buy December futures at $50 for $5 per hundredweight. At the same time, that hedger could have bought, for $1.50 per hundredweight, an option that would have allowed him to say yes or no to selling December futures at $46. That, notes Wagenknecht, "would have effectively fenced the producer into a $49.40 to $53.50 per hundredweight selling range."

How? The hedger who would have sold the choice to buy December hogs got $5 per hundredweight for it. He turned around and spent $1.50 to construct his price floor by buying the option to sell December futures at $46. If the market trended lower, the hedger had his floor at $46 plus the $3.50 profit. On the upper end, the market would have had to have gone beyond $50 plus the $3.50 profit before there would have been any margin requirements.

It is important to note that while the options fencing strategy described above was available, December futures actually only traded as high as $51.70. Therefore, the market didn't even reach the profit potential for the fencer who was daring the market to make his day and trade as high as $53.50.

We have presented but four options strategies here. There are no doubt countless more, probably some that have not been discovered yet.

The important thing is that you become

Varying Tax Treatment for Options Strategies

The Internal Revenue Service has strong opinions about what constitutes a "legitimate" hedging strategy. Unfortunately, those opinions tend to be rather restrictive.

When a hedger loses money on an IRS-approved futures or options hedge, the IRS allows that person unlimited capital loss deductions to be put against ordinary farming income. However, for those strategies the IRS does not recognize as legitimate hedges, capital-loss deductions are limited to $3,000 in a single year, unless there are capital gains to offset the remainder of those losses.

As it stands now, only two market hog hedging strategies would safely qualify for unlimited capital loss deductions. Those would be a straight futures sale and the purchase of a put option to build a price floor. The IRS is very strict on the idea that any position taken in futures and options markets cannot significantly exceed the position or expected position in the cash market.

For example, the purchase of the option in strategy No. 1 would be seen as a legitimate hedging strategy by Uncle Sam. But using strategy No. 2, the floating price floor, may raise some eyebrows if more than $3,000 is deducted with the purchase of the second set of options.

Likewise, any capital-loss deduction involved with the purchase of the option in strategy No. 3 would also be limited to $3,000. Why? Because as far as the IRS is concerned, purchase of an option to reduce risk of a futures sale is not a bona fide hedging activity.

Any margin call requirements brought about by the sale of the option in strategy No. 4 would also fall ulnder the $3,000 limitation.

Does all this indicate you should shy away from the various strategies because of tax ramifications? Probably not. Just don't count on any favorable tax treatment for losses you take on anything more than the most conservative of hedging strategies.

If you're interested in learning more about taxes and hedging, *PORK '86* recommends a bulletin published by the Virginia Polytechnic Institute Ag Economics Department. For information on how to get a copy of the bulletin (No. 448-340) write to: Cooperative Extension Service, Virginia Polytechnic Institute and State University, Blacksburg, VA 24061.

---

aware of as many of the profitable opportunities as possible for making your marketing more flexible through options. It's probably equally as important that you avoid those strategies that aren't suited for you.

"You can't use futures or options to totally eliminate risk because farming is a risky business," says Illinois lender Strom. He adds, "The best we can do is to reduce and manage risk, and options are one of the tools that can do that very nicely."

If you haven't looked at using these tools yet, it might pay to do so. Maybe you won't be able to assess an immediate dollar impact on your operation, but you might quickly find out how much a good night's sleep is worth. ■

Sears: The Family Store

Murray Forseter
EDITOR

Steve Malanga
EXECUTIVE EDITOR

Faye Brookman
SENIOR EDITOR

Rick Gallagher
ASSOCIATE EDITOR

Nanci Brickman
ASSOCIATE EDITOR

Michael Hartnett
ASSOCIATE EDITOR

This study provides a comprehensive analysis of the directions being taken by Sears, both as a retail entity and individually by many product lines. It evaluates the marketing challenges facing Sears as well as the responses being made by the nation's largest general-merchandise retailer.

Chain Store Age General Merchandise Trends serves the general merchandise industry, which includes department and discount stores, national chains, specialty stores, and their suppliers. "Sears: The Family Store" first appeared in the December 1985 issue of *Chain Store Age GMT,* published by Lebhar-Friedman. © 1985. Reprinted with permission.

Sears Family Stores Leap into New Century

On a planning chart, Sears can draw a straight line between its Store of the Future program, debuted two years ago, and an experimental regional buying office it recently opened.

On the surface, the two do not appear all that closely related. Store of the Future, after all, has come to be known primarily as a program to upgrade presentations and rework adjacencies. The new buying office, on the other hand, is an attempt to get some headquarters merchandising personnel into the field where they will presumably do a better job of reading the customers' pulse. Whatever their individual goals, both programs are also apt expressions of the direction Sears knows it must follow if it is to prosper as a family-oriented, full-line store in an age of specialists. Still the world's largest retailer, the company whose well-paid, highly regarded merchandisers fashion their strategies from the lofty heights of the Sears Tower, Sears wants to get closer to its customer and do a better job of tailoring its stores to individual markets.

"We want to sell the customer what she wants, not build the kind of stores we want," says William Bass, chairman of the Sears Merchandise Group.

The idea hardly seems startling or revolutionary. It is one of those things which nearly every retailer which has prospered in the last 10 years has done well—scrutinize the customer closely and fashion stores which operate with the efficiency of a chain but still address the needs of particular markets.

But most of these retailers have had two distinct advantages over Sears. They were small enough to manage such a strategy and they did not have the burden of Sears' retailing history to mold their thinking.

GENERATION OF SPECIALISTS

As Sears drove into regional shopping malls in the 1960's and early 1970's the company reinforced its image as the country's most familiar retailer, a true full-line family store. But life was easier back then. Consumers were not so brand conscious, small retailers often were not efficient enough to take advantage of their superior local market knowledge, and most vendors still had enough leverage to force retailers to maintain full markups.

All of that, of course, is different today. A whole generation of specialists has grown up to sell consumers brand name goods, and most of them can operate less expensively and target customers more precisely than Sears. How can Sears stores, which need at least a 28% total store margin to break even, compete with electronics superstores whose margins can dip into the mid-20's, or with discounters selling photo products at 15% gross margin, or toy specialists taking virtually no profits on the kind of high-visibility items Sears likes to have in stock to draw in a family trade?

"You don't get an expense structure until you're 100 years old," jokes Joseph Batogowski, Sears' executive vice president of merchandising.

As Sears' expense structure made it difficult to compete with emerging specialists on price, the company's national marketing and merchandising orientation distanced it from many of its customers.

While many smaller regionals were banding

together into buying groups, slicing into some of the advantage Sears' enormous buying power gave it, Sears did not do much to offset the regional's greatest strength—their closeness to the markets in which they operated.

As recently as a few years ago Sears was still fashioning stores which varied only by size. Assortments barely differed within stores of the same type, and Sears paid little attention to the kinds of demographic characteristics which might influence how a mix should change to fit a particular market. Even merchandising refinements based on regional weather patterns, the most obvious influence on assortments were not always well executed. So Sears wound up selling space heaters in Hawaii or distributing catalogs in Miami which featured heavy winter coats on the cover.

"Back in the old days," says Batogowski, "we could put up a store because we knew exactly what it was. We knew what a 'B' store was—so many departments and so many lines. Those are the stores we put everywhere."

ON THE ROAD

During the regional shopping-center boom, that may have been the best way to build a network of large general merchandise stores, but in today's competitive specialty store–dominated environment it could be fatal. So Sears finally began bearing down on local markets, looking closely at niches it had ignored and admitting it no longer simply had to be somewhere to be successful.

There is no clearer expression of this new attitude at Sears than its small store program, which Batogowski calls "the most refreshing idea we've had in the company in a long time."

There is nothing surprising about the notion that Sears wants to go into many small markets where it is not represented or operates just a catalog outlet. But how Sears plans to attack those markets is the most significant element of the program and will likely affect the company's overall merchandising strategy for years to come.

In January of 1984, before Sears had opened a single small store, it sent its national merchandise managers on the road to small town America with the charge that they should study retailing there and come to understand how it differed from retailing in Sears' traditional markets. Traveling through the ice and snow and staying in $25-a-night hotels, some of the merchants wondered if Sears had a future in this kind of environment.

"When they first went out they were a little skeptical that we belonged in those markets," says Bass. "But when they came back they were like kids with a new toy."

The first, and doubtless the most important, conclusion of the national merchandise managers was there was no way Sears could "cookie-cutter" the stores or assortments. There are just too many regional differences and not enough room in smaller markets for mistakes.

"In a small town the accuracy of your merchandising is critical because your target audience is smaller. Your merchandising mistakes are amplified," says C. W. Hildebrand, director of planning for the small store program.

With that in mind Sears resolved to study each market carefully, so it put merchandising people on the road again, this time to Alma, Mich., chosen as the site of the first small store.

"In Alma we worked backward," says Bass. "We looked at the demographics, looked at the general merchandise sales, what market penetration we could expect, and how much volume we could expect to do. Then we broke that down into how many feet we should have."

The number came to only 8,300 square feet of selling space, which did not leave much room for the 100,000 sku's that nestle within a full-sized Sears store. So each merchandiser was asked for an honest appraisal of his category's prospects in Alma.

"We built that store line by line," says Bass. "Some merchandise managers came back and told us, 'I don't belong there. I can't be important to Sears and to the town'."

For Sears this was a revolutionary way to fashion a store, but it was also a method which tended to play to the company's strengths—male-oriented hard lines. So Sears sent its merchandisers on the road again, this time to a small town in Ohio—Piqua—where it wanted to create a small market store to attract women shoppers. The result, a store retrofitted just two months ago, is in many ways surprising for Sears and points to further changes.

For one thing, Sears decided that it does not just want to attract more women shoppers; it wants them to come more often. So the chain devotes about one-eighth of its 43,000 square feet in Piqua to consumables—H&BA, household chemicals, candy, even soda. By contrast the typical full-line Sears store gives about 2% of its space to consumables.

Sears took a closer look at assortments in Piqua, which had been a full-line 'B' store, and began tailoring them to local demographics. More than 30% of the workers in the market are machinists or precision tool craftsmen, so Sears eliminated men's suits from the mix, but increased the leisure apparel assortment to the size of a typical 'A' store.

Where it cannot be dominant in Piqua, either because of local competition or space limitations, Sears eliminates lines. Home textiles contains a full assortment of five lines, including towels, but no bath accessories.

With most of its full-line stores in regional malls, little of Sears' assortment is oriented toward convenience. But Sears wants to build convenience back into the mix of the small market stores. In hardware at Piqua, for instance, about 900 sku's were added to the typical 'B' store mix, and most of these items were convenience oriented.

"WE'RE THE BEST"

When Piqua was done, Sears had created a store which may be as aptly suited to the market it serves as any Sears store.

"It's much more sophisticated than saying, 'This town is 250,000 people, 'A' store'," says Batogowski.

To most retailers, this had been an elementary strategy for years, but Sears, the $23-billion giant, had too imposing a bureaucracy and too embedded a corporate culture to adapt swiftly. For years the chain suffered from what one financial analyst called a "'we're the best' ethnocentricity." Store of the Future had begun to shake that up, and the rumblings are still being felt in programs like the small store strategy.

But how quickly can this kind of thinking impact on a chain whose sales already account for about 5% of volume in the top 20 general merchandise categories? Sears is moving swiftly with its small stores and plans to add 50 smaller stores—akin to the Alma unit, in each of the next five years, for a total of 250 stores. Some of them may be slightly larger than Alma, perhaps 20,000 square feet, says Bass.

Over that same period Sears will add 70 small stores like the Piqua store. Add to that another 50 or so specialty paint and hardware stores a year, and Sears could wind up with a network of nearly 600 specialty stores serving small markets by 1990.

If Sears can indeed reach those opening goals, what kind of contribution will the newer, presumably more tailored stores, have? Right now Sears shoots for $300 per net square foot of sales in small store prototypes. If those 570 small stores were part of the chain today, they might be producing as much as $2 billion a year in sales, which would represent about 8% of total Merchandise Group revenues.

THINKING DIFFERENTLY

The total effect of the small store strategy, however, may be more than just in the kinds of numbers these stores generate. Sears is thinking differently about itself, admitting it no longer simply can open a store to be successful. The upshot is something which goes beyond the simple revamped presentations which have come to be known as Store of the Future.

"More than being a physical plant, Store of the Future is a rallying point," says Batogowski. "Store of the Future said to the buying staff, 'It's time to get into the stores, time to see on the receiving end what's happening to your goods once they get here. Does it make sense? Is it logical?'"

That kind of self-examination has already produced some 200 line changes and plenty of hopeful energy throughout the organization. But Sears is working to fine-tune itself during a problematic period for every major retailer, so consumer response to the Store of the Future has not been overwhelming.

By the end of this year some 207 full-line Sears stores will be in the Store of the Future format. Sales at Stores of the Future through the first three quarters ran slightly more than 5% ahead of sales at other Sears store. Gross margins were about 0.4% higher than the typical Sears store.

Bass calls those results "pretty gratifying," but Sears will have to do better to make Store of the Future pay off. Initial projections called for new Stores of the Future to do 12% better than other full-line stores the first year and 6% in their second year.

The typical Sears store last year had sales of slightly less than $20 million. A 5% gain amounts to another $1 million or so. Considering that it takes some $3 million to remodel a Sears store, according to some estimates, is 5% enough of a gain to make this investment pay?

For the program to succeed, gross margins have to continue rising, and that means a better job in the fashion categories. But the going here remains tough. "We're beginning to hedge our way into women's apparel and home fashions. Our balance of sales has obviously improved with our gross margins," says Bass.

Still, Sears does not expect substantial results from Store of the Future strategies until next year, or maybe even 1987. "This is a female-oriented program, and that takes a while to develop from a marketing standpoint," says Wayne Holsinger, vp, marketing.

"Women have established shopping patterns, and that won't change overnight or by running a corporate ad or opening a store, but by giving a satisfying shopping experience that gets rewarded a second and a third time," says Batogowski. "Sears has spent 99 years trying to alter its balance of sales. Finally in the last year we've begun to succeed."

NEW FOCUS ON MERCHANDISE

If Sears is to succeed with Store of the Future in the next few years it will be because the program has evolved away from a simple retrofitting plan toward something broader, something encompassing marketing and merchandise. Store of the Future, in short, can succeed only if it sells merchandise of the future.

Two years after the first Store of the Future opened, Sears is bringing the focus back on merchandise. That is evident in the specialized shops. Sears is putting in many stores. These shops target well-defined customers which the specialty stores have grabbed. Many Sears Stores of the Future are getting Big and Tall men's apparel shops, maternity departments and broader selections of career women apparel.

Sears' advertising next year will clearly reflect a new emphasis on product. Those familiar television ads focusing on the entire Sears store are giving way somewhat to flights of magazine ads featuring new merchandise. In some cases Sears plans to use its buyers in the ads explaining why they chose this product and what its particular benefits may be.

Sears is looking for a merchandising thrust that can encompass all departments, not just specialized areas where it is perceived to be weak or absent. The heart of this new direction is the New Century products program, also known as the Chairman's Centenary Values program.

Sears initially showed about 160 new products in the program, ranging from a $900 home guy system to a car compact disk player, from the Stefanie Collection of professional clothing for women to solid paint, from digital remote control televisions to an iron which marks the beginning of the Kenmore line of small appliances.

What is perhaps most significant about New Century is that it is essentially private label. Most products in the line are either house brand or exclusive to Sears. That serves as a reminder that despite all of the publicity Sears brand name tests have gotten lately, the retailer intends to remain primarily a house brand merchant.

"Department stores are running as fast as they can to private label. We're already there," says Batogowski.

And yet, despite that, Sears has also clearly lost some of its "we're the best" attitude. Gone are the days when a Sears buyer was told that he was not much of a merchant if he could not create a private label line to compete with any brand.

"We love brands," says Bass, in what 10 years ago would surely have been a startling exclamation for a Sears chairman. "At the right price and for the right reason. We look to fill the needs of our customer that, frankly, we're unable to satisfy. I think we have to be honest about that."

In some cases, like licensed toys or the new Minolta Maxxum camera, Sears is clearly selling goods that it can not match in private label offerings. But Sears is also filling in assortments with brand name items it can offer in private label.

In such cases Sears is admitting that it does not have the reputation to match the branded goods. But Sears is also hoping that once it gets branded goods on the floor next to private label goods, many consumers can be persuaded to walk out with Sears brands. This is clearly one intention of the much noted Sears test of brand names in consumer electronics.

"There was a time when at Sears our television set wasn't the best, and we have been paying for that for a good, long time—a decade or more. Today we have the very best—an excellent television, yet our market share is very difficult," says Batogowski.

So Sears has brought in the market leader, RCA, and one of the prestige names; Sony.

"Now we get a chance on our store's floor to show the difference between a Sears television and RCA and Sony, and we welcome that opportunity," says Batogowski. "This is a chance to provide our salesmen with more customers to have a discussion with, rather than having the salesman at some superstore tell them about our television."

Sears will need to convert many potential brand name cusotmers to its label because profitability on name brands will be small. Sears knows it must remain competitive on those brands with other retailers, or risk forging the wrong kind of pricing image in consumers' minds.

"Sears will accept the low markup [on national brands] and be content with it. But that will be a relatively small part of our mix," says Batogowski.

WHAT THE ECONOMY GIVES

Sears is clearly showing more signs of life, more energy, more of a willingness to admit the need for change and then execute it, than at any time in its recent history.

Through it all, however, Sears continues to battle the vicissitudes of the American economy. Perhaps no other retailer's fortunes are tied as closely to that economy. No other chain, no matter how much it reshapes itself, must be content with what the economy is willing to give.

The question then becomes, can Sears expect to do anything but continue to grow at the rate the economy grows? Even now, despite all of the retrofittings and the line changes, most analysts continue to tie Sears' prospects for growth to such obvious signposts as housing starts and consumer installment debt. More than one-fifth of Sears' sales come from big ticket durables. Even single digit percentage sales gains must be measured in billions of dollars.

To some observers it is doubtful Sears could ever do better than keep pace with the overall movement of general merchandise sales through its present network of stores. Even a vigorous small store opening program will have minimal impact on the chain's balance sheet within five years, as was suggested above.

Is the Sears Merchandise Group, then, poised to go on a retail diversification spree, as K mart did last year? The company is characteristically mum.

"Strategies we have put in place over the next five years . . . will enable us to move at the rate of the general merchandise industry, and that's pretty doggone good," says Bass. "To move at a rate in excess would require some other thinking."

What other type of thinking? Sears' vice chairman, Richard Jones, responding recently to a question about competition from appliance/consumer elctronics superstores, said Sears must be more concerned with how product is distributed as opposed to how product is sold. A possible translation of that statement: Sears is thinking about opening freestanding stores to compete with specialists in certain categories.

The paint and hardware stores, the business system stores and even the small stores all suggest that Sears may one day become a vast network of specialty chains whose growth was supported by a base of full-line family stores.

"Look at who has experienced the most growth percentagewise in the last decade. The specialty stores, not the generalists," says Bernard Brennan, ceo of Montgomery Ward and certainly no impartial observer of Sears' fortunes. Ward, of course, has had more obstacles to overcome than Sears, and Ward's executives have taken to calling it a chain of specialty stores. "Today, the generalists lose and the specialists win," says Brennan.

The mix of a network of Sears specialty store chains would be intriguing. Certainly some of those chains, like the paint and hardware stores, or appliance superstores, would sell Sears brands. But in other categories where Sears has no national product reputation, like business systems, the mix might tend toward national brands. In such cases Sears might just as well purchase small already established operations and seek to grow them rapidly.

The industry is frequently abuzz with just such Sears takeover rumors, the latest of which links the company with the retailing units of W. R. Grace.

"We are contemplating new businesses," is all Bass will say. "We are always contemplating them." ∎

Sears: More Than a Men's Store?

Is Sears just a men's store, and not a family store? Has the retailing giant reached the limit in squeezing profits out of its strongest departments? Can Sears turn its weaknesses into strengths? These are some of the questions raised by an extensive statistical study of Sears conducted for *Chain Store Age* by Leo J. Shapiro & Associates.

The core of the study results from 1,008 telephone interviews in the Atlanta, Chicago, Dallas, Los Angeles and Philadelphia markets. Additional information on housewares and home electronics is provided by over 10,000 telephone interviews conducted throughout 1985.

Though households in the *CSA*/Shapiro's study report shopping Sears more than any other single retailer, consumers are picking and choosing selectively from among its de-

Which Store Would You Say Has the Best Value For . . . ?						
	Sears	Penney	Ward	Department Store	Discount Store	Other
Women's wear	8.5%	8.0%	2.0%	54.1%	8.5%	19.0%
Men's wear	14.1	9.6	3.0	46.4	6.9	20.0
Children's wear	22.1	14.7	2.7	30.9	16.2	13.4
Cosmetics	6.2	4.6	1.1	52.1	11.5	24.4
Domestics	18.5	13.3	2.4	39.2	15.2	11.4
Home electronics	20.0	4.5	3.1	19.5	9.9	43.0
Photo	17.3	5.2	2.0	14.6	19.0	41.9
Housewares	22.3	9.2	4.2	33.3	21.9	9.1
Hardware	31.2	2.8	2.0	5.2	11.2	47.6
Sporting goods	20.1	4.5	2.6	10.2	15.8	46.8
Toys	10.6	4.2	1.8	6.5	19.0	58.1
Stationery	7.3	4.7	1.6	20.9	20.3	45.1

Base: Atlanta, Chicago, Dallas, Los Angeles and Philadelphia markets; all who named a store.
Source: *Chain Store Age*/Leo J. Shapiro & Associates

partments and are shopping Sears less frequently.

In the five market survey, 79.2% of households polled say they have shopped Sears within the last year. This correlates nearly exactly with the 80% figure reported in Sears' own national image polling. But among those who have visited a Sears store within the last year, 39.6% report that they are shopping Sears less frequently than in the past. This compares to the 31.4% who say they are going to Sears more often this year, and 29% who report going about the same.

For comparison, department store shoppers are going to these outlets more often. Of those who have shopped a department store in the last year (97.9% of the total sample), 38.6% say they are going more frequently, compared to 29.9% who report that they are shopping department stores less frequently this year.

"There are very few people who buy everything at Sears," says Sears research manager Donald Hughes. Sears' own national polling reveals that men rate hardware, major appliances and portable electric tools as the top three departments. Faring less well, according to the Sears survey, is men's dress clothing.

Women in the Sears' poll rank children's clothing, domestics and major appliances the top three departments, with fashion wearing apparel the weakest, says Hughes.

The *CSA*/Shapiro poll confirms the Sears' results. Consumers in the five market survey rank hardware, housewares, children's apparel, sporting goods and home electronics as the top value departments at Sears (see chart). The departments delivering the least value, according to the study, are cosmetics, stationery, women's apparel and men's wear.

A STORE FOR MEN

Sears' undeniable strength in hard lines and traditional weakness in soft lines, especially fashion wearing apparel, point both to the chain's biggest problem and its tremendous potential. Sears is, quite simply, a man's store. If the retailing leviathan is to grow, it must find a way to attract more female customers.

"How many times will the female shopper

Who Really Shops Sears?

Upscale Customers Not Shopping the Whole Store

	\multicolumn{5}{c}{NAMED SEARS AS HAVING THE BEST VALUE FOR}
	Hardware	Housewares	Domestics	Children's Wear	Sporting Goods
Mean number in household	2.99	3.00	3.17	3.25	3.15
Presence of children:					
▪ None	54.6%	56.3%	54.0%	48.9%	50.3%
▪ Under 12 years	33.8	33.5	34.7	36.2	37.9
▪ 12–17 years	19.0	16.0	21.6	23.0	21.3
White collar	52.5	47.1	51.1	51.7	49.7
Blue collar	24.3	26.7	27.3	25.9	30.2
Total family income:					
▪ Under $20,000	17.3	22.3	22.2	20.7	16.6
▪ $20,000–$30,000	27.1	21.8	19.9	22.4	29.6
▪ Over $30,000	44.0	41.3	45.5	44.3	43.8
Male	44.7	46.6	46.5	37.4	40.8
Female	55.3	53.4	53.4	62.6	59.2

Source: *Chain Store Age*/Leo J. Shapiro & Associates

Who is the Sears core customer? "The best core customer that I ever ran across," says Sears research manager Donald Hughes, "was a fellow in Philadelphia, who, when he bought his Cadillac, bought it stripped down so that he could go to Sears and have all the accessories put on—that's a loyalty we ought to reward some way."

Perhaps it was with this customer in mind that in October Sears took a 1979 Chevy Camaro and installed 50 items of Sears auto parts and accessories as part of its New Century product line promotion. However, not all Sears customers are as loyal as that fellow in Philadelphia.

"The frequent Sears customer is just slightly younger than the national average," says Hughes. "They will be somewhat more affluent. They're not rich, but a little bit above the national average. Definitely, they are more likely to be married, have children and be living in a single-family home."

While the *CSA*/Shapiro survey confirms much of what Hughes says, it also reveals significantly different customer profiles for each of Sears' departments.

Children's apparel presents the most attractive customer profile, a white-collar worker earning over $30,000, female, aged 30 to 44, married with a child under 12 years old—in short, the traditional department store customer.

The women's apparel shopper, on the other hand, is more likely to have a greater number of children, to be part of a two-income family, yet is disproportionately likely to have a family income under $20,000.

"A lot of the department store people think of Sears as blue collar," Hughes says, "and that's not true."

SEARS: THE FAMILY STORE

			NAMED SEARS AS HAVING THE BEST VALUE FOR			
Home Electronics	Men's Wear	Photo	Toys	Women's Wear	Stationery	Cosmetics
3.18	3.16	3.23	2.93	3.51	3.05	3.39
52.1%	50.8%	49.6%	60.0%	40.8%	56.7%	51.0%
36.7	36.4	38.0	30.0	39.5	30.0	35.3
23.1	20.5	22.5	22.2	31.6	21.7	25.5
49.1	40.2	39.5	48.9	40.8	43.3	39.2
29.0	34.1	32.6	31.1	32.9	35.0	37.3
20.7	18.9	22.5	22.2	25.0	23.3	21.6
24.9	29.5	25.6	25.6	25.0	21.7	29.4
43.8	35.6	41.9	41.1	40.8	45.0	31.4
42.0	43.2	45.7	41.1	43.4	50.0	39.2
58.0	56.8	54.3	58.9	56.6	50.0	60.8

Yet in the *CSA*/Shapiro study, blue-collar workers are more likely to name Sears as the best value for the store's weakest departments—cosmetics, stationery, men's clothing and women's apparel. In contrast, white-collar workers name Sears' stronger departments—hardware, children's apparel and domestics—as delivering the best value.

The same relationship occurs along every demographic line. Those with incomes under $20,000 name women's apparel, stationery and photo as the top departments. Families with incomes over $30,000 cite domestics, children's apparel and stationery as the best value at Sears.

Larger families are more likely to value Sears for children's and women's clothes. Smaller families name hardware and toys. Men cite stationery, housewares and domestics as the top departments. Women name children's apparel, toys and cosmetics.

come into a store for an electric drill, or even a washing machine?" asks Merchandising Group chairman/ceo William I. Bass.

Men just enjoy shopping at Sears more than women do, according to the *CSA*/Shapiro poll. Though the survey sample is divided equally between males and females, it is men who disproportionately and consistently give Sears higher marks.

In the study, 64.7% of those who rank Sears highest as an enjoyable place to shop are men. Of those who rate Sears high for "always have

Cosmetics, Women's and Children's Apparel: Best Opportunities to Increase Core Customer Shopping

	All Respondents	NAMED SEARS AS THE BEST VALUE FOR . . .				
		Women's Wear	Men's Wear	Children's Wear	Cosmetics	Domestics
Shopping Sears:						
More	24.9%	42.1%	39.4%	40.2%	54.9%	36.4%
Less	31.3	22.4	28.8	26.4	21.6	27.3
The same	22.8	34.2	29.5	32.8	21.6	33.0
Don't shop Sears	21.0	1.3	2.3	0.6	2.0	3.4

Source: *Chain Store Age*/Leo J. Shapiro & Associates

what I want," 59.3% are men. An almost equal number (57.4%) who rank Sears high for "big selection" are men.

In fact, for 11 of the 12 store attributes measured in the survey, those who give Sears the highest marks are men. The sole exception is "great sales," where those who rate Sears the highest divide equally between males and females.

"One has to wonder how many of the women shopping at Sears are really just on the arms of men," says Shapiro & Associates president George Rosenbaum. "Men are more successful in finding in the store what they want than women are," he says.

Sears' high value perception by men—who are usually department-specific shopers—and lukewarm reaction by women—who generally shop a total store—creates another problem revealed in the consumer study.

Though hard lines are the store's greatest strength, a high value perception of these departments by consumers does not automatically translate into increased shopping of the rest of the store (see chart).

In the *CSA*/Shapiro study 31.2% of households polled say that Sears provides the best value for hardware, literally blowing away the competition. However, consumers who rate Sears the best value for hardware are not shopping the chain any more frequently.

Only 35.9% report going to Sears more this year, compared to 33.1% who say they are going less. A surprising 6% of those who rank Sears highest for hardware report they have not even shopped the chain in the last year. The result of a high value perception, then, is actually a net loss in shopping frequency.

The same disturbing relationship occurs in home electronics, another department which consumers rate as delivering high value. Though 20% of households in the *CSA*/Shapiro poll rank Sears as the best value for home electronics, of that group only 36.7% say they are going to Sears more often this year. This compares to 33.1% who are going less, and 6.5% who have not shopped Sears.

For housewares, the best that can be said is that a high value perception results in an even shopping pattern. In the five market sample, 22.3% report that Sears provides the best value for housewares. Only 35.9% of this group is shopping Sears more, compared to 30.1% who are going less, and 5.4% who have not shopped Sears at all.

Though Sears may have a high value perception and a healthy share of the consumer's mind in its strongest departments, neither of

NAMED SEARS AS THE BEST VALUE FOR . . .						
Home Electronics	Photo	Housewares	Hardware	Sporting Goods	Toys	Stationery
36.7%	41.9%	35.9%	35.9%	37.9%	48.9%	46.7%
33.1	27.9	30.1	33.1	28.4	25.6	26.7
23.7	24.0	28.6	25.0	28.4	23.3	23.3
6.5	6.2	5.3	6.0	5.3	2.2	3.3

these perceptions necessarily turns into market share. The problem may be a lack of national brands.

For example, of those in the *CSA*/Shapiro study who say they intend to buy a video cassette recorder in the next year, 17% say they expect to buy at Sears. In fact, according to the study, only 8.7% actually do end up buying their VCR at Sears. For toaster ovens, 15.9% say they expect to buy at Sears, compared to 3.2% who actually do buy there.

In some key areas Sears is losing market share. In 1982, Sears, according to the *CSA*/Shapiro poll, Sears took a 13% unit market share in televisions. By this year, Sears' market share had fallen to 11%.

POTENTIAL

The real challenge for Sears, however, will be to raise both its share of mind and its market share in those lines where it does not already enjoy tremendous strength. The *CSA*/Shapiro survey offers a glimpse of the payoff if Sears can succeed.

The chain's best model for success is children's apparel, which enjoys a high value rating, is a high female customer base and is a department that increases shopping frequency.

In the *CSA*/Shapiro study, 22.1% of households polled cite Sears as the retailer offering the best value in children's apparel. Of those who choose Sears for children's apparel, 62.6% are women. More importantly, 40.2% say they are shopping the chain more often, compared to 26.4% who are shopping less often, and the less than 1% who do not shop Sears.

Cosmetics, women's apparel, men's clothing, toys, stationery and domestics offer Sears the same potential, according to the survey. Only 6.2% in the poll rank Sears as the retailer providing the best value for cosmetics. Yet this relatively small group of customers is shopping the store far more frequently than the norm.

In this group, 54.9% say they are shopping Sears more frequently this year, compared to the 21.6% going less and 2% who have not shopped Sears.

Only 8.5% of the households polled rate Sears as the best value for women's apparel. But once again, this group is shopping the store with increased frequency. Some 42.1% report shopping Sears more frequently this year, compared to only 22.4% who are shopping less and 1.3% who have not visited Sears this year.

How else can Sears broaden its customer base to include more women and to increase shopping frequency? The *CSA*/Shapiro poll provides one strong answer—more sales. When Sears runs a sale, according to the survey, it becomes more of a women's store.

Women in the poll who rank Sears as the best value retailer for "great sales" equal the number of men. This is the only place in the survey where females rank Sears as high as their male counterparts do.

This group is also shopping Sears more frequently. Of those who rank Sears high for sales, 37.3% report that they are shopping the chain more frequently this year, compared to 24.6% who say they are going less and 1.7% who have not shopped Sears in the last year. ■

Bigger Things from Smaller Books

There is no getting around the facts. Over the past five years, Sears catalog sales have declined as a percentage of total company sales and have shown only a slight overall gain of 14.7%. The consumer mail-order industry, on the other hand, grew by 44.1% during that time period.

Some industry sources predict Sears will follow Montgomery Ward's lead and retire some or all of its catalog operation. Maxwell Sroge, catalog consultant at Colorado Springs–based Maxwell Sroge Publishing, says, "Sears will eliminate its basic catalogs in the next three to four years."

Already Sears has downsized its general catalog to 1,400 to 1,500 pages from its once mammoth-size of 1,800 pages. Like the Store of the Future, many lines that did not make sense for Sears to carry anymore were dropped. Building materials, for example, were eliminated because of the high freight costs and competition from home center warehouses.

Additionally, nonproductive pages that were crowded with tiny print and illustrations were deleted. Pages offering car mufflers looked like telephone listings with an occasional sketch of the product. Now one page replaces five.

Moreover, indications are that Sears will continue to shift emphasis away from its catalog sales. Some catalog stores in smaller Sears markets such as Alma, Mich., have been converted to Sears small stores. While the catalog desks still remain offering all merchandise lines, the addition of hundreds of Sears stores serving smaller markets over the next few years will continue to shift the balance of sales away from catalog and toward retail.

"The day of the general catalog is over," says Jo-Von Tucker, another catalog consultant at New York–based Jo-Von Tucker & Associates.

The reason: specialty niche merchandising. "The strength is in specialty areas—very much the same trend we see in retail," says Sroge.

Only nobody can convince Sears management that its general catalogs are dinosaurs. Despite the picture Sears' numbers paint, Sears still accounts for the largest percent of consumer mail-order sales when compared with the other general catalogers. According to Sroge Publishing, Sears represents 11.1% of the total vs. J. C. Penney at 4.6%, Montgomery Ward at 3.9% and Spiegel's at 1.7%.

It is no wonder, then, that Sears' management is determined to hold onto its catalog business. Instead of abandoning it, Sears is aggressively responding to the changing mail-order industry.

The general catalog has been revamped to resemble a collection of specialty books while Sears directs specialogs, targeted mailings, seasonal catalogs and sales booklets to specific market needs.

The 20 to 24 specialogs Sears publishes

yearly go head to head with the thousands of specialty catalogs available today. Specialog topics include a wide range of subjects including petites, crafts, camping and uniforms. They were developed as a means to reach specific consumers of key products. Sears' general merchandise manager of national catalogs Ted Weldon says, "It's a very efficient way to get customers."

However, many of the specialty catalogs on the market today target the high-end consumer while few appeal to those with more moderate means. Sears fills this middle niche with its specialogs. For example, a popular maternity catalog, *Mothers Work,* features a 100% wool pleated jumper for $93 compared to a similarly styled jumper of polyester and rayon from Sears in its *Mothers-To-Be and Baby* specialog at $32.

Sears targeted mailings, too, provide an efficient way to increase business. But, unlike the specialogs which are sent out mainly on request, targeted mailings are sent to customers who have recently made purchases of similar merchandise.

Additionally, fewer merchandise categories are covered by Sears targeted mailings than by its specialogs. The three topics for targeted mailings are lawn and garden, back-to-school, and home fashions (which is published for the summer and again for winter).

The advantage to targeted mailings, as the name implies, is that these catalogs may be adapted to key in on specific products in specific locations. For instance, this merchandising tool may be implemented to attract former Montgomery Ward catalog customers.

In the general catalogs (which are comprised of spring/summer, fall/winter and the *Christmas Wish* books) Sears now merchandises by lifestyles, breaking with its long-time tradition of presenting similar lines together. This gives the impression of a group of specialty catalogs compiled into one.

Additionally, each section aims at a particular customer by using models that represent that market segment. Juniors feature young, trendy teenagers while women's wear models are older and more sophisticated.

Sears recognizes that certain social factors have strongly influenced the retail and mail-order industries over the past deade. The catalog customer (who is the same customer who shops Sears stores) has become more knowledgeable and discerning over the past five years, says Weldon. She is married, family-oriented and lives in suburbia. Moreover, since many women have returned to the work force, there is an increase in dual-income families and less time for the new trends in leisure-time activities.

To address many of these issues, Sears introduced the "catalog within a catalog" strategy to its big books. The first of these appeared in the 1984 fall catalog and was called *Fashion Expressions.* It was aimed at the contemporary career woman and featured such items as a leather skirt for $75 and a 100% wool suit with the jacket priced at $85, the skirt at $45 and the pants at $45.

Fashion Expressions' unique 50-page format made it stand out from other pages in the general book. Its pages were smaller than pages in the regular catalog and the graphic design differed.

Get Fit was Sears' second catalog within a catalog effort. It too had special graphics but this catalog targeted the fitness buff with exercise equipment and apparel. Both *Fashion Expressions* and *Get Fit* are now regular sections in the big book.

The time and money crunch issues were dealt with by instilling a sense of urgency into the general catalogs.

In the 'Catalog of the Future' (the company's nickname for the recently revised big book), Sears creates a sense of urgency by offering merchandise at a reduced price for a limited time.

Other incentives include reduced prices for multiple purchases. For example, a customer could buy one pair of socks for $2.75 but if she buys five or more, each pair would retail for $2.29.

Moreover, several pages now carry the flag, "No lower price this season." Weldon says this instills customer confidence that Sears prices are competitive with other retailers and catalogers.

In all, 90 to 150 pages of the general catalog offer an incentive. According to Weldon, these pages do better than other pages in the same catalog.

But the real question remains: Are Sears' general catalogs viable merchandising vehicles for the future? Sears' management thinks so. Weldon points out that the average purchase from the 'Catalog of the Future' has increased like it did with the Store of the Future concept.

Additionally, 14 million copies of each big book are distributed in the U.S. every year and 40% to 50% of all Sears catalog sales result from these three volumes alone. Under these circumstances Sears execs are not willing to relinquish such a large portion of the business.

Interesting to note, however, is that 50% of all the catalog orders placed are done through the retail store instead of the catalog division. This suggests that the general catalog's mission is to supplement Sears in-store sales. Weldon adds, "The catalog is the best advertising for the store."

As the stores scale down or are out of stock, the catalog provides the answer. Weldon estimates that this fall's catalog had 150,000 sku's compared with the average store assortment of 70,000.

Not only does the catalog contain more sizes and colors of items than a Sears store, but it also features some categories that the stores do not, such as musical instruments and an occasional test item.

Additionally, the catalog operation bolsters the small store concept by providing a means to one-stop shopping of all merchandise lines. Presumably, catalog sales stand more of a chance to grow from these stores than by being hurt by them. ■

Ad Strategy: Divide and Conquer

How can a family store, one that carries many different kinds of products and has many strengths and weaknesses, create a consistent image for itself through advertising?

Sears' strategy is to divide and conquer. The chain makes its pitch to one family member at a time, informing dad of a new electronic tool, or trying to convince mom or the kids that Sears apparel is fashionable, after all.

That kind of strategy has been evident in its "total store" advertising, which has been Sears' focus since the Store of the Future program began two years ago. But now Sears plans to target individual niches even more carefully with product-oriented ads which allow Sears to make very specific statements, sometimes using moods or techniques which might not seem appropriate in its total store ads.

This month, for instance, Sears will debut a series of commercials featuring Stefanie Powers touting her new career apparel line. The almost austere spots are in the form of a personal chat between Stefanie and the viewer. As each commercial draws to a close a single piano lightly plays the familiar, "There's more for your life at Sears" tune.

Using product-oriented ads in this manner will enable Sears to play to its strength in hard lines or attempt to refashion its image in apparel without having to blend both of those messages into one ad. A Craftsman tool television commercial, for instance, confidently assures customers that each of the chain's line of hand tools is guaranteed forever. The ad, says Sears national retail general merchandise manager Ralph Hoch, mirrors the chain's position as the "pre-eminent merchant of hardware."

Meanwhile, with women's apparel, Sears can admit to a gray past and promise a brighter present. A magazine campaign for Bold Spirit and Cheryl Tiegs lines carries the question, "Who says Sears isn't . . ." and follows with such words as "classy," "fresh" or "a riot."

This new focus on product in Sears' advertising is consistent with the move by the entire chain to stress innovation in its mix in the 100th anniversary year. The strategy will also give Sears a chance to do some corporate cheerleading by letting its buyers and store merchandisers step out into the spotlight.

A series of magazine ads set to debut around the country will feature buyers and store department managers talking about products. Ads for New Century products, in fact, will allow the buyer to explain why he chose the product, what he feels are its strengths and why it offers the customer a good value. In regional ads Sears will feature local store personnel.

Advertising in general will shift a bit toward magazines as Sears increases its product-oriented focus. Working in specialized magazines, Sears believes it will be able to do a better job telling its product story, especially in cases where it is featuring innovative entries.

The look of print ads, meanwhile, continues to improve as Sears shifts toward them. Full-color newspaper inserts increased to 47 last year, up from 26 the year before and only 11 in 1982. Sears intends to keep its focus on those better-quality pieces.

As part of a new corporate effort to tailor its offerings, Sears is also doing a better job of regionalizing print ads. This fall, for the first time, a substitute was found in Florida inserts for winter coats.

These new directions do not mean Sears is about to abandon its total store ads. As a true full-line retailer, Sears still needs to move people through the entire store and reflect the better shopping experience Store of the Future gives.

Store of the Future, in fact, is described by Hoch as the "trigger" for store-oriented ads. These ads attempt to answer the question, "How do we reflect in our advertising the real personality and the impact of Store of the Future?"

One way is to create a commercial featuring a young girl wandering through a Sears store, wondering who Evonne Goolagong is, passing through the automotive department and finally getting the bike she wants. Another is to feature a father looking to buy a cooler but admiring a Harris tweed sportsjacket and a compact disc player.

Sears means high-tech and fashion, too, the ad featuring the father says. This is a full-line store. The music suggests the pleasant shopping experience of the SOF, and the quick cuts convey increased ease of movement through relayed Sears stores.

Sears feels that is an important message for a large, family store to deliver. So the company has gone to its first promotions agency to get assistance in in-store point-of-purchase programs that build traffic between departments. ∎

Electronics: Watchful of Superstores

Earl Signer shoots back his answer with an alacrity which betrays an issue already much discussed and already answered. "Our major competition," says the Sears senior video buyer, "are the superstores."

At first, Signer's answer smacks of the elephant who fears the mouse. With over $2 billion in sales for home electronics last year,

Sears Electronics Market Share (by units)

	1981	1982	1983	1984	1985
VCR	7.1%	7.9%	3.0%	8.3%	8.7%
Telephone	2.3	0.3	N.R.	0.7	7.2
Computer software	N.M.	N.M.	N.R.	3.8	7.2
Blank videotape	N.M.	N.M.	3.5	3.0	4.1
Telephone answering machine	4.2	2.6	7.4	4.0	5.5
Car stereo	N.M.	3.3	8.3	2.9	5.1
CD player	N.M.	N.M.	N.M.	N.M.	16.7
Home computer	4.0	4.1	2.3	8.5	9.3
Personal headphone stereo	N.M.	3.7	7.6	5.6	11.5
Stereo	N.M.	9.0	8.3	N.M.	11.2
Boom box	N.M.	N.M.	N.M.	6.2	11.5
Television	N.M.	13.0	N.M.	N.M.	11.0

N.M. = Not measured N.R. = No response
Source: *Chain Store Age*/Leo J. Shapiro & Associates

Sears is, at worst, four times bigger than its largest superstore rival. With 6,000 fewer stores, its sales of home electronics approach even Radio Shack's $2.4-billion volume.

In every minute of every shopping day, according to *CSA*/Leo J. Shapiro & Associates MarkeTrends research, 12 customers buy a television at Sears, adding up over a year's time to an estimated 2.1 million sets last year. Add to that over 600,000 VCRs, two million telephones and 150,000 telephone answering machines. In all, Sears sells about 6% to 7% of the entire market for home electronics in the U.S. in dollar volume.

During the past year, Sears sold more than 1 in every 10 personal headphone stereos, boom boxes, televisions, stereos and compact disc players (see chart). In addition, it sold more than 1 in 20 VCRs, telephones, home computers and telephone answering machines. Sears sold only 4.1% of blank video tape last year, but even that amounted to an estimated 500,000 units.

Sales per square foot for home electronics averaged an estimated $625 to $675 in 1984. Market share for nearly every category increased, with video cassette recorders, telephones, home computers, stereos, blank video tape and computer software hitting historic highs. Sears has taken a commanding chunk out of the emerging market for compact disc players.

With such overwhelming success, why does Sears keep such a watchful eye on the superstores? "I think you just have to look at where the mass market for electronics is being bought," Signer says, "and you have to say that if you're going to compete in that arena, you have to compete with the people who are successful.

"If you want to be a dominant outlet in electronics, you can't ignore the people who are the major players selling electronics today— you have to focus in on them as your competition," he says.

Though home electronics continues to post the highest year-to-year sales gains for any Sears department, each passing year finds superstores gaining ground. In 1983, combined sales for Circuit City, Silo and The Federated Group amounted to only a little over one-third of Sears' electronics sales. Last year, the top three superstores turned in a combined sales increase of 71%, for a total equal to about 60% of Sears' sales. This year the three will be breathing down Sears' neck.

In markets where superstores establish a foothold, the tendency is to take sales away from Sears. From 1981 to 1984, Sears' share of the Los Angeles television market fell from 9.7% to 8.9%, according to *Los Angeles Times Marketing Research*. At the same time, The Federated Group's share has risen from less than 2% to 2.9%. In 1984 The Federated Group overtook Sears in VCRs with 8.5% of the market, compared to 4.3% for Sears.

A more ominous example is Circuit City's home market of Richmond, Va., where the superstore holds the top market position for both VCRs and color televisions. According to *Media General Marketing Analyses,* Circuit City takes an astounding 32% share for color TVs and a 26% share of VCRs. This compares to Sears' 6% portion of color television sales and 3% for video cassette recorders.

Interestingly, the presence of an established superstore competitor has little or no effect upon market share for either crosstown rival Montgomery Ward or fellow cataloger J. C. Penney in any of the markets studied (see chart). In every case, the real target is Sears.

SURVIVAL

Despite the geometric growth in the home electronics industry over the last five years, Sears cannot assume either that the market is endlessly elastic, or that its superstore competitors will end their rapid expansion. The spector of a Toys "R" Us–like electronics competitor gobbling up market share must haunt every decision Sears makes.

Paradoxically, Sears' very strength represents its greatest weakness in facing the superstore competition. In a brand-conscious retailing environment, Sears may have already milked the last drop of profit from its private label electronics lines.

According to *CSA*/Shapiro research, 20% of households rank Sears as the best value for home electronics, a number slightly above department stores and more than discount stores Montgomery Ward and J. C. Penney combined.

When asked where they intend to buy specific electronics categories, consumers reveal that Sears also owns a hefty share of the customer's mind. According to MarkeTrends research, 17% of those who expect to buy a VCR in the next year name Sears as the place where they will but it.

Yet only 8.7%, about half that total, actually end up buying a video cassette recorder at Sears. Normally, a share of mind which outpaces a share of market is a signal that more advertising would boost sales. However, Sears already advertises VCRs heavily.

Barring that Sears is hitting the wrong price points or does not offer product with the right features—both of which are unlikely answers—the only conclusion is that customers are not finding the brands they want at Sears.

Radio Shack operator Tandy, the other giant private label electronics retailer, is mapping out a plan which addresses the same problem. While not abandoning its traditional Radio Shack customer, Tandy has aggressively entered the branded side of the business with the acquisition of both VideoConcepts and Scotts-McDuffs.

Sears may one day find itself walking down that same path. Recently, soon-to-be Sears corporate president Richard Jones stated that Sears must become more of a company concerned with how products should be distributed, as opposed to how products should be sold. This leaves the door open for Sears to explore the possibility of free-standing consumer electronics stores, but does not hint at whether or not they would include brand names.

The time for such a venture, however, may already have come and gone. With a leveling in growth for home electronics projected, the market already faces the real threat of overstoring. In addition, Sears' corporate culture of careful research, testing, more research

Head-to-Head Against the Competition
(market share by units)

Los Angeles	Sears	Penney	Ward	Zodys
Television	8.9%	3.1%	6.8%	6.0%
VCR	4.3	2.3	2.9	2.4
Oklahoma City	Sears	Penney	Ward	House of Sight & Sound
Television	10%	3%	6%	10%
VCR	5	5	2	8
Stereo	7	3	4	1
Richmond	Sears	Penney	Jeff. Ward	Circuit City
Color TV	6%	3%	6%	32%
VCR	3	6	3	26
Tampa	Sears	Penney	Ward	Oldt-Waring
Color TV	15%	1%	8%	8%
VCR	8	4	7	22

Source: *Los Angeles Times Marketing Research, The Oklahoman and Times Marketing Research*, Media General Marketing Analyses.

and more testing makes any bold moves unlikely.

"This is a very, very expensive business to make a mistake in," says home electronics national merchandise manager Daniel Danhauer, "and Sears does not like to make mistakes."

BRANDED ENTRY

Unlike major appliances, where the Kenmore name dominates the market, or hardware with Craftsman tools, Sears has never developed a private label brand presence in home electronics. The right time for that move would have been 20 or 30 years ago, but market conditions in the 1950's or 60's did not require an electronics brand name. Creating a new brand now would be next to impossible.

"Realistically speaking," Signer says, "there isn't enough money in the Bank of England to accomplish that now."

So Sears has decided to throw its lot with already established national brands. Beginning in June, Sears started tests in both the Atlanta and San Francisco markets of branded electronics. In Atlanta, Sears is testing RCA televisions and VCRs, while in San Francisco it is Sony TVs and audio equipment. In each case a Sears sku is deleted, and a branded one put in its place.

Though the tests are scheduled to run through the end of next month, and early results are not absolutely conclusive, the smart money is betting that Sears will add national brands to its television, VCRs and audio assortments.

"We're looking at where we're going from here to become a dominant outlet in this industry," says Danhauer. "We asked ourselves the question, 'Are we talking to all the customers we could be talking to?' The Sears core customer—are we attracting all of those people?"

Sears decided that it was not. "In the mature lines of goods," Danhauer says, "we found out that an awful lot of those customers are brand predisposed, and that if we included in our mix some national brands, an awful lot

Fedco	Broadway	Adray's	Gemco	Federated	May Co.
4.7%	4.6%	4.2%	3.5%	2.9%	2.2%
3.4	3.6	3.3	2.0	8.5	3.6
Silo	T.G & Y.	OTASCO	Wal-Mart	Target	John A. Brown
5%	4%	3%	2%	2%	2%
4	1	1	1	1	3
2	2	3	2	1	1
Thalheimers	Best	Bill May	K mart	Miller & Rhodes	Lawes
11%	9%	5%	3%	2%	2%
5	8	N.M.	N.M.	14	1
K mart	DeSears	Maas	Stereo Town	Zayre	Burdines
8%	7%	5%	5%	4%	3
5	5	5	7	1	2

more people would begin to shop our departments for those products."

The move to national brands, however, will not mean that Sears will be abandoning private label. "We're dedicated to private brand dominance in our departments, and that will always be the case," says Danhauer.

Sears strategy in home electronics will be different, then, from its strategies in other departments, such as hardware or major appliances. "The dominant outlet strategy is what's critical here," Danhauer says. "Not a domi-

A Red Flag for VCRs
Sears Share of Mind vs. Share of Market

	Share of Mind*	Share of Market**
VCR	17.0%	8.7%
Telephone	9.8	7.2
Computer software	8.5	7.2
Blank video tape	2.2	4.1
Telephone answering machine	6.5	5.5
Car stereo	1.9	5.1
CD player	2.6	16.7
Home computer	3.9	9.3
Personal headphone stereo	9.0	11.5
Stereo	5.6	11.2
Boom box	4.9	11.5
Television	8.6	11.0

*% likely to buy at Sears   **% actually bought at Sears
Source: *Chain Store Age*/Leo J. Shapiro & Associates

nant brand, but a dominant outlet and what mix does it take to bring that off. That doesn't mean a mix of brand and private label cannot coexist successfully."

Not everyone is convinced that Sears can bring off the move to branded electronics. "We welcome Sears' entry into branded electronics," says the chairman of a discount chain with sales in excess of $1 billion. "With their expense structure, I would have the price advantage."

Sears, however, is willing to accept the lower margins for branded products. "We will continue to be street price competitive," Signer says. "It's one of the realities of the branded business."

Changes in distribution and warehousing, according to Signer, will significantly reduce inventory levels and provide economics which will allow Sears to remain profitably price competitive, though surely at margins below historic levels.

If the result of brand names is added business from customers who would not have bought in the department without them, Sears can easily accept the new found profit dollars. The inherent danger in the strategy is cannibalization—branded products with lower margins going out the door with customers who would have been content to buy private label.

In such a worst-case scenario, sales do not increase significantly, or only marginally, and profit dollars for the deaprtment actually drop. When Sears says that results from its San Francisco and Atlanta tests are as yet inconclusive, it is perhaps this fear which stalks their results.

Yet the worst-case scenario looks like an unlikely result. Despite the attention given to the introduction of brand name audio and video products, Sears already is—and has been for years—a brand name electronics retailer.

Sears routinely features national brands in its catalog as a way to test the waters for new products or for declining categories where it wishes simply to maintain a presence in the business. Among others, it already carries branded telephones, answering machines, blank video tape, home computers and computer software in its stores.

A telephone assortment dominated by AT&T product has helped Sears grow its share of the market from only 2.3% in 1981 to 7.2% this year, according to MarkeTrends research. It is this kind of growth potential which Sears hopes to replicate using a similar strategy in audio and video.

UNKNOWN FUTURE

The question which no one can answer with convincing authority is what place a family store—with or without branded product—will have in the emerging market for home electronics.

Up until recently, the four private label giants—Sears, Radio Shack, the old Montgomery Ward and J. C. Penney—have taken close to a 20% slice out of the electronics industry pie and have been able to dominate a market where the majority of their competitors were small, independent dealers.

With the market for home electronics growing explosively by over 100% from 1980 to 1985, the growth curve itself has given most retailers a free ride on the upward spiral.

All that is about to change. Growth in the next five years will be considerably slower. The market for private label electronics, while not shrinking, has reached its limit. By 1990, at least 25% of electonics sales will be turned in by sophisticated superstore operators.

Can a 3,600-square-foot Sears electronics department become a dominant outlet in an emerging retail environment where 30,000-square-foot superstores filled with 10,000 sku's are the norm? In the upcoming battle between this modern David and Goliath, the smaller rival once again has a good shot at the giant superstore.

A superstore's greatest strength is its broad assortment. Yet, perhaps 80% of sales in the average superstore come from about 20% of the assortment. Sears, which assorts only to that core section, should certainly continue to compete effectively in the broad center.

The role of broad assortments in winning customers, though the superstore's bread and butter, has been oversold. In the *CSA* Value Study (May 1985), consumers rank assortment near the bottom of the value equation, ranking it ninth out of 12 components.

According to consumers in the poll, the top three determinants in figuring value are quality merchandise, prices and location. If Sears makes a move to more branded goods, it will be on an equal footing with the superstores on quality.

If it retains its determination to street pricing on branded goods as it has in both its San Francisco and Atlanta tests, then Sears can run even with the superstores on price.

On location, Sears has the definite advantage. Most superstores are either free-standing or situated in secondary malls. In contrast, Sears stores occupy prime locations in most markets. As a family store, it also can bank on the advantage of increased customer traffic.

Sears and home electronics will have a place in the era of the superstore. Though Sears has lost market share in some markets with strong superstore competition, the chain thinks the addition of more name brands gives it an excellent shot at becoming the dominant electronics retailer. ∎

Computer Stores in for the Long Haul

John Rollins is proud to be a merchant. In a business littered with technical talk, the Sears Business Systems Centers national manager is more likely to wax nostalgic about his days as a Sears store manager.

Or Rollins will speak with pride about arranging computer printers in a familiar "good, better, best" product presentation. He is equally apt to boast about introducing deep blue work stations in his stores to contrast with the now *de rigueur* ivory color for nearly all personal computers.

Not too heady stuff, but it is the glue of merchandising that Rollins thinks will help hold Sears Business Systems Centers together as the shakeout among his competitors continues. And, above all else, John Rollins is a merchant.

Still, it may be the depth of Sears' pockets, and not merchandising skill, which will determine if Sears Business Systems Centers will outlast the competition in a volatile and overstored marketplace.

In 1984 Sears raced to open 50 new units. In 1985 it added only four more. Today, Sears operates 105 Business Systems Centers in 59 markets, but at least for the next six months, the emphasis will be on expanding its outside sales force, and not on opening new storefronts.

In the early days, the personal computer market was a walk-in business, according to Rollins, and convenience of location was considered important. In contrast, up to 30% of the chain's $262.5 million in sales for 1985 will be turned in by his outside sales staff. Next year Rollins expects that outside sales will amount to half the chain's total volume.

The change in emphasis will also change the configuration of Business Systems Centers themselves. At present, the typical 3,500-square-foot location is divided approximately 60% to personal computers, 10% monitors, 10% printers, 8% software and 5% to communications devices.

As he adds more sales staff, who will pursue business consumers at their place of business rather than in the store, Rollins expects to shift some space in the relatively small area he has to work with. Additional closing areas may be added. Plus, even an outward bound salesman will need a desk to call home.

In an effort to find an identity which would distinguish it from its largely look-alike computer store competitors, the Business Systems Centers have tried a number of merchandise assortments and strategies.

Typewriters were an early part of the mix, but were later dropped as inappropriate for the market's new corporate customer base. Magazines and books were tried at some locations, primarily as lunch hour traffic builders, but they, too, were dropped. With the exception of AT&T's Merlin telephone system, communications products have not been a success.

Though originally conceived as a more broad-based business store, the Business Systems Center customer apparently reacts to the chain primarily as a computer store. Even there, its perception needs some sharpening.

According to a poll conducted for *Computer+Software News* (Dec. 2, 1985), only three-fourths of business consumers in the San Francisco, Chicago, Atlanta and Dallas markets report recognizing the Sears Business Systems Center name in aided responses. About one-fourth say that they have actually shopped Sears, according to the trade publication survey.

This compares to the 93% of business consumers in the survey who reported they were aware of ComputerLand, and the 53% who had shopped at ComputerLand.

Rollins, however, is not unaware of the problems which surround both Sears Business Systems Centers and the personal computer industry itself.

"It [the industry] is not wonderful today because of the rapid expansion of selling outlets," he says. "Everybody has gotten into the business, and it's a hell of a lot more competitive."

Yet Rollins is equally committed to making a success out of the personal computer business, trading in on Sears' traditional strengths of both quality and service. "Sears is in this for the long haul," he says. ∎

Housewares: Strong Image, Fair Sales

Sears' greatest challenge in housewares as it continues to refine the Store of the Future will be to translate a strong value image in the category into actual sales.

Shoppers often think of Sears when in the market for housewares items, according to research from *Chain Store Age*/Leo J. Shapiro & Associates. However, the retailing giant loses some luster when it comes time to buy. Even Sears officials admit housewares, specifically small appliances, rank high in national image studies but not in actual market share in the category.

CSA research finds that once Sears wins over a customer to housewares, the shopper actually increases shopping trips to the department. Of those who consider Sears to have the best value in housewares, 35.9% reported they were shopping Sears more in 1985 then in 1984. Thirty per cent are shopping Sears less, 28.6% the same.

What makes Sears' need to entice more customers so imminent is the threat of losing other shoppers. When *CSA* surveyed all consumers about shopping habits in 1985 vs. 1984, 12% responded they were visiting Sears less for housewares. Only 7.2% are going to Sears more for housewares and 6.1% the same as 1984.

Further research from *CSA*'s MarkeTrends suggests Sears must turn strong consumer intentions-to-buy at Sears into actual cash register rings.

For example, in *CSA*'s June MarkeTrends research on toaster ovens, Sears scored well with 16% of the households surveyed indicating they would go there to purchase. But, when consumers were asked where their last toaster oven was bought, Sears dropped to only a 3.2% response rate. The biggest shift by consumers was to discount stores where the mix often features national brands at sharp prices.

In a similar study conducted on Cookware in August, Sears was mentioned by 20.2% as the outlet they would shop, but only 12.3% said they last purchased cookware at Sears.

ROMANCING WOMEN

One reason for the retailer's shortfalls in housewares is its failure to draw women. When conceiving the SOF, Sears formed focus groups of women and found they did not like how Sears merchandised household chemicals with cookware and kitchen appliances near major appliances.

The first SOF prototype brought together all items for the home—which in some cases were scattered on three floors—into one home area. Now kitchen appliances are found near food prep, clocks have been removed from jewelry and located in housewares and, most recently, kitchen textiles have been moved from domestics to housewares.

Yet, the housewares department still lacked spark. Suppliers say it still required something to draw female shoppers. Realizing that, Sears has embarked on the following programs to make the department more compelling:

- Use of the Kenmore name for kitchen appliances rather than the lesser known CounterCraft
- Greater advertising of table appliances
- A sprinkling of key brand names
- Addition of a line of casual products designed for the way customers now eat and entertain
- And, the lowering of the gondola heights and the additional use of terra-cotta flooring, gridded fixtures and clearer signing.

Executing these plans is Pam Nelson, national merchandise manager for housewares. Nelson was brought into housewares three years ago from apparel. ■

The Curious Case of Dr. William Jory

Derek Cassels
EDITOR

Dr. William Jory is a British Columbian eye surgeon whose political activism subjected him to persecution by his enemies in the College of Physicians and Surgeons in British Columbia, which monitors physicians' practice of medicine and disciplines doctors when necessary. This series of editorials was written to expose the ways in which the College was using—and abusing—its authority.

The Medical Post is circulated to all licensed physicians practicing in Canada. "The Curious Case of Dr. William Jory" first appeared in the January 14, 1986, February 11, 1986, March 25, 1986, and July 22, 1986, issues of *The Medical Post,* published by Maclean Hunter Limited, Toronto, Canada. © 1986. Reprinted with permission.

Part I

It is the job of the various colleges across the country to keep order and discipline.

There has always been grumbling about the way some of them do this. Many doctors see the colleges as being high handed and out of touch with the day-to-day realities of front-line medicine. And there has always been the complaint that professionals have to contend with double jeopardy . . . they can be penalized by their college *and* by the criminal or civil courts.

While it is difficult for the individual doctor, it is also difficult for the colleges which, after all, must guard the public interest. They must have the respect of the profession by being seen to be scrupulously fair to both public and profession. And they must, like Caesar's wife, be above reproach.

Above all, they must not set themselves above the law of the land. There must be no bias.

Recently, both the Ontario and B.C. colleges have had a rough ride in the appeal courts of their respective provinces where judges have taken them to task about the way they have gone about the job of regulating the profession.

Ontario has had a couple of judicial black eyes. But in B.C. the damage is much more serious. This province's college has, to the best of our knowledge, been upheld only once in the six or seven cases that have come to appeal.

The latest case to come up is perhaps the more celebrated.

We refer, of course, to the curious case of Dr. William Jory.

Dr. Jory, you will remember, is the B.C. ophthalmologist and political figure who faced four charges arising out of his practice among the Indian populations of remote areas of the province.

The matter was first brought up in the House of Commons by an NDP member who charged Dr. Jory had carried out hundreds of quickie eye exams among Indian children.

The matter eventually landed in the lap of the B.C. College of Physicians and Surgeons, which decided there was a case to answer . . . four cases in fact.

So far so good.

But it is at this point that the case against Dr. Jory becomes very curious indeed.

But first, some background.

Dr. Jory is a man who inspires deep feelings in B.C. For the last 15 years or so he has taken a keen interest in medical politics. For a time, he was among the leaders of a group of neoconservatives, who called themselves The Reform Group.

Due to the pressure brought by the group as a whole, the British Columbia Medical Association (BCMA) started to change from a rather cosy, old-boys club to one that thrived on confrontation politics. In a way, the reformers made the association much more answerable to the membership at large. Possibly the single biggest contribution Dr. Jory and his colleagues made was to force the BCMA to set up referendum provisions on major political decisions, including the election of officers.

For the most part, the reformers were British expatriates who saw a drift towards the type of socialized medicine that was being practised in the U.K. And they were determined to stop, and if possible, reverse that drift.

Many of the reformers, including Dr. Jory, were elected to high office within the BCMA.

Not only did Dr. Jory serve as the BCMA president, but he was picked as the province's man to take his turn as president of the Canadian Medical Association (CMA) at its annual meeting in Toronto.

Normally, the person picked by a province for the CMA job is elected by acclamation. But at that fateful Toronto meeting, the anti-Reform group persuaded delegates from other provinces to head a revolt. As a result, Dr. Jory was pushed aside, while another B.C. doctor took over as head of the CMA.

It looked as though Dr. Jory's political life was over. And, indeed, for a while he retired to his practice and took little interest in BCMA politics. But this didn't last long. He again rose to the leadership of the BCMA and was again elected as its president.

By some curious coincidence, just as he was to take the chain of office the subject of the quickie eye exams was raised. There were demands that he step aside until the matter was settled by the college. Dr. Jory refused, saying that while these cases were usually dealt with quickly he suspected that the college might drag its feet. (At the time we said that we thought Dr. Jory was making a mistake by not stepping aside until the air was cleared.)

Normally, the B.C. college acts with a proper air of dispatch. The majority of cases are disposed of, one way or another, in about six months.

In Dr. Jory's case this was not to be. In retrospect, it could be said his initial suspicions were correct. It has taken the best part of four years to hear the complaint and take the matter through appeal . . . with most of the time being taken up by the college's investigation.

In the three charges that were quite specific, it found Dr. Jory not guilty. On the fourth, the least specific of all, he was found guilty.

The punishment was severe. He was fined $10,000 and told to pay $20,000 in costs. He was also suspended from practise for a year.

The college must have known—in fact we pointed out on this page ("Swinging in the wind with Bill Jory," Jan. 8, 1985)—that the extraordinary time taken to investigate the case had ruined Dr. Jory's once-thriving practice. This, obviously, was not taken into account when his punishment was handed down.

We said at the time, and we see no reason to change our tune, that the college must be cognizant of the attrition factor when dealing with members. The resources of an organization of this kind are beyond that of any individual. By drawing out the investigation, a college can impale a member on a lethal legal bill.

Surely, if a doctor is going to "done," 'tis better he be "done" quickly.

There is a fine line between prosecution and persecution. Dr. Jory's supporters have claimed there is more persecution is his case than prosecution. And their view has gained validity with the comments of the appeal court judge, Madam Beverley McLachlin.

After reading the 33-page judgment through, it is apparent the trial judge sees again and again evidence the college was prejudiced in this case against Dr. Jory. Inferences are made by the college that are not sustainable by the evidence, the judge says.

In short, the court found the college took what it wanted from the evidence it had before it and dismissed or conveniently overlooked evidence that could be seen as supporting Dr. Jory's defence.

A typical comment made by the judge appears on page 24 where she looked at the question of the credibility of witnesses aside from Dr. Jory.

"The committee (of the B.C. college) stated that it accepted the evidence of (another doctor). It did so where that evidence was adverse to Dr. Jory. Where it was not the committee either ignored the evidence or refused to accept it."

And on the next page the judge again notes: *"Similarly, the committee erroneously exaggerated the differences between* (a second medical witness) *and Dr. Jory and failed to mention factors which supported Dr. Jory's views of their differences of professional opinion."*

But the most chilling excerpt comes when the judge quotes the college's assessment of Dr. Jory as a witness.

The college's report says:

"On several occasions the counsel for the college charged Jory with being the perpetrator of a scam. The committee finds that Jory's performance as a witness contained all the elements of a confidence man who would be guilty of Charge 4. The committee found him to be smooth and glib, pompous and condescending. At times he feigned a certain deference and humbleness, but at all times his egoism and feeling of self importance and superiority was [sic] very apparent. The committee found his contrived performance irritating and obnoxious. In addition, the committee was not impressed with Dr. Jory's credibility or his integrity as a witness, which will be discussed at greater length in this report."

The judge reminds the college that issues, not personalities, are paramount. Or, as the Madam McLachlin says: *"While the committee in this case is not bound by the rules of evidence which govern court procedures, it is bound NOT to convict without convincing and cogent evidence. Therefore, any conclusions based on Dr. Jory's personality traits should have been made with great caution, so as to be certain that the committee was not convicting Dr. Jory because it found his general character or demeanor repugnant."*

Furthermore, says the judge, the lawyer of the college, *"dwelt at great length on a picture of Dr. Jory as a shrewd, manipulative person, a politician par exellence. The committee appears to have adopted the same tone in much of its report, although it did not expressly refer to Dr. Jory's political activities in the college. In my view, the committee by its report revealed itself ready to castigate Dr. Jory, to draw inferences against him whenever possible, and finally to place significant weight on the fact that his testimony contained "all the elements of a confidence man who would be guilty of Charge 4."*

There is the impression all through the judgment that the judge feels the college had it in for Dr. Jory.

B.C. doctors would certainly seem to have a right to demand an investigation into the way the college is being run and advised. There can be no doubt that bias played a large part in this case.

It may be the college is itself in contravention of the B.C. Medical Practitioners Act. As we read the act, the college must hold a meeting every calendar year or within 18 months of the last meeting.

Last year, the college by custom should have held its meeting during the week the BCMA held its annual meeting. (Last year, the BCMA met with the Yukon Medical Association in Whitehorse). It cancelled the meeting at the last minute. There has not been another meeting of the college since—which means that it is now over 18 months since the college last met.

Regardless of where and when the college decides to hold its next meeting, it has almost guaranteed itself a hot time of it. ■

Part II

When we wrote the editorial titled "The Curious Case of Dr. William Jory" (*The Medical Post,* January 14) we little realised the drama was about to become curiouser and curiouser.

We left the sad narrative at the point where Dr. Jory seemed to have come to the end of a long painful fight for his professional life and personal reputation.

His appeal against a conviction by the British Columbia College of Physicians and Surgeons had been successful. The judgment was highly critical of the way the college had conducted its investigations and hearings. It was in no way equivocal.

The judge, Madame Justice Beverley McLachlin, left no doubt she thought the college seemed more interested in pursuing Dr. Jory than in the case against him. (The college itself had earlier found Dr. Jory not guilty of two specific charges. The appeal was against a third "guilty" verdict on a much vaguer charge. He was suspended from practice for a year and fined $10,000 with $20,000 of court costs being assessed against him.)

It was the last judgment of Madame Justice McLachlin in the B.C. Supreme Court. Just before she filed her judgment she was promoted to a higher court. She is widely acknowledged to be one of the brighter up-and-coming jurists in B.C.

So here we have a clear-cut judgment delivered by an extremely clear-minded judge.

Convictions. On the face of it we could be forgiven for believing that this was the end of the story.

Not so, as our story on the first page indicates.

Certainly the college and its advisers had some explaining to do to the profession in British Columbia . . . not only over the Jory case but over a whole string of convictions which had been reversed in recent years. In fact the college's batting average in the appeal process is dismal.

As in all judgments there is a set time given for appeal. In the Jory case this period of time came and went. No appeal.

To put matters into perspective we would point out that the *College v Jory* case has lasted longer than World War I.

Despite the fact that the college has taken its good time to pursue its case, it filed an appeal *after* the deadline. And after a two-day hearing it won the right to appeal on the basis that it was a college lawyer and not the college itself which had missed the bus. (We cannot tell you at the moment if this curiously tardy legal aide still works for the college.)

To give some idea of the future costs involved (costs to this point must run well into the six figures), a B.C. lawyer says the appeal will cost a minimum of $75,000—a third of which will be spent copying all the testimony for the panel of judges!

We again question the college's judgment here. Enough, surely, is enough. It has taken more than four years for the college to make its best case against Dr. Jory . . . and it has failed, at least so far.

The college cannot but be aware of the attrition factor. As we said in an earlier editorial, we feel Dr. Jory has been hung out to dry. The most recent decision by the college merely reinforces that belief. His practice is ruined, he is on the edge of personal bankruptcy and he is forced to rally again to face a foe with unlimited financial resources that can draw its case out interminably.

The whole spectacle is unnervingly repugnant.

As we said a few weeks ago there is a growing suspicion in many minds that prosecution in this case is another word for persecution.

And the thought has more than once crossed our mind that much of this whole matter may be motivated by Jory's personality.

Dr. Jory comes from an English upper-middle-class background. He can often give the impression of being arrogant and condescending. Certainly there is some sense of this in the way the college saw him as a witness.

But personalities must, and should, be set aside here.

There may be those in the college who feel they have nothing to lose by appealing. It gets the matter tidily out of the way for a while . . . particularly during its annual meeting where it cannot be discussed as it is now *sub judice.*

Enemies. We still maintain that when the day comes when doctors can ask the college for an accounting on this and other cases there should be some very pointed questions—if on nothing else but the enormous cost and the bungling.

Even Bill Jory's enemies must be awed into a state of shocked disbelief as they contemplate the persistent and pressing behavior of the college.

There is one way that doctors in B.C. can indicate some measure of support for Dr. Jory. They could consider sending referrals. It is one way of showing the college that not everyone is in agreement with its curious crusade. And no one can fault his professional competence. ∎

Part III

The curious case of Dr. William Jory keeps right on getting curiouser and curiouser.

The latest chapter starts, we suppose, where our last editorial left off a few weeks ago ("The curious case of Dr. William Jory" [cont.], Feb. 11).

Followers of the saga will remember that we commented negatively on the decision of the college to appeal the successful appeal of Dr. Jory to a conviction by the College of Physicians and Surgeons of British Columbia . . . if you follow us . . . We wondered whether the college had given any thought to some pretty major and substantive issues.

Among them:

∎ *The attrition factor.* Here we have a powerful body with unlimited financial resources slowly grinding down an individual who, no matter how well fixed before the ordeal, is almost certain to be wiped out financially and professionally in the long haul—which brings us the second issue.

∎ *The long haul.* We have repeatedly pointed out that the usual time for a hearing and decision is (or should be) measured in months. The Jory affair has now dragged on longer than the First World War. Apart from the financial burden mentioned above, there is the immense psychological trauma of having this very serious matter hanging over a person's head literally for years. This kind of sustained stress imposed by a group of fellow physicians must be all but unbearable. Families have broken up over much less. Yet fortunately, the Jory family has been unshaken in its resolve to see the thing through together.

∎ *The legal procrastinations.* The decision to appeal the Jory case, considering the strong judgment against the college and the lacklustre performance of its legal help in almost missing the appeal, is curious. The lawyers, you will remember, were strangely tardy in seeking leave to appeal . . . in fact, were so late they had to go to court again to make a case for proceeding. Needless additional expense all round.

These are very important issues. No matter how unpleasant and obnoxious a defendant is perceived to be by his accusers, he must be given, and appear to be given, due process. Personalities cannot be allowed to intrude, otherwise the whole system will suffer and be the poorer. (Remember Dreyfus!)

The message is beginning to get through. It was a lonely fight for a while. But we have now been joined by both a grassroots movement of physicians in B.C. who are petitioning for an extraordinary meeting of the college, the resignation of its 11-member council and a financial accounting.

And the lay press is beginning to comment on the issue, much to the consternation of the college and its registrar. *The Vancouver Sun* has raised the spectre of the college being opened to nonphysicians (see below).

For reasons easily understood, the college is less than pleased by the adverse publicity. It took the unusual step of circulating a letter to the profession in B.C. attacking *The Medical Post* and *The Vancouver Sun* for "many inaccurate statements." (See *The Medical Post,* March 18). The letter, signed by college president Dr. John R.C. LeHuquet, is curious for its omissions. It takes three pages and does *not* even try to tackle the substantive issues we have raised.

It says we have underestimated its legal batting average. Yet, using the college's own figures, this reduction is marginal at best. We said they had lost five or six appeals and it looks as though the college is saying it is only four or five, two of which were in the 1960s

Part IV

We hope regular readers of this page will bear with us while we remind you of the background to this continuing saga.

Most will be familiar with the broad details of the curious case of Dr. William Jory, the B.C. ophthalmologist and medical politician who was charged by his provincial college on three counts arising from his practice in northern B.C. On two of the charges he was aquitted by the college itself. On the third and least specific charge he was found guilty, fined heavily and suspended from practice for a year.

He appealed this finding to the B.C. Supreme court and this appeal was upheld. The college had 30 days to appeal this finding. It was only after the 30-day limit had come and gone that the college decided to appeal and won the right to do so only after a two-day court appearance.

In May, without any reason being given, the college announced it was dropping its hard-won appeal. Following news reports and a series of editorials in *The Medical Post* on the case the B.C. College of Physicians and Surgeons took us to task in a letter to its members for what it described as a series of mistakes in our assessment of the situation. In fact they challenged us on two counts which we dealt with in our May 25 issue.

In its first meeting in two years, during the British Columbia Medical Association's series of conferences earlier this month, the college turned to meet its accusers and we learned some other rather curious facts that, we contend, need some further examination.

When a member tried to open the cases of Dr. Jory and another member whose appeal was upheld in the B.C. Supreme Court the meeting was told these two cases were *sub judice*. This meant, of course, they could not be discussed in any way.

. . . the letter is not too clear on the point.

And the college admits to facing "a formidable array of legal challenges." (If the college is perceived by its members as being scrupulously fair, would this array be as formidable, one wonders.)

The letter also makes a pretty weak attempt to defend itself against the charge made by us that it appears to be contravening the Medical Practitioners Act. The college says its members could not get to Whitehorse last May (where there was a joint meeting of the British Columbia Medical Association and the Yukon Medical Association) because of an air strike that affected CP-Air.

The facts are, however, that dozens of doctors made the trip to Whitehorse on specially chartered aircraft. *The Medical Post* managed to get two staff members *from Toronto* to Whitehorse via Vancouver to attend the meeting.

Yet here we have the college saying it couldn't do the same thing. Let's not forget either that the BCMA and the college literally share the same roof.

The college must have known of alternative travel arrangements, yet it did not take advantage of them. And even if it did not make the meeting there, curiously, it made not the slightest attempt between May and December last year to hold a substitute meeting open to the general membership.

All it needed to do was book a hall and let people know the time and place. It really is no big deal, considering the funds and staff the college has at its disposal.

There are indications, too, that the college is getting more than a little twitchy about criticisms about some of the legal decisions that have been coming its way.

It also makes curious people like ourselves a deal more curious as to the real reason for the urge to secrecy.

We will not be silenced on this issue and will continue to give it the publicity it so richly deserves as the case unfolds.

Stay tuned. ■

We are puzzled by this ruling. There is nothing pending that we know of in either case. The Jory case was dropped by the college and the other case, regarding Dr. William Hirt, was disposed of May 10 of last year.

If we are in error we hope the college will clarify what actions are being taken that make either case *sub judice.*

We also learned with some sadness that the vast majority of doctors in B.C. could care less about what happens in the college. Certainly they stayed away that day in droves.

Frankly, we think this was a huge mistake. What happens to their governing body and how it conducts its business is of concern to every doctor in that province . . . and indirectly to every doctor in the country.

One delegate who did attend, Dr. Richard Davidson, made the point that many of the issues raised by the Jory case and others had not truly sunk home with many members. Dr. Davidson's charge should not be dismissed lightly. This B.C. neurologist knows more than a little of what he speaks. At age 27 he became the youngest man ever in Britain to qualify both as a doctor *and* a barrister.

The plain fact of the matter is that Dr. Davidson is right . . . the vast majority of doctors are still unaware of the issues raised in the way colleges have recently been conducting their businesses.

They are largely unaware of the language used by senior jurists who have been very disturbed at what they find after looking at the way colleges work. There seems to be the idea among doctors that the rulings which have gone against colleges have been on minor, rather technical points.

In fact judges have criticized in very strong language indeed the largely undesirable way colleges have been running the store.

Some sense of this was gained when we printed some excerpts of the judgment of Madame Justice Beverly McLachlin in her December 13, 1985, ruling in the Jory case.

For instance in her summing up Justice McLachlin left no doubt that she found solid evidence of bias toward Dr. Jory.

"Only by emphasizing motive, bad character and Dr. Jory's lack of credibility—none of which survive close scrutiny—and by ignoring much of the testimony could the committee arrive at its conclusion."

We won't go into the tongue lashing Madame McLachlin gave the college here. More details can be found in our earlier editorial ("The Curious Case of Dr. William Jory," Jan. 14).

Dr. Jory's innocence or guilt are no longer the issue. The issue is how the college went about its prosecution.

Nor is Dr. Jory alone is having a serious complaint against the college upheld by the B.C. Supreme Court.

Let's go back to the earlier Hirt case.

Here another judge, Mr. Justice Gibbs who upheld Dr. Hirt's appeal, makes it quite clear a charge of sexual intimacy with one patient should never have been made. Not only should the college never have laid a charge against its member but it used evidence from that case to help convict on a second case . . . an inexcusable error in practice. And, says the judge, quite improper questions were asked during the hearing which also allowed clear hearsay evidence.

In other words the college acted in much less than a fair and judicial manner.

At one point Mr. Justice Gibbs says: *"What the council did, or permitted, was more than a mere technical breach of the rules. It was a grave and prejudicial error."*

And at the end of his 36-page judgment Mr. Justice Gibbs says: *"In my opinion, for all the reasons I have given, both on the basis of the evidence and because of fatal procedural errors, Dr. Hirt was unjustly deprived of his reputation and unjustly punished."*

Justice, we all accept, must not only be done but must be seen to be done.

With quotes like that from the Supreme Court hearings can justice be seen being truly done in B.C.?

There is at least one other facet worth pondering. It not only takes a brave man to take on the college. He has to be a rich one. It takes between $50,000 and $100,000 to have your say in court . . . a real, and fair, court that is.

Nor are costs limited to the individual defendant. The college's legal bill was $166,000 two years ago. Last year the bill had grown to $260,000. What next year's account will be is anyone's guess. It will reflect the lengthy Jory case and Supreme Court hearing plus the two days in court arguing for that appeal which was later dropped, presumably because of a contrary second opinion.

The college now has to face countersuits by Dr. Jory. And if he sues, and wins, the college could be in very big money trouble indeed.

At its long-delayed annual meeting the college also served notice it intended to open the Medical Practitioners Act for revision.

One of the curious changes it wants to make is to drop the written report that is required of the investigating committee. This report goes to the college council which debates it before deciding if any punishment is justified. That debate can be seen as an in-house appeal hearing.

It is the written reports that seem to have got the college into most of its recent troubles and so it is natural that it wants to drop them. But this would have the effect of denying the larger council its debate of a case. In other words the appeal process within the college would no longer be there.

We hope the college thinks again before passing that one. And we hope it knows what it is doing when it requests the Medical Practitioners Act be opened. Because once it is open some people in Victoria might want to have a go at making some of their own amendments . . . one of which might question the need for the college, as it is now constituted, in the first place.

Whether it denies it or not there is still a great deal of suspicion that the B.C. college is not above settling old scores and singling out its critics. Wise heads in the college know that actions talk louder than words. If as a result of a fishing expedition it lays more charges in the Jory case the clouds of suspicion will only grow darker.

There was, however, one bright spot on the horizon that week in Vancouver. Before the college's annual meeting a member of the BCMA was brought into the room to identify members of the press in order that they get their marching orders at start of business.

At the last moment, with the prospect of closing its doors on the public via television cameras, the college decided to hold its first open meeting.

Once open they are difficult to close.

At least that was one move in the right direction. ∎

State of the Food Industry

Charles Haberstroh
EDITOR IN CHIEF

Kevin Hannigan
FEATURES EDITOR

Ann Przybyla
TECHNICAL EDITOR

Charles Morris
MIDWEST EDITOR

Dianne Taylor
CONTRIBUTING EDITOR

Scott Stephens
ART DIRECTOR

This report permits the management of food companies to evaluate how they stand in relation to the performance of both individual segments and the industry as a whole. As a planning document, the report allows companies considering diversification into new areas to see how those areas are faring. The report contains an economic forecast and information on marketing trends from local, state, and federal government agencies, as well as from sources in the private sector.

Food Engineering is edited for manufacturing marketing managers at food and beverage processing operations. "State of the Food Industry" first appeared in the August 1986 issue of *Food Engineering,* published by ABC Publishing. © 1986. Reprinted with permission.

Surviving a Strong Market

During 1985, the food industry demonstrated why it has become so attractive for investors and mergers/acquisitions specialists over the past several years—it is steady, predictable, and not prone to the kinds of cyclicality other manufacturing industries experience. Growth in '85 ran at about 1.7 percent when adjusted for inflation and at a total shipment value of $307.4 billion.

The continuing strength of the market was reflected in stock performance. For the fifth consecutive year, the companies that make up the Standard & Poor's food index outperformed the S&P 400. In fact, 1985 was the year in which the performance of the food stocks index actually passed the S&P 400 in absolute terms, as well as relative performance.

As the Standard & Poor's Industry Surveys reported: "Generally speaking, food processors have managed to forge ahead from an earnings standpoint, while averting any major disasters. Clearly, lower costs of certain raw materials have helped. But other costs also have been favorable. Declining interest rates and energy prices, along with only small increases in wage and packaging expenses, more than offset higher marketing costs in 1985. . . . Similar factors, plus the benefit of a weaker dollar (for those companies with a substantial exposure to foreign markets), should lead to an even better showing in 1986, with the food group projected to post a 19.7% EPS gain."

There is little doubt that two other factors will help to keep EPS fat. For one thing, the new tax bill (if it goes into effect intact) will raise bottom lines significantly because of the large real tax rate food companies currently pay. The other factor will be divestiture, as food conglomerates begin to spin off their less stellar divisions.

Apparently, while many have their doubts about the efficacy of mega-mergers, the 1985 acquisitions of Nabisco by R.J. Reynolds, of General Foods by Philip Morris, and of Beatrice by Kohlberg Kravis Roberts & Co. did push stock prices up, having a ruboff effect on the attractiveness of food stocks generally.

But more than anything else, it was the

Mergers/Acquisitions Scorecard, 1984–1985

PLAYERS	1984	1985
Total Activity	583	658
Selected Segments:		
Food Processors	89	95
Diversified Firms with Food Interests	48	39
Meat Packers	8	5
Poultry Processors	11	12
Soft Drink Bottlers	14	14
Wholesalers	36	39
Dairy Processors	13	21
Packaging Suppliers	25	26
Foreign Firms Buying U.S. Firms	40	55

Source: The Food Institute

New Product Introductions

Doubled since the seventies and still going strong.

AVERAGE	
1970–81	1,026
1982	1,510
1983	1,803
1984	1,988
1985	2,206

Source: Dancer Fitzgerald Sample

matter that once again the food stocks proved their dependability.

If stock prices seem to bode a bright short-term future for the industry, improvement in companies' performances is still going to be largely a matter of trench warfare and very careful positioning. Per capita food consumption has been increasing very little. For example, dry grocery tonnage, as measured by Selling Areas-Marketing Inc. (SAMI), shows an average growth of less than one-half of one percent per year since 1980. Refrigerated and frozen products, generally considered one of the important growth categories over the last five years, have done better, but have been averaging only about 2.2 percent according to SAMI. True, this 2.2 percent increase has been delivering about a 7.3 percent average increase in dollars generated, largely because of the increase in upscale products which deliver more dollars per ton. But even that number is starting to taper off. Even though average dollar growth has been 7.3 percent, it went from 10 percent five years ago to 4 percent in 1985.

This doesn't mean anyone has to despair about the food business, but it does mean that more is going to have to be spent in market research, in developing a talent for exploring and exploiting niche markets, in regionalizing marketing, and in advertising.

For one thing, the trend toward consolidation goes on. This means that the lone food processor will increasingly be competing against companies with more resources, diversification, and market access than he possesses. The big mergers get a lot of attention, as they should, considering the fact that four conglomerates control probably 15 percent of the value of all industry shipments. But in a rush to focus on the major mergers, processors should not lose sight of the fact that for the last ten years the trend in the industry generally has been toward realignment of businesses through mergers and acquisitions. For example, between 1976 and 1985, according to The Food Institute, there were 5,680 merger and acquisition activities—an average of 568 per year. In just the food processors area, between 1980 and 1985 there were 499, or 83 per year. There are no indications that this trend will slow down.

At the same time, market share will be the name of the game. Processors cannot depend on increasing the size of the market. This will mean more expenses on the marketing side, which in turn will mean that companies not prepared to spend more on marketing will see themselves getting squeezed.

Lastly, if the 2,206 new products that Dancer Fitzgerald Sample charted as they entered the market in 1985 were an indication, there is not going to be any abatement in product technology, packaging creativity, or marketing aggressiveness. And even though new supermarket construction is showing a clear trend to more floor space and more sophisticated product selection, the competition, particularly with the introduction of direct product profitability (DPP), will only get more intense. With DPP the retailer now has a way to quantify his decision-making; so, in addition to everything else, the manufacturer will have to meet hard and fast demands for a certain numbers profile on his products.

In the face of this ever-more-difficult competition, several strategies will continue to evolve. For one thing, target and niche marketing will become more important than ever. Product differentiation and development by region, or demographic and even psycho-

STATE OF THE FOOD INDUSTRY 121

Wholesale Grocers' Sales (in billions)		Food Store Sales (in billions)	
1982	$174.7	1982	$245.3
1983	190.3	1983	254.9
1984	208.9	1984	270.4
1985	216.1	1985	282.2

Source: The Food Institute

Grocery Store Price Index (1982=100)		Eating & Drinking Place Price Index (1982=100)	
1982	100.0	1982	100.0
1983	101.5	1983	104.3
1984	105.1	1984	108.5
1985	107.9	1985	112.6

Source: The Food Institute

Producer Price Index for Finished Consumer Foods (1967=100)		Farm Price Index (1977=100)	
1982	259.2	1982	133.2
1983	261.8	1983	134.7
1984	273.3	1984	141.9
1985	271.4	1985	128.4

Source: Bureau of Labor Statistics
Source: USDA

Food Products Balance of Trade, 1984–1985 (in millions)

	Exports	Imports	Balance
1984	$16,103	$17,727	$−1,624
1985*	14,467	18,343	−3,877

*Estimated.
Source: U.S. Industrial Outlook 1986

graphic group will be essential. Also important will be looking for improvements in productivity. This will come partly through processors reassessing manufacturing operations; partly by choosing suppliers of machinery and ingredients who can help processors be more productive in their operations on an ongoing basis rather than just being the up front "lowest cost" supplier; and partly by continuing to make sure their businesses are carefully defined.

The market in 1986 is tougher than it was in 1985, and will be tougher in 1987. The key is to be tougher than the market—not always easy, but always necessary. ∎

Juices, Soft Drinks

There's a lot to drink in the U.S. these days. In fact, there may be too much. The flurry of new product activity in 1984 has created a glut of drinks on supermarket shelves, and many in the beverage industry expect the competition will be too tough for some brands. Bottled water, for example, is still a fast-growing beverage market with profit margins running as high as 25 percent. But the many brands now available suggest that profits may have to be shaved to buy shelf space.

In carbonated soft drink marketing, the emphasis has been on new products, discounting and heavy advertising. In some cases, as with flavored colas and chocolate-type soft drinks, the new products have become new categories. The positioning of juice-containing soft drinks such as Pepsico's *Slice,* for example, as a healthy modern beverage in several fruit-juice-containing versions—as opposed to traditional "bellywash"—prompted a horde of similar products. Now, juice-containing carbonated soft drinks account for nearly 3 percent of carbonated beverage sales and should grow to about 15 percent by 1990.

The continuing interest in dieting, fitness

Changing Tastes for Soft Drinks

	NATURALLY SWEETENED		NON-CALORIC		TOTAL	
	1983	1984	1983	1984	1983	1984
Colas	51.2	53.2	13.9	16.7	65.1	69.9
Lemon-Lime	9.6	10.0	2.3	2.8	11.9	12.8
Other Flavors	17.6	12.9	2.8	1.5	20.4	14.4
Mixers	1.1	1.2	0.8	0.9	1.9	2.1
Total Market	79.5%	77.3%	19.8%	21.9%	99.3%	99.2%

Source: U.S. Dept. of Commerce

and health, say some industry experts, is the primary cause for the rise of the beverage industry since about 1975. The use of aspartame in new diet drinks, for instance, actually expanded the total market, bringing in new consumers who wouldn't touch carbonated beverages before that. Presumably, these "new" consumers previously drank still-drinks such as *Kool-Aid* because they could add whichever sweetener they preferred. Diet soft drinks should continue to grow over the next decade, and plateau at about 33 percent of the total carbonated drink market.

In 1985, reports Cornelius F. Kenney of the Commerce Department, Office of Consumer Goods, soft drink demand increased because of new product introductions, favorable demographics, and improved economic conditions. The value of total bottled and canned soft drink industry shipments reached about $20 billion. That's about a 3.4 percent rise in real dollars, following a 2.4 percent rise in 1984. By comparison, the carbonated soft drink industry had been relatively stagnant during the 1980–84 period.

Per capita consumption of soft drinks increased about 5.5 percent in 1985, to 43.1 gallons. But most of this increase belonged to *Pepsi-Cola* and *Coca-Cola*. There was considerable new-product activity in 1985, but the two giant cola companies drew the attention of both media and consumers via marketing moves, on-again/off-again acquisitions, and clever television commercials. Most lesser-known brands, overwhelmed by heavy advertising, lost market share in 1985 and resorted to discounting to stay alive.

Meanwhile, the total aseptic juice drink market passed the $600-million mark at retail in 1985. Current trends to increase this figure include early efforts to market aseptic packs through vending machines. Aseptically packaged drinks are tending to higher juice content, also. In fact, says one major packer, you can expect the little paper/plastic packs to go to 50 percent juice soon—followed in time by 100-percent-juice packs. His thinking? Flavored and 10-percent-juice drinks are acceptable for children, but not for adults. They're ideal, for example, as school lunchbox drinks. To capture the larger adult market, however, and put aseptically packaged juices on the family table, the industry will have to increase the juice content. In Europe, for example, where per capita consumption of single-serve aseptic packs is more than six times the U.S. average, this evolutionary process has already taken place.

That's good news for primary suppliers of apple, orange and other popular juices. But not very cheering to the customers. It may increase the pressure on juice supplies, which already has been squeezed by a recent flood of new juice-containing products. Frozen fruit juice bars, for example, are one of the fastest growing of current trends. And, along with the introduction of juice-containing carbonated soft drinks, it may create a cost/supply problem for smaller packers. Thus, it seems likely, we can expect some shakeout in the aseptic drink category.

In 1986, says Commerce Department's Kenney, the value of bottled and canned soft drink product shipments should increase about 4.5 percent, in real dollars. Demand for soft drinks is expected to continue increasing, but at a somewhat lower rate, because of promotional efforts to secure firm market share for recent new products. Drink companies are likely to continue new product development efforts and increase promotional efforts. But packaged goods discounting practices are unlikely to abate. Thus, bottlers' margins will remain strained.

Total and per capita soft drink consumption should continue to rise, but at a slowing rate, during the next five years. Some observers believe that per capita consumption will top 50 gallons by about 1990. The value of soft drink industry shipments is forecast to increase about 2.3 percent a year. ∎

Seafood

Continuing the trend toward lighter foods, Americans in 1985 consumed a record 14.5 lbs. (net edible raw weight) per capita of seafood products, up 0.8 lbs. from an adjusted previous record of 13.7 lbs. per captia in 1984.

The National Marine Fisheries Service estimated value of U.S.-processed edible seafood at $4.7 billion—down 2 percent from 1984—while imports of edible seafood reached a record 2.8 billion lbs. (product weight) valued at $4.1 billion, up 12 percent in quantity and 9 percent in value over '84. U.S. firms exported 648.1 million lbs. of edible seafood products valued at $1 billion, an increase of 74 million lbs. and $168 million over last year.

Breakdown of U.S. production in 1985:

■ Raw fillets and steaks: 245.1 million lbs. valued at $436.6 million, down 7.2 million lbs. from 1984 but valued $26.2 million higher.

■ Fish sticks and portions: 426.7 million lbs. worth $476.9 million, slightly up from 1984 production of 425.7 million lbs. which was valued, however, at $523.5 million.

■ Breaded shrimp: 90.4 million lbs. valued at $347.9 million from 38 reporting plants, vs. 94.5 million lbs. valued at $369.4 million from 34 reporting plants last year. (Plants which report production quarterly accounted for 90 percent of 1985 production, says NFMS.)

■ Canned products: 1.2 billion lbs. worth $1.4 billion, down 250 million lbs. and $185

Seafood Highlights

	1985	1984
Per-capita consumption: (adjusted)	14.5 lbs.	13.7 lbs.
Fresh & frozen:	9.0 lbs.	8.5 lbs.
Fillets & steaks	3.24 lbs.	2.99 lbs.
Sticks & portions	1.76 lbs.	1.83 lbs.
Shrimp	1.98 lbs.	1.90 lbs.
Canned:	5.2 lbs.	4.9 lbs.
Tuna	3.3 lbs.	3.2 lbs.
Salmon	0.6 lbs.	0.6 lbs.
Shellfish	0.5 lbs.	0.4 lbs.
Sardines	0.3 lbs.	0.2 lbs.
Cured	0.3 lbs.	0.3 lbs.
Farm-raised catfish	195 million lbs.	150 million lbs.
Per-capita consumption	0.4 lbs.	0.3 lbs.
Surimi analogs	90.4 million lbs.	61.8 million lbs.

Sources: NMFS, NFI, AFDF, USDA

million from 1984. Of this, 911.7 million lbs. valued at $1.3 billion was for human consumption, the balance for bait and pet food.

Breakdown of edible imports: 2.2 billion lbs. of fresh and frozen products valued at $3.5 billion; 414.4 million lbs. of canned products worth $465.8 million; 65.2 million lbs. of cured products valued at $75.1 million; 11.8 million lbs. of other products valued at $17.7 million. Just about every import category set a record: Shrimp, for example, reached a record 359.9 million lbs., accounting for 28 percent of total import value at $1.2 billion—down $63.4 million, however, from last year.

According to the NFMS report *Fisheries of the United States, 1985*, imports of analog surimi products last year amounted to 33.7 million lbs. valued at $48.2 million. Using data reported in Japanese media, however, NMFS staffers estimate 1985 imports of surimi analogs at 72.8 million lbs. Add to this 17.6 million lbs. of analogs made by U.S. producers from imported surimi and the total is 90.4 million lbs. Breakdown: Imitation crab legs from Japan, 68 million lbs.; other seafood analogs from Japan, 2.6 million lbs.; seafood analogs from South Korea, 2.2 million lbs.; analogs produced domestically from imported surimi, 17.6 million lbs. Applying the finished-product value of $1.40 per lb. used in the NFMS report would raise the 1985 value of surimi analogs to $126.5 million. Reason for the tremendous surge in analog crab legs: King crab landings plummeted from a 1980 record of 190 million lbs. to only 15.4 million lbs. last year, down 1.4 million lbs. from 1984.

The rate of surimi imports slowed late in 1985, however. Reasons: The fall of the dollar against the yen; limited availability of raw material to Japanese producers because of pollock quotas in U.S. fishing waters and a prohibition on fishing for pollock in Soviet waters; the FDA requirement for "imitation" labeling on surimi analogs. These factors boosted the price of raw surimi to $1.40 per lb. by mid-June, 1986.

According to Chris Mitchell of the Alaskan Fisheries Development Foundation, Alaskan production of raw surimi last year reached about 375 metric tons (825,000 lbs.) from a single plant at Kodiak, which is boosting capacity. With two more surimi plants plus a factory ship starting up this year at Dutch Harbor, Mitchell projects 1986 Alaskan surimi production at 7,000 to 8,000 metric tons (15.4 to 17.6 million lbs.).

While surimi allows low-value fish to be marketed in forms simulating high-value products, cultured "farming" promises increased availability of high-value fish. Ecuador in 1984 shipped more than 46 million lbs. of cultured shrimp to the U.S.; cultured shrimp from the Philippines and Taiwan will soon follow. U.S. cultured shrimp is still in its infancy but the Commerce Department reports "about a dozen companies in five states" now active in shrimp culture. Farm-raised salmon from Norway and New Zealand are making inroads. USDA reports U.S. farm-raised catfish soaring 30 percent last year. ∎

Milk & Dairy Products

The year 1985 was a mixed bag (udder?) for the dairy industry. On the negative side, milk production soared to a record 143.7 billion lbs., up 6 percent over 1984 and nearly 3 percent over the previous record set in 1983. Herds grew by 1.8 percent and milk-per-cow surged 4.2 percent. At the end of 1985, USDA projected 1986 milk production to spurt 2 to 5 percent higher than last year and indeed the trend continued into the first quarter with production running 7 to 8 percent ahead of the year-earlier period in spite of support prices averaging $1.00 per cwt lower.

All of this was bad news to taxpayers: The Commodity Credit Corporation last year pur-

Milk and Dairy Products Per Capita Consumption (lbs.)

	1985	1984	% CHANGE
Fluid milk			
Whole milk	116.3	122.7	−5.2
Lo-fat milk	84.9	80.8	+5.0
Skim milk	13.0	11.9	+9.2
Flavored milk/drinks	10.7	10.9	−1.8
Buttermilk	4.3	4.3	0.0
Yogurt	3.9	3.6	+8.3
Manufactured products			
Butter	3.8	3.8	0.0
American cheese	9.5	9.7	−2.0
Cottage cheese	4.0	4.1	−2.4
Other cheese	10.1	9.5	+6.3
Dry whole milk	0.4	0.4	0.0
Non-fat dry milk	1.8	2.0	−10.0
Evaporated/condensed milk	7.6	7.5	+1.3
Frozen desserts			
Ice cream	18.1	17.8	+1.6
Ice milk	6.9	6.9	0.0
Net milk used per capita	53.9	53.5	+0.7

Source: Milk Industry Foundation

chased 13.2 billion lbs. of surplus dairy products, up 4.5 billion lbs. from 1984 (but 3.6 billion below the 1983 record). CCC removals for the first two months of '86 totaled 4.4 billion lbs., well over 2.8 billion for the same period last year, and on March 1 the CCC set a new weekly record by buying 632 million lbs. of surplus products.

But the impact of the herd buyout program, enacted by Congress last December as part of the 1986 Farm Bill, started to register during the second quarter and on June 13 USDA reported that milking cows had declined by 2 percent since January 1 although yield-per-cow was up 3 percent. This prompted USDA to lower its 1986 milk forecast to only 1 percent higher than '85.

On the bright side, commercial disappearance of milk in 1985 surged to a record 131 billion lbs., up 3.3 percent from 1984 and 7.7 percent from 1983, reflecting continued economic growth, more aggressive promotion, rising incomes and falling retail prices. Relative to the Consumer Price Index, retail dairy prices have fallen 13 percent since 1980 and should continue to decline slightly through 1986. "Unless the economy falters, commercial disappearance probably will increase 2 to 4 percent in 1986," said USDA in March. Sales for the first four months confirmed that prediction by running 4 percent ahead of last year.

The Commerce Department *(U.S. Industrial Outlook, 1986)* estimated total value of 1985 dairy shipments at $42.7 billion, up 4.5 percent from $40.8 billion in 1984 and 6 percent from $40.2 billion in 1983. The top four producers captured an estimated 18.3 percent of the total, down 1 percent from a year earlier. Kraft led with a 6.8 percent share, Beatrice was next with 4.6 percent, Borden third with 3.7 percent, Nestle (after its 1984 acquisition of Carnation) fourth with 3.2 percent.

Consumers continue to show concern about fats and cholesterol evidenced in declining consumption of whole milk and rising consumption of low-fat and skim milk.

Total fluid milk consumption, however, remained static at 230.2 lbs. per person, said *Industrial Outlook*. Flavored milks declined slightly, perhaps reflecting lack of acceptance of aseptic milk products. Yogurt, positioned by producers as "healthful," continues to boom. Top four producers of fluid milk products: Southland, with 6.8 percent of sales; Beatrice, 4.6 percent; Borden, 4.3 percent; Dairymen's, 3.6 percent.

Butter, after eroding in favor of margarine from 11 lbs. per capita in 1950 to 3.8 lbs. in 1984, plateaued as new butter/margarine blends became popular.

Total cheese consumption edged up as Cheddar, other American varieties and Cottage cheese dipped slightly in favor of Italian varieties, which gained 2.9 percent. Mozzarella, sparked by the booming pizza market, led with per-capita consumption rising to 4.2 lbs. from 4 lbs. a year earlier. Top cheesemakers: Kraft, with 21 percent of sales; Schreiber Foods, 5 percent; Land O'Lakes, 4 percent; Beatrice, 3 percent.

Consumption of ice cream and other dairy products has leveled off but the premium segment gained with the 1983 acquisition of Haagen-Dazs by Pillsbury and the 1985 acquisition of FrusenGladje by Kraft. Last year, four producers dominated the ice-cream and frozen-dessert market with 31 percent of sales: Southland, 11 percent; Kraft, 8 percent; Borden, 8 percent; Beatrice, 4 percent. ∎

Poultry & Meat

After a few years of increased consumption but stifled net earnings, poultry processors are back on the profit track. But for red meat processors, the situation is not so good. Consumption is declining, and industry economics are worsening.

Poultry consumption has risen steadily since 1979. Poultry production grew 5 percent last year and economists predict this trend will continue for the next few years. And even with these larger supplies, retail poultry prices decreased only about 1 percent in 1985—after a double-digit increase in 1984—suggesting strong consumer demand, according to USDA.

Despite this market potential, producers are only beginning to reap benefits, according to the U.S. Commerce Department. Between 1981 and 1983, average profits declined nearly 1 percent compared to previous years. Since then, feed costs declined and overall production efficiency increased substantially, and poultry industry profit margins rebounded to pre-1980 levels of 1.3–2.0 percent of total earnings.

In addition, consumer demand for poultry is increasing—keeping retail prices at 1985 levels and suggesting a strong consumer interest.

Reports USDA: poultry firms are funneling more earnings into product development and marketing. A "new-wave" of convenience chicken items has entered the market, including Tyson premium chicken entrees, sticks and chunks and "Perdue Done It!" fresh-prepared nuggets, cutlets and tenders. The $375-million further-processed poultry market, adds National Broiler Council Economist Bill Roenigk, has doubled in the last five years and now accounts for about 20 percent of the poultry industry.

Why such growth? "There is great demand for convenience foods," says a Perdue spokeswoman, "and poultry is the better buy." Economists agree: retail poultry prices are much lower than red meat prices, due to widespread production efficiency advances.

The setting for 1987? Poultry firms can look forward to large supplies and cheap feed prices, product prices in excess of production costs and a rising U.S. economy—according to USDA economists.

Beef prices should increase. The reasons:

■ Herd liquidations will stop. Because of poor returns to livestock producers, and thus their need to generate cash flow, farmers "liquidated," or slaughtered, many herds in 1983–85 to receive government subsidies. This year, herd liquidations are phasing out—a factor experts predict will tighten supplies, increase beef prices and decrease producer profit margins. And economists agree: higher prices and tight supplies predictably mean decreased demand.

■ Cattle feed supplies are low, a condition that causes feed prices to increase.

The total red meat price increase, however, will be a "constrained" 3–5 percent for 1986 over 1985, says USDA, since other price-altering factors—consumer purchasing power, sensitivity to relative meat prices, and tastes and preferences—are expected to remain relatively unchanged from last year.

A predicted 1.3-percent decrease in 1986 red meat supplies, however, will ultimately reduce this year's red meat consumption by at least 3 percent over 1985, says USDA. And, adds pork-producer Thorn Apple Valley: "All segments of the red meat industry continue to be bogged down with excess production capacity," one factor hurting profit margins.

Since 1984, says American Meat Institute Economist Bill Harold, red meat slaughterers have not met their traditional 1 percent of sales profit margin. In June 1985, retailers captured 43.4 percent of the retail beef dollar—compared with 39.8 percent last year. But, predicts Harold, the longer-term future will not be so grim for red meat processors.

The red meat industry, he says, has adopted a new marketing orientation that should boost the bottom line: adding value through further processing. "Today you see tighter trims, and deboned and pre-cooked items in the fresh case. Red meat is not a commodity business any more," says Harold.

Swift just introduced *Lite Pork*—a product containing 25 percent less fat than comparable products. Thorn Apple Valley introduced its "lower-salt, no-sugar-added" pork product line, and a new "Lean 'N Trim" boneless pork product, which the firm believes "represents a growth segment."

U.S. hog inventory is at its lowest point ever, down 9 percent from last year—due to a sharp decline in hog herd liquidations. A decrease in the number of hogs available typically results in higher prices and lower profit margins for processors. Says Harold: "Hog production will increase again during the second quarter of 1987." ■

Alcoholic Beverages

Beer sales continued flat in 1985. According to The Beer Institute, malt-beverage production edged-up 0.1 percent to 193.3 million barrels from 193 million in 1984. Cunsumption (taxable removals), however, slipped 0.2 percent from 175.5 million bbls. in '84 to 175.1 million bbls. last year. Beer drinkers seem to be consuming more at home and less away from home: Packaged beer removals increased 0.5 percent to 153.4 million bbls. while draught-beer removals decreased 4.7 percent to 21.8 million bbls. Per-capita consumption of malt beverages, after reaching an all-time high 24.6 gals. in 1981, dropped to 24 gals. by 1984 and plateaued at that level last year. The U.S. Department of Commerce estimated 1985 value of malt-beverage shipments at $12.1 billion, down 0.4 percent from '84.

Light beers continue to gain market share, moving-up from 19.1 percent of total beer sales in '84 to 20.3 percent last year, according to Business Trend Analysts. Miller *Lite*—the top-selling light beer and the No. 2 brand (after Budweiser) among all beers—achieved higher volume in '85, and Anheuser-Busch reported that its three light beer brands surged 22 percent last year. But the American beer drinker still prefers some bite in his brew: Analysts see slow acceptance of light alcohol beers, which niched 0.3 percent of the market in '84 and remained at that level in '85. Anheuser-Busch's *LA* brand dominates this segment, too, with 70 percent of sales. Coors, Stroh and Heileman tapped a new market last year with malt coolers positioned against wine coolers. Coors learned what it needed to know, took its *Colorado Chiller* back to the drawing board after a three-month test and "remains committed to the segment," said a spokesman. Watch for it to return. Two new no alcohol "beers"—*Kaliber* from Guiness and *Barbican,* also made in the U.K. and imported by Stroh—joined several Swiss and German entries in the no alcohol segment, which surprisingly picked up 0.3 percent of the beer market in '85 and continued to grow into early '86, says David Whitman of Business Trend Analysts. In the draught segment, Miller introduced *Genuine Draft*—nonrefrigerated in bottles via a "unique cold-filtration process"—to test markets in '85 and national rollout is now in progress.

Anheuser-Busch boosted its share of a flat market by another 2 percent in 1985 to 36.6 percent of U.S. beer sales—"40-percent market share by the late 1980s," said Chairman August A. Busch III. At the same time, Coors scored a remarkable 11 percent gain in shipments in 1985 through geographic market expansion and increases in California and Texas.

According to The Wine Institute, per-capita wine consumption grew 3.4 percent last year. As shown above, however, the gain was entirely due to wine coolers—which surged 155 percent to 86.2 million gals. from 34.2 million gals. a year earlier—while consumption of wine per se declined in every category. Consumption of American wines grew 2 percent at the expense of imports, which fell 2 percent. California wines entering distribution in 1985 were up 0.7 percent; wines from other states gained 1.3 percent.

According to the Distilled Spirits Council of the U.S. (DISCUS), consumption of distilled spirits—after peaking in 1981 at 450 million gals—declined for the third consecutive year to 426.1 gals. in 1984 and the slide continued into '85. Per-capita consumption steadily declined from a high of 2.88 gals. in 1974 to 2.46 gals. in 1984, down 1.3 percent from '83. Higher federal and local "sin" taxes contributed to the decline. Whiskey sales fell 5 percent in '84 from a year earlier, with domestic down 8 percent and imports by 2.2 percent. Even blended whiskies dropped, but in line with the trend toward lighter drinking the decline slowed to 0.5 percent. Among imports, only Canadian whiskey gained (4 percent) while Scotch fell 9 percent. Vodka and gin, both domestic and imported, also declined. One bright spot: Cordials rose 12 percent, with domestic up 15.1 percent and imports up 7 percent. Distillers, too, hope to boost sales by riding the cooler wave. One example: *Schnapps Spritz,* a fruit-flavored 5.5-percent alcohol beverage from Fletcher & Oakes. ∎

U.S. Wine Consumption (Millions of gallons)

TYPE	1985	1984
Table wines	377.3	401.3
Dessert wines	34.3	37.7
Champagnes, sparkling wines	45.6	47.0
Vermouth	6.9	7.0
Special natural wines	26.8	27.2
Wine coolers	86.2	34.2
Total	577.1	554.4
Per capita consumption (gal.)	2.42	2.35

Source: The Wine Institute

Breakfast Cereals

Breakfast cereal manufacturers can see the dawn of a new marketing era. After the turmoil of the past 10 years, the industry seems to have nothing ahead but smooth, steady growth.

Consider: Most cereal manufacturers have changed their products' image from one of sugar-laden, tooth-rotting junk to one of healthy, natural, nutritious food products. Many new cereals are enriched with fiber, sweetened with aspartame and/or contain real fruit. And even sugar-containing cereals contain less sugar than before.

The public has responded to this effort by buying more cereal than ever before. Other consumer trends may have helped, though. The growing interest in fresh fruits, for example, which are eaten with many cereals, and the turn away from high-fat and high-cholesterol products such as bacon and eggs, may have affected the type of breakfast being eaten today.

Whatever the reasons, the cereal market looks strong and should stay that way. What it all adds up to is a growth market for manufacturers who can adapt quickly to changing consumer tastes.

In 1985, estimates Commerce Department's William V. Janis, Office of Consumer Goods, about 1.8 percent—or $5.6 billion—of all food shipments were cereal breakfast foods. And the industry's real gain in shipments, about 8.2 percent, was the largest since 1973. There were several reasons for this gain, Janis says. Most production costs either declined or rose only slightly, for instance, helping to hold producer prices down. And, of the eight principal ingredients used in producing breakfast cereals, only flour and prepared flour mixes recorded a slight rise in 1985.

On average, retail prices for all breakfast cereals increased about 5.5 percent in 1985—the same change as in 1984—while prices of all food rose 2.9 percent. Producer prices for corn meal, grits, and hominy fell 4.4 percent, while prices of all other hot cereal gained 2.6 percent. That may reflect a change in regional tastes, toward conformity with national preferences. Producer prices for cold cereals, the major breakfast cereal segment, rose 5.5 percent over 1984.

Recently published Bureau of Census data show that many consumers have gradually changed their breakfast food preferences. While total per capita consumption of cereals rose about 2.9 percent in 1985, to 14 pounds, that growth varied by type of cereal. Cold cereal, for example, gained 2.1 percent, reaching 9.8 pounds per capita, while corn- and wheat-based ready-to-serve products both advanced 3 percent, to 3.3 pounds per capita. Meanwhile, oat- and rice-containing cereals were static at 1.6 and 1.2 pounds, respectively. Hot cereals fared slightly better, up 3.3 percent in per capita consumption, to 3.1 pounds. Consumption of farina and other wheat breakfast food moved up 20 percent, to 0.6 pounds per capita, while oatmeal remained unchanged at 2.5 pounds.

In 1986, breakfast cereal shipments should increase 3.5 percent—although mid-year data from SAMI indicates this estimate may be too modest. Stable ingredient costs will help to hold down increases in consumer prices. Per person consumption of all breakfast cereal will probably rise 3.1 percent in 1986, with consumption of all cold cereal matching that increase and corn-based cold cereals remaining unchanged. Per person consumption of wheat, rice, and oat cereals should rise 2.9 percent, 7.7 percent and 5.9 percent, respectively. By comparison, consumption of hot cereals should gain 3.2 percent.

During 1985–1990, says the Commerce Department, the value of breakfast cereal shipments should expand 2.5 percent annually, while total population will increase 0.9 percent per year. Estimated per capita consumption of all breakfast cereal will gain 2.3

percent per year. And, since demand will grow slowly while consumer tastes and purchasing patterns are changing rapidly, we can expect a steady flow of new products to keep pace with changing tastes.

Sales of presweetened cereal should increase as the number of children aged 5–14 grows at a rate of 1.6 percent a year. The use of nonsugar sweeteners will probably increase, too. From 1985 to 1990, the population aged 20–49 should continue to prefer unsweetened cold cereal. Firms also are expected to incorporate more fruits and nuts into their products.

Demand for hot cereal also may increase. Children aged 5 and under and persons aged 65 and over, the main consumers of hot cereal, will likely contribute to an estimated 2.4 percent yearly increase in per capita consumption of hot cereal. Although population of children aged 5 and less will rise only 0.5 percent annually, the affluent elderly will gain in numbers by about 2 percent a year. ∎

Canned Foods

POUNDS (IN MILLIONS)

	1982	1983	1984	1985
Pork & Beans	988	989	964	940
Pasta	532	526	535	527
Chili	234	244	240	240
Beef Stew	105	118	127	129

Information provided by Selling Areas Marketing, Inc. (SAMI)

CASES (IN MILLIONS)

	1982	1983	1984	1985
Golden Corn	59.5	50.1	56.2	55.2
Tomatoes	33.1	29.1	32.6	32.5
Peas	20.5	20.6	23.3	29.1
Asparagus	2.4	2.3	2.6	2.8
Peaches	0.9	1.0	1.1	1.3

Information provided by the National Food Processors Association.

Canned Foods

Sales of canned food (or food preserved by heat processing) began to increase in 1985 after being sluggish for the past few years. The increase was not a dramatic one, though. Canned speciality foods were among the items showing the largest sales gain. Aseptic packing has also boosted sales of canned foods.

"The value of production of canned fruits, vegetables, and specialties rose to an estimated $22.4 billion in 1985," according to *U.S. Industrial Outlook 1986*. After adjusting for price changes this reveals a 2.2 percent production increase which is the first meaningful increase since 1978.

The *Outlook* went on to point out that most of the real growth was attributable to increased demand for aseptically packaged foods, sauces, and ethnic foods. "Consumer demand for most canned goods remained sluggish; shoppers apparently prefer fresh and frozen goods," continued the report. Canned single-serving soups, and canned foods with low sodium or sugar content also are doing well.

But customer demand is not the only factor, much of the flux in canned fruit and vegetable production can be attributed to availability of crops in any given year. For example, the decline in processed vegetables between 1984 and 1985 is largely attributable to an 8 percent reduction in annual tomato acreage, Shannon R. Hamm, Agricultural Economist pointed out at the Annual Agricultural Outlook Conference, last December in Washington, D.C.

On the other hand, the other three major processing vegetables—sweet corn, green peas, and snap beans—are up an average of 7 percent. This is translating into larger 1985/86 packs of these vegetables, while domestic tomato pack will be reduced. Imports of processed tomatoes will partially offset reductions in domestic supply.

"The important issues for vegetable producers become: (1) the future growth in demand for vegetables, and (2) the continuing response of imports to the strong relative dollar in competing nations," Hamm concluded.

In the area of canned fruits, the increasing popularity of fresh fruit as a popular snacking item has contributed to the sluggish sales. Although wholesale prices of most canned fruit were higher at the beginning of 1986 than a year previously, prices could be reduced to stimulate sales.

Commodity items are not the only type of canned foods showing sluggish growth, another area of canned foods with low growth is soup where growth has been just 2 percent a year since 1983, reports *Outlook*. The real growth for soup has been in the dry mix area which is growing at 14 percent a year.

Campbell Soup Co., the country's leading canned soup producer, now offers dry and frozen soup lines. The company did boost its 1985 canned soup sales with several new product introductions. The new *Gold Label* line of *Creamy Natural Soups* was rolled out nationally in 1985, and the *Home Style Soup* line was expanded during the same year.

Sales of canned pasta, pork & beans, chili, and beef stew have not shown any significant changes over the past four years. Chesebrough-Ponds Inc. is hoping its 1985 introduction of *Ragú Pasta Meal* in glass jars will contribute to sales growth in 1986.

One method used by the canned food industry to battle sluggish sales has been to establish a marketing program. It is sponsored by the industry under the canned Food Information Council, and marks the first time that various segments of the industry have joined together to communicate positive information about canned products. The program recently launched its third year with a $2 million advertising and public relations effort.

"Our goal is to reach the consumer with an integrated advertising and public relations message that canned foods are high quality, convenience products that meet the needs of contemporary consumers," said John Porter, Vice President of Dole Processed Foods Company and Chairman of the Canned Food Marketing Committee. ■

Frozen Foods

The increasing number of women in the work force continues to be a major driving force behind accelerating frozen food sales. But a close examination of frozen food sales during late 1985 and early 1986 reveals changes in the buying patterns established several years ago.

The market for frozen entrees, which exploded in 1982 when Stouffer Foods' *Lean Cuisine* captured $125 million in sales during its first year in national distribution, is no longer sustaining double-digit increases. Tracking of frozen entree sales by A.C. Nielsen reveals a slowing of growth beginning in late 1985 and early 1986. Frozen entree sales for December 1984 through November 1985 reached $2.4 billion—or a 17 percent increase over the previous year, reports Nielsen. But sales for the first quarter of 1986 (December 1985 through March 1986) are even with sales for the same time period one year earlier.

Frozen dinners sales are also slowing. Reaching $1.2 billion in sales during 1985, or 5 percent growth from a year previously, frozen dinner sales registered a -2 percent growth for the first quarter of 1986.

This shakeout was expected, although the exact timing was not known. "One possible problem which could arise is in terms of freezer space at retail food outlets . . . The limited space, coupled with a glut of new entries into the market, should bring about a shakeout in the near future," predicted Business Trend Analysts, Inc. (BTA) in its report, *The Market for Frozen Dinners and Entrees*.

This is not to say that frozen dinner and entree sales will not continue to rise, but the rise will not be as rapid as in the past. Many of the reasons for the popularity of these items still exist. In particular, time constraints which have made frozen meals coupled with microwave ovens an increasingly popular phenomenon, will continue to be a driving force as the number of women in the work force grows.

"People have displayed a willingness to pay good money to make food preparation as painless as possible," states the BTA report. This is also seen by looking at microwave ovens usage. Microwave ovens are in use in 40 percent of the U.S. households, with an expected increase to 75 percent by the turn of the century, predicts Business Communications Co., Inc.

While frozen entree and dinner sales are no longer increasing at double-digit rates, frozen breakfast sales are. Introduced in many cases to compete with fast food chain items, frozen breakfast entree sales for 1985 were up 29 percent from 1984 according to Selling-Areas Marketing, Inc. (SAMI). Frozen breakfast entrees include french toast, pancakes, quiche, and toaster items.

The excitement in frozen food sales is clearly in further processed, value added foods rather than in commodity items like various fruits and vegetables. But these items do play an important role in the frozen food industry. For example, today Americans are eating about 11 pounds of frozen vegetables per person per year—up from 9.6 pounds in 1970, according to the October 1985 issue of FDA Consumer. Although approximately 30 different vegetables are available, still corn, broccoli, peas, and snap beans account for half of the total consumption. In contrast to increased frozen vegetable consumption, frozen fruit consumption has declined steadily.

And consumption of frozen potatoes has jumped more than fourfold over the past two decades, reports the FDA Consumer. This is mainly due to the increased use of frozen French fries, hash browns, and other frozen potato products in food service outlets.

Frozen French fries are the most popular frozen potato item. They accounted for 4,384 million pounds of the 5,118 million pounds of frozen potato sales in 1985, according to the American Frozen Food Institute. And, of the 4,384 million pounds of frozen French fries sold in 1985, 3,907 million pounds were sold to food service establishments.

The overall frozen food market should continue to grow—especially since expected growth of one- and two-person households, and number of women in the work force are expected to grow. ■

Snack Foods

Snack food sales—including potato chips—are rising despite the emphasis on good health and nutrition. In fact, potato chips showed an 8.2 percent increase in sales from 1984 to 1986 which was second only to popped popcorn in the salty snack area.

Greg Overman of Frito-Lay gives several reasons for potato chips' popularity. "People's eating habits have changed. Fewer families sit down to meals, leading to more grazing or eating on the run, and potato chips offer consumers convenience."

A new study by MRCA Information Services, Stamford, Conn., confirms that eating habits are changing. Between 1977 and 1985, the number of people eating lunch at home dropped 18 percent from 51 million to 42 million. The study pointed out that this occurred despite a growth in population. Many of these lunch skippers are likely to eat some type of snack during the day.

As consumers continue to eat smaller, more frequent meals and supplement their diet with snacks, potato chip consumption is expected to continue its climb. Business Trend Analysts predicts that the "chip" industry will grow at a compound annual rate of 9 percent through 1990.

Frito-Lay's Overman credits new product introductions for part of the growth within the potato chip category. While regular chips represent about 78 percent of total potato chip dollar sales, flavored chips represent the highest growth segment. No-salt potato chips have found a small niche with 5 percent of chip sales.

Pricing strategy is critically important to the success of the snack food industry, according to Frost & Sullivan. This is because snacks do best when prices of snacks rise less than other consumer goods. F&S predicts that the overall salted snack food industry will see moderate growth, and that product category growth will depend on development of new products, pricing strategies, and overall demographic and economic trends.

In the area of warehoused canister snacks, Pringles is the category leader with 50 percent market share. This segment of snack foods represents about $295 million a year in sales. Shoestring potatoes account for $40 million or about 14 percent.

Pretzel sales only increased 4.3 percent in sales from 1984 to 1985. But dieters ate 59 percent more pretzels in 1984 than in the early 1980s, according to a Menu Census study. The study by MRCA Information Services compared eating behavior of dieters and non-dieters, both at home and away from home. Pretzels are baked in an oven rather than fried in oil like chips and extruded snacks, and this may account for their appeal to dieters.

Health consciousness is having its effect on the snack food industry, though. Many people are turning to "natural" snacks. But these sales are in addition to salty snack sales rather than detracting from them. For example, Americans spent $600 million on fruit snacks alone in 1985, reports Del Monte.

"Del Monte has long been a leader in the production of dried fruit—traditionally used seasonally, mostly as an ingredient in cooking," said Ted Taft, a marketing director at Del Monte USA. "We've taken that product, added convenient packaging and variety, and produced a high quality snack that fits with a modern lifestyle."

Del Monte USA first introduced Fruit Snacks a year ago in two varieties—fruit mix and yogurt covered raisins. Six varieties including Sierra Trail Mix, Pineapple Nuggets, Tropical Fruit Mix, and Strawberry Yogurt Covered Raisins are now available.

"The instant popularity of fruit snacks snack category points to a growing demand on the part of the public for nutritional and convenient snacks that deliver taste and variety," Taft added.

Raisins have always been a popular fruit snack. And they continue to be, even though the Food Institute Report quoted trade estimates for California raisin production at 300,000 tons this year, down from 360,000 tons last year.

Sun Diamond Growers, a co-op comprised of walnut, raisin, prune, fig, and hazelnut growers, reports that the tonnage of products sold in 1985 was the highest ever, yet sales revenue and net proceeds were the lowest ever. Lower priced foreign imports are the main reason for this. Sun Diamond did recently receive a concession from the union which reduced base pay and fringe benefits of the workers by 35 percent, though. In addition, the company plans on focusing more on value-added products which contain its basic commodities and are sold under its own brands. ■

Bakery Products

For a market that grew only .5 percent in 1985, the situation for bakers is surprisingly good.

U.S. Department of Commerce economists predict industry growth will pick up to about 1.5 percent yearly into 1990.

Raw material costs have been stable since early 1985 and will remain so for 1986, predicts American Bakers Association President Bob Wager. A 1985 ABA survey concluded that these stable prices helped to increase bread bakers' pretax profits by 4.6 percent on a single one-pound loaf—their largest profit margin since 1977. In fact, in 1985, prices for nine out of ten principal baking ingredients declined or remained stable, says the U.S. Department of Commerce. Only shortening edged up 1.5 percent over 1984.

Certain segments within the bakery market, too, show much promise for growth: variety breads, specialty items, soft cookies, and refrigerated/frozens.

In the $5.4-billion dark-bread industry, per capita consumption rose 5.9 percent annually between 1977 and 1984; in 1985, consumption rose 1.1 percent to 8.9 pounds per person. Rye and pumpernickel bread consumption has been level for two years.

According to a Ph. Orth Company baking industry survey conducted at the 1985 International Baking Industry Expo, 74 percent of those surveyed feel variety bread sales will continue to grow. Respondents also felt that "new lines will be added" to the variety bread category, and that whole or multigrain breads hold the most potential to grow in sales.

Ph. Orth survey respondents also strongly agreed: specialty items (muffins, biscuits, cookies and croissants) have the "greatest demand for new product development and the highest potential for bakery sales." Fifty percent think the croissant, in particular, will enjoy continued sales growth.

The cookie market, too, is growing. In 1985, shipments in the $3-billion cookie market advanced 4.4 percent, according to the Commerce Department. Frost & Sullivan predicts the cookie category will grow about 2 percent per year in volume into 1990.

Soft cookies seem to be faring best. According to the Commerce Department, soft cookie introductions have cannibalized the sandwich cookie segment. Sandwich cookies, which held 31 percent of the cookie market in 1977, now hold about 26 percent. Other cookie types—including soft cookies—held 65 percent in 1977 and now comprise 70 percent.

Industry sources estimate 1985 shipments of refrigerated and frozen bakery products sold directly to consumers totaled $1.6 billion. Commerce Department analysts say this area holds "enormous potential" for food firms. Many top food firms agree. Pillsbury recently introduced its *Crusty Loaf* refrigerated bread dough, a product that capitalizes on the frozen 'convenience' trend. Sara Lee, as well, recently introduced its own frozen bagels to compete with Dart & Kraft's newly acquired Lender's frozen bagels.

Within the stagnant cracker segment, flavored crackers show the most promise. "Crackers are preferred by adults, and the adult market is growing steadily," says Frost & Sullivan. The firm predicts crackers will score an annual growth rate of about 1.6 percent through 1990, to reach a retail value of about $2.2 billion (in 1984 dollars).

White bread and rolls, which comprise 31 percent of the bakery category, have been losing market share since 1977. Consumption in 1985 decreased 1.8 percent over 1984 to total 26.8 pounds/person. Analysts predict these decreases will slow as the white-bread-eating, over-65 population grows. They are expected to increase 2.1 percent annually. Industry representatives believe, however, that variety breads will continue to be favored over white.

For sweet goods consumed at home, the picture looks dim. Says MRCA Information Services, a research firm: "For dessert, Americans ate 1.9-billion fewer cakes and pies in the last seven years." The number of cakes eaten in one MRCA census study decreased by one-third since 1973. Pies, too, are down substantially. The only gain: individually wrapped sweet goods, which grew just moderately. ■

Confections & Desserts

In the confectionery and desserts category, "premium" is where the action is. For candy makers, this news is both good and bad.

The Bad: Competition from foreign manufacturers is heavy. Since 1982, confectionery imports have risen dramatically. In 1985 alone, U.S. candymakers' share of the domestic market declined about 2 percent, according to the U.S. Department of Commerce. Specifically, the U.S. share of domestic chocolate consumption reportedly declined less than 1 percent while the U.S. share of the nonchocolate market dropped about 3 points.

The value of all candy imports reached an estimated $325 million in 1985, increasing 28 percent from 1984. The reason for this foreign success? After 1982, the dollar appreciated substantially and the U.S. restricted sugar imports—two factors that opened the door for foreign candy makers to undercut domestic manufacturers.

The Good: But since March 1985, the value of the dollar has been declining. The drop came too late to affect the first half of 1986, but not the second. Retail prices of confectionery imports are now on the rise.

"We expect price increases of imported chocolates to force a leveling off in growth in the super-premium market, which now constitutes 5 percent of the total market for chocolate confections . . . smaller American manufacturers may be able to seize this opportunity to establish themselves in the premium market," says Godiva Chocolatier President Tom Fey.

"Premium" chocolates represent the greatest growth area in the entire $7.1-billion confection industry right now, thanks mostly to an increase in 35- to 54-year-olds and disposable income. In 1984, the boxed chocolate category (the chocolate segment comprises 65 percent of the entire confection industry) was worth $1.8 billion, and, says research firm Frost & Sullivan, this figure will double by 1990.

The market for highly expensive, "super-premium" chocolates, however, "seems to be reaching maturity," according to Find/SVP. But, analysts agree, medium-priced boxed chocolates, or just plain "premium" items, will really grow. By 1993, almost one-half of all boxed chocolate consumption will be in the middle-priced segments, according to Find/SVP.

On another note, the $1.5-billion chewing gum market showed "uncharacteristically weak" sales in 1985, according to Warner-Lambert. Sugarless gum, however, is by far the fastest-growing segment, thanks to a proliferation of gums containing aspartame. Says Frost & Sullivan: The sugarless gum segment grew 25 percent last year.

For the many candy producers purchasing sugar, however, prices should remain relatively stable for 1986. At this writing, bulk sugar prices checked in at 23½ cents per pound, and no sharp price increases are expected soon, according to Eiler Ravnholt, Hawaiian Sugar Planters Assn. Predicts Ravnholt: Prices will go up another "½ cent or so."

As in confectionery, the buzzword in the frozen novelty business is "premium."

Frozen novelty producers are enjoying a growing $150-million retail market that is expected to double by 1990, thanks to a proliferation of premium, frozen fruit bars, says Find/SVP. Premium frozen novelties, adds the research firm, are expected to cannibalize the non-premium novelty segment.

According to A.C. Nielsen Co., the entire frozen novelty market grew 14 percent in 1985 over 1984. MRCA Information Services found, too, that the 5,500 individuals they tracked substantially increased their consumption of in-home frozen novelties. In this study, the 5,500 people are representative of the U.S.

census. "The past few years have seen the entrance of large, well-financed food firms into the frozen snack business," comments the Eskimo Pie Corporation. "And we expect this intense competition to continue in the forseeable future."

Recently, Jell-O embarked on a "shrewd" marketing course and introduced its own fruit bars and gelatin pops—after the extremely successful introduction of its pudding pops some years ago. ∎

Dressings & Sauces

What had been just a product category has grown up. As salad manufacturing is now an industry, so is the production of salad dressings and sauces. And it's a booming industry.

According to The Association for Dressings and Sauces in Atlanta, total 1985 production of dressings and sauces increased 62 percent over 1975 figures to an estimated 445.2 million gallons—about 45 percent of it mayonnaise, 25 percent salad dressing and 30 percent other products. Estimated dollar sales for salad dressing products in 1985 were set at more than $2.6 billion. Forty-five percent of those sales were retail, 55 percent were foodservice.

What's more, the future looks as bright as the present for this new industry. "Fresh vegetable consumption is expected to increase 35 percent by the year 2000," says Larry Noble, President of T. Marzetti Company and Board Chairman of the Association for Dressings and Sauces. "Fresh fruit consumption will rise 23 percent. And, as all sorts of salads continue to surge in popularity, so will salad dressings."

Noble points out that "consumers now accept that a salad can be hot or cold, served as an appetizer, entree, side dish or dessert. In effect, salad time is any time." Salads are on almost every menu, he says, whether at home or away from home, in outlets from fast food to white tablecloth. "And there's a dressing right there beside every one served."

The most recent figures available support this view. Per capita consumption of salad dressings has increased 48 percent since 1975. Last year, on average, we each consumed 14.9 pints of salad dressing—up from 10.1 pints in 1975. And a lot of that increase was new types of dressings.

For example, 12-week data from Selling Areas-Marketing Inc. in early 1986 showed that low-calorie salad dressings tonnage gained 23 percent, while refrigerated salad dressings and sauces rose 12 percent in the same period. The category as a whole increased about 7 percent—or over 25 million gallons.

Those figures are backed up by many consumer research studies. A *Better Homes and Gardens* survey, for example, found that 82 percent more consumers are more calorie/weight conscious today. And 53 percent are eating more salads. A Gallup poll conducted for *American Health* reports a trend toward vegetarianism, and a survey by Vance Research Service shows that nearly one-third of surveyed households said they ate more fresh vegetables than they had the year before. Salad bars are popular with 60 percent of restaurant patrons, says another Gallup poll, especially the self-service feature. Also, says the Brown Bag Institute, salads (pasta, fruit or green) are very popular among brown-baggers today.

Foodservice sales are sharing the strong action. A 1984 study by the National Restaurant Association found main dish salads were the sixth fastest growing menu item with 31 percent more restaurant patrons ordering them in 1984 than in 1982.

French, Thousand Island, Italian, Blue Cheese and Oil & Vinegar, respectively, remained the most popular non-diet menu dressings in 1985. Sweet & Sour and low-calorie dressings led the pack in terms of growth as a popular menu item followed by buttermilk-based, Caesar and Creamy Garlic.

Eating trends uncovered by these and other studies included an increased interest in nutritious foods, shifts to more roughage, less consumption of cholesterol, and a marked increase in "grazing." Salads and flavorful dressings supply the "natural" solution to these consumer concerns and desires.

In response to this growing interest in "fresh" foods, many manufacturers have introduced refrigerated dressing lines that are as fresh as the salads. In keeping with the low-cal craze, "light" versions of refrigerated lines are being introduced. And, prompted by the continuing popularity of blue cheese dressing, many manufacturers have new cheese dressings on the market, such as Creamy Parmesan, Italian with Cheese, and Romano, etc. Buttermilk-based products are also moving up strongly in this category.

Condiment manufacturers are making strong advances into the gourmet/specialty foods market also. Whole seed and flavored mustards, flavored mayonnaise and oils such as barbecue basters and dressings positioned as dips and marinades are finding their way onto gourmet shelves and into specialty shops.

"Right now," sums up Noble, "dressing manufacturers are meeting consumer needs by introducing new category segments such as reduced-calorie, refrigerated and more cheese flavors. And, with new packaging techniques such as the squeezable plastic bottle, how can our industry do anything but prosper?" ∎

Patient's Advocate

Sigrid Nagle
ASSOCIATE EDITOR

Jean Arbeiter
DEPARTMENTAL EDITOR

Marianne Dekker Mattera
MANAGING EDITOR

James A. Reynolds
EDITOR

These three columns show what can happen when nurses err in attempting to fulfill one of their most crucial obligations: that of acting as advocates for hospitalized patients. Through the use of three case histories, the columns deliver the message that a nurse can succeed as a patient's advocate only by gaining a thorough understanding of the patient's needs.

RN serves registered nurses, particularly those who work in hospitals. "Patient's Advocate" first appeared in the November 1985, February 1986, and August 1986 issues of *RN*, published by Medical Economics Company, Inc. © 1986. Reprinted with permission.

What Rosie Taught Us About Dying

Rosie died of cancer just before dawn. She was only 15.

She'd been unresponsive for some time, but her family and I had maintained a bedside vigil. Together, we'd listened to her labored breathing for what seemed like a lifetime.

One of her brothers had removed the Bruce Springsteen posters from the wall before she died. There remained only her crucifix, a Bible, and a well-worn, stuffed bear to be taken home.

After the family left, Rosie's nurses and I—a hospital chaplain—sat for a long time over coffee. Along with our sadness, we were distressed by feelings of relief. Everyone on the staff had loved Rosie. She was good-natured and kind. Although she papered her door, as teenagers will, with "do not disturb" signs, she told us all that they didn't apply to us, her special friends.

But Rosie had not been an easy patient. We preferred dealing with Joe, whose family cursed everyone they encountered, or Melanie, a lovable eight-year-old who talked openly about her fear and pain. What made Rosie difficult, you see, was the fact that she absolutely refused to discuss what was happening to her.

Our training had equipped us to face the emotions of dying children without flinching. But Rosie maintained that she didn't have any questions about her disease and that she was not afraid. She professed to have total confidence in her father's reassuring words, "You'll be all right; I won't let anything happen to you." He steadfastly refused to allow the doctors to tell Rosie what the final stages of her illness might be like.

What, we wondered, could be done for the daughter of a man who simply would not face the truth? Could the words "you'll be all right" have any real meaning at a time like this?

WE MISJUDGED ROSIE'S ATTITUDE

To us, her father's statement, and Rosie's apparent acceptance of it, implied deception. So we redoubled our efforts to help Rosie and the family come to terms with death. Denial, we knew from our courses on dying, was bad. Communication was good.

Every day, the doctor carefully framed open-ended questions to encourage Rosie to express her feelings. The nurses spent extra time with her father, hoping their concern would help him "confront" the illness. But our determination to make sure that Rosie died "the right way" blinded us to what was really going on. It prevented us from offering her the kind of support she needed.

The key to understanding Rosie lay in the family's history, not in our preconceptions about dying. Rosie's father had been orphaned as a young child. His wife was killed in an automobile accident shortly after Rosie's cancer was diagnosed. For him, the normal parental responsibility of providing security for his children was tinged with desperation.

To admit openly that Rosie was dying would be to admit failure as a parent. Rosie, for her part, felt an obligation to protect her father from yet another loss. So, instead of expressing their feelings, the family dealt with her illness in an oblique manner that we interpreted as denial.

Actually, they were involved in an acceptance process that we could not see, because it did not match our expectations. For example, when Rosie's grandmother presented her with a frothy blue gown, we thought she was denying the fact that her granddaughter would not live long enough to attend a prom.

What we were witnessing was not an evasion, however, but the cementing of a bond between generations. In Rosie's family, each girl's first long dress was a treasured gift. Her grandmother, in bringing the dress to the hospital, was acknowledging the fact that rites of passage had to be performed quickly because Rosie was soon to die.

When Rosie asked whether her older brother could return home from college, "because it doesn't hurt so much when he lifts me," her family did not need a more explicit statement that she knew her death was near.

HOW WE CAN HELP DYING PATIENTS

Rosie's story demonstrates that families evolve complex ways of communicating with one another about death. The question we must ask is not whether their behavior is appropriate but why they need to act as they do.

As caregivers, we emphasize feelings and relationships as well as physical needs. We attend, often at our own expense, workshops on dying and grief. Unfortunately, we've come to believe that there's only one proper way to die, and we concentrate on making sure our patients conform to it. In so doing, we may miss the subtle ways they've chosen to handle the situation.

If we are to be useful to dying patients like Rosie and their families, we must allow them to confront death in their own ways. Instead of imposing our values, we must be open to their words and gestures, their moods and silences. We should be able to empathize with them, no matter what form their grieving takes. If we have the courage to listen to our own fears, we will be able to recognize theirs.

Our role is to share the dying process, however our patients define it. From them and their families we can learn about the harmony —if not the beauty—of life. The gift can be both theirs and ours. ■

How Hospitals Hurt Old People

I always enjoyed visiting Mrs. Simmons, my spirited 80-year-old neighbor. Proud of managing on her own, Mrs. Simmons refused to let occasional memory lapses or arthritis get her down. She used a timer to remind herself to take medications, and she exercised regularly. She was alert and happy in spite of her problems.

Then Mrs. Simmons spent six weeks in the hospital. When I visited her at her daughter's home, she was scarcely recognizable. The independent, lively woman I knew had become fearful and depressed. Her mind wandered, and her arthritis had become so bad that she had difficulty walking. She sobbed that she had become a burden to her daughter—and indeed she had.

It's not unusual for hospital stays to turn functioning old people into helpless dependents. To understand why, consider what happens to an elderly person when he becomes a patient:

If the patient seems confused, we put up the side rails to keep him from falling. We may not be able to answer the call light immediately, so he climbs out of bed to reach the bathroom. When we catch him, we apply a chest restraint. If his bladder control is poor, we may insert a catheter. To avoid nutritional problems, we start IV fluids or feeding tubes. When he tries to pull out the tubes, we restrain his hands.

Now we have the patient tied up and helpless. No wonder he's too disoriented to realize what's going on. He's lost part of his humanity.

EXPLAIN PROCEDURES TO THE PATIENT

What can we do to prevent that loss? Certainly we must take measures to protect the patient, but we shouldn't overdo them. Remember that each procedure, although it may be routine to us, invades the patient's privacy. Every time he loses control, he becomes more confused and depressed. That's why we must tell the patient what we're doing and why, even if he doesn't appear to care. Chances are he cares a lot—he's just too apprehensive to communicate.

Young patients ask questions all the time because they assume they'll recover. Old people, however, expect the worst. To them, the very word "hospital" can mean the end. No wonder they have little to say; they're walled in by anxiety.

WE NEED TO MAKE A SPECIAL EFFORT

We can break through that wall. It's up to us to buoy the elderly patient's spirits, to counter his fears, and to keep him in touch with his surroundings. Busy as we are, we must make use of every available minute to talk to these patients.

While setting up a breakfast tray, for example, we can mention the day, the time, and what the weather is like outside. Because such information is specific, it orients the patient to reality. When coupled with a cheerful greeting, it also makes him feel cared for.

Bath time provides another opportunity to impart concern and information. You might tell a stroke victim: "I know you can't move your left arm and leg, Mr. Green, but you'll be having physical therapy today. The exercises will help you regain your strength."

In addition to giving patients information, we can encourage them to function on their own. If possible, allow a patient like Mr. Green to bathe himself. To be sure, you can probably give him a bath more quickly than he can do the job for himself, but being independent preserves his sense of self-worth. When, for example, you help a patient from his bed to a chair, let him take a few steps on his own. Be generous, too, with praise for his small successes. He needs all the encouragement he can get.

Include the patient's family in your efforts. They can help him feed himself or get out of bed. But, don't make the mistake of discussing problems with the family and treating the patient as if he were invisible. To preserve his self-esteem, you need to treat him as an individual.

BE AWARE OF SPECIAL NEEDS

Another way to bolster the self-esteem of old people is to accommodate their physiological problems. For example, since an elderly patient tends to react more slowly, encourage him to sit on the edge of the bed before he tries to stand up. Those few extra moments can do more than just keep him from losing his balance; they may actually relieve him of the fear of falling.

Remember, too, that old people have brittle bones and require gentle treatment. When you handle them, do so carefully or you run the risk of causing a fracture.

Since the elderly have a reduced tolerance to drugs, look for hidden reactions. Before deciding a patient has lost his appetite, make sure the problem isn't really drug toxicity. Instead of being lazy, a patient who refuses to walk may be suffering from an accumulation of sedatives.

Even though old people feel pain less acutely,

their restlessness may signal discomfort instead of confusion. So don't assume that a state of unease is purely mental. Assess the patient's need for additional medication. If confusion is the problem, you can curtail it by reassuring the patient about his surroundings.

Providing that reassurance is just one way of handling the elderly patient with respect. If we give him sensitive care, he can leave the hospital with his self-esteem intact. On the other hand, if we pay more attention to procedures than we do to his needs, we can destroy his ability to function at home.

The elderly patient needs more than nursing from us: He needs emotional support. The hospital should not be the place where the patient loses his independence. With our help, it need not be. ■

Your Duty When Doctors Browbeat a Patient

Brenda was a 21-year-old Medicaid patient in an inner-city hospital. She had been in labor with her first child for 16 hours. She was completely exhausted, very frightened, and very much alone.

Since her contractions were not effective, the residents decided that a labor-stimulating drug they were investigating might prove helpful. They explained the research study to Brenda in some detail, but her questions showed that she didn't really understand what they were talking about.

At first she resisted the idea of trying the experimental drug, saying that she didn't want to be a guinea pig. But when the residents pressed her to the point of tears, she gave in.

Five minutes after nurses began the infusion, Brenda started feeling nauseous and began to vomit. She also complained of being very hot. She asked why she felt so ill and was told she was experiencing side effects of the drug. At those words, Brenda begged the nurses to have the infusion stopped.

But Brenda's labor was progressing steadily, so the doctors wouldn't hear of ordering the infusion to be discontinued. Brenda's symptoms did not abate. She continued to vomit and still felt hot, but she stopped complaining. Two hours later, she delivered a healthy, seven-pound boy. She suffered no lasting effects from the experimental drug.

Despite the happy outcome, Brenda's story raises ethical questions about the conduct of the physicians who pushed their own research interests over the comfort and express wishes of the patient. It also raises questions about the role played by Brenda's nurses, who apparently never attempted to intercede beyond a single request to stop the infusion, despite the patient's protests and obvious, continued distress.

DID BRENDA GIVE INFORMED CONSENT?

Clearly, the answer to that question is No. In order for consent to be valid, the patient must understand a research study's purpose and procedures. To be sure, the residents gave Brenda an explanation, but she was in no condition to comprehend what was said.

Although the residents stressed the benefits that Brenda could expect from participation in the study, they said nothing about the risks. They did not mention alternative forms of treatment, and they did not tell Brenda that she could withdraw her consent at any time. All of these points must be covered if the patient is to give truly informed consent. Even a signed consent form is invalid if it is based on incomplete information.

DID BRENDA CONSENT VOLUNTARILY?

Again, the answer is No. The doctors' insistence that she take part in the study, at a time when she was particularly vulnerable, could be interpreted as coercion rather than consent. Instead of agreeing freely, Brenda merely acquiesced. Maybe she felt powerless. Perhaps she thought a refusal might jeopardize her baby. Maybe she was just too tired to fight further.

WHAT SHOULD BRENDA'S NURSES HAVE DONE?

They should have intervened on her behalf. They had three opportunities to do so:

- When they realized that Brenda did not understand what the drug trial involved, they should have asked the residents to give her a clearer explanation. Legally and morally, they were obligated to make sure that the patient knew what she was getting into before they ever began administering the treatment.

- When Brenda said she didn't want to participate in the drug trial, her nurses should have backed her up. If the residents persisted in harassing the patient, the nurses should have taken the matter to their supervisor.

- When Brenda became hot and nauseous and begged to withdraw from the study, they should have stopped the infusion immediately. If the residents tried to continue it, the nurses should have gone to their supervisor.

This episode, unfortunately, is not an isolated one. I have heard many such horror stories in my work as a nursing research coordinator. There seem to be too many doctors who attempt to override a patient's expressed wishes because they think they know what's best. And there seem to be too many nurses who, through ignorance or passivity, go right along with such doctors.

But ignorance doesn't protect nurses who "go along." They can be held liable for contributing to the violation of a patient's right to refuse treatment, not to mention assault and battery.

Research is a means to an end—not an end in itself. The patient is much more than a subject for study. She's a human being whose rights must be protected. When more nurses are willing to understand that responsibility, they'll be fewer unhappy experiences like Brenda's. ■

Retail Sales Training

Rosemarie Kitchin
EDITOR

Philip Katcher
RESEARCH EDITOR

John Wirebach
SENIOR NEWS & FEATURE EDITOR

Gail Krueger-Nicholson
SENIOR EDITOR

This article provides guidelines for retail sales personnel in the area of automotive parts and related items. It includes a basic overview of the automotive system, operation, or work category; a glossary for each subject; and answers to questions most commonly asked of the retail clerk by the customer who wishes to accomplish his or her own auto repair.

Automotive Marketing is read by automotive parts, accessories, and chemicals retailers serving those who maintain and repair their own vehicles. "Retail Sales Training" first appeared in the June 1986 issue of *Automotive Marketing,* published by ABC Publishing. © 1986. Reprinted with permission.

Introduction

"We don't sell auto parts here. We provide solutions to people's problems."

No matter where that statement is heard . . . whether it be in an auto parts store pushing for volume DIY sales, a traditional jobber making an effort to service walk-in trade, a home center stocking automotive SKUs, or a department store or other outlet, the salesperson speaking is the result of an effective training program.

He or she may not "sell parts," but the training which has fostered that problem-solving attitude has built the foundation for better employees, greater sales, and contented return customers.

That same training program has undoubtedly provided enough current information about products to allow the employee to confidently face customers on the floor.

The company's management has made a commitment to expend effort to meet the training needs of its employees. It's used management time and skill to develop a program which meets the needs of the new hire and the veteran sales person. It's implemented that program . . . possibly naming it Corporate College or Store School . . . bolstered its effectiveness with incentives, and recognized that once the program's launched, it's already obsolete. The company constantly monitors the program, modifying it as new technology becomes important, changing the pace as required, and reviewing its results in terms of the bottom line.

The training needs of the automotive aftermarket are considerable. Training shows up near the top of every industry poll asking about major concerns.

No doubt this concern stems from the ever-changing technology, the constant employee turnover, and the cyclical advance and retreat of training availability.

The 16-year-old, no matter how "car crazy" he is, can't help but be overwhelmed at the realization that he's responsible for helping the customers choose the right parts, tools, and chemicals from an average of 20,000 SKUs. And that very wide of array of catalogs doesn't instill confidence, unless he's been taught how to use them properly.

The veteran auto parts clerk struggles to keep current with the changing information about the cars' needs. Although he's an expert, new technology requires new parts, and the customer may not even know that his new turbocharged car requires things different from his previous vehicle. Chances are that the turbo owner won't mention "turbo" in his conversation with the salesperson unless he is asked.

There's too much information available. Beginners can't absorb it all. An effective training program provides enough information, selling skills, and product knowledge to give the trainee confidence while whetting his interest in the next skill level.

Step-by-step education, with constant reviews of previously learned information, is the most effective program, just as it was in school.

In this issue, *Automotive Marketing* has gone step by step, too, asking our Retail Panel for their most commonly asked questions. AM's panel provided the questions, and AM provides the answers.

Knowing that every good text has a glossary to make the vocabulary familiar, AM provides a glossary for each training module. The training modules are approached in a classic way . . . product or system features and owner benefits.

The beginner has a cheat sheet; a picture of the system and other needed information, the test questions from the customer, answers from *Automotive Marketing*, and a glossary for an open-book test.

The veteran has a brush-up review, easily scanned for information new to him.

There's much more available. Manufacturers provide more than lip service to the marketplace's training needs these days with hotlines, clinics, films, videotapes, interactive learning programs, and technical reps available to answer questions and to teach. Trade groups are working to systematize the training material so that it will be somewhat consistent in format and allow the prospective student to qualify himself. APAA's new retail training program is slated to debut at the August show in Atlanta.

Automotive Marketing's sister Chilton publication, *Motor/Age,* has compiled an extensive list of hotlines, clinics, films, literature, and other training aids. The list will be ready within weeks: More information about quantity and price is available from Trudy Kolb at 215-964-4000.

Training can provide answers to informational needs of the people who have the responsibility to help the DIY customers, and the parallel responsibility to sell parts. ■

longer. While a DIY repair will probably not serve as a permanent repair, it will keep a car on the road for an extra few years.

Rust and corrosion occurs chiefly under and above the wheelwells and along the rocker panels because of water and salt washed up from the road. The main challenge for the DIYer is to eliminate as much of the rust as possible with a grinder and sandpaper, then treat the remaining metal surface with a metal conditioner. This is an acid that will etch away rust that can't be seen.

Once the metal is as clean as possible, it can be filled with aluminum tape, which serves to bridge any holes in the bodywork. A coating of plastic comes next to level the area and gives the primer coat a surface to adhere to. The repair can be completed with a coating of primer paint and a coat of paint to match the original paint.

The major suppliers of body repair products will have extensive training materials both for the clerk and for the DIYer. The store can best serve the DIYer by providing him or her with the correct information and make sure he has the right tools to complete the job. ■

Body Work

Although body repair products such as paint and body fillers are seldom major categories in auto stores (our studies show DIY levels at about 10–15% of DIYers), these products are growing in popularity.

One spur to DIY body repair is the number of older cars on the road today. The average car is 7.5 years old and all indications are the average age will increase in coming years. Because many cars rust out long before the engine wears out, a DIYer willing to do some body repair can keep a car on the road even

Glossary

Body filler: *A plastic compound used to fill small holes, dents and creases in the metal surface of a car after it has been sandpapered smooth.*

Ferrous oxide: *The technical name for rust — iron and oxygen.*

Grit number: *The degree of abrasiveness in a sandpaper — the higher the number, the finer the paper.*

Primer: *Substance used after body filler is applied to seal the surface of sanded metal against rust, air, and moisture. It provides a surface for the paint to adhere to and also fills tiny holes and imperfections in the metal.*

The Three Most Commonly Asked Body Repair Questions

1. What sandpaper should I use?
The degree of abrasiveness of sandpaper is noted by its grit number which is on the manufacturer's label. The lower the number (such as 36 and 40), the coarser the sandpaper. Conversely, the higher numbers have finer grains (80 and 100 are typical fine sandpapers). Use the grit number recommended by the body repair equipment manufacturer. Too coarse a sandpaper will scratch and too fine a paper will not remove enough material.

2. Will body filler stop rust?
For a large rusted section, body filler will not stop rust permanently. For a permanent repair you must cut away all the rusted metal, weld in new sheet metal, then undercoat and repaint the section. But aluminum tape covered with plastic body filler will serve as a quick, easy way to repair small rust outs and it will serve for some time. You can maximize the time the repair lasts by grinding away all visible rust and treating the remaining metal with metal conditioner.

3. How do you mix and apply body filler?
Carefully follow the directions on the product's package. Mix the filler thoroughly with a putty knife or paint mixing stick until the resin on top is completely blended. Put enough filler to cover the repair area with one thin coat on a piece of cardboard and mix in the specified amount of hardener. Mix until no color streaks show. For flat surfaces, use a firm plastic squeegee; for other surfaces, use a flexible squeegee. Work filler in one direction only; work in a thin coat over the entire repair area. But don't get filler on undamaged paint. Allow filler to dry and then sand.

Cooling Parts

The cooling system is the system that keeps the car's engine from becoming little more than a block of molten metal. This is not to say that heat isn't removed from the engine by anything but the cooling system. In fact, about a quarter of the heat energy is needed to drive the car; about 35% is removed through the exhaust system; 10% disappears because of internal friction and heating the lubricating oil; only the remaining heat is removed by the cooling system.

The system is a fairly simple one that is built around a mixture of coolant (antifreeze and water) that is pumped by the water pump through hoses between the engine combustion chambers and radiator, where it is cooled. A fan goes on when needed (in older cars the fan works constantly) to pull cooling air through radiator and cool the coolant in it. The water pump, actually misnamed since there is usually more coolant (antifreeze) than water in the system, serves like the heart to keep this mixture moving.

The same mixture of hot coolant and water is also circulated through heater supply and return hoses into the heater core to heat the car in the winter.

Of course, this heat puts much stress on the cooling system components. Hoses and belts wear out and should be checked regularly. The concentration of coolant should be checked with one of the inexpensive gauges available for that job at least twice a year (spring and fall). And the entire system should be checked for leaks on a regular basis—at least

The Three Most Commonly Asked Cooling Parts Questions

1. Will a cooler thermostat make my car run cooler?

Having a thermostat set cooler will indeed make a car run cooler. But this is not an advantage. Engines that run cooler than they are designed to run waste gasoline. A cooling system that should run at 180° could have a thermostat that allows it to run at 125°, for example. But that system's engine will take 10% more gas to run it. At 100°, the engine uses 25% more gasoline. And at 125° the engine is wearing at a rate 2½ times faster than normal. It is running nearly six times faster than normal at 100°. Therefore, the thermostat should be in good running order and set to run the cooling system, and, therefore, the engine, at the temperature the manufacturer designed it to run.

2. How can I tell if my hoses are bad?

A simple eyeball inspection will show if the hose is flaking or cracked. Beyond that, the car-owner should squeeze each hose in his hand to see that it has not gotten too hard or become too oil softened.

3. How do I solve overheating problems?

Basically, car overheating problems can be caused by bad coolant, incorrect proportion of antifreeze, air in the system, defective coolant recovery system, loose or broken belts or fans, debris on radiator, defective or broken thermostat, defective radiator cap, too great a load being pulled, late ignition timing, clogged fins on engine or oil cooler, too little coolant, frozen coolant, cooling system clog or leak, loss of pressure, leaking core plug, cracked block or cylinder head, leaking cylinder-head gasket, thermostat stuck closed, faulty water pump or heater control valve, dragging brakes, blocked system, too low idle speed, too lean air-fuel mixture, or misadjusted damper door. Each possible problem area should be checked. Some can be easily fixed, others require professional help.

when the oil is changed. The radiator cap should be checked to see that it's still doing its job, and the thermostat to see that it's not stuck open (a thermostat stuck open will not allow a cool engine to warm up as quickly as it should).

Lately, as engine temperatures have risen—engine temperatures can now reach 5,000° F—additional equipment has been added to many cooling systems. These include special coolers for transmissions—needed when heavy loads like trailers are added—and various types of energy-efficient fans. You should let your customer know these products are available to solve his heavy-duty cooling problems.

So make sure your customers have considered every possible way of making their car's cooling system as efficient and hardworking as possible—both through constantly checking the system's present condition and considering adding on additional or different cooling system equipment. ∎

Lighting

The customer who comes into your store for lighting products will be seeking either a replacement for his car's headlamps or for additional lighting—fog lights on cars or extra driving lights for off-road vehicles and trucks.

Glossary

Afterboil: This is when the engine coolant boils after the engine in turned off. It's caused by the inability of the shut-off engine to get rid of excess heat.

Belts: The belts are driven off engine pulleys and drive the car's water pump, fan, alternator, power steering pump, and air conditioner. They should be checked frequently for condition and tension, as shown below.

Coolant and recovery system: This system, found in most newer cars, provides a reservoir for coolant that has heated and expanded to the point where it would overflow from the system. When cooler, it is drawn back into the system by means of a vacuum. Such a system can be retrofitted on most older cars that lack one.

Core plug: A metal plug fit tightly into an opening in the engine block water jacket. If the coolant freezes, core plugs pop out, thus relieving pressure and preventing engine block fracture. These are also called freeze-out plugs.

Cross-flow radiator: In this radiator the coolant flows through horizontal rather than vertical tubing.

Fan: The fan pulls cool air through the radiator. Some, although this is rare now, run constantly. Electric fans have a thermo-switch that turn them on when the car is idling or going slowly in heavy traffic. Variable pitch fans have blades that change position to cut down the power needed to drive them as car speeds change.

Fan clutch: This clutch shuts off the fan when it is not needed e.g., when driving at high speeds in cool weather, thus saving the as-much-as 10 horsepower needed to drive the fan.

Fast flushing: Cleaning out the cooling system with a pressure machine that runs faster than the engine's water pump and a special chemical solution.

Hoses: Coolant runs from the engine to the radiator and heater though hoses. These often develop leaks and should be checked often and replaced when necessary. It is best for the customer to bring in his old hose to be sure of getting the right size when getting new ones.

Hose clamps: Clamps are made of metal and screwed tight at each hose connection. Clamps should be replaced, rather than reused, when hoses are replaced. Generally, it is best for the customer to bring in his old clamp to match the correct size when getting a new one.

Headlamps may seem like a pretty straightforward replacement item. However, the actual products can differ. Over the past few years more types of headlamps have been made legal on American roads. They now come round and rectangular, conventional sealed beam and halogen. Assuming the customer knows the type and year of car, and which headlamp he's replacing, you can look up his exact model number in one of your lighting catalogs.

In some cases, he may balk at replacing a halogen headlamp—which comes as original equipment on many new U.S. and most foreign cars—because of cost. He can replace it with a cheaper sealed beam but he'll have to replace the other, good, headlamp at the same time to have the beams light in the pattern they should. And, he'll lose the advantages offered by halogens. In some cases, he can be sold one of the newer sealed beam halogens that use replaceable bulbs so future halogen headlamp replacement will be cheaper.

AUXILIARY LIGHTING

The shopper wanting auxiliary lights generally wants to expand his vision at night,

Glossary

Oil cooler: *A small radiator through which oil passes to be cooled.*
Radiator: *The radiator actually cools the coolant by the passage of air through it, exchanging the engine heat in the coolant with the cooler external air. When leaks develop in these now, it is often best to simply replace the entire radiator with one of the new replacement models — a task many DIYers can do themselves.*
Radiator cap: *The radiator cap not only keeps the coolant in the radiator, it also maintains the system at a constant pressure, usually 12–18 pounds, to raise the coolant boiling point. Higher coolant temperature gives higher engine temperatures and, therefore, greater efficiency.*
Thermostat: *Thermostats maintain engine temperature. They are found in the thermostat housing, usually just behind where the hose connecting the radiator and the engine is clamped to the engine.*
Transmission cooler: *The transmission cooler is generally a separate cooling system that brings transmission fluid out of the transmission and passes it through a small, separate radiator where the heat is passed out into the external air. These are useful when the car is used to pull heavy loads or special stress is placed on the transmission.*
Water jacket: *The coolant flows, collecting excess engine heat, through these passages that wrap around the cylinders.*
Water pump: *The water pump keeps coolant circulating within the system.*

usually for off-road driving. Such lights can be placed as low as below a front bumper and as high as over roll bars. However, the customer —and the salesperson who sells the customer if he doesn't want him coming back angry— should be careful that the auxiliary lighting that is bought is legal. Most states limit the number of auxiliary lights used and where they can be placed. Check with your local police department before selling elaborate auxiliary lighting.

Of course, standard fog lights—white or yellow—are legal virtually everywhere, and these are installed on regular cars as well as on light trucks and vans. ■

Chemicals

Sales of chemicals is one category in which the retail auto parts stores and mass merchandisers have always dominated the automotive aftermarket, so much so that there are still old jobbers who refer to volume retailers as the "snake oil and fuzzy dice" stores. Although retail auto stores now sell quite a bit more than chemicals and accessories to DIYers, chemicals are still a major category for most retailers.

DIY STUDIES

The chemical shelves serve as traffic builders on sale and high-margin items day to day despite keen competition for chemical sales from other volume retailers. These were some figures for chemical product purchases and installation by DIYers in the past year, according to the 1985 *Automotive Marketing* Consumer Automotive Repair Study (CARS):

- Antifreeze 73%
- Wax/polish 68%
- Functional fluids 59%
- Oil/gas additives 50%
- Appearance chemicals 48%

Furthermore, a 1984 *Automotive Marketing* study of DIY vehicle maintainers found that 89% had bought some kind of chemical product in the past year, a percentage exceeded only by tune-up products and motor oil.

Obviously, retail clerks should be knowledgeable about chemicals in order to service the many customers these products will draw to the store.

WHAT'S ON THE SHELVES

At first glance, the chemical category is a bit intimidating. Even on the best planogrammed shelves, the new clerk may only see a hodgepodge of colors and containers. What are they used for? Who buys them and why? The best way to break down the category is examine chemicals by use.

Functional fluids have the highest purchase levels so let's take these chemicals first. They do just what the name suggests: they perform a needed function inside some part of the vehicle's engine and they must be replaced on a regular basis, which is why they are the leading seller. Without functional fluids, the vehicle will simply not work properly. Antifreeze/coolant is the most obvious functional fluid, but such chemicals as brake fluid, automatic transmission fluid and power steering fluid are also chemicals that must be checked and topped off regularly. Most major chemical suppliers provide a line for each of these areas that are engineered to meet OE specifications.

Good weather will bring in scads of DIYers buying appearance chemicals of all sorts to clean and protect their car's finish. The biggest sale items in this category are vinyl cleaners and protectants, although DIYers will probably ask more questions about waxes and polishes. The reasons for this are simple: virtually every major appearance chemical supplier has a line of wax and polish and competes rigorously with new products. There are poly waxes, premium waxes, spray-on waxes, and special waxes designed for special paints. Other appearance chemicals include tire cleaners, wheel cleaners, tar removers, and general purpose cleaners for the car's interior.

The Three Most Commonly Asked Lighting Questions

1. What are the advantages of using halogen headlamps?
The advantage of the halogen headlamp is that its filament is heated to a higher operating temperature which results in a more powerful, whiter light than older, conventional American-made headlamps produced. Some halogens produce 400% more light than conventional sealed beam headlamps. Seeing distances can be increased by more than 50%.

2. What lights are legal to install?
It's impossible to say generally what is legal to install because requirements differ tremendously by state. For example, most states allow only two driving lights, but some allow three and others one. Several states totally prohibit driving lights for on-road use. There's not even any uniformity among those states that do allow driving lights as to where they can be placed. Some say between 16" and 42", while others say 12" to 42", and others say "a minimum of 24". Some states also require auxiliary lighting to be hooked into the high-beam circuit of the dimmer switch so they go on only when high beams are on. The would-be driving light installer (or retailer) should check local regulations to find out what's legal where he will be driving.

3. How easy are they to install?
Headlamps are easily replaced generally with nothing more than a screwdriver. Most auxiliary lights come in kits now that include instructions, wiring, relays, and, of course, the lights themselves. Any DIYer with average mechanical abilities and normal tools available should be able to install them quickly and easily.

Glossary

Aiming screws: *The spring-loaded screws that permit headlamps to be aimed horizontally and vertically. They hold the headlamps to the support frame.*

Courtesy light: *The small light inside the car, usually on the roof, that comes on when the door is opened.*

Dimmer switch: *A switch, now often hand-operated but earlier usually foot operated, that turns the highbeam headlamp filaments on or off.*

Flasher: *Device in the turn-signal and hazard warning systems that causes the proper signal light(s) to turn on and off by opening and closing the circuit.*

Halogen lights: *The halogen light uses a halogen gas (iodine, bromine, chlorine, fluorine, or astatine) in which evaporated filament particles continuously go from one chemical chain to another. This "regenerative cycle" causes evaporated tungsten particles to be deposited on the coolest parts of the lamp, usually filament and support wires. This allows a higher filament temperature; bulb wall temperature often reaches 500°C. Because of the heat, the bulb is made of quartz rather than glass.*

Relay: *Relays are used in lighting systems, starters, horns, and other electrical systems to prevent large currents from flowing through the dashboard mechanical switches. Each relay is an electromechanical switch operated by a mechanical switch. A small current passes through the mechanical switch and activates a solenoid in the electromechanical switch. This closes a set of heavy contacts and allows a large current to flow.*

Schematic: *A "road-map" of an electrical system that uses various symbols to represent its components.*

Sealed-beam: *A complete headlamp containing the lens, reflector, and filaments with no separate bulb.*

Solenoid: *Sometimes synonymous with relay, this is an electromagnet that moves a metal rod or strip as a switch or relay.*

Third brake light: *A single red light, linked to the brake lights, placed in the center of the car level to the top or bottom of the rear window. Mandatory in new cars from 1986 on, but installed as aftermarket accessories on earlier cars.*

ADDITIVES AND OTHERS

In recent years, additives for the gas tank and the crankcase have shown significant increases in sales. One reason is the DIYer's desire to get better gas mileage; another is the growing number of older cars that DIYers try and keep going for another year or two. Because there are so many gas/oil additives and so many claims for these products, we suggest that clerks make a point of reading labels closely for manufacturer's claims of benefits, directions for use, and any warning about the product's use. It goes without saying that the DIYer should read the label carefully also.

Today's motor oil is composed of as much as 30% additives to fight wear, absorb moisture, and keep internal engine parts clean. But additives wear away as the car is driven, and most oil additives serve to replace the worn away additives. Oil additives that contain viscosity improvers to thicken oil are often used by DIYers on older engines to close various clearances. Oil additives also serve to clean older valves and piston rings for longer wear. Leaking seals can sometimes benefit from stop-leak additives that can seal in oil bearings and seals. There are also oil additives that are

RETAIL SALES TRAINING

designed to reduce friction by coating internal engine parts with a super slippery oil.

The single most popular gas additive is a gas line antifreeze, which is mainly bought in winter to prevent icing in the fuel tank. However, more DIYers are now buying this chemical year round to soak up moisture between the gas tank and the carburetor. Most other gas additives are designed to clean the fuel system in various ways. There are also cold starting sprays, made of a highly combustible liquid and sprayed directly into the carburetor. Finally, because many oil companies are no longer producing regular leaded gas for their stations, chemical companies are now providing a lead additive for older cars designed to run on leaded gas.

Serious DIYers will buy large quantities of maintenance chemicals. The most popular is penetrating lubricants which serve to help loosen corroded or rusted nuts and bolts. DIYers working under the car on the suspension and steering systems will also buy lubricating grease to protect undercar parts from water and wear. In this category, there are also numerous cleaners, solvents and degreasers especially designed for almost every engine part or system. Most DIYers will buy a flush and possibly a cooling system cleaner every year or so when changing antifreeze. But the most popular of these for older cars will be carburetor cleaners that clean the inside of the carburetor, the choke and the linkage, and aid in engine efficiency for more power and better gas mileage.

OTHER CHEMICAL PRODUCTS

Though this may sound like a complicated list of chemicals, it does not nearly complete the list of chemicals a store might sell. For example, to name just a few, there are tire sealants and aerosol cans of air for motorists with flat tires; windshield washer fluids and antifreezes for the windshield washer. And any auto store should stock a hand cleaner especially formulated to clean grease from the DIYers hands.

Knowing what chemicals are designed to do is not an easy job but it will benefit the store and the customer. ■

Glossary

Additives: *Chemicals added to oil and gas to improve their performance.*

Antifreeze/coolant: *An ethylene glycol solution that raises the boiling point and lowers the freezing point of water in the cooling system, prevents rust and corrosion, and also lubricates the water pump.*

Appearance chemicals: *Chemicals a car owner will use to maintain and improve the appearance of the car such as waxes, polishes, and vinyl cleaners.*

Functional fluids: *Chemicals a car owner will use on a regular basis. Without these chemicals, the systems they are designed for will not work. Examples are brake fluid, automatic transmission fluid (ATF), and power steering fluid.*

Maintenance fluids: *Chemicals used as aids to DIYers, mainly cleaners and degreasers of various types.*

Penetrating lubricant: *A chemical lubricant used to loosen rusted or corroded nuts and bolts.*

Ignition

The ignition system is the system that provides the spark that ignites the gasoline/air mixture in each cylinder that in turn provides the power to move the car.

This is not as simple a job as it may seem. The mixture that actually reaches the cylinder is highly compressed and it takes a very high

> ## The Three Most Commonly Asked Chemicals Questions
>
> **1. Should I recommend a gas additive? Do they work? Should I use them?**
> This is a tricky area because there are many additives and many claims. You should read the labels carefully and should recommend that the customer does the same. Check the benefits, the directions, and the warnings closely. Most gas additives are designed to clean the fuel system. However, particularly in winter, you'll sell a lot of gas line antifreeze or dry gas — an additive that soaks up moisture collected in the gas tank.
>
> **2. Should I recommend oil additives? Do they work? Should I use them?**
> The same warnings hold true for oil additives as for gas additives. No two engines are identical; all engines will react differently to additives. Motor oil contains as much as 20% additives to begin with. But the original additives wash away over the miles and some oil additives replenish them. Some oil additives are useful for cleaning valves and piston rings. Older engines with leaking seals can benefit from engine stop-leaks additives that seal oil bearings and seals. Some newer products are designed to reduce friction by coating internal parts with a super slippery oil.
>
> **3. Should I use a carburetor cleaner?**
> If the carburetor is performing correctly, you probably should not. If it isn't, a carburetor cleaner might cure its performance problems. Both spray and liquid versions clean the inside of the carburetor, the choke, and the linkage, removing gum and varnish that accumulate on the carburetor over a period of time. Again, read the labels carefully for benefits, directions, and warnings. Some cleaners may contaminate catalytic converters. If the cleaner does not cure the problem, the carburetor must be rebuilt or replaced.

voltage to produce a spark that can ignite it. Yet the average car battery supplies only 12 volts. To find out how 12 volts becomes the spark that can ignite the mixture one has to follow the entire ignition system.

Electricity comes from the battery. The battery has one cable that is grounded to the car frame. This is necessary for the electricity to flow through the system. The other cable goes to the ignition switch. When this (which is actually the car key switch) is turned on, electricity flows to the coil.

The coil is the key to boosting voltage. It actually has two wire coils, the primary winding with a few hundred turns of fairly thick wire, and a secondary coil with thousands of turns of fine wire. Electricity passes through the primary winding first and then through the secondary winding by which time it can reach as many as 40,000 volts.

This seeming magic is created because when electricity flows through a wire it produces a magnetic field around that wire. When the magnetic field is broken down, electricity is generated in any wire within the field's lines of force.

In cars made before 1975 (or Chrysler cars made before 1972), ignition systems use breaker-points as part of the ignition system. These have a resister in the wire from the ignition switch to the primary winding which cuts the primary voltage from 12 volts in half (generally). When the points open, electricity jumps from one point to the other until the gap

Glossary

Advance: A manual or automatic adjustment to the distributor that produces an ignition spark earlier in relation to the piston position.

Alternator: A device that changes mechanical energy to electrical energy to keep the battery charged.

Center electrode: Often called the stationary electrode, this metal rod passes through the center of the ceramic insulation of a spark plug to complete one side of the circuit path to the high-voltage ignition circuit.

Coil: The device that amplifies a small current from the battery into a large surge by means of induction to fire the spark plugs. Coils contain primary windings, made of relatively heavy wire, and secondary windings of a fine wire.

Distributor cap: A component of the ignition system having a center tower that connects the high-voltage transmitting coil to the rotor.

Dwell angle: The number of degrees the distributor cap rotates while the contact points are closed. In electronic ignitions, this is the time the primary circuit is completed by transistorized circuitry. It is expressed in degrees of distributor shaft rotation.

Gap: Also known as air gap, a space between spark plug electrodes, the distributor points, the armature and pickup coil of a distributor, or rotor, that can be often adjusted to obtain optimum performance.

High torque: A type of starter that draws additional amperage to produce more torque and turns over hard-to-start engines.

Rotor: A part of the ignition system that relays voltage to the distributor cap's corresponding spark plug wire inserts.

Timing: Making sure the surge from the coil reaches the plugs at exactly the time needed for the power stroke in the piston.

Voltage regulator: Either an electromechanical or solid-state component that controls the amount of voltage and current applied to a circuit.

becomes too wide. At first this induces a voltage of about 250 from the initial 6 volts in both windings. When the field completes its collapse, the 250 volts is boosted to as much as 40,000 volts—enough for ignition.

However, this constant electric arcing eventually erodes the points and they have to be replaced during the tune-up.

REPLACING THE BREAKER POINTS

In the older, conventional systems the breaker points are found in the distributor, in which is found the rotor and condenser.

Even though 1975 may seem like a few years ago, you'll be astonished at how many people will come into your store asking for points and other parts for breaker-point ignitions.

However, cars made since then in America generally have electronic ignition systems that use transistorized electromagnetic or photoelectric devices to interrupt the primary current flow through the coil. These are not generally touched by the average do-it-yourselfer.

From the secondary winding, electricity is sent to the rotor which is driven by the distributor shaft and sends current to each spark plug once during every four-stroke engine cycle.

The Three Most Commonly Asked Ignition Questions

1. What will solve my car's ignition problem?

Generally, the owner's manual will describe basic potential problems. Beyond that, books like those produced by Chilton are useful in ignition troubleshooting, defining what is needed for each specific problem. Many problems, such as cars not starting or dying after running, often are not ignition problems but problems in fuel or other systems.

2. How often should I replace ignition parts?

Spark plugs can go up to 30,000 miles before being replaced, although they should be replaced every 10,000 to 15,000 miles for best performance. Points, in cars without electronic ignition, should be replaced every 10,000 miles. Wires should be checked for wear at the same time and replaced if necessary.

3. Are OE ignition products the best for my car?

Not necessarily. Non-OE manufacturers make products that generally meet OE specifications (this usually will be mentioned on the box), and often incorporate improvements beyond specifications that they have developed themselves. One manufacturer of spark plug wires, for example, says that its wires are thicker and tougher than OE wires.

HOW SPARK PLUGS WORK

When the current reaches the spark plug through its terminal, it flows down the center electrode and arcs across a small gap to the side electrode (that small piece of metal that is attached to the side of the plug and curves to cover the center electrode). This small gap is one of the most important aspects of the whole ignition system. If it's too narrow, the spark won't be large enough or last long enough to ignite the gasoline/air mixture. If too wide, it may require more voltage (as more is needed to jump a larger gap than a smaller one) than the system can produce.

Therefore, in any tune-up, the spark plugs should be removed and the gaps checked against the recommended distances that are generally listed in every car owner's manual or repair guide. Simply bending the second electrode to the correct gap will work for setting the correct gap distance. However, older plugs will often have the side electrode eroded by the constant arcing. When the gap is more than .01" there generally will not be enough secondary electrode for the plug to be of any value.

In addition, the removed plugs will tell the do-it-yourselfer a great deal about how his car is running. Red deposits, for example, are caused by some lead-free fuels and do not indicate damage. But dry black deposits indicate too rich a fuel mixture, faulting timing, low compression, a weak spark, or wrong heat range. Wet black deposits often indicate a leak involving either transmission fluid, brake fluid, or oil. Brown spots on a white insulator may indicate pinging, too lean a fuel mixture, faulty installation, wrong heat range, or overly advanced timing.

In some cases, such as the wrong heat range, different types of plugs are indicated. These are "colder" as opposed to "hotter" plugs. The difference between the two is that "colder" plugs dissipate heat faster than "hotter" plugs. "Colder" plugs have a shorter insulator nose than "hotter" plugs. Generally, the do-it-yourselfer should use the plugs recommended by the car manufacturer. However, there can be times when he would consider changing. For example, a colder range plug could be used when a trailer is pulled often so the extra heat generated by this extra work can be dissipated quickly. In the same way, cars used for only short trips (under ten miles), might benefit from hotter plugs which will not foul as quickly.

In addition, spark plug types vary widely, too. Surface gap tips are used with capacitor discharge ignition systems only. They offer excellent fouling resistance with an extremely low heat range. Extended tip plugs have the insulator and electrode extending into the combustion chamber for efficient combustion and self-cleaning action to help control fouling. Copper core tip plugs use copper in the center electrode which allows the use of a longer insulator nose to resist fouling for longer periods of time. Long reach plugs are used where the cylinder head is very deep, while short reach plugs are used in engines with thin cylinder heads. Tapered seat plugs eliminate the need for a gasket. And wide gap plugs produce a larger spark needed to ignite the lean gasoline/air mixtures found in some modern smog-controlled engines. Then, too, motorcycles, lawnmowers and similar products, and racing cars also require specialized plug types.

In any case, generally manufacturers recommend changing plugs every 12,000 to 15,000 miles. Installing them in the fall, to provide better cold-weather starting, is a good idea, too.

Ignition system components are among the most common products sold in automotive aftermarket retailers. Learning as much as you can about them will be very helpful in dealing with your customers. ■

The Three Most Commonly Asked Sunroof Questions

1. Can I install a sunroof myself?
Anyone with a standard collection of home-workshop tools and average mechanical ability can install his own sunroof. As a result, most of them come in kit form with complete home installation instructions. The DIYer will need an electric drill, electric shear, screwdriver, and hammer.
2. Doesn't the sun coming in through the roof make the car unbearably hot?
Most sunroofs today come with some form of reflective material that cuts out as much as 30% of the sun's illumination and 75% of its ultraviolet rays. Separate window screens that roll up when not in use are also available for sunroofs. These keep the car's inside cool. And air circulation can often actually be improved by keeping the sunroof open, both drawing air from the car's heating and air conditioning systems up and out and taking with it stale tobacco smells.
3. Won't they leak eventually?
Most sunroofs come with a one- or two-year warranty guarantee against leakage due to faulty materials. Beyond that, however, today's materials, manufacturing techniques, and sealing products have made leakage problems virtually things of the past.

Sun Roofs

There are times when the customer has to be sold on the idea of chopping a hole in his roof to put a sunroof in. This can be done by impressing on him the benefits of the sunroof. What benefits? Easy. Sunroofs give a sense of openness to the ever-smaller cars now on the roads. They help ventilate the car by pulling stale air and smoke through the open sunroof, as well as pulling up cool air from the air conditioner or warm air up from the heater. This is especially useful now when few cars are made with once common vent windows. They can, one maker says, actually add to the roof strength in case of an accident.

Glossary

Air deflection: A sunroof design or accessory that cuts down wind resistance and noise.
Dot matrix coating: A coating forged to the outside of tempered glass that blocks the sun's heating light.
Laminated glass: Glass that consists of two layers of glass with reflective vinyl in between.
Moonroofs: Sunroofs that mechanically or electrically slide inside the roof when open. These are generally larger than pop-ups, running between 17" and 32". These tend to be the most expensive type of sunroof.
Pop-ups: Sunroofs that open up, often being removeable. They generally have framed glass and a mechanical handle allowing the roof to be opened from the inside.
Solar cool: A type of glass that is similar to the mirror glass used in office buildings that relects the sun and keeps the car interior cool.
T-tops: Sunroofs using two reflective glass plates on the right and left side of the roof. They usually pop out when opened.

And, the sunroof can give the car a new, sporty look, even adding to its resale value.

You may not have thought of selling sunroofs when you began as an automotive retailer, but sunroofs are another product that you'll help your customer and your store by selling right. ∎

Suspension

When cars were first introduced, they used the spring suspension system then in use on horse-drawn wagons. This was handy for manufacturers, but rough on riders. Since then, suspension systems have become much more sophisticated, allowing a smooth ride over pothole pitted roads as well as giving the car safe and good handling properties.

The main parts of the suspension system are the shock absorber and the spring.

The spring is generally made in the spiral shape of a coil although sometimes leaf springs (multiple springs that are curved at each end) are used. Other cars use torsion bars which are connected rigidly to the frame. These twist as the wheel, to which they are indirectly attached, moves up and down.

Regardless of the type of spring, all of them compress, twist, or straighten out when the wheel hits a bump, and then expand, untwist, or curve. However, the reaction to the initial compression, twisting, or straightening is greater than the spring's resting position. This would cause the car to continue to bounce up and down wildly unless checked. It is the shock absorber that checks this movement. It does it by means of a cylinder that is partially filled with hydraulic fluid or gas that slows a piston that rides up and down through the cylinder.

This shock absorber can be separate from the spring, or combined as in the new invention designed to save weight and space (and money for the car manufacturer), the MacPherson strut. There are, besides, more than one type of shock absorber.

KNOW YOUR SHOCK TYPES

The *adjustable shock* can be adjusted by hand to give a harder or softer ride as desired. Different models are adjusted different ways, and the installer has to consult the manufacturer's instructions to see how a particular model works.

Air shocks use air pressure to support heavier than usual loads. They are preferred on cars that occasionally tow trailers or on cars that sometimes are lightly loaded and other times have heavy loads. This is because air can be bled from the chambers in the shock to reduce or even eliminate the extra support needed for heavier-than-usual loads. Then, when a trailer is hooked up or a heavy load is put into the car, air pressure can be increased, through a standard tire air valve. Some air shocks have automatic level sensors that automatically adjust their air pressure as needed. Others are adjusted by means of a switch usually mounted on the dashboard. Both use compressors powered by the engine vacuum.

Heavy-duty shocks are designed for off-road or high-speed use, having stiffer valving and larger fluid capacity than the average shock. They offer increased control.

In much the same way, *overload shocks* are designed for heavy loads or trailer towing. They incorporate coil springs wrapped around heavy-duty shocks for help in support. They should not be confused with MacPherson struts.

In many cases, a customer coming into your store doesn't know exactly the type of replacement shock he wants. All he knows is what his problem is, and, perhaps, the kind of ride he wants. It's your job to know and suggest the type of shock that will solve that problem.

SUSPENSION SYSTEMS

Whatever type shock is used, it appears as the centerpiece of the *suspension system*. In most of today's cars, the system includes independent front suspension, in which each wheel operates separately from each other, and either independent rear suspension or live-axle rear suspension.

Generally, MacPherson struts are used as the front suspension, or, if separate shocks and springs are used, the most common front suspension is the double A-arm suspension. In this form the coil spring is also wrapped around the shock. If the customer doesn't know which type of suspension his car uses, he can easily find out from his owner's manual or a repair manual for his car model. Virtually any do-it-yourselfer can replace the shocks in a double A-arm suspension, but a special spring compressor is required to replace the MacPherson strut.

In some cars stabilizer, sway, or antiroll bars are used. These products allow the car maker to use softer springs because the bars increase roll stiffness even though they don't affect the quality of the ride seriously. They also transfer some of the braking forces from the wheel to the frame.

The live-axle rear suspension includes an axle housing that runs between the wheels. Independent rear suspension, however, is generally marked by independent trailing arms on which shocks and springs rest.

Glossary

Alignment: *Either front-end or four-wheel, alignment involves using special equipment to measure the relationships of the wheels and suspension parts to each other and the road and then correcting the relationships with adjustments or by installing shims.*

Ball joint: *A sphere on one side and a matching socket on the other that joins two members, permitting rotation in all planes.*

Camber: *The angle at which a wheel-tire assembly meets the ground vertically, either negative (leaning inward) or positive (leaning outward).*

MacPherson strut: *A combination of a spring and shock absorber that links chassis and the lower control arm.*

Shock absorber: *A device that limits the spring's travel and stops it from continuing to oscillate after hitting a bump through hydromechanical means.*

Stabilizer bar: *Often called roll bar, antisway bar, sway bar, or antiroll bar, this links the two front suspension systems to prevent sway.*

The Three Most Common Suspension Questions

1. Do I have to replace a good suspension item when I replace a bad one?
In the front or the back, with shocks or MacPherson struts, the pair must be replaced even if only one is bad. The car's handling will be affected if only one is replaced. Ball joints, tie rod ends, and bushings should be replaced in pairs since the failure of one suggests an imminent failure of the other. With other suspension items, such as idler arms, only bad parts need be replaced.

2. Can I replace it without special tools?
Shocks can be replaced with the typical handyman's tools. MacPherson struts, however, require the use of a special spring compressor. These can often be rented at auto supply stores. A taper breaker is needed to replace tie rods and related parts such as idler arms. A pitman arm puller is needed to remove an old pitman arm. Ball joint replacement requires a press (for press-in ball joints), a taper breaker, and a gauge to check the looseness of worn ball joints.

3. Can I replace MacPherson struts with conventional (and cheaper) shocks?
MacPherson struts, in saving space, have combined features of both shocks and the conventional suspension system. They are a part of the car's engineered suspension system, and can be replaced only by new MacPherson struts.

UNDERSTANDING ALIGNMENT

Regardless of the suspension system or shocks used, every car eventually has to have its wheels aligned. This is something that the do-it-yourselfer will not attempt to do because it requires specialized and very expensive equipment. Basically, alignment means making sure the wheels, frame, front (or front and rear in four-wheel alignment), and steering components are placed in the relationship to each other specified by the car's manufacturer. If this isn't done, the car won't have the tire life and fuel efficiency it was designed for. Nor will it steer or handle as well as it should.

Suspension parts are sold to the serious do-it-yourselfer who comes into your store having a fair idea of what he wants. But you will be able to help him by pointing out the different types of suspension products available and how they can best be used. ■

Training

Success in any store training project revolves around the recognition that we are dealing with two important considerations: the technical and the human. This is just as true when you teach someone how to quickly, accurately, and productively use parts catalogs.

To a new employee, catalogs can be very intimidating. The sheer number of catalogs is overwhelming. The prospect of coming to grips with many thousands of part numbers is frightening. And the knowledge required to determine customer needs and to select the right parts seems staggering.

Instead of helping, we can continue to complicate these fears with a haphazard approach to parts catalog training: a few minutes here, a few minutes there; no logical order; covering too much or too little; leaving out important concepts; passive learning by the trainee; and very little of the right type of feedback to determine just how much learning has taken place. (To avoid such training pitfalls, see the training article in our May issue.)

You can effectively organize your approach to catalog training and apply sound principles of learning to the technical subject matter at hand.

USE A PROBLEM-SOLVING APPROACH

You should have at least two major objectives when it comes to parts catalogs training:

■ To have your new counterman help customers solve their auto problems.

■ To have your new counterman look up the right part the first time around.

Some parts people become very proficient in using the catalogs, and they take great pride in coming up with the right part in record-breaking time. But, as they push the part across the counter to the customer, they should ask themselves: "Is this part alone going to solve this customer's problem?"

CATALOG ORGANIZATION

Looking at four or five linear feet of catalogs can really be intimidating to the novice. So spend a few minutes describing how the catalogs are arranged; this will help the trainee get to the right catalog with a minimum of time and effort.

If your store uses the Weatherly Index system, pick up a few examples to show the trainee the steps followed to get from the index pages to the right catalogs. If the catalogs are arranged alphabetically by product categories, spend some time with the trainee reviewing the tab dividers that separate the catalogs in the rack.

Just remember not to get into too much detail in this introduction. Do not point out all the exceptions to the rules. The objective at the start is to get the trainee feeling comfortable—not lost. Save the specifics for the right kind of examples that will lead the trainee through the catalogs in an orderly and efficient way. And use the systems selling flow charts.

It should go without saying that the catalogs must be properly organized and kept up-to-date no matter what system you use if you want your training efforts to be truly productive.

USING THE CATALOGS

Mastery of the parts catalogs is a never-ending job. New catalogs arrive frequently, automotive systems keep changing, and new part numbers are the rule rather than the exception.

So don't try to teach the new employee everything you know about catalogs in the first training session. Your objective should be to build basic skills and discipline in using catalogs. The mastery of each catalog will come over a much longer period of time as the trainee gains knowledge and experience in dealing with a variety of customer needs.

As you train, select catalogs that best illustrate the sequence of events that the trainee must follow in handling a customer's request for a part. Then present those catalogs in an organized format so the trainee builds good thinking and work habits right from the start. Here are some important points to cover:

■ Index and front pages. Not all manufacturers' catalogs are the same. They vary according to layout and format. But catalogs do provide an index that enables the user to get to the right page quickly and easily and they also provide hints on use. It is important that you instruct the trainee to look at the beginning of each parts catalog for helpful information rather than thumbing aimlessly through the pages.

■ Reading a catalog page. Another important point to emphasize is patience and care in reading each catalog page. Getting the right part the first time around depends on being on the right page, in the right column, and on the right line. A ruler or a piece of cardboard can be used to insure that the trainee moves across the page in a straight line.

- Footnotes. Footnotes play a critical role in determining the right part application and they also provide cautions or suggestions on installation. Select a catalog or two where footnotes are especially important and where they illustrate the point you are trying to make. Remember, use only a few examples at the start—too many will only confuse rather than enlighten.

- Interchange listings. Interchange listings (often found at the rear of the catalog) are vitally important in locating the right part for a customer in certain applications. The oil and air filter catalogs serve as good examples. Different manufacturers will have different numbers for the same part application, and the trainee must be able to convert one part number to the number you carry. Another good example is the carburetor catalog, where the cross reference or interchange list can be vital.

- Illustrations. Many parts catalogs provide part illustrations. It may be an illustration which shows the arrangement of drive belts in the engine, front end parts, brake parts, ignition parts, etc. Sometimes customers call a part by the wrong name, and the illustration can be used to properly identify the part. Illustrations are also used to show what cores are acceptable or not acceptable in certain transactions.

- Price lists. Looking up the right part is not complete without pricing the part correctly. There are a number of variations on how this is accomplished through price lists, computers, or individually priced marked parts. No attempt will be made here to present details. Your own pricing system should be reviewed along with instructions on how to use the catalogs.

- Catalog maintenance. Keeping catalogs up-to-date and organized is a day-to-day job, and trainees must be taught how to do this efficiently and correctly. Don't assume they know which catalogs to keep or which to discard. If you do, you may lose valuable catalogs which are necessary for certain part applications. Also do not assume that everyone knows how to remove a catalog from the rack and insert a new one. If you do, catalogs will continue to stack up on the parts counter waiting for a home.

WRITE IT DOWN

Accuracy and efficiency in arriving at the correct part application can only be achieved if you have complete and accurate information to work with. Yet we see some parts people looking for paper and pencil to write with when a phone request comes in—or they write the information on a scrap of paper or catalog page.

Sometimes the information is incomplete or inaccurate because the parts person is disorganized or hurried. And nothing irritates a customer more than to be asked over and over again for the same information simply because what they said was not written down.

Figure I shows a part request form, which obtains information in a logical, orderly, and permanent manner. Such forms are not universally used and many counter people rely on their memories to generate customer orders.

If you have any turnover at all, if you do your share of hiring and training, and if you want to do it in the most efficient and productive way, I strongly encourage the use of such a form so good parts catalogs skills are developed early.

Much of catalog training is directed at the new employee, but there is also a need to continually up-grade the knowledge and skill of experienced employees and a need to create high levels of involvement and motivation.

You can do this by assigning certain catalogs to individual employees and having them become proficient in their use. Then they can share their knowledge and expertise with other

Figure 1

PART REQUEST	NAME:	DATE:
Vehicle Data	Part Requested	Part Number
Make: _____	_____	_____
Model: _____	_____	_____
Year: _____	_____	_____
Engine _____	_____	_____
_____ Notes:		
_____		
_____		

employees either during formal or informal training sessions. Your role will be to encourage this "pursuit of excellence" by routing special training materials and technical bulletins to the appropriate trainer.

CUSTOMER RELATIONS SKILLS

No parts catalog training should be considered complete without emphasizing the customer relations skills that are so necessary in developing a loyal customer following.

Successful sales transactions depend not only on selling customers the right part, but on making them feel good about it in the process. Customer relations skills in using the parts catalogs revolve around:

- Recognizing customers as quickly as possible.
- Asking the right questions and listening to what the customer says.
- Greeting customers by name whenever possible.
- Using good eye contact and positive body language to successfully influence how the customers think and feel.
- Not using technical knowledge to belittle the customer or to prove him wrong when a difference arises.
- Being patient and understanding even with the most difficult customers.

This is not all there is to customer relations training, of course, but it will encourage you to build some solid customer relations skills into your parts catalog training.

THE HUMAN SIDE OF TRAINING

Training does not occur in a vacuum, and a trainee's behavior pattern is determined as much by the actions of the trainer and the other employees in the store as it is by the training program.

If you preach good customer relations, then you should serve as a role model in greeting customers, determining their needs, and satisfying their needs.

If no one in the store practices systems selling, the trainee will soon forget the problem-solving approach you taught and sell the way other employees sell.

The human side of selling begins, then, with creating the right store environment for training—an environment within which the store management staff shapes behavior as much by their actions as by their words.

For your training to be truly effective, it must be based on the needs of the individual and on sound learning principles:

- Get to know your people as individuals. Each individual is different and learns at a different rate.
- Set realistic goals and objectives for your training. People learn better when they know where they are going, what's expected of them, and how long it should take them to get there.
- Get the trainee actively involved in the learning process. The trainee should "do the doing" while the trainer provides the direction.
- Recognize and reinforce desired behavior with some positive words rather than concentrating on errors and negative comments.
- Follow up. Feedback is essential to be sure that learning has taken place.

So there it is: an overall concept and approach to learning how to use the parts catalogs accurately and productively.

Looking up the right part in a catalog is not an end in itself. Customer satisfaction and employee satisfaction must be part of every transaction. ■

Nutrition and Primary Care

Ethelyn N. Fuller
SENIOR EDITOR

Lucy H. Labson
EXECUTIVE EDITOR

Robert L. Edsall
DEPUTY EDITOR

Clayton Raker Hasser
EDITOR

Judith A. Cash
MANAGING EDITOR

Elizabeth R. Pollack
ART DIRECTOR

Medical school is not the best place to learn about nutrition, and heightened awareness from nutrition-conscious patients has made physicians increasingly aware of their relative ignorance. These articles resulted from the efforts of a panel of experts in a variety of nutrition-related fields to analyze an enormous body of conflicting information. They constitute a practical primer of nutrition issues for the physician.

Patient Care serves primary-care physicians, particularly those specializing in family practice or internal medicine. "Nutrition and Primary Care" first appeared in the June 15, 1986 issue of *Patient Care,* published by Medical Economics, Inc. © 1986. Reprinted with permission.

The Diet-Heart Connection

Although not accepted by all, the consensus report on the treatment of hypercholesterolemia issued in December 1984 by the National Institutes of Health gives clear-cut recommendations for modifying the typical American diet to reduce hypercholesterolemia and its presumed risk for coronary heart disease (CHD):

- Patients with blood cholesterol levels above the 90th percentile should be treated intensively by means of dietary changes and, if response is inadequate, drug therapy (see Table 1).
- Patients with blood cholesterol levels between the 75th and 90th percentiles should be treated intensively by dietary changes. Drug therapy may be necessary.
- All Americans except children under age 2 should be encouraged to adopt a cholesterol-lowering diet.
- Ideal weight should be achieved and maintained by a combination of reduced caloric intake and regular moderate exercise.

Part of the rationale for such sweeping recommendations is the conclusion that a causal relationship does in fact exist between blood cholesterol levels and CHD. When the blood

TABLE 1. Plasma Cholesterol Levels by Age and Percentile

	PERCENTILES				
AGE (YRS.)	5	50	75	90	95
Male					
5–19	115 mg/dl	155 mg/dl	170 mg/dl	185 mg/dl	200 mg/dl
20–24	125	165	185	205	220
25–29	135	180	200	225	245
30–34	140	190	215	240	255
35–39	145	200	225	250	270
40–44	150	205	230	250	270
45–69	160	215	235	260	275
69+	150	205	230	250	270
Female					
5–19	120 mg/dl	160 mg/dl	175 mg/dl	190 mg/dl	200 mg/dl
20–24	125	170	190	215	230
25–34	130	175	195	220	235
35–39	140	185	205	230	245
40–44	145	195	215	235	255
45–49	150	205	225	250	270
50–54	165	220	240	265	285
54+	170	230	250	275	295

*Gotto AM, Bierman EL, Connor WE, et al: Recommendations for treatment of hyperlipidemia in adults: The Nutrition Committee and Council on Atherosclerosis of the American Heart Association. *Circulation* 1984:69:1067A-90A.

> Risks of hypercholesterolemia: A National Institutes of Health consensus report recommends dietary changes and weight control to reduce the incidence of hypercholesterolemia. The panel concluded that elevated blood cholesterol levels do in fact increase the risk of coronary heart disease (CHD) by causing a buildup of plaque in the arteries and blocking the circulation, and that reducing existing hypercholesterolemia or preventing its development can cause a reduction in the incidence of CHD.

carries more cholesterol than can be properly metabolized, cholesterol is deposited in cells that line the arteries, leading to inflammation and scar formation. Once damage begins, more cholesterol, calcium, and cellular debris collect. Plaque build-up eventually blocks the circulation.

While the amount of plaque found in the arteries is generally related to the degree of hypercholesterolemia, the relationship is not strictly linear. Other conditions compound the risk for atherosclerosis. The lipoprotein fraction in which the cholesterol is carried seems to make a difference in that elevated levels of low-density lipoprotein (LDL) do more harm than elevated levels of high-density lipoprotein (HDL). Indeed, HDL may be protective. Because triglycerides are part of the molecular aggregate that includes cholesterol, the two are often elevated in parallel. It is not clear whether an elevated serum triglyceride level by itself increases the risk for atherosclerosis and CHD.

Hypertension, diabetes, and obesity further increase the risk of CHD, especially in patients who also have hypercholesterolemia. But since obesity is a risk factor for both hypertension and diabetes, its threat to cardiovascular health may be secondary to these other conditions.

Another conclusion of the NIH consensus report is that reducing elevated cholesterol levels in patients with hypercholesterolemia decreases the risk of CHD. Results of a number of clinical interventional trials have determined that the incidence of CHD can be significantly reduced in some hypercholesterolemic patients by lowering the level of serum cholesterol. The most recent study, the Lipid Research Clinics Coronary Primary Prevention Trial (LRC-CPPT), recorded a 19% decrease in CHD among nonobese middle-aged men whose blood cholesterol levels were reduced an average of 9% by a combination of diet and drug therapy with cholestyramine (Questran).*

The mechanism of cholesterol reduction with cholestyramine is promotion of cholesterol excretion through binding of its bile acid metabolites in the intestinal lumen. As is the case with a diet low in cholesterol and fats, LDL receptor activity is enhanced. The conferees therefore suggest that the LRC-CPPT results can and should be extrapolated to a recommendation for cholesterol reduction by diet for all Americans.

Some cardiologists criticize the consensus conference for extrapolating recommendations from a limited target population to all Americans. If the results of the Lipid Research Clinics Coronary Primary Prevention Trial are interpreted narrowly, they imply only that nonobese middle-aged men with serum cholesterol levels above 265 mg/dL could benefit from dietary modifications plus treatment with bile acid sequestrants.

A broader interpretation is that the benefits of dietary modifications extend to men *and* women who are in the top quintile of serum cholesterol levels. The most far-reaching directive the results might imply is that the diet of all Americans should be modified, not only to lower elevated blood cholesterol levels but

---

*Gotto AM, Bierman EL, Connor WE, et al: Recommendations for treatment of hyperlipidemia in adults: The Nutrition Committee and Council on Atherosclerosis of the American Heart Association. *Circulation* 1984:69:1067A–90A.

TABLE 2. Extrapolations from Results of the Lipid Research Clinics Coronary Primary Prevention Trial
(Depending on how broadly the results of this study are applied, they could have implications for the diets of anywhere from 1 million to 239 million Americans.)

Interpretation	Population Affected	Possible Number of Americans	Intervention
Narrow	Middle-aged men with cholesterol levels >265 mg/dl	1–2 million	Diet plus therapy with biliary sequestrants
Limited	Men and women of any age who are in the top quintile of cholesterol levels	48 million	Diet with or without drugs
Broad	Entire population	239 million	Diet alone

also to prevent hypercholesterolemia (see Table 2).

Serum cholesterol is normally maintained at an acceptable level by a feedback mechanism that turns off hepatic synthesis of cholesterol when the dietary supply is adequate. A genetic susceptibility or acquired metabolic defect may be operative in those patients who develop hypercholesterolemia. Either the cholesterol feedback mechanism becomes inoperative or an insufficient number of cell receptors are available to take up the cholesterol-rich low-density lipoproteins (LDL). With either an oversupply of cholesterol or impaired ability to dispose of it, a diet high in cholesterol and saturated fats will produce atherosclerosis. But others seem able to consume relatively high quantities of lipids without experiencing any adverse effects.

Though an association has been demonstrated between increased levels of cholesterol in the blood and increased mortality from coronary artery disease, a reduction in serum cholesterol does not automatically reduce mortality. While, in general, the higher the level of serum cholesterol, the more arterial plaque, a desirable lower limit of blood cholesterol has not been established. People with lifelong serum cholesterol levels as low as 120 mg/dL do not have cholesterol streaks in their arteries.

Furthermore, the fact that the incidence of coronary disease varies continuously with serum cholesterol, LDL, and high-density lipoprotein levels demonstrates that no single level of plasma cholesterol separates those at risk from those who are not. Controversy exists, therefore, as to the necessity of aiming for a cholesterol level as low as possible for all patients.

Indeed, the American Academy of Pediatrics questions the recommendations as applied

---

Dissenting views: Extrapolating study results from a limited patient population to all Americans may not be justified. While some people may have a defective feedback mechanism for control of cholesterol synthesis or may lack sufficient cell receptors to dispose of blood cholesterol, others are able to consume cholesterol without experiencing any adverse effects. Adequacy of a low-cholesterol diet for growing children has not been established.

TABLE 3. Dietary Modifications to Reduce Hypercholesterolemia (NIH Consensus Conference)

NUTRIENT	RECOMMENDED AMOUNTS		
	Phase 1	Phase 2	Phase 3
Fat	<30% of calories	<25% of calories	<20% of calories
Saturated	<33% of fats	<33% of fats	<33% of fats
Polyunsaturated	>33% of fats	>33% of fats	>33% of fats
Monounsaturated	33% of fats	33% of fats	33% of fats
Carbohydrate	55% of calories	60% of calories	65% of calories
Protein	12–15% of calories	12–15% of calories	12–15% of calories
Cholesterol	<300 mg/d	<200–250 mg/d	<100–150 mg/d

to children who are not at high risk for coronary heart disease (CHD) because:

- A diet low in calories, regardless of its fat content, may be all that is required to protect children from developing CHD.
- Dietary cholesterol may be needed during the entire growth period—indeed, throughout life—to supply substrate for the formation of bile acids, hormones, and other special tissues.
- A low-fat diet may be detrimental in other ways to children with normal fat metabolism. Children may need a full complement of lipids for neurologic development. Since no population of children has been raised that way, no confirmatory epidemiologic data exists. In addition, mineral and vitamin deficiencies may develop along with the dietary reduction of nutrient-rich foods containing saturated fats.

When dietary modification seems advisable, the patient can restrict fats and cholesterol progressively until an acceptable blood cholesterol level is reached (see Table 3). If diet alone is not enough, drug therapy may also be necessary.

To reduce dietary cholesterol to 300 mg/d from its current average of about 800 mg/d in the typical American diet, encourage a decrease in foods of animal origin, the only dietary source of cholesterol (see Table 4). Because of the cholesterol feedback mechanism, a reduction in dietary cholesterol may stimulate increased synthesis of hepatic cholesterol.

Since the substrate for endogenous synthesis is partly derived from fatty acids, a reduction in total fats in the diet to no more than 30% of daily calories is desirable. Furthermore, the rate of cholesterol synthesis seems to be somewhat dependent on the ratio of saturated to unsaturated fats in the diet. The consensus conference recommends that no more than 33% of fats be saturated. Until recently, monounsaturated fat was considered neutral with respect to cholesterol metabolism. According to current studies, it seems to offer some protection against hypercholester-

---

Dietary cholesterol and fats: When it seems advisable to reduce dietary cholesterol to 300 mg/d, foods of animal origin, especially organ meats and eggs, must be limited. The substrate for endogenous cholesterol is partially derived from fatty acids. On average, total fats should compose no more than 30% of daily calories, with only 33% of the total in saturated form. Both polyunsaturated and monounsaturated fats confer some protection against hypercholesterolemia.

TABLE 4. Dietary Sources of Cholesterol

Food	Portion Size	Cholesterol (mg) (approximate)*
Brains	3 oz.	1,700
Kidneys	3 oz.	700
Other organ meats	3 oz.	166–400
Egg yolk	1 medium	250
Shrimp	3 oz.	130
Sardines	3 oz.	120
Crabmeat	3 oz.	85
Herring	3 oz.	80
Red meats and dark-meat poultry	3 oz.	75–85
Lobster	3 oz.	70
White-meat poultry	3 oz.	65
Fish	3 oz.	40–70
Ice cream	½ C	50
Butter	1 tbsp.	35
Hard cheeses	1 oz.	25–30
Cream	1 tbsp.	20

*Cholesterol content varies because of variations in animal breed, types of feeds, water temperature, and age of the animal.

olemia by increasing blood levels of high-density lipoproteins.

While all fats and oils are mixtures of saturated and unsaturated fatty acids, the degree of hardness generally correlates with the degree of saturation. Thus, beef tallow, which is highly saturated, is solid at room temperature, whereas highly polyunsaturated safflower oil is liquid even when refrigerated.

To increase monounsaturated and polyunsaturated fats in the diet, the patient can include legumes, nuts, and, in particular, seeds. Seeds and their oils are the highest source of polyunsaturated fat, while monounsaturated fat is abundant in nuts and olives and their oils (see Table 5). Peanut butter made from nothing more than ground peanuts is a particularly good food, but many commercial peanut butters are partly hydrogenated—that is, saturated—to make them smoother and keep them homogenized. In most cases, however, the final product is still more unsaturated than saturated. It may, however, contain unnecessarily high additions of salt and sugar.

Apparently, the degree of saturation is not the only characteristic of a fat that determines its atherogenicity. Populations that consume fish at least three times per week have a lower incidence of coronary artery disease than currently occurs in the United States.

Some fish contain Ω-3 polyunsaturated fatty acids—compounds with a double bond located

TABLE 5. Degree of Saturation of Edible Fats and Oils

Fat or Oil	Saturated (%)	Monounsaturated (%)	Polyunsaturated (%)
Beef tallow	52	44	4
Butter	65	31	4
Chicken fat	31	47	22
Cocoa butter	62	34	3
Coconut oil	92	6	2
Corn oil	14	25	61
Cottonseed oil	27	19	54
Goose fat	29	59	12
Lard (pork)	41	47	12
Margarine, hard	74	10	16
Margarine, soft	18	42	31
Olive oil	14	77	9
Peanut oil	18	48	34
Safflower oil	9	13	78
Soybean oil	15	24	61
Sunflower oil	11	21	69

> Other dietary considerations: Although some fish and presumably their Ω-3 polyunsaturated fatty acids have recently been discovered to be protective against atherosclerosis in certain defined populations, fish liver oils and Ω-3 fatty acid supplements should not be substituted for fish as food. Soluble fiber, garlic, and some beers have been suggested as hypocholesterolemic. Excessive consumption of brewed coffee may increase cholesterol levels. Isolated hypertriglyceridemia probably does not increase the risk of heart disease.

at the third carbon from the end of the chain. These fatty acids, particularly eicosapentaenoic acid, are competitors in the synthesis of prostaglandins and leukotrienes and thus inhibit or modify platelet aggregation and the inflammatory process such aggregation causes. While this mechanism does nothing to reduce cholesterol buildup in the arteries, it interferes with the portion of the atherosclerotic process that depends on responses mediated by prostaglandins and leukotrienes.

In addition, because the Ω-3 fatty acids are polyunsaturated, increased consumption of fish containing these acids increases the ratio of polyunsaturated to saturated fats in the diet. Fatty saltwater fish, such as mackerel, salmon, tuna, herring, sardines, and swordfish, contain abundant amounts of Ω-3 fatty acids. Shellfish, sole, cod, and red snapper contain little if any. Supplements that contain Ω-3 fatty acids in the form of fish liver oils or pills—usually a mixture of eicosapentaenoic and docosahexaenoic acids—are not acceptable substitutes for the fish. They may contain toxic amounts of vitamins A and D.

Dietary constituents other than cholesterol and saturated fats may also influence the serum cholesterol level. Brewed caffeinated or decaffeinated coffee in excess of two cups a day seems to be hypercholesterolemic. There's less evidence with filtered coffees. Soluble fiber tends to be hypocholesterolemic, possibly by interfering with absorption of bile salts or dietary cholesterol. Types of soluble fiber—lignin, pectin, and guar—are contained in oat bran, barley, and most fruits and vegetables; they are distinguished from crude fiber in that they have a polar side chain.

In addition, garlic and some brands of beer have been credited by some with reducing elevated blood cholesterol levels. Moderate alcohol intake may preferentially increase high-density lipoprotein levels without affecting the total blood cholesterol levels.

While moderate hypertriglyceridemia does not seem to be a risk factor for atherosclerosis unless the patient is also hypercholesterolemic, hypertriglyceridemia approaching 1,000 mg/dL is a substantial risk factor for pancreatitis. Triglyceride elevations over about 500 mg/dL are usually associated with a disease entity, such as diabetes mellitus, alcoholism, or the nephrotic syndrome, and require treatment to protect against pancreatitis.

The recommended dietary approach for reducing hypertriglyceridemia is to achieve or maintain normal weight; slowly reduce dietary fats, especially saturated fats; choose more complex carbohydrates over simple sugar; and restrict alcohol intake. When weight loss is necessary, a process of slow loss is preferable.

The exact amounts of these nutrient limitations should be determined empirically. If the percentage of fat in the diet is restricted too severely and the amount of protein is kept constant, the percentage of carbohydrate will increase automatically. This might tend to increase the triglyceride levels, and the cycle could be perpetuated in susceptible patients—increased carbohydrate, leading to increased secretion of insulin, leading to increased triglyceride synthesis. ∎

REFERENCES

1. Ahrens EH: The diet heart question in 1985: Has it really been settled? *Lancet* 1985;1085-7.

2. Callaway CW: Nutrition. *JAMA* 1985;254:2388–40.
3. Glomset JA: Fish, fatty acids, and human health. *N Engl J Med* 1985;312:1253–4.
4. Goldbourt U, Holtzman E, Neufeld HN: Total and high density lipoprotein cholesterol in the serum and risk of mortality: Evidence of a threshold effect. *Br Med J* 1985;290:1239–43.
5. Gotto AM, Bierman EL, Connor WE, et al: Recommendations for treatment of hyperlipidemia in adults: The Nutrition Committee and Council on Atherosclerosis of the American Heart Association. *Circulation* 1984;69:1067A–90A.
6. Grundy SM: Comparison of monounsaturated fatty acids and carbohydrates for lowering plasma cholesterol. *N Engl J Med* 1986;314:745–8.
7. Hoeg JM, Gregg RE, Brewer HB Jr: An approach to the management of hyperlipoproteinemia. *JAMA* 1986;255:512–21.
8. Kirby RW, Anderson JW, Sieling B, et al: Oat-bran intake selectively lowers serum low-density lipoprotein cholesterol concentrations of hypercholesterolemic men. *Am J Clin Nutr* 1981;34:824–9.
9. Kritchevsky D: NIH Consensus Conference: A dissenting view. *Nutrition & the MD* 1985;11(October):5–6.
10. Levy RI: Cholesterol and coronary artery disease. What do clinicians do now? *Am J Med* 1986;80(suppl 2A):18–22.
11. National Institutes of Health Consensus Conference on the treatment of hypertriglyceridemia. *JAMA* 1984;251:1196–200.
12. National Institutes of Health Consensus Development Conference statement: Lowering blood cholesterol to prevent heart disease. *JAMA* 1985;253:2080–6.
13. Oliver MF: Consensus or nonsensus conferences on coronary heart disease. *Lancet* 1985;I:1087–9.
14. Schaefer EJ, Levy RI: Pathogenesis and management of lipoprotein disorders. *N Engl J Med* 1985;312:1300–10.

How Cancer Affects Nutritional Status

Cancer can exert a profound effect on a patient's nutritional needs, both by increasing caloric demands and by interfering with the patient's ability to meet those demands. And malnutrition itself may paradoxically increase a patient's anorexia. Oncologists estimate that cancer cachexia is among the most predominant causes of death in patients with neoplastic disease.

To get an idea of the degree to which the stress of cancer increases a patient's normal caloric requirements, consider 1.0 to be the standard for a person who is healthy and sedentary. Then multiply by the factors that are provided below for the same person if he or she:

- Is healthy and active — 1.2
- Has had minor surgery — 1.3
- Has had major surgery — 1.5
- Has major sepsis — 1.6
- Has leukemia, lymphoma, or lung cancer — 1.3–1.6
- Has another cancer — 1.0–1.3

The mechanisms by which cancer increases a patient's energy requirements involve fundamental metabolic aberrations that are not fully understood but may be due in part to elevated levels of circulating catecholamines. The metabolic effects of cancer also create a high turnover of lactic acid and shifting of other metabolic processes. These various metabolic derangements, in combination with the characteristic anorexia of cancer (which may be due to disruption of the CNS appetite center by cancer metabolites) can devastate a patient's nutritional status.

> **Malnutrition from cancer:** The stress of cancer increases caloric requirements at the same time that the disease produces anorexia and metabolic alterations that make it difficult to meet those needs. Cancer therapies further compound the problem. Not only do they exacerbate anorexia, but by damaging the digestive tract and causing widespread systemic disruptions of metabolic processes, they produce specific nutrient deficiencies.

Inadequate intake, diarrhea, vomiting, and urinary elimination lead to deficiencies of vitamins, minerals, and other nutrients. A tumor anywhere in the digestive tract can be expected to impair nutrient absorption and utilization profoundly. Lymphatic obstruction may cause an isolated protein deficiency. Interference with bile salt production or transport may cause a deficiency of essential fatty acids and fat-soluble vitamins. Severe and prolonged malnutrition may result in atrophy of the intestinal villi and create lactose intolerance.

In addition to metabolic aberrations set in motion by the cancer itself, many aspects of cancer therapy disrupt the patient's nutritional state. In the overwhelming majority of patients treated for cancer—by means of surgery, chemotherapy, or radiotherapy—appetite is adversely affected. Many, if not most, patients find that food loses its appeal. Nobody is quite sure why this is so, but it's probably multifactorial.

Some cancer therapies not only distort sensory perceptions but may more fundamentally impair nutrient acceptance and utilization. Radiotherapy to the head or neck and chemotherapy that affects the mucosa of the mouth are almost certain to interfere with the patient's ability to salivate and swallow. Radiotherapy affecting the small intestine is likely to cause malabsorption, which is often severe. Resection of a large portion of the small bowel inevitably disrupts digestion and absorption. Prolonged chemotherapy, particularly with toxic drugs, can be expected to have far-reaching systemic effects, which may affect the patient's ability to ingest, digest, or absorb food.

High-dose radiation to the abdomen almost invariably causes acute radiation enteritis. Characteristically, the patient suffers from diarrhea and malabsorption and rapidly loses weight. Vitamin deficiencies, lactose intolerance, and steatorrhea are typical. But these signs of radiation enteritis sometimes do not occur until ten years after the radiation exposure and can easily be confused with other entities, including tumor recurrence. Your awareness of this insidious effect of radiation therapy may save the patient from the trauma and expense of unnecessary reoperations.

Nutritional intervention is almost always appropriate for the patient who has become malnourished from cancer or its treatment. Preventing cachexia is preferable to trying to correct it after body tissues have already broken down. You needn't fear that by feeding the patient you'll feed his or her tumor. Feeding also doesn't interfere with therapy.

While the oncologist does not usually delay tumor chemotherapy or radiotherapy to await nutritional therapy, it's occasionally advisable to feed a high-risk, malnourished patient before a surgical procedure or in anticipation of extended radiotherapy that will interfere with the patient's ability to eat properly. In such cases it's often considered better to permit a ten-day delay in cancer therapy than to submit a severely malnourished patient to the rigors of intensive therapy that is itself debilitating.

For patients who should be able to eat but don't, a variety of subtle interventions may help. Encourage the homemaker to present the patient's food as attractively as possible. There's anecdotal support, although no hard evidence, that the appearance of food can affect the appetite.

The timing of meals sometimes makes a

Preventing cachexia: Nutritional intervention can prevent serious problems in the malnourished patient with cancer. It is occasionally advisable to delay potentially debilitating therapy until the patient's nutritional status is improved. Indulge the patient in his or her food preferences and eating times. Early satiety is a frequent problem, as is alteration in responses to tastes and odors. The patient should avoid favorite foods on a day when he is scheduled to undergo nausea-producing chemotherapy.

difference in total intake. The patient will often tolerate food better early in the day, preferring breakfast and lunch to supper or a bedtime snack. Most patients who are disinterested in eating benefit from having 5 to 6 small meals daily. This is especially true for patients who experience early satiety, a frequent complaint of patients with cancer. Still, some patients may find sitting and eating with the family at their regular mealtimes three times a day to be the incentive they need to eat better. Indulge the patient's preferences in this as well as in food choices. If one brand of food, or even water, tastes better to the patient, recommend that the family make every possible effort to provide it.

Patients with cancer often develop a hypersensitivity to odors. The smell of foods, particularly hot protein foods such as meats, can cause immediate nausea and vomiting. Sometimes an adverse reaction to a specific food stems from an association between eating that food and becoming nauseated from chemotherapy. It's best, therefore, for the patient to avoid eating his favorite foods on any day in which nausea-producing chemotherapy is anticipated.

Though it is far more difficult to renourish a cachectic patient than to maintain adequate nutritional status in the presence of cancer, various devices might persuade a debilitated, even bedridden, patient to make the considerable effort to eat. The patient's description of how food tastes and smells can be useful. In some cases, his or her sensory responses may have altered so much as to seem bizarre. There are several interventions you can suggest to the caregiver.

■ If food tastes bitter, avoid red meats, coffee, tea, chocolate, sour citrus juices, and foods cooked in metal pans. Instead, use plastic utensils and glass pots and pans. If the patient normally prefers meat to other sources of protein, choose more delicately flavored meats, such as veal and poultry, instead of beef, or marinate meat in juices, wine, or beer.

Reversing cachexia: Any of several interventions might encourage a cachectic patient to try to eat. The patient's description of how food tastes and smells can guide you and the caregiver in substituting foods he or she finds acceptable. Also consider the textures and temperatures of foods with respect to an irritated mouth or gastrointestinal disturbances.

■ If food tastes too sweet, avoid highly sweetened foods or dilute the flavor with lemon, other sour juices, mayonnaise, vinegar, or soy sauce. Patients sometimes find the sweet taste less objectionable when the foods are served cold or frozen instead of warm or at room temperature.

■ If food has little or no taste—patients commonly complain that all food tastes like cardboard—add herbs and spices, salt, sugar, and prepared sauces. Encourage experimentation. Because the sensations of taste and odor are so intimately related, some patients find that foods taste better because they smell better. Serving food warm instead of cold increases the aroma. Adding odorous foods, such as garlic, onions, and cabbage-family vegetables, may help if the patient will accept them.

■ If dental problems or stomatitis or mucositis secondary to chemotherapy or radiotherapy makes the texture of foods particularly important, serve soft, ground, or puréed foods, preferably at room temperature—never hot or frozen. Avoid extremely salty or sour foods, especially with liquids.

■ If milk products seem to be poorly tolerated, experiment by eliminating them from the diet. At least some degree of lactose intolerance is to be expected in patients who have had radiation therapy to the abdominal, pelvic, or pancreatic areas or who have had abdominal surgery. Cachectic patients may also lose their tolerance for lactose.

- If diarrhea, nausea, or vomiting seems to be a frequent accompaniment to meals, limit fluids during a meal of solid foods. Some patients seem able to take liquids one hour before or after the meal. Others may benefit from a glass of wine with their meals. It also often helps to limit consumption of food fiber, which may be irritating to a sensitive digestive tract. In particular, avoid whole grain flours, nuts, seeds, dried fruit, and fruit with tough skin. Some patients react badly to mixing hot and cold foods. If gastrointestinal disturbances occur, serve all the hot foods first, and permit a short delay before serving the cold foods.

When the patient cannot consume an adequate diet despite the family's best efforts, nutrients might be increased by means of one of the following devices:

- Giving snacks of liquid nutritional supplements in flavors selected by the patient. Limit quantities to 4 oz/h.
- Adding 2 tbsp of dry skim milk powder to recipes calling for milk.
- Using grated cheese as a condiment.
- Adding a tablespoon of sour cream to food whenever possible (it would take almost ½ C of plain yogurt to equal the 70 calories in 1 tbsp of sour cream).
- Sprinkling chopped hard-cooked eggs on salads or cooked vegetables. Uncooked eggs, as in homemade eggnogs, carry some risk of contamination.
- Keeping snack foods readily available—especially those that can be eaten without a delay for preparation. In the time it takes to prepare food, the patient may lose interest in eating.

If the patient cannot secure adequate calories through oral feedings, you may want to supplement intake with enteral or parenteral feedings, at least early in the course of the disease. At the terminal stage of disease, the patient who seeks only relief of pain and has no interest in prolonging life may interpret such interventions—or even encouragements to eat more—as interference. ■

REFERENCES

1. DeWys WD: Pathophysiology of cancer cachexia: Current understanding and areas for future research. *Cancer Res* 1982;42(suppl 2):721S–6S.
2. Jonsen AR: A concord in medical ethics. *Ann Intern Med* 1983;99:261–4.
3. Newell GR, Ellison NM (eds): *Nutrition and Cancer: Etiology and Treatment.* New York, Raven Press Pubs, 1981.
4. Nielsen SS, Vickers ZM, Theologides A: Food odor perception and food aversions in cancer patients, abstracted. *Proc Am Assoc Cancer Res Am Soc Clin Oncol* 1980;21:377.
5. Schloen LH, Rivlin RS: Cancer, in Paige DM, (ed): *Manual of Clinical Nutrition.* St Louis, CV Mosby Co, 1983, pp 5.1–25.4.
6. Shils ME: Nutritional problems induced by cancer. *Med Clin North Am* 1979;63:1009–25.
7. Theologides A: Cancer cachexia. *Cancer* 1979; 43(suppl):2004–12.
8. Trant AS, Serin J, Douglass HO: Is taste related to anorexia in cancer patients? *Am J Clin Nutr* 1982;36:45–88.

Who Is Malnourished?

A global assessment of your patient's nutritional status starts with his or her general appearance—hair, skin, energy level, and apparent underweight or overweight. You'll easily recognize extreme undernutrition without making any measurements: Is there evidence of muscle wasting, particularly in the proximal musculature of the upper arms and the temporal musculature? Does the patient's face look gaunt? Malnutrition presents more often as overnutrition than undernutrition, even in low socioeconomic groups, and that, too, you'll recognize easily.

Growth curves over time are almost foolproof for identifying the malnourished child, but they are not so useful over the short run because children do not normally grow along their percentile curves all the time. Weight/height data also are useful. A child whose weight is over the 95th percentile and whose weight to height ratio is over the 50th percentile is probably eating too much. If his weight is below the 5th percentile for height, the child is probably undernourished.

A specific nutritional deficiency is unusual in Americans of any age. Nevertheless, alcoholics may suffer extreme deficiencies of vitamin B complex. Patients with various types of malabsorption may develop a deficiency of fat-soluble vitamins, calcium, zinc, magnesium, or iron. An occasional deficiency disease has been reported in other populations, most notably the elderly who, for a variety of socioeconomic and medical reasons, develop a "tea-and-toast" nutritional pattern. Deficiency diseases to consider in various populations include beriberi, cretinism, pellagra, rickets, and scurvy.

Subtle undernutrition generally poses no major risk as long as no insult is superimposed. If a marginally undernourished person experiences the stress of a surgical procedure, an automobile accident, or an acute infectious illness, however, his recovery may be jeopardized. A diet and drug history can help identify such at-risk patients (see Table 6).

To elicit pertinent information quickly, ask the patient whether his eating has changed recently. A particularly useful question is "Is the way you eat now different from the way you ate six months ago?" You won't get precise answers, but you should get a general idea. Members of the patient's family may have useful observations about the patient's eating pattern, too. Any dramatic loss or gain of weight over the past six months may also be significant.

The most efficient single question may be, "What *don't* you eat?" You will learn immediately whether the patient consumes milk products, whether he's philosophically opposed to eating meat or eggs, and whether he habitually follows one fad diet after another. The response that uses phrases like "organic foods" or "natural foods" *might* signal the patient's rejection of an adequate diet. But remember, concerned laymen deserve at least as much of the credit for the current interest in nutrition in the United States as the medical profession does. Patients tend to tell you honestly what they normally eat—except in the case of excessive alcohol consumption.

> Initial assessment of nutritional status: The patient's appearance can give you a broad nutritional overview. The most efficient question in the diet history is probably "What don't you eat?" Major, recent changes in eating habits or weight may be significant. For more detailed information, consult a dietitian or use a diet history form as necessary.

The ethnic or racial background of a patient often influences his food choices. Black, Italian, German, and Greek Americans tend to eat diets high in fat. The typical Oriental, Indian, and vegetarian diets are high in fiber. Sodium restriction is difficult for people who follow Oriental, Mexican, Black, Spanish, Italian, Jewish, or German diets.

A thorough nutrition history, which would take an experienced dietitian close to an hour, is not cost-effective as part of a regular office visit. As needed, however, you can make use of nutritionists and dieticians who are able to spend the necessary time with a patient. And as part of an office visit, you can ask your secretary, receptionist, or nurse to help patients complete a questionnaire on nutrition.

Your knowledge of a patient's preexisting medical condition or disease can serve as a clue to either impending or existent malnutrition.

■ Expect multiple nutritional deficiencies in patients with gastrointestinal (GI) problems,

TABLE 6. Examples of Nutritional Deficiencies That May Result from Drug Use

Drug	Possible Deficit	Mechanism
Alcohol	Potassium, magnesium, zinc Vitamin B$_1$, others	Malabsorption Insufficient intake
Amphetamines	Many	Appetite suppression
Anorectics	Many	Appetite suppression
Antacids	Phosphates	Fecal loss
Anticoagulants	Vitamin K	Antagonism
Anticonvulsants	Calcium	Accelerated metabolism of vitamin D
	Folic acid	Decreased absorption
Aspirin and nonsteroidal anti-inflammatory agents	Iron	Blood loss
Cholestyramine (Questran)	Fat, fat-soluble vitamins	Fecal loss
Colchicine	Fat, fat-soluble vitamins, lactose	Enzyme damage
Contraceptives (oral)	Vitamin B$_6$	Metabolic interaction
Cytotoxic agents	Folic acid Many others	Antagonism Appetite suppression
Glucocorticoids	Calcium	Reduced calcium transport
Glutethimide (Doriden)	Calcium, potassium	Impaired transport
Laxatives	Many	Fecal loss
Penicillamine (Cuprimine, Depen Titratabs)	Copper, zinc	Chelation
Sulfasalazine (Azulfidine)	Folic acid	Malabsorption
Thiazides	Potassium, sodium	Urinary loss

Clues to nutritional deficiencies: Medical conditions that foster malnutrition include gastrointestinal problems, cancer, and depression. Pregnancy, lactation, infancy, and old age may place a person at risk for nutritional deficiency. Health-food enthusiasts may also be at risk. Various laboratory data, evaluated in association with the clinical picture, can help identify malnutrition before clinical lesions become obvious. Hair analysis is of little diagnostic value.

such as inflammatory bowel disease, especially with diarrhea and fever, or other GI conditions that cause malabsorption.

- Patients with cancer are at risk for nutritional deficiencies from both the disease and its treatment.
- Depressed patients are often anorectic and may become malnourished.
- Some elderly patients, especially those who live alone, may be at special risk for malnutrition.
- Patients receiving medication may be at risk for specific deficiencies.
- People on fad diets may be at risk.

Certain life stages may render a person especially sensitive to poor nutrition. This would include not only old age, but also pregnancy, lactation, and infancy. Teenagers, while constitutionally robust, may be cavalier about their eating habits.

Nutritional imbalances also are sometimes seen in health-food enthusiasts who take megadoses of nutritional supplements. Age is no selector. Some elderly people in retirement communities subscribe to such excesses, as do college students. Sports enthusiasts sometimes overdo both exercise schedule and dietary supplements. Some of these people have developed chronic diarrhea from their altered diets and don't recognize the relationship.

An apparently deficient diet is not sufficient evidence of malnutrition unless you also find chemical and/or clinical abnormalities. Nutritional deficiencies develop along a predictable sequence, starting with reduced oral intake of or increased requirements for certain nutrients. The first subclinical effect is reduced tissue saturation, which you might detect by means of changes in blood and urine tests. Biochemical imbalances then follow. You might see alterations in enzyme levels and urine and blood metabolites. Finally, clinical lesions occur. During a physical examination, you would see changes in weight and in the appearance of hair, skin, mouth, and gait (see Table 7).

Various laboratory data can help identify

TABLE 7. Clinical Features That Suggest a Nutrient Imbalance

Clinical Signs	Possible Nutrient Imbalance	Specific Patients at Risk
Hair		
Dull, dry, brittle	Protein-calorie malnutrition Iodine deficiency Selenium excess	Undernourished people Rare in United States today Food faddists
Hair loss	Vitamin A excess	Patients overtreated for severe acne, food faddists
Eyes		
Night blindness	Vitamin A deficiency	Undernourished people, especially children
Optic neuritis	Vitamin B_{12} deficiency	Vegetarians
Photophobia	Vitamin A or B_2 deficiency	
Mouth		
Inflamed, burning lips	Vitamin B_1 or B_2 deficiency	Alcoholics, generally undernourished people
Gingivitis	Vitamin A, niacin, or vitamin C deficiency	Alcoholics, elderly poor
Aphthous stomatitis	Folic acid deficiency	Patients receiving cancer chemotherapy
Pale mucosa, depapillated tongue	Iron or vitamin B_6 deficiency	Women of reproductive age, infants, patients with chronic blood loss
Painful tongue	Vitamin B_6 or niacin deficiency	Alcoholics
Mottled tooth enamel	Fluoride excess	Children
Poorly formed teeth	Vitamin D deficiency	Children, especially those receiving prolonged antibiotic therapy

TABLE 7. Clinical Features That Suggest a Nutrient Imbalance

Clinical Signs	Possible Nutrient Imbalance	Specific Patients at Risk
Skin		
Dehydration	Sodium deficiency	Patients using diuretics or vomiting
Edema	Protein deficiency	Not usual in the United States, except for cachectic patients
Pallor	Iron, folic acid, or vitamin B_{12} deficiency	Women of reproductive age, vegetarians, patients with chronic blood loss
Increased yellow-orange pigmentation	Carotine excess	Food faddists
Dry, scaly, or acneiform lesions	Vitamin A or fatty acid deficiency	Dieters
Petechiae	Vitamin C deficiency	The elderly, especially those living alone; alcoholics; infants whose mothers ingested megadoses of vitamin C
Musculoskeletal		
Weakness, fatigue	Potassium	Patients using thiazides
	Vitamin B_1 deficiency	Dieters, alcoholics
Decreased bone mass	Calcium deficiency	Postmenopausal women, patients with lactose intolerance
	Vitamin D deficiency	Patients confined indoors
Swelling of long bones	Vitamin A excess	Food faddists
Swollen, painful legs	Vitamin C deficiency	The elderly, especially those living alone; alcoholics; infants whose mothers ingested megadoses of vitamin C
Gastrointestinal		
Bleeding	Vitamin K deficiency	Patients who eschew green, leafy vegetables
Diarrhea, flatulence	Fiber, fruit or vitamin D excess	
	Niacin deficiency	Dieters, alcoholics
Nausea, cramps	Selenium or zinc excess	Food faddists
Neurologic		
Ataxia	Vitamin B_{12} deficiency	Vegetarians
Dementia	Niacin deficiency	Alcoholics
Depression	Vitamin B_6 deficiency	Women using oral contraceptives
Irritability	Protein-calorie deficiency	Persons on starvation diets
	Selenium excess	Food faddists
Footdrop and wristdrop	Vitamin B_1 deficiency	Alcoholics
Peripheral neuropathy	Vitamin B_6 deficiency	Alcoholics
Tremor	Magnesium deficiency	Alcoholics

Clinical Signs	Possible Nutrient Imbalance	Specific Patients at Risk
Metabolic		
Obesity	Caloric excess	Common
Anemias	Iron, folic acid, or vitamin B_{12} deficiency	Vegetarians, patients with chronic blood loss
Anergy	Protein deficiency	Patients with infection (rare in ambulatory patients)
Goiter	Iodine deficiency	Residents of "goiter belt" (rare in United States today)
Hypertension	Sodium excess (?)	
Siderosis	Iron excess	Transfused patients
Slow healing	Linoleic acid deficiency Zinc deficiency	Patients on fat-restricted diets
Vascular		
Flushing, burning, and tingling in neck, face, hands	Niacin excess	Patients overtreated for hyperlipidemia

subclinical malnutrition. Microcytosis in the RBC differential may indicate iron deficiency for instance, while macrocytosis may indicate vitamin B_{12} or folate deficiency. Evaluate the laboratory data in association with the total clinical picture. A patient with a normal serum iron level might still be iron deficient because of diminished iron storage in the bone marrow not yet reflected in blood iron levels. Similarly, a malnourished patient may have a normal serum albumin level. Total protein is of little diagnostic value.

Hair analysis is frequently advertised in the lay press as a method for evaluating nutritional status. Since the hair may be affected by age, sex, natural hair color, hair conditioners, sprays, shampoos, and environmental pollution, however, hair analysis is not a reliable test for dietary vitamin or mineral deficiencies.*

Cytotoxic leukocyte testing has been declared by the Health Care Financing Administration of the Department of Health and Human Services to be of no value in detecting food allergies. For most allergies, only a painstaking elimination diet can identify the specific foods that may be causing problems. Though a breath test is available to confirm a suspected lactose intolerance, it is perhaps simpler to try dietary lactose restriction. ■

REFERENCES

1. Goodhart RS, Shils ME (eds): *Modern Nutrition in Health and Disease*, ed 6. Philadelphia, Lea & Febiger, 1980.
2. Grant JP, Custer PB, Thurlow J: Current techniques of nutritional assessment. *Surg Clin North Am* 1981;61:437–63.
3. Hubbard VS, Hubbard LR. Clinical assessment of nutritional status, in Walker WA, Watkins JB (eds): *Nutrition in Pediatrics: Basic Science and Clinical Application*. Boston, Little Brown & Co, 1985, pp 121–150.
4. Nestle M: *Nutrition in Clinical Practice*. Greenbrae, Calif, Jones Medical Pubns, 1985, pp 64–72.
5. Reuler JB, Broudy VC, Cooney TG: Adult scurvy. *JAMA* 1985;258:805–7.
6. Roe DA: Effects of drugs on nutrition. *Life Sci* 1974;15:1219–34.
7. Roe DA: Nutrient and drug interactions. *Nutr Rev* 1984;42:141–54.
8. Winick M (ed): *Nutrition and Drugs*. (Current Concepts in Nutrition, vol 12). New York, John Wiley & Sons Inc, 1983.

---

*Barrett S: Commercial hair analysis: Science or scam? *JAMA* 1985;254:1041–5.

What the Hell, I Can Always Drive a Truck!

D. P. Eigo
EDITOR

Scott E. Henjum
MANAGING EDITOR

Steven C. Taylor
ART DIRECTOR

Peggy S. Navarre
ASSOCIATE ART DIRECTOR

Marcie Tibbling
COPY EDITOR

Although the trucking industry has had a fair record of success in modernization, fuel conservation, and the provision of service to an increasingly complex economy, growing accident figures and negative public attitudes are an indication that there has not been matching success in upgrading driver quality and training. This series of editorials attempts to make trucking management and the general public aware of the importance of maintaining professional standards and mature behavior among drivers.

Fleet Owner is circulated to owners and executives of trucking fleets. "What the Hell, I Can Always Drive a Truck!" first appeared in the September 1986, October 1986, and November 1986 issues of *Fleet Owner,* published by McGraw-Hill Financial Services Company. © 1986. Reprinted with permission.

The problems with driver safety, driver licensing, and driver training —once you begin investigating them— are like an onion: when you remove one layer, you find more layers, more problems.

There are enough facts now available to demand that a major, and multifaceted, effort be brought to bear upon all aspects of driver quality. The public pressure for tougher controls and stricter law enforcement on trucks is as strong as ever.

For a long time, segments of the trucking industry have been happy to "let George do it." And "George," in the person of the more conscientious fleet operators, trucking-group professionals, manufacturer or supplier leaders, or in the ranks of state and federal governments, has worked to improve the quality of trucks, truck drivers, and the trucking environment.

NINETEEN TO GO

But, in 19 states today, says a report of a National Highway Traffic Safety Administration National Forum on the Driver License Compact and Classified Licensing, "any person licensed to drive an automobile can legally drive a tractor-trailer." What's worse, in some of those states the driving test is little more than a demonstration of the notorious World War II Army physical: "If you can see lightning and hear thunder, and if the body is warm, you're in!" (Incidentally, the number of states used to be 20, but Oregon recently adopted a classified licensing system for drivers of heavy rigs, to go into effect Oct. 1. See FO—8/86.)

In our research for this and the next couple of editorials, we have begun to isolate some problems and causes.

There are very few villains in the story; and a lot of dedicated men and women among the "good guys." But there are also some historic conflicts.

For instance, just about everyone realizes that to get a uniform licensing and classification system, a federal-type standard must be created.

But since the states depend upon licensing revenue and—more important—since they are, and must be, responsible for enforcement, they must not give up their responsibility.

And right now, because each has had to "grow its own," we lack a unanimous 50-state definition even of what constitutes a "commercial driver." By the same token, the states also don't agree on what constitutes a reportable vehicle accident.

If we still can't define an accident, consider the chances of defining a "good driver." The quality of the driving schools—the starting-point for our most recent research—is "all over the lot," and we mean that intentionally.

There are a number of state-run or state-authorized schools of high quality, yet three or four states do not even maintain schools. There are some good commercial schools, yet organizations of the "blue suede shoes" character exist that manage to attract both students and government financing. There are schools that offer minimal practice time behind the wheel of a heavy-duty rig, and some that never take a student out of the parking lot, and never conduct a single nighttime exercise.

Says Robert Knoop, founder and executive director of the National Assn. of Truck Driving Schools, fleet executives must understand that many a driving school graduate, if hired, "will drive more miles for you in the first week on the job than he drove for his entire training period."

MORE THAN ONE BEGINNING

The needs are many, and the effort can't wait for each goal to be met one at a time. There are needs for coordination (and state authorities, fleets, driver groups, insurance experts, and industry executives are joining together). There are needs for standards of licensing, of instruction, and of testing (and we see a beginning there). There are existing and historical barriers of state/federal separation that must be thoughtfully approached (and that has begun). There must be curriculum standards for the schools themselves (and an expert group is at work on that problem).

As Jim Johnston, president of The Owner-Operator Independent Drivers Assn. of America, said: "The professional truck driver is damned tired of taking the rap for the conduct of hundreds of thousands of unqualified individuals turned loose by the states each year who tarnish the image and the reputation of the entire industry." Correcting that is only going to come through a cooperative effort unlike anything seen before in trucking. ∎

We Don't Have to Wait to Start Improving Driver Training

The chorus is growing: We as a nation and as an industry must take every step necessary—no matter how expensive it may appear to be in the short term—to get the irresponsible, unprofessional driver off the road.

About 95% of the problem, we're afraid, is not "killer trucks" but "killer drivers." However, as we observed last month, the federal agencies, the Congress, and some potent industry groups are attacking that basic problem.

THE EFFORT IS PAYING OFF

We can expect to see—within the next several months—help from Washington. There is a Bureau of Motor Carrier Safety "proposed minimum standards and model curriculum for training tractor-trailer drivers," and the National Highway Traffic Safety Administration has a Truck Operators Road Qualifying Exam" (TORQUE). There is a state-participation program to drastically increase roadside inspections of commercial vehicles. There is a real push for a single commercial driver's license, with standards for testing, qualification, and classification of drivers. There are elevated skill demands for operators of rigs hauling hazardous materials.

Then there are the laudable efforts of the Trucking Industry Alliance, the Commercial Vehicle Safety Alliance, the National Assn. of Driver Training Schools, the National Safety Council, and, the most promising, the Professional Truck Driver Institute of America, all of which are bringing pressure to bear on improving the quality of the training available to the beginning driver.

The fleets are virtually unanimous in their support of the effort, even as they warn us that trucking cannot afford to demand experienced drivers at all levels of the industry. Every one of us who is acquainted with young people entering the work force has heard the complaint: "They all want me to have experience, but no one wants to give me a chance to get some."

But given all that, we strongly suggest that while fleets work toward that longer-term objective, there is no need for them to hold off from taking the first steps to improve the "state of the art" of their drivers.

We recently visited with two fleets in preparation for an article on driver training for next month's issue. In those preliminary visits alone we came across clear evidence of success in "retraining" of current drivers.

Retraining doesn't mean putting a veteran employee or contractor through kindergarten.

The assumption is that most such drivers are professionals, and to infer otherwise would harm the whole idea.

Rather, two of the fleet we talked to indicate that retraining of the professional usually takes the form of refresher talks, films that jog the thoughtful driver into reexamining some ingrained driving habits, and flat-out training courses for new and unfamiliar equipment. (All trucks and tractors are not the same, and no true professional could be trapped into thinking so.)

THE WILLING PROFESSIONAL

In most training programs, the veteran drivers seem to join the newer employees in the classroom without any reluctance. Most of us are pleased to find that our management is willing to spend money and effort to help us do our jobs better. It's no different with the drivers who have responsibility for all that expensive equipment and cargo; they like recognition of their influence on the company's success. And, like most of us, they're often willing to help newcomers learn the ropes.

As one truck-fleet executive put it: "Retraining seems to affect our veteran drivers more directly in terms of attitude. They'll come up to you after the course and say they've discovered areas in which they think they can improve."

In both cases, the fleet executives in charge have already seen stronger evidence than simple attitude. Both had been holding their accidents/million miles ratio at about the national level of 11; both have cut the ratio to below six! That means lower insurance costs, fewer insurance claims, less damage to cargo, and better driver and customer relations all around.

Above all, let's keep working toward those better schools, better curricula, and better drivers. But let's not wait to start the effort "at home." ∎

Okay, Who Wants to Volunteer to Be the Chief S.O.B.?

It has been popular for public speakers to decry the passage of trucking's "knight of the road" and the intrusion of the "cowboy," or the reckless, incompetent driver. It has also been fashionable to point the finger at a breakdown in the national moral fiber and "young people today." It has been popular, fashionable, and pointless.

Pointless because lots of us who deal with young people today know most of them to be as dedicated, as principled, and as hardworking as any of our contemporaries. We also know them to be devoted to their friends, their communities, and their work. (They may be a little more outspoken about their jobs and their bosses than we were raised to be, but that ain't necessarily bad.)

We would suggest that it is more to the point to try to see what is really happening to the driver community, and then encourage and develop the true professionals while doing everything we can to eliminate the bad, irresponsible, and dangerous driver.

DIFFERENT TIMES, DIFFERENT PEOPLE

We haven't undertaken a national survey of drivers to establish these data, but we have talked to enough industry experts to have built some ideas.

Consider the "source" of most untrained drivers. Talk to a 30-year veteran driver and he'll tell you of years growing up on the farm, where a young man learned how to keep the equipment running because "my old man told me I had to," and who learned to run tractors, harvesters, and trucks at an early—sometimes tender—age. Very often, if that young person came of age in the 1940s, the farm experience got expanded through the courtesy of Uncle Sam, with some time in an Army motor pool. For such a veteran, the climb into the cab of an 18-wheeler was not so forbidding.

Talk to some of the younger truck drivers today and you may well find that they are small-town or even big-city people, who may have tinkered with cars while they were growing up, but who generally don't have their predecessor's depth of experience.

We recently spent some time among driver trainers and driver-training-school personnel. Those people all recognize some basic truths that many of us have forgotten: 1) learning something new is difficult, and retaining what one has learned usually calls for refresher work; 2) individuals who choose to sign up with a "professional driving school" frequently have already tried other careers and are looking for another opportunity; 3) even the best of training schools is able to do little more than conduct a basic screening of the student, acquaint him or her with the rudiments of driving, and combine that with a minimum of "hands-on" experience; and 4) some driver-training schools seem more dedicated to taking advantage of available government student funding than they are to producing qualified graduates.

As every veteran driver knows, the vehicle population on the road has changed—with bigger commercial vehicles and smaller private cars, most of them traveling the same speed. In addition, the equipment itself has changed, with reductions in rolling resistance, with lighter-weight vehicles, and with longer and wider configurations.

The climate in which many of today's drivers work once they get behind the wheel has also changed. For good or ill, many modern drivers are locked into tight pickup and delivery schedules. No driver who stands to lose his place at the loading dock if he is late is likely to stop en route to assist a stranded motorist. (Before he went to the rescue of the damsel, the knight of yore had to feel pretty sure that the king wasn't going to lop off his head for showing up late at the Round Table.)

If the highway was ever a place for an amateur to learn "on the job," it sure isn't now.

THE MANAGEMENT BURDEN

U. S. economists rank truck driving as a future "growth industry," and predict a need for many more drivers. The industry, the government, and the public today share a concern for the professionalism of those drivers.

Unfortunately, fleet management is the only final control, the only barrier to protect the public, the cargo, and the industry itself. That means that when an unqualified driver tries to get behind the wheel—no matter how eager or how well-intentioned—it is fleet management who must be "the s.o.b. who says 'no'." ∎

Toxic Waste

Marcia Ruff
MANAGING EDITOR

Most automobile repair shops are generators of small amounts of hazardous waste. A change in the Resource Conservation and Recovery Act brought this problem into the spotlight, and for the first time these shops had to deal with complex environmental regulations and their substantial legal and financial liabilities. This article attempts to explain how the law affects shop owners, what their obligations are, and how they can best comply.

Motor is written for professional auto mechanics. "Toxic Waste" first appeared in the December 1985 issue of *Motor,* published by The Hearst Corporation. © 1985. Reprinted with permission.

A Shop Owner's Survival Guide to the Latest Hazardous Waste Laws

When your third-grader comes home from school and tells you the cover story of *My Weekly Reader* is about hazardous waste, you can be sure the fear of poisoning our countryside has penetrated deeply into the nation's consciousness.

It seems as though everybody knows someone who was forced to abandon a well because poisons leached into it from the local landfill, or someone who found a hidden cache of old chemical drums and didn't know what to do with them, or someone else who discovered that a landlord in town was burning used oil laced with an unholy mixture of chemical residues. These situations make people afraid. They don't know what's safe and what isn't. They don't know how to handle problems that arise, or even who to ask for answers to their questions.

The upshot of this public fear and confusion is the desire to put the responsibility for solving the problem on someone. And that someone is going to be businesses that generate hazardous waste—including your business. It used to be environmental laws were directed at the Big Guys like chemical manufacturers, mining companies and utilities. But that's no longer the case.

New laws that became effective August 5, 1985, require companies that generate only 100 kilograms (220 pounds) of hazardous waste a month—that's about half a 55-gallon drum—to begin meeting some of the same waste handling regulations as larger companies. Almost 40% of auto repair shops now come under federal hazardous waste laws, according to one government survey. Chances are, your business is one of these.

Companies in this new category are called small quantity generators, a group that includes all businesses that generate between 100 and 1,000 kilograms of hazardous waste a month. The federal Environmental Protection Agency (EPA) estimates that about 175,000 businesses fall into this group. The largest single group is motor vehicle repair shops, which encompasses about half the newly affected companies. Dry cleaners, printers, photography processors and small manufacturers are among the remainder.

Repair shops, body shops and fleet-servicing facilities generate hazardous waste primarily through two operations: cleaning and painting. The problem chemicals include spent solvents, ignitable wastes like paint thinner and enamel reducers, strong acids and alkalis used for degreasing and rust removal, and heavy metal pigment in paint.

Under the new regulations, waste that you may have been pouring down the drain or dumping into the dirt behind the shop will have to be disposed of properly. In many cases, this will mean filling out a manifest to track the waste, and contracting with a licensed hauler to take it to a certified hazardous waste disposal facility.

Yes, the new rules are probably going to cost you money. You'll have to pay more for transportation and disposal. There will be records to keep. You'll have to setup a container system to store your waste and teach your employees to use it properly.

But you don't have a choice. These requirements are only the beginning of a tough new

EPA Regional Contacts

EPA Region 1 (Connecticut, Maine, Massachusetts, New Hampshire, Rhode Island, Vermont)

Waste Management Division
State Waste Programs Branch
John F. Kennedy Federal Building
Boston, MA 02203
(617) 223-1922

EPA Region 2 (New Jersey, New York, Puerto Rico, Virgin Islands)

Air and Waste Management Division, Solid Waste Branch
26 Federal Plaza
New York, NY 10278
(212) 264-0504

EPA Region 3 (Delaware, District of Columbia, Maryland, Pennsylvania, Virginia, West Virginia)

Hazardous Waste Management Division, Waste Management Branch
841 Chestnut Street
Philadelphia, PA 19107
(215) 597-0980

EPA Region 4 (Alabama, Florida, Georgia, Kentucky, Mississippi, North Carolina, South Carolina, Tennessee)

Air and Waste Management Division, Residuals Management Branch
345 Courtland Street, NE
Atlanta, GA 30365
(404) 257-3016

EPA Region 5 (Illinois, Indiana, Michigan, Minnesota, Ohio, Wisconsin)

Waste Management Division, Solid Waste Branch
230 South Dearborn Street
Chicago, IL 60604
(312) 886-7435

EPA Region 6 (Arkansas, Louisiana, New Mexico, Oklahoma, Texas)

1201 Elm Street
InterFirst Two Building
Dallas, TX 75270
(214) 767-9885

EPA Region 7 (Iowa, Kansas, Missouri, Nebraska)

726 Minnesota Avenue
Kansas City, KS 66101
(816) 374-6534

EPA Region 8 (Colorado, Montana, North Dakota, South Dakota, Utah, Wyoming)

Waste Management Division, Hazardous Waste Branch
(8HWM-ON)
One Denver Place, Suite 1300
999 18th Street
Denver, CO 80202-2413
(303) 293-1502

EPA Region 9 (Arizona, California, Hawaii, Nevada, Guam, Marianas)

Toxics and Waste Management Division
Waste Programs Branch
215 Fremont Street
San Francisco, CA 94105
(415) 974-7472

EPA Region 10 (Alaska, Idaho, Oregon, Washington)

Hazardous Waste Division, Waste Management Branch
1200 Sixth Avenue
Seattle, WA 98101
(206) 442-2777

---

approach toward hazardous waste. Far from fading away, such regulations are likely to become even tougher. Already the EPA is preparing the next tier of rules for small quantity generators, to be implemented next year. Fortunately, if you set up systems now to comply with current regulations, you shouldn't find it too difficult to accommodate any new ones that come along.

And in any case, the cost of compliance pales next to the cost of non-compliance. Penalties for failing to handle your waste properly could total $50,000 and two years in prison. Add to that punishment the stratospheric cost of being involved in a cleanup should your hazardous waste wind up where it is not supposed to be. Few if any small businesses could survive the fine, legal fees, and cleanup cost.

There are also other reasons to comply with the law. The years spent ignoring hazardous waste have left Americans with a cleanup bill of some $100 billion, according to the Congressional Office of Technology Assessment. One way or another, taxpayers will have to foot this bill. In addition, there are not enough disposal sites to hold the hazardous waste already in existence. So it's in everyone's best interest to reduce the amount of hazardous waste produced in this country, and to handle the remaining waste responsibly.

In the following article, we'll give you a practical guide to the new regulations, explain how to comply with them, and look at ways to cut your cost of compliance as much as possible.

NEW REGULATIONS

Giles Mason (not his real name), the owner of an auto body shop in Maryland, thought he was doing the right thing when he hired an experienced transporter to remove his drums of waste paint thinner.

But rather than take the thinner to a disposal facility, the hauler took it to his uncle's farm in suburban Maryland. His uncle thought waste thinner would be just the ticket for killing weeds along the roadside and fence line.

A year or so later, the uncle sold the farm. When the new owner surveyed his 160 acres, he found a pile of empty drums in a gully. Neatly stenciled on the drums, courtesy of the company that had sold them, was Giles Mason's name and address.

The Maryland Department of Health informed Mason that not only did he have to take the drums away and dispose of them properly, but he also had to remove the contaminated soil beneath them. The final bill was $25,000 for the cleanup plus a $10,000 fine from the state. Mason's liability insurance didn't cover environmental damage. The cost forced him out of business.

It hardly seems fair that Mason had to suffer for the bad judgment of his hauler. But that's the law. The current approach to pollution control is that businesses that generate hazardous waste never lose responsibility for that waste. Even if the transporter or the disposal site operator makes a mistake, the generator still bears financial responsibility.

The federal legislation controlling hazardous waste is the Resource Conservation and Recovery Act of 1976 (RCRA), known familiarly as "Rick-Rah." The heart of the legislation is a manifest system to track hazardous waste at every stage, so that the identity of the generator is always known.

The original RCRA legislation required businesses that generated more than 1,000 kilograms of toxic waste a month to have an EPA identification number, fill out a manifest describing the specific wastes they are shipping, and make certain a licensed hauler takes them to a certified treatment, storage or disposal facility.

Businesses generating less than 1,000 kilograms a month merely had to make certain they disposed of their waste properly, which in most cases meant sending it to the local landfill with the rest of their garbage.

In November 1984, Congress directed the EPA to write new regulations for small quantity generators. The new toxic waste regulations took effect August 5, 1985. Now, all small quantity generators must complete portions of the Uniform Hazardous Waste Manifest when they ship more than 100 kilograms of hazardous waste off their premises.

Unlike the law covering larger businesses, the small quantity generator law doesn't currently require businesses to use transporters licensed by the EPA to haul hazardous waste, nor does it require them to send it to facilities certified to accept hazardous waste. However, in reality, few ordinary waste haulers or landfills will accept materials accompanied by a manifest, which all small generators *are* required to complete.

As a result, the new regulations do in fact force many small auto repair and body shops to use the same procedures as any large quantity generator of toxic waste.

The law may soon catch up with this reality. The EPA is preparing further regulations for release by March 31, 1986. The regulations are not yet available in final form, but will probably require small generators to use licensed transporters and to send their waste to a hazardous waste disposal facility.

Also, in complying with hazardous waste

laws, keep in mind that federal rules only set minimum standards. States are permitted to set stricter standards if they choose, and many do. For example, 15 states already require small generators to ship waste to hazardous waste facilities. Others require a state manifest and generator identification number. Still others have set their own standards for amounts and types of waste to be regulated.

It is imperative that you contact your own state environmental protection agency. All state agencies are listed in the box on pages 200–203. When you call or write for information, ask for the person responsible for small quantity generators. He or she will tell you about the applicable state regulations.

COMPLYING WITH RCRA

In general, hazardous waste displays one or more of the following characteristics:

- **Ignitable**—substances that catch fire easily, such as solvents or paint thinner;
- **Corrosive**—chemicals that can eat through metal or other containers, or burn skin on contact, such as strong acids or alkalis;
- **Reactive**—materials that bubble on contact with water or may explode upon contact with air or water, such as perchlorates or peroxides;
- **Toxic**—compounds that are poisonous to humans and other organisms, such as metal-bearing solutions or pesticides.

The table on page 205 lists the most common automotive repair processes that generate hazardous waste. You will need to review the products in your particular shop to find out which of these chemicals you use.

In addition, some states require certain wastes to be manifested even though the federal government does not. Illinois, for example, requires a manifest for antifreeze, transmission fluid and brake fluid. Check with your state agency for special requirements.

We suggest that you collect the applicable information from the EPA and your state agency, and do a careful inventory of your shop. If you have questions about whether or not a chemical is considered a hazardous waste, check with the supplier. Also, the Material Data Safety Sheet that comes with many products lists any hazardous substances present.

Then take your inventory and compare the hazardous substances with those listed in the table on pages 206–7. This will give you the hazard class and UN/NA identification number. Make a note of these, as they are required for hazardous waste manifests.

After you have identified which hazardous wastes you produce, you need to determine if you produce between 100 and 1,000 kilograms (220 to 2,200 pounds) a month, the federal definition of a small quantity generator. Depending on the weight of the wastes, the lower limit works out to about half a 55-gallon drum. The federal EPA estimates that about 37% of auto maintenance shops across the country are small quantity generators.

Shops that produce less than 100 kilograms per month are called very small quantity generators and are exempt from the federal requirement to use a manifest. However, some states, including California, Louisiana, Minnesota and Rhode Island, have no lower limit and regulate all generators.

Very small quantity generators still need to dispose of their waste properly, which means sending it to an approved disposal site, not pouring it onto the ground or down the drain. Both of those methods could contaminate groundwater, which more than half the nation depends upon for its drinking water. In environmentally fragile areas of the country like Florida or Cape Cod, the water table may be only three to five porous feet below the shop.

Small quantities of hazardous waste should be disposed of a little bit at a time along with the rest of your trash. "Sending a gallon of solvent a week with the garbage isn't a problem," said James Moran of the New York State Department of Environmental Conservation. "However, if you've accumulated a drum of ignitable solvent, that's different. That could blow up a bulldozer operator at the landfill."

Also, if you allow your small quantities of hazardous waste to accumulate over several months, your hauler may demand a manifest. The laws and regulations governing hazardous waste are still evolving, so it's no surprise that many transporters and landfill operators are taking a "better safe than sorry" attitude and demanding documentation to cover themselves.

CUTTING DOWN WASTE

It is obviously to your economic advantage to lower your monthly output of hazardous waste to below the 100 kilogram threshold. Reducing your output is also better for the country, which is struggling to find ways to dispose of waste that already exists.

One strategy is to recycle as many wastes as possible. If these are handled by an EPA-licensed recycler, you are permitted to deduct them from your monthly total. The most readily recycled wastes include:

- lead acid batteries;
- solvent in a parts washer that is serviced on a regular basis by a solvent recycler;
- used paint thinner that is distilled and reused;
- used crankcase oil.

Take care to keep these wastes from becoming mixed with other substances. A recycler won't accept used oil that has had paint thinner mixed in, for example. If your wastes are too impure for a recycler to handle, then you must treat them as hazardous wastes.

As MOTOR Magazine went to press, the EPA severely restricted burning waste oil in furnaces and heaters. You are now prohibited from burning oil that contains more than 5 parts per million (ppm) of arsenic, 2 ppm of cadmium, 10 ppm of chromium, 100 ppm of lead, or 4,000 ppm of halogens. You are also prohibited from burning oil that ignites at a flash point less than 100°F.

In addition, the EPA has proposed future regulations that would treat all used oil as a hazardous waste. This may eliminate recycling as an option. The biggest problem with used oil, according to Matt Strauss of the EPA, is not the oil itself, but rather that used oil is so frequently blended with other toxic substances to disguise them. The agency will hold hearings on the proposed regulations, and issue final rules before March 31, 1986.

THE MANIFEST

This is the heart of the system, the form that identifies you as the generator of a particular shipment of hazardous waste. Consequently, it is vital that you fill it out accurately and keep track of what happens to both your waste and your paperwork.

Current federal regulations only require you to use the single-copy Uniform Hazardous Waste Manifest, and to complete lines 3, 5, 9, 11, 12, 13, 14, and 16. However, many transporters and disposal sites insist upon a multiple-copy manifest and require more information than the lines cited above.

The additional information gives the transporter more flexibility. States vary widely in their hazardous waste regulations, and since many states don't have any hazardous waste disposal facilities, there is a good chance your waste will be transported to another state. You then must comply with both the requirements of your own state and those of the state for which your waste is destined.

One additional item frequently required is an EPA generator identification number. The agency currently requires numbers only for large generators, although that may change next March, too. And many states already insist that small generators have either a state number or a federal number. To apply for an identification number, write to the EPA and

State Hazardous Waste Management Agencies

Alabama
Alabama Department of Environmental Management
Land Division
1751 Federal Drive
Montgomery, Alabama 36130
(205) 271-7737

Alaska
Department of Environmental Conservation
Hazardous Waste Program
Pouch O
Juneau, Alaska 99811
(907) 465-2666

Arizona
Arizona Department of Health Services
2005 North Central, Room 301
Phoenix, Arizona 85004
(602) 257-0022

Arkansas
Solid and Hazardous Waste Division
Arkansas Department of Pollution Control and Ecology
P.O. Box 9583
Little Rock, Arkansas 72219
(501) 562-7444

California
Department of Health Services
714 P Street
Sacramento, California 95814
(916) 324-1781

Colorado
Waste Management Division
Colorado Department of Health
4210 East 11th Avenue
Denver, Colorado 80220
(303) 320-8333 ext. 4364

Connecticut
Hazardous Materials Management Unit
Connecticut Department of Environmental Protection
165 Capitol Avenue
Hartford, Connecticut 06106
(203) 566-5712

Delaware
William Razor, Supervisor
Solid and Hazardous Waste Management Branch
Delaware Department of Natural Resources and Environmental Control
89 Kings Highway
P.O. Box 1401
Dover, Delaware 19901
(302) 736-4781

District of Columbia
Department of Consumer and Regulatory Affairs
Pesticides and Hazardous Waste Branch
5010 Overlook Avenue, S.W., Room 114
Washington, D.C. 20032
(202) 767-8414

Florida
Solid and Hazardous Waste
Florida Department of Environmental Regulation
2600 Blair Stone Road
Tallahassee, Florida 32301
(904) 488-0300

Georgia
Georgia Department of Natural Resources
Land Protection Branch
270 Washington St., S.W. Rm. 723
Atlanta, Georgia 30334
(404) 656-2833

Guam
Jim Branch, Administrator
Guam EPA
P.O. Box 2999
Agana, Guam 96910
(Overseas Operator) 646-8863

Hawaii
Hawaii Department of Health
Environmental Protection and Health Services Division
Noise and Radiation Branch
P.O. Box 3378
Honolulu, Hawaii 96810
(808) 548-3075

Idaho
Department of Health and Welfare
Solid and Hazardous Waste Section
450 West State Street
Boise, Idaho 83720
(208) 334-4060

Illinois
Division of Land Pollution Control
Illinois Environmental Protection Agency
2200 Churchill Road
Springfield, Illinois 62706
(212) 782-6761

Indiana
Hazardous Waste Management Branch
Division of Land Pollution Control
Indiana State Board of Health
1330 West Michigan Street
Indianapolis, Indiana 46206
(317) 243-5021

Iowa
U.S. EPA, Region 7
726 Minnesota Avenue
Kansas City, Kansas 66101
(816) 374-6534

Kansas
Waste Management Bureau
Kansas Department of Health and Environment
Forbes Field
Topeka, Kansas 66620
(913) 862-9360 ext. 297

Kentucky
Division of Waste Management
Department for Environmental Protection
18 Reilly Road
Frankfort, Kentucky 40601
(502) 564-6716 ext. 151

Louisiana
Office of Solid and Hazardous Waste
Louisiana Department of Environmental Quality
P.O. Box 94307
Baton Rouge, Louisiana 70804
(504) 342-1227

Maine
Bureau of Oil and Hazardous Materials Control
Maine Department of Environmental Protection
State House—Station 17
Augusta, Maine 04333
(207) 289-2651

Maryland
Waste Management Administration
Office of Environmental Programs
201 West Preston Street
Baltimore, Maryland 21201
(301) 383-5734

Massachusetts
Division of Solid and Hazardous Waste
Department of Environmental Quality Engineering
One Winter Street, 5th Floor
Boston, Massachusetts 02108
(617) 292-5851

Michigan
Hazardous Waste Division
Department of Natural Resources
P.O. Box 30038
Lansing, Michigan 48909
(517) 373-2730

Minnesota
Minnesota Pollution Control Agency
Solid and Hazardous Waste Division
1935 West Country Road B2
Roseville, Minnesota 55113
(612) 296-7340

Mississippi
Department of Natural Resources
Bureau of Pollution Control
Division of Solid Waste Management
P.O. Box 10385
Jackson, Mississippi 39209
(601) 961-5171

Missouri
Missouri Department of Natural Resources
Division of Environmental Quality
P.O. Box 1368
Jefferson City, Missouri 65102
(314) 751-3241

Montana
Department of Health and Environmental Sciences
Solid and Hazardous Waste Management Bureau
Cogswell Building, room B-201
Helena, Montana 59620
(406) 444-2821

Nebraska
Department of Environmental Control
Hazardous Waste Management Section
P.O. Box 94877
Statehouse Station
301 Centennial Mall South
Lincoln, Nebraska 68509
(402) 471-2186

Nevada
Department of Conservation and Natural Resources
Division of Environmental Protection
Capitol Complex
Carson City, Nevada 89710
(702) 885-6470

New Hampshire
Division of Public Health Services
Office of Waste Management
Health and Welfare Building
Hazen Drive
Concord, New Hampshire 03301
(603) 271-4609

New Jersey
Division of Waste Management
Hazardous Waste Advisory Program
Department of Environmental Protection
32 E. Hanover St., P.O. Box CN028
Trenton, New Jersey 08625
(609) 292-8341

State Hazardous Waste Management Agencies (cont.)

New Mexico
Hazardous Waste Section
New Mexico Environmental Enforcement Division
P.O. Box 968
Sante Fe, New Mexico 87504-0968
(505) 984-0020

New York
Division of Solid and Hazardous Waste
Department of Environmental Conservation
50 Wolf Road
Albany, New York 12233
(518) 457-0530

North Carolina
Department of Human Resources
Solid and Hazardous Waste Management Branch
P.O. Box 2091
Raleigh, North Carolina 27602
(919) 733-2178

North Dakota
Division of Hazardous Waste Management and Special Studies
Department of Health
1200 Missouri Avenue, Room 302
Bismarck, North Dakota 58501
(701) 224-2366

Ohio
Division of Solid and Hazardous Waste Management
Environmental Protection Agency
361 Broad Street
Columbus, Ohio 43215-1049
(614) 466-7220

Oklahoma
Waste Management Section
State Department of Health
P.O. Box 53531
Oklahoma City, Oklahoma 73152
(405) 271-5338

Oregon
Department of Environmental Quality
Hazardous and Solid Waste Division
522 S.W. 5th Avenue
P.O. Box 1760
Portland, Oregon 97207
(503) 229-5913

Pennsylvania
Department of Environmental Resources
Bureau of Solid Waste Management
P.O. Box 2063
Harrisburg, Pennsylvania 17120
(717) 787-6239

Puerto Rico
Land Pollution Control Area
Environmental Quality Board
P.O. Box 11488
Santurce, Puerto Rico 00910-1488
(809) 722-0439

Rhode Island
Division of Air and Hazardous Waste Management
Department of Environmental Management
Solid Waste Management Program
204 Cannon Building
75 Davis Street
Providence, Rhode Island 02908
(401) 277-2797

South Carolina
Bureau of Solid and Hazardous Waste Management—RCRA
Department of Health and Environmental Control
J. Marion Sims Building
2600 Bull Street
Columbia, South Carolina 29201
(803) 758-5681

South Dakota
Office of Air Quality and Solid Waste
Department of Water and Natural Resources
Room 217, Foss Building
523 E. Capitol
Pierre, South Dakota 57501
(605) 773-3329

Tennessee
Division of Solid Waste Management
Customs House, 4th Floor
701 Broadway
Nashville, Tennessee 37219-5403
(615) 741-3424

Texas
Industrial and Industrial Service Facilities:
Industrial Solid Waste Section
Texas Department of Water Resources
P.O. Box 13987, Capitol Station
Austin, Texas 78711
(512) 475-2041

Commercial Service, Municipal State and Federal Facilities:
Texas Department of Health
Bureau of Solid Waste Management
1100 West 49th Street
Austin, Texas 78756
(512) 458-7271

Utah
Bureau of Solid and Hazardous Waste
Division of Environmental Health
P.O. Box 45500
State Office Building, Room 4321
Salt Lake City, Utah 84145
(801) 533-4145

Vermont
Agency of Environmental Conservation
Air and Solid Waste Division
State Office Building
Montpelier, Vermont 05602
(802) 828-3395

Virginia
Department of Health
Division of Solid and Hazardous Waste Management
Monroe Building, 11th Floor
101 North 14th Street
Richmond, Virginia 23219
(804) 225-2667

Virgin Islands
Hazardous Waste Program
Division of Natural Resources Management
Department of Conservation and Cultural Affairs
P.O. Box 4340
Charlotte Amalie
St. Thomas, Virgin Islands 00801
(809) 774-3320

Washington
Department of Ecology
Office of Hazardous Substances
Mail Stop PV-11
Olympia, Washington 98504
(206) 459-6299

West Virginia
Solid and Hazardous Waste/Ground Water Branch
Department of Natural Resources
Division of Water Resources
1201 Greenbier Street
Charleston, West Virginia 25311
(304) 348-5935

Wisconsin
Department of Natural Resources
Bureau of Solid Waste Management
P.O. Box 7921
Madison, Wisconsin 53707
(608) 266-1327

Wyoming
EPA Region 8
Waste Management Division
Hazardous Waste Branch (8HWM-ON)
1860 Lincoln Street
Denver, Colorado 80295
(303) 293-1502

---

request a Notification of Hazardous Waste Activity Form (EPA Form 8700-12).

One advantage of using a multiple-copy manifest is better record keeping. The first and any subsequent transporters each keep a copy. The disposal facility keeps a copy and sends one copy back to the generator. This notifies the generator that the wastes have been properly handled. If you choose to use only the single-copy manifest, you should at least make a copy of the completed form for your files.

If your state requires its own version of the manifest, you can obtain it from your state agency. For a federal manifest, check with your EPA regional office or state agency. However, you will probably find it easier to order manifests from a commercial stationer. One source is Labelmaster, 5724 N. Pulaski Road, Chicago, Ill. 60646.

There is a difference of opinion over the question of who should fill out the manifest. Some believe only the owner should fill it out. "You are responsible for the accuracy of the manifest," said Don Randall of Automotive Service Councils. "Generators of hazardous waste should complete the manifest themselves."

In contrast, some transporters believe they can offer a service by helping the shop owner fill out the manifest, since they are more knowledgeable about the procedures. For example, Hazco International, a large East Coast hauler of used paint thinner, sends out a preprinted manifest for each customer on its regular route. At the shop, the only item that needs to be completed is the quantity being removed.

In any case, since the transporter generally makes the arrangements with a disposal facility to accept your waste and arranges for any subsequent haulers—information you will need to complete the manifest—you will have to work with the transporter to fill out the manifest. Just make certain you check it over carefully before you sign, since the manifest makes you responsible for the materials listed.

HIRING A TRANSPORTER

If you are shipping more than 100 kilograms of manifested hazardous waste, you will probably need to hire a transporter that has been licensed by the EPA and the Department of Transportation to haul hazardous waste. As we noted earlier, you are not now required by federal law to have a hazardous waste hauler. But for fear of their own liability, few ordinary haulers will accept manifested waste.

One good source for names of transporters in your area is your state environmental agency. Other shops and trade associations also may be able to refer you to a qualified hauler.

Choose your transportation company carefully, since you are dependent on it to handle your waste properly. "The transporter should indicate knowledge of the manifest system," said John Nolan, of Hazco Transporters. "The company should be able to tell you what will happen to each copy and when you will get a final copy back."

The manifest should be completely filled out before you sign it and give it to the driver. To do that, the transporter must be able to tell you where the wastes will be taken, along with the facility's EPA authorization number. You will also need to know if your wastes will be transferred to another transportation company at some point, and if so, the name and EPA number of that company.

"Be very careful on the first shipment," said Nolan, "and keep close tabs to make sure everything goes smoothly. Keep a copy of the manifest in a tickler file, and be sure to check on your shipment if you don't receive a receipt from the disposal site within a couple of weeks."

Don Randall, of Automotive Service Councils, suggested that you contact the Better Business Bureau to check the transportation company's credentials. "Choose a bonded contractor, if possible," Randall added.

He recommended that you sign a written contract clearly indicating that all activities will be done in accordance with local, state and federal laws.

You also should establish a regular pickup schedule with your transporter. Keep in mind that generators are not permitted to store more than 1,000 kilograms of waste on the premises more than 90 days. (That may increase to 180 days next March.)

Store toxic substances properly, keeping them separate and labeled. Check them frequently for leaks. It is a good idea to keep them on a solid surface rather than soil or gravel, to reduce the chance of seepage into groundwater.

The cost to transport your wastes will vary. Nolan estimated that it may run between $150 and $300 to have three to five drums picked up, including the disposal facility fee. It may be slightly less expensive if you live close to a disposal site.

TOEING THE LINE

The federal penalties for failing to comply with the hazardous waste laws are stiff—up to $50,000 for each day of violation and two years in prison. The federal EPA is responsible for enforcement, although the states are generally authorized to enforce the law.

If you have been reading the newspapers lately, you know the federal EPA already has its hands full trying to enforce the law against large generators. Even the agency acknowledges that it will be impossible to inspect all small generators.

Hazardous Wastes in the Shop

Typical Process/ Operation	Typical Materials Used	Typical Material Ingredients on Label	General Types of Wastes Generated
Oil and grease removal	degreasers—(gunk), carburetor cleaners, engine cleaners, varsol, solvents, acids/alkalies	petroleum distillates, aromatic hydrocarbons, mineral spirits	ignitable wastes, spent solvents, combustible solids, waste acid/alkaline solutions
Engine, parts, and equipment cleaning	degreasers—(gunk), carburetor cleaners, engine cleaners, solvents, acids/alkalies, cleaning fluids	petroleim distillates, aromatic hydrocarbons, mineral spirits, benzene, toluene, petroleum naphtha	ignitable wastes, spent solvents, combustible solids, waste acid/alkaline solutions
Rust removal	naval jelly, strong acids, strong alkalies	phosphoric acid, hydrochloric acid, hydrofluoric acid, sodium hydroxide	waste acids, waste alkalies
Paint preparation	paint thinners, enamel reducers, white spirits	alcohols, petroleum distillates, oxygenated solvents, mineral spirits, ketones	spent solvents, ignitable wastes, ignitable paint wastes, paint wastes with heavy metals
Painting	enamels, lacquers, epoxys, alkyds, acrylics, primers	acetone, toluene, petroleum distillates, epoxy ester resins, methylene chloride, xylene, VM&P naphtha, aromatic hydrocarbons, methyl isobutyl, ketones	ignitable paint wastes, spent solvents, paint wastes with heavy metals, ignitable wastes
Spray booth, spray guns, and brush cleaning	paint thinners, enamel reducers, solvents, white spirits	ketones, alcohols, toluene, acetone, isopropyl alcohol, petroleum distillates, mineral spirits	ignitable paint wastes, heavy metal paint wastes, spent solvents
Paint removal	solvents, paint thinners, enamel reducers, white spirits	acetone, toluene, petroleum distillates, methanol, methylene chloride, isopropyl alcohol, mineral spirits, alcohols, ketones, other oxygenated solvents	ignitable paint wastes, heavy metal paint wastes, spent solvents
Used lead acid batteries	car, truck, boat, motorcycle, and other vehicle batteries	lead dross, less than 3% free acids	used lead acid batteries, strong acid/alkaline solutions

"There is no way we can have a traditional enforcement and inspection program for this number of entities," said Barry Stoll of the EPA Office of Solid Waste Programs and Enforcement. "We will depend heavily on voluntary compliance."

But this doesn't mean the EPA intends to ignore small generators. Instead, the agency plans to follow the example of Internal Revenue Service auditors. It will inspect shops on a random basis, and respond to complaints.

"We expect to see a lot of, uh, what's a good word for tattling?" said Stoll. "Small businesses operate on the fringes of profitability. If one small businessman sees another around the corner saving money by not complying, he may be tempted to pick up the phone and call."

Nolan, of Hazco, thinks enforcement of the

Descriptions of Some Wastes[1]

Waste Type	Designations/ Trade Names	DOT Shipping Name	Hazard Class	UN/NA ID Number
Strong Acid/ Alkaline Wastes				
Potassium Hydroxide	Potassium Hydroxide, KOH, Potassium Hydrate, Caustic Potash, Potassa	Waste Potassium Hydroxide Solution	Corrosive Material	UN1814
		Dry Solid, Flake, Bead, or Granular	Corrosive Material	UN1813
Sodium Hydroxide	Sodium Hydroxide, NaOH, Caustic Soda, Soda Lye, Sodium Hydrate	Waste Sodium Hydroxide Solution	Corrosive Material	UN1824
		Dry Solid, Flake, Bead, or Granular	Corrosive Material	UN1823
Ignitable Wastes				
Ignitable Wastes NOS[2] Aromatic Hydrocarbons Petroleum Distillates	Carburetor Cleaners, Ignitable Wastes NOS	Waste Flammable Liquid NOS	Flammable Liquid[3]	UN1993
		Waste Combustible Liquid NOS	Combustible Liquid[4]	NA1993
		Waste Flammable Solid NOS	Flammable Solid	UN1325
Ignitable Paint Wastes				
Ethylene Dichloride	Ethylene Dichloride, 1,2-Dichloroethane	Waste Ethylene Dichloride	Flammable Liquid	UN1184
Benzene	Benzene	Waste Benzene (benzol)	Flammable Liquid	UN1114
Toluene	Toluene	Waste Toluene (toluol)	Flammable Liquid	UN1294
Ethylbenzene	Ethylbenzene	Waste Ethylbenzene	Flammable Liquid	UN1175
Chlorobenzene	Chlorobenzene, Monochlorobenzene, Phenylchloride	Waste Chlorobenzene	Flammable Liquid	UN1134

law will become strict. "The states will find it in their interest to have a vigorous enforcement," he said. "They will find some poor victim, fine him $20,000, and the news stories will scare everyone else."

CLEANUP COSTS

Ultimately, the generator's liability for damage caused by his or her hazardous waste may be the most effective tool for encouraging proper handling.

While the legislature and EPA have been wrestling with new regulations, the courts have been developing case law to force the cleanup of existing waste sites. And the legal principles that have evolved can make it *very* expensive to be involved in a cleanup.

The courts have invoked two legal principles in hazardous waste cases—strict liability and joint and several liability. These two liabil-

Waste Type	Designations/ Trade Names	DOT Shipping Name	Hazard Class	UN/NA ID Number
Ignitable				
Paint Wastes				
Methyl Ethyl Ketone	Methyl Ethyl Ketone, MEK, Methyl Acetone, Meetco, Butanone, Ethyl Methyl Ketone	Waste Methyl Ethyl Ketone	Flammable Liquid	UN1193
Spent Solvents				
White Spirits, Varsol	White Spirits, Mineral Spirits, Naphtha	Waste Naphtha	Flammable Liquid	UN2553
			Combustible Liquid	UN2553
1,1,1-Trichloroethane	Aeothane TT, Chlorlen, Chloroethene, Methyl-Chloroform, Alpha. T, Chlorotene	Waste 1,1,1-Trichloro-ethane	ORM-A	UN2831
Petroleum Distillates	Petroleum Distillates	Petroleum Distillate	Flammable Liquid	UN1268
			Combustible Liquid	UN1268
Paint Wastes With Heavy Metals				
Paints with Heavy Metals Lead Nickel Chromium	Heavy Metals Paint	Hazardous Waste, Liquid or Solid, NOS	ORM-E	NA9189

[1] These descriptions may change given variations in waste characteristics or conditions.
[2] NOS—Not otherwise specified.
[3] A flammable liquid has a flash point below 100°F
[4] A combustible liquid has a flash point between 100°F and 200°F

ity concepts are complex, and their application depends on the details of the individual case. But, in essence, they make generators irrevocably responsible for cleaning up their hazardous waste.

In its simplest terms, *strict liability* means that the generator is financially responsible, without excuse, for damage caused by its waste. The generator may have obeyed the laws that were in existence at the time the wastes were discarded, or may not have known the wastes were dangerous. Or, like Giles Mason, the generator may have had nothing to do with the contaminating act. It makes no difference in the world of strict liability.

Joint and several liability means that the costs created by any damage will be assessed among any responsible parties that can be found. If a dozen businesses, say, had sent toxic waste to a site that later became contaminated, but only seven were still in existence, those seven would have to split the cost of the cleanup.

Consider a hypothetical dump that served one major company, Vile Chemical, and several local auto repair and body shops. Vile, unfortunately, declared bankruptcy 20 years ago. Under joint and several liability, if the government forces cleanup of the dump, the small businesses could be stuck with the entire bill, even though Vile caused 80% of the damage. Not a pleasant prospect.

Also, liability is not limited to business owners. Employees who knew hazardous waste was being dumped without permits have been held liable in the courts. So be sure your employees know their responsibilities.

Rocky Mountain Response

When Congress extended hazardous waste regulations to small quantity generators, it opened up a whole new universe to the EPA and state environmental agencies. They had been struggling since 1976 to cope with an estimated 14,000 large quantity generators in the country. Suddenly they had 175,000 new businesses to regulate, many of which had processes and products that were new to the inspection teams.

A year ago, right after the passage of the small generator law, the Florida Automotive Service Council invited its state environmental agency to do a sample inspection of an independent repair shop. The result? The agents were unfamiliar with the chemicals they ran across and were unable to advise the shop owner on the hazards involved.

Since then, the EPA and the state agencies have been busy familiarizing themselves with the hazardous wastes produced by small quantity generators, and these agencies are now better equipped to handle questions. But local trade associations, concerned about the legal vulnerability of their members, also have been educating themselves. One energetic model for other states is the Colorado Association of Commerce and Industry (CACI).

"We had been training large quantity generators since 1979 and had reached about 1,200 of them," said Olie Webb, director of environmental affairs for the association. "But when the small quantity generator laws passed, we did some math and calculated that between 1,700 and 2,000 more businesses were going to need immediate information. So we expanded our program."

The program is Haz-Ed — Hazardous Substances Education — and it offers seminars in complying with hazardous waste laws, with the emphasis on simplicity.

"The EPA regulations have a one-page definition of the word 'empty'," said Webb. "Once we simplify and boil it all down, people are not so overwhelmed."

It is critical to make the seminars convenient for attendees, said Webb. So during the fall of 1985 CACI held seminars in 10 locations throughout the state.

"I was very surprised by the level of sophistication out there," he said. "We stress in our program that you want to exempt yourself from as many categories as possible by recycling, and people were already presorting and looking into recycling."

The research in developing the seminars was funded by a grant from the EPA via the Colorado Department of Health. With the frontend costs covered, CACI charges just $60 for an all-day session, including lunch and materials. Attendees receive a generic workbook about handling hazardous waste, with a specialized insert for vehicle maintenance. They are also placed on a mailing list to receive updated information about changes in the law or improved ways of handling wastes

INSURANCE

Normally, this kind of situation would send a business owner out shopping for liability insurance to protect against accidents or the mistakes of others. But if you've rewritten your insurance policy lately, you won't be surprised to hear that liability insurance for pollution is prohibitively expensive, if not actually impossible to obtain.

"Availability and price of environmental insurance is a major problem in this country," said Dominick Vezzi, of Insurance Services Office. "Many insurers are already excluding all environmental coverage."

According to Vezzi, insurance companies don't like writing environmental insurance policies because of three unknowns. First, there is no time limit on when the pollution occurred. A policy-holder could be held responsible for something that happened 50 years ago. Second, joint and several liability means that, at the time of writing the policy, the company has no way of knowing what proportion of cleanup costs the insured party might ever have to assume. And third, there is no limit to cleanup costs.

As a result, many underwriters are excluding environmental liability coverage for any business they consider to have a major pollution exposure. And that seems to be a pretty broad category these days. When Vezzi was asked for an example of a business without a major pollution exposure, he replied, "A Hallmark card shop . . . maybe."

"The insurance situation is very bleak," said Olie Webb, of the Colorado Association of Commerce and Industry, which has taken an active role in training businesses to comply with hazardous waste regulations. (See box.) "It's the most critical issue government, businesses and the insurance industry must face today."

Congress has been holding hearings this fall about the availability, or lack thereof, of liability insurance for small businesses, but there have been no breakthroughs so far. Frankly, at this point, there are no good answers for shop owners. The best advice we can offer you is to go over your policy carefully with your insurance agent so you know what coverage you do have, and to go about handling your waste as responsibly as possible.

---

in the shop.

"We're training people who have never been under any kind of government regulation in their lives. There's a lot of animosity at first," said Webb. "But state environmental inspections are going to be done randomly, and we think there is a good chance for any shop to be inspected. We want to prepare them."

CACI is trying to ease the pain of compliance with more than seminars. There are few local sources for manifests, so the organization buys them in bulk to sell at cost, Colorado has no licensed hazardous waste disposal facility, and waste must be transported to Oklahoma and California. So CACI is trying to establish a network of EPA-authorized transfer points throughout the state, where wastes will be stored until they can be economically combined and shipped. It is also providing assistance to manufacturers developing processes to neutralize or recycle hazardous wastes.

The organization has been active in lobbying the Colorado legislature to keep the state laws in line with the federal laws, for easier compliance. It is also studying the liability insurance situation.

For more information about the program, write to Olie Webb, CACI, 1860 Lincoln St. #550, Denver, Colorado 80295-0501, or call (303) 831-7411.   — *MR*

CUTTING THE COST

There's no doubt that handling hazardous waste properly will cost you more than throwing it out with the trash or pouring it down the drain. But you can cut costs by recycling as many products as possible, coordinating waste pickups with other shops in your area, and passing costs directly along to your customers.

The major benefit of recycling is that it could easily bring you under the small quantity generator limits and exempt you from the manifesting and shipping requirements. Dead batteries, waste oil and used solvent are all recyclable, and are the three biggest sources of hazardous waste in most shops.

Recycling also cuts down on the total amount of hazardous waste produced in the country. For instance, Safety-Kleen, the largest maker of recycling parts washers, reclaims about 70% of the solvent it originally gives to its customers and only has to buy about 30% virgin solvent. This cuts down dramatically on the amount of solvent that ultimately must be disposed of.

Some kinds of recycling are beyond the scope of a single shop but are possible when several shops organize. For instance, a paint shop needs substantial amounts of solvent to thin paint and to clean the spray guns. Instead of pouring the used solvent onto the waste can, it could be distilled. The distilled solvent would probably not be pure enough for making with paint, but it could be used to clean the guns and could save on the overall amount of new solvent required.

Setting up a still in the backyard would be a risky proposition for most paint shops, due to the heat and flammable vapor involved. But several shops together might have the clout to demand that their solvent supplier distill the used solvent.

Several shops in an area also could get together and have a hazardous waste transporter make a regular circuit through the area. The increased efficiency could lower the cost per pickup for each shop.

Shop owners also can pass the cost of compliance along to the customer. Many shops already add a hazardous waste disposal fee to the estimate, right along with parts, labor and shop supplies. Recent polls have shown that the majority of Americans are concerned about hazardous waste, even to the point of being willing to pay more taxes. So if you take the time to explain the charge to your customers, you may not find much resistance.

Still Have Questions?

The EPA has opened two hotlines: the RCRA Hotline — (800) 424-9346 (382-3000 in the Washington, D.C., area), and the Small Business Hotline — (800) 368-5888. You also can ask questions of your regional EPA office, which is listed on page 196.

The EPA has published a helpful brochure about small quantity generators and the hazadous waste laws. You should request publication number EPA/530-SW-010 with a vehicle maintenance insert. Order it from the U.S. Environmental Protection Agency, Office of Solid Waste and Emergency Response, Washington, D.C., 20460.

When you have a drum of waste and you don't know what to do with it, you'll probably find that your state environmental protection agency is the most helpful source for answers to the real nuts-and-bolts questions.

It may also be helpful to contact state and local trade associations to see if they have developed workshops or information.
— *MR*

FUTURE REGULATIONS

It is generally bad practice to predict the future, but in this case we feel pretty confident saying that the future holds still more regulation of hazardous waste. Already, the fit between regulation and reality isn't very good. The government has brought small quantity generators into the mainstream of hazardous waste management, even though there aren't yet enough treatment, storage or disposal sites to handle the wastes from the large generators. And the insurance dilemma is enough to give any honest business owner nightmares.

Nonetheless, the direction of regulation is going to be forward, not backward, as society seeks practical ways to control the toxic products of an industrial economy. Small generators shouldn't think they will be relieved sometime in the future of their obligation to properly handle hazardous materials. We have thoughtlessly poisoned our neighbor's well for many years. But that age of innocence is over, even for third-graders. ∎

American Express Headquarters

Beverly Russell
EDITOR IN CHIEF

Karin Tetlow
BUSINESS ROUNDUP EDITOR

Wolfgang Hoyt
PHOTOGRAPHER

Colin Forbes
ART DIRECTOR

Maryann Levesque
ART DIRECTOR

The new American Express headquarters in Manhattan sets a world record for its size: 2.2 million square feet of space designed for 9,000 employees. This series of articles explains how the enormous task was accomplished.

Interiors is circulated to architects, interior and industrial designers, corporate clients, manufacturers, and students. "American Express Headquarters" first appeared in the June 1986, August 1986, October 1986, and November 1986 issues of *Interiors,* published by Billboard Publications, Inc. © 1986. Reprinted with permission.

The cover story for this issue involving the record-breaking American Express headquarters, is the first of a series of articles which will be focusing on this giant corporate tower. Back in the Fall of 1985, when Swanke Hayden Connell Architects initiated a meeting with *Interiors* to discuss the project, we suggested that there was too much material to do justice to their work in one article. A total of 100 photographs were being taken, more than we could show in an *entire* issue.

Thus the story was conceived as an ongoing serial. It begins this month with the employee workspaces and amenities, with an adjunct article on how CADD was used in the planning. In July, we will devote another article to the intelligent systems of the building. In August, we will cover the Shearson Lehman Brothers units of the building, including the executive floors and the trading rooms, which were added midway into the planning, when American Express–owned Shearson bought the Lehman Brothers Kuhn Loeb operation. In October we will follow up with a look at the top floors, 50 and 51, showing the corporate executive offices.

Aside from the major order for 4,000 Ethospace workstations from Herman Miller, 91 other manufacturers in 50 different categories of furniture were specified. A grand total worth over $30 million. We are told that 1,450 separate furniture orders with up to 1,000 pieces of furniture per order and 550 fabric orders were written.

Furniture Consultants Inc., the New York–based firm which has grown from seven people to over 100 personnel in the last seven years, was retained by the American Express corporation early along to coordinate purchasing of furniture other than the systems furniture, and interface with the designers at SHCA, the in-house facility managers and purchasing officers, and the construction management teams. The firm dedicated a 12-person project team to this assignment, headed by partner Larry Itkin, with Mark Hemphill, Project Manager, Nancy Goldstein, Account Manager and Mark Grove, Field Coordinator. According to partner David Itkin, the "dynamic quality of American Express" was experienced all through the job. Revisions were constantly being made, as the company expanded with employees and acquisitions. "It was awesome in its scope," says Itkin. "But now that we have worked on this scale, we will never be intimidated by anything again."

In all, the FCI team estimates it handled 100,000 pieces of information relating to purchasing and installation. Office mockups for the nine floors of executive offices were done at the firm's headquarters and very often contained selections from a minimum of seven different manufacturers.

As far as corporate culture image is concerned, the American Express headquarters is an example of the pursuit of traditional formality that is marking the interiors of a multi-billion-dollar corporate headquarters now nearing completion. Equitable Insurance, Barclays Bank, Merrill Lynch, all reflect a rich, Jeffersonian approach to the workspace. This is only to be expected, perhaps, from conservative financial institutions selling services.

Since the quality of construction in these buildings ensures longevity, however, it seems clear that the year 2000 may not be ushering in the space-age odyssey previously imagined, but a solid recapitulation of design from previous centuries: a significant thought for all those professionals currently engaged in creating new work environments today. The reality of the upcoming era of supertechnology is undoubtedly causing a reaction: a search for familiar signals in a world of unchartered experiences. ∎

How CADD Expressed the American Express Headquarters

Without question the key to Swanke Hayden Connell Architects' successful completion of the American Express project in New York's World Financial Center (see cover story) is the firm's CADD system. More than a series of design and drafting stations, it is a carefully planned operation that *integrates* data management, word processing, publishing and printing, and reprographics. Since more and more clients—American Express being a prime example—are interested in computer tapes of completed installations for facility management purposes, it is a significant marketing tool. With 40% of the firms total work on computer accomplished by 10% of the staff in 4% of the space, it is also very productive.

The overall system consists of four integrated functional levels. First, Data Base Management that tracks accounting, personnel management, job costing and design-related services such as programming, stacking and purchasing. These programs are run on a very user-friendly McDonnell Douglas supermini (formerly called Microdata and not to be confused with the manufacturer's CAD system) by data specialists; 80 of the 83 terminals are in New York. Second, a variety of CADD workstations that provide different levels of sophistication; these include 17 (15 in New York and one each in Chicago and Washington) Calcomps with 256 levels, 16 colors and 5 second screen repaint for design and drafting, and PCs for architectural detailing and workstation development; faster electrostatic plotters have replaced pen plotters. Third, NBI word processing multi-type and multi-font equipment that generates Swanke's printed matter. The fourth component of the network is a reprographics service center operated by an outside firm, GSO Graphics, Inc. Almost all programs for data base management and for software enhanced Calcomp operations were written in-house and by consultants.

Breaking the basic rule never to initiate CADD with a big project, Swanke, two days after receiving its first 3 Calcomps in January 1983, started entering the American Express project. Four months later, with 3 workstations running one shift, 800,000 square feet of drawings were completed.

Crucial to the system's success, explains its mastermind Bradley Meade, Director of Computer and Reprographic Operations, is the way CADD was conceived. Not as a mysterious magic black box but as electronic equipment that combines all the concepts of sophisticated systems design and drafting, such as overlay, photodrafting and cut and paste—an approach that Swanke had taken 5 years to refine before its decision to purchase CADD.

Since reprographics was an essential element of its systems operation the firm opted for an in-house service center. Meade reiterates the advantages: A saving in turnaround time; mylar sheets are maintained at stable humidity and temperatures to ensure overlay alignment; and standardization of methods, materials and sheet punching procedures.

Swanke has built its own CADD and data base libraries of systems components for Steelcase, Knoll Zapf, Sunar-Hauserman, Gunlocke, Hiebert and the newer Herman Miller Ethospace. For the American Express project, it efficiently used its data base equipment to enter component attribute data—such as dimensions, manufacturer, type, lead time, expected ship date, which therefore left Calcomp available for design and drafting. Each drafted component, e.g., a sprinkler head or chair, was created and coded as a symbol with an 8-digit "intelligent" code. Upon completion of floor plans, the data base management system would transfer and link the symbol with its appropriate attribute data to generate a purchase order. A three-inch-thick Herman Miller order based on seven floors of the American Express project took 15 minutes to process and two and a quarter hours to print.

The three 5-day, 4-day and weekend CADD shifts, includes a half-hour communication overlap during regular office hours, can reduce a project's time span between 40 and 80%. "The hardest part," says Meade "is getting answers fast enough from the client. That is one of the reasons we developed design drafting methodology so people could contribute to a number of projects in the same time frame. "Architects and interior designers who operate the system need to participate in project meetings so they can understand design concepts. The CADD environment is critical. SMCA has task lamps but no ceiling lights. Designers sit in high back Vecta chairs; terminals face away from the window.

An added benefit from Swanke's commitment to CADD is the capacity to provide facility management service. This includes facility use reports from as-built plans such as charge back reports. American Express, for instance, can track costs for its facilities.

A frequent speaker at A/E systems shows and lecturer abroad, Meade believes that CADD at the present time is a better tool for the design of interior projects than for the design of buildings because of the multitude of layers and repetitive elements. "The degree of organization and preplanning of work is the key to CADD success." Swanke's operation certainly proves that point. ∎

Expressing an Image, I

Largest single private interiors project. Fastest track record. Greatest number of construction drawings for an interiors project. Biggest carpet contract let at one time. Records abound at the Swanke Hayden Connell Architects' (SHCA) recently completed American Express Tower in New York's World Financial Center. But in addition to being a milestone in quality design and construction techniques, the 2.2-million-square-foot Tower is an expression of a new urban corporate attitude towards employee needs that deserves applause and should provoke attention from board rooms, the design community and the employed.

Gone are the days when building height alone was enough to bestow headlines and substance to its executive occupants. Now, aware critics and environmentalists look to content and context. Amenities for its occupants, accessibility and appreciation for setting are valued characteristics.

Fifty-one stories high and tallest of the four Cesar Pilli–designed office towers in the largest private development in New York since Rockefeller Center, the Tower adjoins a glass-vaulted Winter Garden, complements the New York skyline and will have rare urban access to green space and the waterfront.

The American Express Company with $75 billion in assets has paid special attention to its people—a concern reiterated in its annual report—in wanting thoughtfully designed workstations and *two* entire floors devoted to its 7,500 employees' needs. Both floors are conveniently accessible by both escalator and elevator from the second-floor lobby which is secured via the computerized security system with SHCA-designed card-access turnstiles. They comprise a full-range cafeteria and restaurant service, a physical fitness center, medical facilities, employee credit union, travel store and financial services offices and employee lounge.

Mandatory for new suburban and rural corporate headquarters physical fitness centers occupying valuable square footage that are available to all employees are seldom seen in New York. The 15,000-square-foot facility staffed by eight specialists is handicapped accessible. It has two aerobics rooms and two equipment rooms with a variety of machines, video monitors and head sets. Definitely not a drop-in service, employees are required to sign up for a course of exercise based on individual needs.

The employee lounge is another unusual amenity. A place to relax and socialize, the comfortable room has card tables, chairs but no sofas (sleeping is discouraged).

When the corporation, which has a total of nearly 2,400 offices worldwide, sought a designer for its new international headquarters, it had two crucial requirements in addition to a demand for quality. First, that a computerized facilities package be handed over at the end of the project to the corporation's in-house facilities management team. Second, that work schedules be kept because Olympia & York (O&Y), developer and contractor for the World Financial Center and contractor for the shell and core of the American Express Tower, had arranged to purchase and then lease American Express's old quarters at 125 Broad Street; heavy penalites were on the cards if the American Express schedule fell behind that of O&Y.

SHCA, who had recently completed the American Express–owned Shearson offices at the World Trade Center and was gearing up for CADD, (that is Computer Aided Design and Drafting), came on board in August 1982. Interiors construction was to start in October 1983 and the staggered move-in begin a year and a half later. But as facilities managers and any reader of the financial press can testify, little in billionaire corporations stays the same. In May 1984 Shearson acquired the investment banking firm Lehman Brothers Kuhn Loeb and came to be known as Shearson Lehman Brothers Inc. Completed floors were torn out and the designers went back to their terminals to restack and redesign. Hundreds of con-

---

Olympia & York's $1.5-billion World Financial Center, the world's largest single office development in progress, is an integral part of what is expected to be New York's newest chic 92-acre neighborhood — Battery Park City.

First fully occupied and 51 stories high is the American Express Tower. Between it and the 34-story tower with a ziggurat roof that will be completed this summer and occupied by Merrill Lynch is a covered over glass courtyard dedicated to restaurants and retail. Adjoining the Tower to the south is the centerpiece of the development, a 120-foot-high glass-vaulted Winter Garden on the scale of grand Central Station. Controlled for temperature and humidity, the Garden will be host to concerts, exhibitions, restaurants and an array of plants including sixteen palm trees being acclimated under cheesecloth in the Mojave Desert. Merrill Lynch has also taken the domed-roof, 44-story tower bordering the southern wall of the Garden. The southernmost 40-story tower houses Dow Jones and Oppenheimer.

For the first time in history, there has been a planned collaboration between a landscape architect and artists. M. Paul Friedberg & Partners, Scott Burton and Siah Armajani. Burton, best known for his stone furniture sculpture, has designed public seating; Armajani is responsible for decorative gates that serve as entryway to the grass area.

By early 1988 the waterfront should be complete.

struction drawings were voided during the project due to changes in business plans and operating strategies.

SHCA's initial task was to analyze over eleven thousand building documents in terms of both investment for its client, who had decided to purchase rather than lease the building, and interior-design concepts. Significant base building modifications were made that included changing the ceiling height, the electrical distribution system, a corner skin detail flipping the building's core and the amount of cooling capacity available. In all, SHCA produced nearly 8 million square feet of drawings, 25 stacking plans and 2,100 construction documents representing 5.7 million square feet.

SHCA followed its usual practice of pairing design and management functions. Heading the project, which involved some 70 people, were Managing Principal Richard Seth Hayden, Principals Richard A. Carlson, in charge of Design, and George Alexander, Project Director. Kathryn Noles and Henry Kurz were Design Directors and Doug Coombs, Production Director.

Because of time constraints, textbook sequential phases of design had to be abandoned. Base building modification, programming and design leapt ahead simultaneously.

The base building with its wide interior corridor determined circulation patterns and the rationale behind the central design concept of the "street"—the community entry and information space to each floor. Rather than have visitors walk past workstations on their way to meeting areas, the team sited conference rooms at both ends of the street. The architectural grid—a theme repeated in different colors and finishes throughout the building—was developed early. "We were looking for continuity," recalls Carlson.

With their choice of open plan office systems furniture limited to a handful of large manufacturers with a history of design and manufacturing quality, SHCA and American Express established a relationship with Herman Miller and selected the brand new as yet unreleased Ethospace workstation package with its grid system of flexible opaque and transparent tiles. The design team learned the system's quirks and benefits and developed its own coding system so layouts could be developed and purchase orders issued. Ethospace was used for all open plan offices; the foothigh purchase order (generated by SHCA and negotiated by the client) was the manufacturer's largest purchase. The 175,000 square yards of modular carpet contract with Milliken/Shehadi was also a record.

SHCA gained an extra 6 inches to the height of the original building's planned 9-foot ceiling height by deciding to hang lights rather than place them in the ceiling—and to develop a new ambient system which was especially important since American Express planned to have a video display terminal on every desk by 1990. Using a new Sylvania 1″ 32-watt octane fluorescent lamp, equivalent to the older 40-watt 1¼″ model, and selecting a new electronic ballast (the device that adjusts current and frequency) that served four lamps instead of the usual two, SHCA, in collaboration with the lighting consultant, designed a light-weight, thin profiled fixture and a softer more economic field of light. The fixture is now in the process of being patented by SHCA with the lighting consultant as co-inventor.

Office standards for the client's corporate offices and three of its four major subsidiaries, American Express Travel Related Services Company, Inc. (TRS), Shearson Lehman Brothers Inc. and American Express Bank Ltd., were developed in liaison with the client. Perimeter private offices have interior demountable full height partitions that include a clerestory and an ingenious SHCA-designed custom-built storage wall that has reversible components. Partitions were attached to a fineline ceiling grid in order to make quick changes to offices and at the same time to prevent ceiling tile degradation. Lacquer colors, wood and fabric add variety; executive floors and areas with a significant level of visitors, for example, have a mahogany wall finish.

The four-color palette, blue, red, green and tan, was another early development. By varying colors on the systems furniture, carpet tile (custom colors were created) and finishes, it was possible to accomplish considerable variety and an unusual level of color throughout the building.

When designers, who were grouped according to area, started on Shearson or TRS, they would use the standard design, vary colors and report and resolve problems at the several weekly client and consultant meetings. "Things had to go on without a lot of interdependence. We had to take a chance and in some cases had to proceed with documentation prior to final approval so we could meet the construction drawings deadline," recounts Alexander. A full-scale mock-up with six different furnished offices and several open plan systems configurations was built in a nearby rented loft to evaluate layouts and elements such as window treatments, perimeter walls, lighting and graphics in addition to construction sequence and time schedules. The majority of design decisions were passed on by both client and design team; one change that resulted from the mock-up was the decision to revise the pattern of ceiling lighting requiring in four floors of drawings being redone.

Because of the fast track schedule, interiors construction work had to go forward before the building was enclosed. On the cafeteria floor, for instance, wood grounds for paneling were installed before the exterior walls. Costs of replacing some materials due to damage were a small price to pay for staying on track.

Records speak for themselves, but don't do justice to the professional contribution of the people concerned. The American Express project is top quality and was completed on schedule because both client and designers knew what they wanted, revolutionized traditional techniques and took risks—definitely a personal commitment that will not be forgotten by those involved or by those who are professionally curious. ■

Expressing an Image, II

Behind every record breaking achievement is a story of how people united to accomplish their goals. The 2.2 million square foot American Express Tower designed by Swanke Hayden Connell Architects is no exception. The design and completion in 3½ years of 51 distinctive but thematically similar floors—four were designed and built twice—fitted with trading floors, 'intelligent' communications, exceptional amenities, art, open plan and private offices and mahogany panelled executive floors is a record indeed. But equally impressive are the managerial strategies behind the project's success.

While some moves called for rewriting design and construction practice or taking advantage of newly developed computer expertise, others involved brand new ways of doing things. Of the latter, the most innovative—and one that should profoundly affect real estate development—was the client's approach to financing the purchase of the building. For years, mortgages on single family homes have been secured by the home itself. Not so in commercial real estate where instruments have traditionally been rated on the credit standing of the issuer. American Express was the first to follow the housing market example and issue bonds based solely on the collateral of the building. (Due in 2000 with a face value of $450 million, the bonds are well below the Tower's appraised value of $700 million.) The corporation gained an additional advantage in 'retaining' its portfolio collateral for other market purchases which otherwise would have been assigned to the bonds.

But the single most important strategy that led to the project's completion on schedule, was the early decision by top American Express executives to acquire a construction company—one familiar to the corporation, Herbert Construction. It would, thereby possess proven management expertise while keeping profits in-house, and, most important, by avoiding the traditional adversarial relationship, have informed control over budgets and streamlined decision making. In charge of the overall project was Herbert's President, Ted A. Kohl, American Express Senior Vice President, Real Estate.

In addition to revising construction sequence such as installing sheetrock and carpeting before the skin of the building, Herbert invested thousands of dollars in restructuring its management practices. An in-house programmer developed software packages and American Express auditors devised fast track approval and budgeting methods.

Liaison between SHCA and American Express and lead contact with the many corporate user groups was Richard F. Macauley, American Express Vice President, Headquarters Facilities. Macauley, as former facilities head of Shearson Lehman Brothers, the brokerage and investment banking arm of American Express, had worked closely with Kohl when Herbert installed Shearson's trading floors at the World Trade Center. With both men working for American Express, Kohl in charge of the budget and link to top management and Macauley working closely with all project participants including design consultants (a minimum of 35 key people met Wednesday mornings at SHCA and on every Sunday Kohl and Macauley walked the building), quick personal decisions were possible. "Otherwise I don't think we would have met schedules unless we had written a blank check for a cost plus job," recalls Macauley. The experience of working with a contractor who was also the client was a new one for SHCA. "It was a great benefit," remembers George Alexander, SHCA Principal and Project Director, "there was an immediate appreciation and overview of the scale of the project."

"American Express never paid rent on two places for the same space," reports Kohl. "This job was an example of how you get so consumed that you lose sight of everything else. Everyone had a love for doing this building that I have never seen in 25 years in the business."

One of the team's many accomplishments was creating an American Express 'oneness.' The goal was to effect more 'cross pollination' amongst its banking, trading, travel and financial services companies, and have, for instance, the marketing and advertising minds of Travel Related Services spark the financial brains of Shearson Lehman Brothers—yet still have each subsidiary operate in its own distinct manner. The conference and training room floor with its smart A/V systems was a special challenge since it served the entire corporate hierarchy. Design concepts, such as the grid theme, and the SHCA-designed storage wall for private offices, which helped solve different subsidiary's square foot standards, all contributed to an overall corporate look.

Along with its new CADD operation, SHCA changed its organizational systems. To avoid wasting meeting time, project manager and designer teams attended SHCA 'classrooms' to learn about document, drawing and design standardization; a special plan desk operated by 5 people processed and filed the 16,000-plus sketches and drawings; two typists concentrated on paperwork, and, to prevent overdistribution, channeled documents by functional level; twice daily deliveries were scheduled after one month's monumental messenger bill. But the most useful service for all parties was the firm's "Document Registry." A comprehensive computerized legal record of each of the 15,000 written documents associated with the project was filed in SHCA's data base by date, originator, recipient, type, subject, building, location and brief description. This system eliminated cross-referencing and personal files.

Macauley likens the assignment to relocating a town of 7,500 people with all their possessions. With the project's many vital statistics, unique bond issue and myriad systems, the parallel certainly holds true. And the fact that it occurred in an extraordinarily tight time frame makes it all the more impressive.

THE FINE ART OF LIGHTING AN ARCHITECTURAL PHOTOGRAPH

The design business has expanded rapidly in the last decade, and a major force in this expansion has been the design press. Publishing projects is gratifying to both designer and client, but more important in the long run is the energy added to the ongoing evolution of design itself. Designers and clients need to see the best work being done, and the pages of design publications offer the best possible views.

The most critical element in the presentation for publication in this or any other magazine, after good design, is good photography of that design. Projects published in the pages of this magazine look, for the most part, better here than they do in reality. This is not to downgrade any designer's work, but simply to state a truth of the trade: Architectural photographs do more than justice to a space, if they are done right—they organize, glamorize, and illuminate.

That last word, illuminate, is key. Lighting is perhaps the most critical element in a successful interior photograph.

Photographer Wolfgang Hoyt shot over 70 pictures of the new American Express Tower interiors for the serial article *Interiors* is running of the project. This major job consumed about 35 nights, spread out in sleepless ten-night stints over a period of several months. Using a 4 × 5 inch format camera, Hoyt shot an average of two photographs during each of the nights that he spent at the Tower.

The pictures were taken at night for several reasons, the most critical being that the offices are busy during the day and therefore the photographer could only get access at night. Also, artificial light is easier to control than daylight (almost all office interiors photography is shot at night for these reasons). In addition to Hoyt and two assistants, two or three people from the public relations department of Swanke Hayden Connell, the project designers, were present, to help choose photographic angles as well as clean and style.

Clearly, architectural photography is a time-consuming, technically demanding job. It's also expensive. A photographer's day rate can range from $500 to $2,000 per day, and that doesn't include the cost of assistants, film, processing, etc.—which can increase the cost of the average job by 50%.

It's taken Wolfgang Hoyt over a dozen years to achieve the high level of competence required for such major projects as the American Express Tower. Although other architectural photographers may work faster, Hoyt will tell you that the reason it takes so long (4 to 10 hours) to take a single photograph is, in a word, lighting. Hoyt estimates that on average he is responsible for 75 percent of the lighting seen in his photographs—and unlike some photographers Hoyt's primary purpose in lighting is to "convey the designer's intent on film. To this end," he says, "the photographer should avoid making things look overly dramatic. Rather, one should make the images—the spaces—look uncontrived."

A photographer shooting a space will see that space—particularly the light—differently than will the designer or the client. The photographer has to see it differently, for he or she knows that film "sees" light differently than does the eye. So the space must be lit to suit the film which will in turn reproduce light in a fashion that is pleasing to the eye. To achieve this, the photographer meters light levels and color temperature, then, after hours of careful testing, combines film, lights, and filters to make sure they all match at a level that is eye-pleasing. And brackets—shoots every image at different exposures, or lengths of time—to make sure the correct one is covered.

Because of these critical differences in *seeing*, photographers such as Hoyt have very strong feelings about the way designers use light. For example, Hoyt wishes that there was less fluorescent light in use, because it tends to polarize colors. In a more general vein, Hoyt believes that "light is what makes an interior sing, and the designer doesn't always do it right. Spaces just aren't lit right for pictures! I shouldn't have to walk into a space and totally relight it in order to photograph it, but I almost always do." ■

Expressing an Image, III

Traditional but with a rationale that meets both demands of design and bottom line, the top floors of New York's American Express Tower clearly express the late 20th-century look of the nation's newest corporate executive offices.

Recently completed by Swanke Hayden Connell Architects (SHCA), the 50th and 51st floors of the tallest building in Cesar Pelli's World Financial Center in Battery Park City are also an instance of innovation in ways of accomplishment. Encouragement of client involvement, design approach and purchasing methods all took on fresh meaning.

The SHCA designers, Todd De Garmo and Holly Haeringer, directed by the client's wish for a traditional concept, focused on continuing building architect Cesar Pelli's Beaux-Arts theme. Traditional materials and a traditional progression of spaces characterize the floors. The diagonal pattern of the marble in the downstairs public lobby is repeated upstairs in the carpeting and subtle beige Royal marble with Belgian Black insets.

After viewing mockups of three vignettes with loaned antique furniture and decorations, the client chose SHCA's proposal of flat, rather than heavier, raised paneling. With banding and reveals to suggest crown molding and chair rails, it serves as a strong yet unostentatious architectural background for the traditional dining rooms, and the English, Chinese, French and contemporary themes of the private offices. All wood, with the exception of the English brown oak for the client dining room, came from a single African mahogany log.

One intriguing aspect of the project, the designers report, was gaining an understanding of large-scale space—a knowledge that was familiar to the designers of English stately homes and turn-of-the-century American mansions. So De Garmo and Haeringer paid visits to the Wrightsman rooms at the Metropolitan Museum of Art (the source of an upholstered wall detail), the Frick Museum and The New York Public Library. Scale affected every detail from color to the source of furniture.

But what makes the executive spaces unusual is the choice of fine period furniture—a decision that grew out of the client's positive reaction to the mockups. It was a decision that also made excellent economic sense based on SHCA-prepared budgets of furnishing alternatives, the fact that American Express owned the building and would not be moving in the foreseeable future, and the knowledge that antiques have an intrinsic value—unlike many contemporary pieces whose resale value is a tiny fraction of cost. Selecting examples provided the client with a rare opportunity to become more personally involved in the process and to exercise expertise in reevaluating some earlier design choices.

After identifying half the antiques locally, Haeringer, appreciating the difficulty of finding large-scale items in the U.S. and the devalued pound, went on a trip to England. Efficiently armed with a formal education in the decorative arts, a list and the help of a very knowledgable English dealer, she purchased the remaining items in a lightning ten days at dealer prices which netted considerable savings.

The library with its working fireplace is a successful integration of pieces from all over the world. A Florence Knoll coffee table, French Empire chair, old leather-bound books on travel and a pair of Regency globes reflect the international nature and the Wells Fargo origins of the company. Again, the mix of art selected by Joan Kaplan, art advisor to American Express, and Diane Bliss, Director of the Art Program, complements the ambience and adds a subtle aesthetic tension.

These floors are clearly exceptional. But they are also an expression of the new corporate thinking about its own executive environment that will set a benchmark for the Fortune 500 and other organizations in the 1990s.

COMPUTERIZATION ADDS EFFICIENCY AND CONVENIENCE TO AMERICAN EXPRESS SIGNAGE

The functional criteria for the American Express Company's graphics program were familiar to Swanke Hayden Connell Architects, interior designers for the new 2.2-million-square-foot Tower in New York's Battery Park City. The signage plan should establish standards for identification purposes, be flexible to allow for high employee movement and reinforce the building's overall design themes.

But what made the program unusually valuable to the client was the development of a design approach and choice of fabrication capability that—after the initial move-in order of 25,000 signs—allows American Express to produce most of its own signs in-house. The hardware recommended was a new Hermes 1219 electronic engraver with keyboard and CRT. Using SHCA-adapted cap-and-core ¼" plastic to manufacture individual name plates, directional, base building and informational signs, the machine has already paid for itself.

Employing a modular approach SHCA designed signage in six different sizes, to reflect the elements of the 'street' or elevator lobby grid theme. All signs are magnetized in order to avoid marring surfaces and ease interchangeability. The three custom colors were selected from street end-wall lacquer finishes and the trim colors of the Ethospace open plan systems. A single plate surrounds each setback, similarly aligned elevator call button and incorporates the code-required fire egress diagram—developed from SHCA's CADD-stored 14 varieties of floor plans. Wood paneled executive floors received square code and bathroom signs of polished brass with black fill type. Floor identification panels lacquered and silk-screened in three colors are reusable. They and executive signage are produced by outside vendors.

Granted a more lenient time schedule for the project in which to develop the appropriate software, the designers would have been able to use their own CADD-generated tapes to program the engraving machine, thereby avoiding extra production steps—and adding one more capability to the firm's CADD system. ■

Behind the News

Ralph Emmett Carlyle
SENIOR WRITER

Willie Schatz
WASHINGTON BUREAU MANAGER

David R. Brousell
NEWS EDITOR

Parker Hodges
MANAGING EDITOR

Karen Gullo
ASSISTANT NEWS EDITOR

Kenneth Surabian
ART DIRECTOR

This department analyzes the information-processing angle behind major news stories. The three examples here explore: 1) who will get the lion's share of the huge funds allocated to computers and software for the Strategic Defense Initiative; 2) the cost of technical chaos when dissimilar computer operations must be combined in the course of huge mergers; and 3) the role played by inferior automatic warning systems at Bhopal, with an examination of similar shortcomings in the United States.

Datamation is read by people who buy, run, and program information systems worldwide. "Behind the News" first appeared in the March 1, 1986, August 15, 1986, and September 15, 1986, issues of *Datamation*, published by Cahners Publishing Company. © 1986. Reprinted with permission.

To Stop Another Bhopal

When Gary Gelinas walked into his office on Dec. 3, 1984, he had no reason to believe that this day would be unlike any other. The 38-year-old president of Safer Emergency Systems expected another not-so-successful day of peddling his computerized emergency response system to apathetic chemical companies. But before the day closed, news reports came from halfway around the world that radically changed the outlook of Safer's business and the chemical industry itself. The reports were headlined with the name of a city in central India that has since become a household word—Bhopal.

"When I first heard of Bhopal," recalls Gelinas from his office at Westlake Village outside of Los Angeles, "I thought, 'My God, it really did happen'. This wasn't a simulation that you put on the computer screen and watch colors change as the cloud moves downwind. I knew what toxic gas could do to a community, and I personally grieved for the people who were killed."

As the statistics filtered in, Gelinas's fears regarding the disaster became dire truth. Of the 200,000 victims who were exposed to the chemical leaked at Union Carbide's pesticide plant in Bhopal, over 2,500 died and 17,000 were left disabled. Today, people are still dying from what is recognized as the world's worst industrial accident.

After Bhopal, Gelinas no longer had to play the role of suitor, courting chemical companies. "Our phone lines were buzzing off the hook for days and days," he says. "There were so many inquiries about the emergency response system that I couldn't even break for lunch."

In the three years before Bhopal, Safer sold 15 emergency systems; less than a year later, that figure had jumped by more than 200%. The chemical industry wanted to demonstrate progress in handling toxic spills to an impassioned public. Safer offered an answer: a computer that predicted the path of an accidental release and promised to give officials time to deliver advance warnings.

The Safer system consists of a customized package of hardware and software with a base price of $60,000. The electronic sentry monitors the air for toxic gases and, in the event of a leak, charts the atmospheric dispersion of the gas, displays a regional map showing the affected areas, and optionally places prerecorded telephone calls to police and fire authorities. Inherent in the system is a three-dimensional model of local terrain, a schematic of the plant's physical layout, and detailed information about critical equipment including pipelines, mixing reactors, and storage tanks. Churning that data through a mathematical model along with weather conditions sensed from a meteorological tower, the Safer computer gives a crystal-ball view of the expected path of an airborne release.

That view has enticed a number of chemical industry heavyweights. Du Pont heads the list of Safer's customers with seven installations. Others include Diamond Shamrock, Olin Chemicals, Ciba-Geigy, Kaiser Aluminum and Chemical, and Union Carbide. Union Carbide chose a Safer system for its manufacturing site in the town of Institute outside of Charleston, West Virginia. The Institute plant is the only domestic producer of methyl isocyanate (MIC), the pesticide ingredient responsible for the deaths in India.

Safer technicians installed the computer at

Institute in February of 1985. Six months later, the system was called to duty for its first live test on an otherwise quiet Sunday morning. A tank ruptured that day, August 11, spewing a milky white cloud of toxic chemicals over the plant. The plume drifted east across the company fence into a residential neighborhood and a golf course. Before the gas dissipated, 135 people were engulfed by the plume. They were later treated at nearby hospitals for eye, throat, and lung irritation.

At Safer's office in California, the phones rang incessantly once again. This time the inquiries didn't come from frantic chemical company officals eager to learn about Safer's system, but from an equally anxious but less welcome source: news reporters demanding to know why Safer's computer had failed to correctly predict the path of the hazardous cloud.

A front-page headline in the *New York Times* proclaimed, "Carbide computer could not track gas that escaped." The Associated Press reported the computer erroneously showed the toxic cloud remaining within plant boundaries. After a four-month investigation, the Environmental Protection Agency reached the same conclusion, claiming the Safer computer's incorrect prediction "misled" officials, skewing their response to the leak.

The Institute incident raises questions regarding the role of computers in safety and processing at chemical plants. Some critics maintain that the effectiveness of plume models like those from Safer, Radian Corp. of Austin, Texas, and Environmental Research Technology of Concord, Massachusetts, is overbilled. Carbide officials counter that Safer's technology is the best available tool for tracking vapor releases.

Furthermore, they stress, plume modeling systems are only one facet of how computers contribute to safety by monitoring and processing hazardous materials. Safer's Gelinas is quick to defend his company's product. He points to a 1984 hydrogen chloride spill at a plant outside of Baton Rouge, Louisiana, where 100 families were safely evacuated.

The environmental engineering manager there said the Safer system "did accurately predict the concentration of the cloud."

Referring to the August mishap, Gelinas states without hesitation, "The computer worked exactly the way it was supposed to."

At that time, the Safer system at Institute was programmed to handle only three chemicals, he explains. If a release occurred, the Carbide employee operating the computer would choose the leaking compound with a light pen from a screen menu displaying the three chemical names. The operator would also point to the source of the leak on a displayed map. Information about chemical properties and storage characteristics related to each substance—such as molecular weight; viscosity; boiling point; heat of vaporization; and valve, pipe, and tank sizes, among other items—are stored in the computer. The operator can override these values by entering specific data.

Combining release volumes and rates with the weather conditions supplied by its meteorological tower, the Safer system simulates the path of the plume in color, showing severity levels in purple, brown, and yellow shades superimposed over an area map on its graphics display. A Motorola 68000-based microcomputer from Wicat Systems of Orem, Utah, handles processing chores within the system.

"On August 11, the operator did not have the leaking chemical on the computer menu, so he selected MIC, a chemical he thought was close," says Gelinas. But the two substances have different dispersion characteristics, he continues, and thus the system gave out wrong information. The incorrect results contributed to a 10-minute delay in notifying local officials.

What actually did leak at Institute was a chemical stew consisting of 3,800 pounds of 23 different compounds. The two main substances that vaporized in the airborne cloud were methylene chloride, a solvent, and aldicarb oxime, a basic ingredient in pesticides. Methylene chloride is a known carcinogen whose applications include decaffeination of some coffees and flame suppression in hair sprays. (The Food and Drug Administration proposes banning its use in hair spray.) Aldicarb oxime is also a component in the formula for Temik, a pesticide that figured in news reports last summer after hundreds of Californians fell ill from eating aldicarb-tainted watermelons.

If the computer had complete descriptions of methylene chloride and aldicab oxime, then, Safer and Union Carbide officials imply, it could have correctly plotted the plume and could have prevented or at least mitigated the injuries due to exposure to the toxic gas.

Others are not so sure. "I wouldn't bet too many lives on it," argues one source who is familiar with the Institute plant and is regarded as an authority on plume modeling. "A lot of funny things can happen with the wind in the hilly terrain of central West Virginia. Averaging the speed and direction from a single meteorological station over a five-minute period as the Safer system did may not give you an accurate picture. A 50% margin of error would not be unusual. For example, in light, variable wind conditions, as prevailed on August 11, a drifting gas can make a 180° turn in the space of five minutes."

In the opinion of this person, the main danger of a Safer-type system is believing the "impressive" picture created on the color graphics terminal without using judgment or looking out the window. "Some officials believe that a plume modeling system permits you to evacuate fewer people in the event of a leak than you would otherwise. But that may not be the right move. When you consider that plume models have only been validated in three basic tests with ammonia, liquefied natural gas, and rocket propellant, a significant error factor could arise, especially in predicting the path of other materials."

Gary Powers, a chemical engineering professor at Carnegie-Mellon University in Pittsburgh, voices similar concerns: "Plume models must take into account complicated dispersion processes. Diffusion, bulk mixing, and possibly reactions and absorption all come into play. It's a numerically demanding problem involving millions of calculations in several differential equations solved over time. It's like weather forecasting—you need a supercomputer to do the computation extremely well."

Powers believes that even if a computer could produce an exact replica of a toxic cloud, the information has limited value. "In essence, we're trying to detect a release, predict its trajectory, and then run ahead and warn people. But the thing gets there in a hurry. The transport mechanism—release and dispersion by winds—carries the material to populated areas in four or five minutes. Maybe 10 to 15 minutes if the wind isn't blowing. Do we actually think that we can get people out of the way?

"This doesn't mean that plume models have no value for planning emergency responses or that we shouldn't do our best to try to get people mobilized," continues Powers. "Ultimately, though, an ounce of prevention is worth a pound of cure. We should try to catch abnormal situations upstream in the manufacturing process before they erupt as leaks."

Carbide itself is reluctant to discuss the Safer plume modeling system. In light of an $88-million lawsuit by Institute residents claiming that Carbide "failed to maintain an adequate warning system," the company's position can be understood. Perhaps actions speak louder than words—in this case, anyway. Since the methyl chloride emission, a second meteorological tower has been connected to the Safer computer to increase the accuracy of predictions. At the same time, seven more chemicals have been programmed into the software, bringing the total number on the system menu to 10. To help streamline evacuations in the event of a major leak, Carbide is supplying engineers, construction crews, and $85,000 to build an emergency access road leading from the town of Institute.

Meanwhile, the admonishment to invest in an ounce of prevention hasn't fallen on deaf ears. The company is committing $220 million to improvements in environmental protection and safety; $5 million of that amount went into leak monitoring systems at Institute, where agricultural pesticides are manufactured.

Conrad Burriss, head of computer systems technology at Institute, calls the assortment of computers there "one of the biggest hardware stores in the East." According to Burriss, few materials enter or leave the plant without coming within the grasp of process control and monitoring computers.

On a tour of the facility, Burriss dons a hard hat and goggles to lead a visitor through the maze of pipes, valves, and tanks that give chemical plants the appearance of oversized printed circuit boards. The metallic arteries conduct the basic utilities of the plant—steam, air, nitrogen, and water—through a network covering a square-mile site on the Kanawha River.

"Many of our materials are handled by Honeywell TDC 2000 process control computers," says Burriss, walking into a dimly lit room where half a dozen operators sit at side-by-side consoles. In this application, Burriss explains the TDC 2000 sequences a 14-step process where a solid, liquid, and reactant are combined in batches to produce a solid. He declines to name the end result, referring to it only as an agricultural product.

Most of the processing steps are initiated by human operators, but a few fall under the control of a Modcomp Classic minicomputer. The Modcomp, manufactured by Modular Computer Systems of Fort Lauderdale, Florida, directs activities on the Honeywell TDC and keeps the process running smoothly, especially during shift breaks. It also serves as a vigilant sentry monitoring the status of the reaction. An operator can at any time request from the Modcomp a graphic depiction of the process. The computer relies on remote sensors to show the status of the mixing reactor and feeder pipes. In this example, ingredients are fed at rates up to 20,000 pounds per hour into a 20-foot-square tank or reactor. During a day-long mixing and "cook" cycle, the reactor is cooled to $-5°$ centigrade by a jacket of circulating brine. The finished product is then pumped from the vessel at 70,000 pounds per hour.

To keep tabs on the pressurized contents, the computer relies on an array of sensors. Tank-level indicators, pressure switches, temperature gauges, and flow meters, among other instruments, many installed as redundant sets, serve as the machine's nervous system. If a measurement falls out of a specified range, then audible and visual alarms are activated. One of the challenges in building these systems, asserts Burriss, is to categorize the alarms by priority so an operator is not inundated by bells and whistles.

Beyond particular processes, computers constantly watch over the environmental quality within the overall plant. Senior environmental engineer Diana Holley cites one water-monitoring system as a "real lifesaver." According to Holley, "The system is designed to catch effluent imbalances long before they leave plant property. It continually samples water cycled from the river for cooling equipment and it checks flows coming in and out of the plant's waste-water treatment unit."

Once a minute, a Hewlett-Packard 1000 minicomputer controlling this system polls eight monitoring stations connected through modems over telephone lines. The sensors at the stations perform checks ranging from simple tests for high levels of acidity and causticity to fine detection of organic carbon, measured by parts per million, in stream flows of up to 50,000 gallons per minute. In the event of an abnormal chemical balance, the computer triggers alarms at three different locations so plant personnel can stop the discharge at its source within an hour. The time required to respond to a leak can spell the difference between routine containment and disaster. As one Carbide engineer points out bluntly, "There's enough toxic material at the plant to poison the drinking water of every community from here to New Orleans."

In addition to monitoring substances within the plant, concern about environmental quality extends to tracking materials in transit, Burriss emphasizes. "One highly technical application involves a system for monitoring a 10-inch underground pipeline. The pipe carries toxic materials from the Institute plant across the slopes and valleys of Appalachian mountains to an industrial consumer 18 miles away. At the heart of the system, a Modcomp minicomputer regularly polls metering stations placed along the entire length of the pipeline. Station readings are transmitted by way of radio signals to the host. At the same time, the host computer runs a simulation model and compares actual pressure, flow rate, and temperature measurements with simulated values. If a discrepancy arises, the computer gracefully shuts down the pipeline and pinpoints a probable pipeline leak to within 100 feet."

Since the pipeline passes through populated areas, the computer also details emergency procedures for handling the leak. This information includes telephone numbers of appropriate government agencies and residents who live near the pipeline.

In any discussion about computers at Carbide's Institute plant, Burriss inevitably must field questions about the Safer system and what caused the erroneous prediction last August. Burriss's staff is responsible for maintaining the system's software. Major changes, such as adding new chemicals to the program's menu, are handled by Safer on a contract basis.

"The Safer system gives you a big bang for your buck," Burriss contends. "Sure, gas dispersion modeling systems may not be perfect, but they're an excellent tool for planning emergency response actions. And in the event of an actual release, they're better than having some guy who raises a wet finger in the wind and tries to guess where the plume's going."

The effectiveness of computerized plume modeling will no doubt be debated among scientists and engineers for some time. The question of whether or not existing dispersion models are valuable in directing an emergency response is one that can perhaps be best answered by those who must shoulder the financial consequences of a toxic leak—the insurance companies.

One of the largest insurance brokers for the chemical industry, Johnson and Higgins of New York, has several corporate clients whose plants line West Virginia's "Chemical Valley," a 25-mile stretch along the Kanawha River around Charleston, where two out of every three of the 15,000 manufacturing jobs depend on 13 major chemical factories.

"Don't expect plume modeling computers to lower liability rates in the near future, because they probably won't," asserts Evan Quarton, vice president of casualty loss control at Johnson and Higgins. "In today's market it's not a question of lower rates. It's a more general problem of finding an insurance carrier who will even touch a chemical plant."

The fact that a plant has installed a plume modeling system shows that management has an emergency response plan, adds Quarton. That factor may be enough to persuade an underwriter to at least consider an otherwise intolerable insurance risk. ■

All Sizzle and No Steak?

The easy part was writing the words in the Report to the Congress on the Strategic Defense Initiative, June 1986: "The purpose of the Strategic Defense Initiative is to establish the basis for an informed decision in the late 1990s on whether or not to develop and later deploy a defense of the United States and its Allies against ballistic missiles."

So much for simplicity. Now comes the hard part.

SDI (AKA Star Wars) is by far the most expensive, complicated, and controversial Department of Defense (DOD) project ever. It's the largest military research program DOD has ever undertaken. At its current level of funding, $2.75 billion, SDI is as expensive as the total technical base efforts of all the armed services. On a difficulty of implementation scale from 1 to 10, we're talking 96. President Reagan proposed a national research project on March 23, 1983, to make nuclear strategic missiles "impotent and obsolete." As the Pentagon sees it, SDI is a network of satellites carrying sensors, weapons, and computers to detect Soviet ballistic missiles and wipe them out before they get too far off the ground.

And while humans can fantasize about experimental rail guns, optical sensors, free-electron lasers, and all the other wonderful new weapons that technology may bring, none of them will work without computers. Without computers, SDI makes as much sense as a race car without an engine.

"Data handling, along with command and control technologies, for layered defenses must maintain a high priority within the SDI program," says the report to Congress. "Clearly, this work is central to the concept of a layered defense against ballistic missiles. No matter what evolves from our research in other areas of the program, reliable, resilient, and responsive data handling and command and control capabilities are requisite."

So where's the Strategic Defense Initiative Organization (SDIO) going to get all this great stuff? The computer companies of America, of course.

Like Gaul, SDI is divided into three parts. The computer industry is most concerned with what the report to Congress defines as the software programs of Systems Analysis and Battle Management (SA/BM) and countermeasures work. Then come the hardware technology programs such as Directed Energy Weapons (DEW), Kinetic Energy Weapons (KEW), Surveillance, Acquisition, Tracking, and Kill Assessment (SATKA), and Survivability, Lethality, and Key Technologies (SLKT). There are also "ancillary areas" that address the threat and threat projections, in addition to "an activity to stimulate innovative science and technology," whatever that means.

But this is serious business, folks. You don't buy this stuff at the hardware store or the local computer outlet for a few hundred dollars. According to the Federation of American Scientists (FAS) in Washington, D.C., the SDIO from 1983 to 1986 has awarded about $255 million to computer companies. It sounds like major bucks, but look again. The number is almost invisible in the grand SDI budget scheme. The nonprofit Center for Budget and Policy Priorities in Washington estimates that since 1983 SDIO has awarded contracts worth $5.97 billion. Major aerospace and government laboratories received the bulk of these contracts. The only computer company among the top 20 SDI contract recipients is Honeywell, at number 18.

SDI money isn't going to make or break the largest individual computer recipients of SDIO largesse. Granted, if SDI flies—a much debated prospect among computer scientists—it will be steady source of income for certain companies, but the initial benefit of being on the SDI payroll is a moderate chunk of revenue and nothing more. Sure, Honeywell probably feels somewhat better about its balance sheet because it has gotten 26 contracts worth $70.1 million. Those dollars, spent mostly on sensors and battle management computing, are more than any other major computer vendor has received. But how much does that really mean when the company's 1985 sales reached $6.62 billion?

Then there's Burroughs, which has gotten 12 contracts worth $38.3 million. Even Michael Blumenthal couldn't tell you where those fit in the company's 1985 total revenue of $5.04 billion. Control Data hit $13.9 million on the SDI scoreboard; compare that with a 1985 total revenue of $3.7 billion. Think IBM has really noticed its four SDI contracts worth $11.6 million in its total 1985 revenue of $50.6 billion? For a real laugh, try Hewlett-Packard, which has gotten a whopping four contracts for the staggering sum of $119,319. You'd need the world's strongest electron microscope to find that in the company's 1985 revenue of $6.61 billion.

"There's maybe $200 million a year in the SDIO budget going purely for computers," says John Pike, FAS's associate director for space policy. "Most of the computer research is coming out of other budget areas. There's no artificial intelligence per se in there. There's a $70 million FY '87 request for gallium arsenide [GaAs], and most of that is just to update DARPA's [Defense Advanced Research Projects Agency] old GaAs production line."

Despite the fact that the money computer companies will get for SDI amounts to little more than loose change, there are those who say the real payoff to the computer industry will come in the form of commercial spin-offs. Estimates of just how much the market for these spin-offs will be worth range from $5 million to $20 trillion, according to research firm Business Communications Co., Stamford, Connecticut. "I think it's a semisecret way of funding the next industrial era," the Center for Budget and Policy Priorities' Gordon Adams says. "SDI is saying, 'Here's the capital to let you acquire a leg up on the software and hardware of the future'. It's a covert industrial policy."

Well, that's one way of looking at it. Others are not so sure. "I don't think [SDI] money is going to have any commercial spin-off," says Pike of FAS. "It's all sizzle and no steak. The innovative software they're talking about is so mission specific that it's not going to be transportable to the private sector. The size of the contracts to the computer industry isn't going to make any difference in the big companies to anybody but the shareholders. SDI might be a good deal for the small software houses, though."

And how. Exhibit A: Adaptive Optics. The 40-person, $5-million firm in Cambridge, Mass., was founded by Julius Feinleib, a PhD in physics from Harvard. He had "a good idea" ten years ago and set up shop in his basement. Feinleib wanted to build a totally programmable, high-speed digital processor with instant input/output. So he hired an electrical engineer and started working.

There was only one problem: money. One small DARPA contract in 1976 led to another and another, which allowed Adaptive Optics to get started on the sensor system for lasers that Feinleib had envisioned. Then along came SDI, and all the firm's contracts were transferred to SDIO. Adaptive Optics is now creating a real-time, high-speed computer that will control a mirror that aims the laser that SDIO envisions traveling through the atmosphere and striking its target. Because atmospheric conditions always change, the sensor aiming the mirror has about a millisecond from input to output.

"We're totally dependent on SDI," says Feinleib, whose "sales" are strictly SDI money. "It's very dangerous for us. If SDI has a hiccup, we're in trouble. We're too vulnerable." As those who once made the vast majority of their living off IBM and no longer do can attest, when the boss doesn't want your business, you're history. As a hedge against that fate, given the political and budgetary uncertainties of SDI, Adaptive Optics is heading into the real world.

"I never thought there would be much commercial use for this." Feinleib admits. "But we've gotten interest from the machine-vision industry. And some oems are interested in our board sets for scanning and image acquisition.

"We've never had to worry about whether a chip was cheap or expensive. Now we do. For the first time, we've got to produce a product at the right price. We've been doing well, so I can't complain too much. But we feel very helpless."

There's more independence from SDI money when you're bigger. Computer Corp. of America (CCA), a Cambridge, Mass–based piece of Toronto's Crowntek Inc., does about $25-million worth of business annually. It has a funded research budget of $10 million. It's into SDIO for about $500,000, and the agency has an option to hit $745,000.

CCA is developing a software tool called Program Visualization (PV), a very sophisticated async distribution system that makes dynamic pictorial representations understandable to users.

"This is generic software technology that we would have done without SDIO," says Diane Smith, co-vice president for research and systems. "We would have been looking for sources of funding. Now, SDIO has made PV much more important and turned it from a minor growth opportunity to a major one. It's a reasonably sized project, given our research budget. We'll give it due importance."

Federal R&D seed money has made a cautious yet faithful SDI believer out of CCA president Ken Draeger. "I'm convinced there will be spin-offs, but not for four to 10 years," he says. "When I see what early federal funding did for my production line, I'm a believer." Years ago, that money helped CCA develop its Model 204 database, which will be used in the first round of the U.S. military's installation of a new Worldwide Military Command and Control System Information System (WIS). Model 204 is also used for Australia's social security system and by the nine largest universities in Japan.

SDI hasn't caused much of a ripple at other, larger companies, however. Take Computer Sciences Corp. (CSC). The El Segundo, Calif., systems integrator did $723.5 million in sales last year. It owes 75% of its existence to the government, but since 1983 has gotten only $33.7 million in SDIO money. More than half of that came last spring, when the Air Force Weapons Laboratory awarded CSC $19 million to harden the electronics in sensing equipment in space.

"It's not going to mean major changes in the way we do business," says Walter Culver, president of CSC's 1,700-employee systems division in Falls Church, Va. "We're only talking $6 million to $7 million a year. That's peanuts. The major impact won't be on earnings per share or overall growth impact.

"I think the greatest impact will be in research and development. It's also speeding up our normal process. We'd be doing this work, but not as intensely. And it's going to give us a tremendous advantage against our competitors that do DOD integration. There's a head and shoulders difference between those who go after SDIO money and those who don't."

That's easy for CSC to say. It's been a beneficiary of government contracts for a long time. But what about the industry as a whole? It's been down so long that it can't see up anymore. A baseball team in a slump this prolonged would be tossed out of its league in the best interests of the game. Will SDI make the slump go away?

"There's certainly enough [SDI] money to have an impact [on the computer industry]," says Lloyd Thorndyke, president of ETA Systems. The St. Paul–based Control Data spin-off is hard at work on the ETA-10 supercomputer (see "Not A Paper Tiger," July 15, p. 26).

"Computers are a small part of SDI," Thorndyke says. "They're an application rather than a salvation. SDI will help inflate the numbers, but it won't be dramatic. It won't provide enough of a transfusion for the industry to be what it was."

Maybe not, but in Thorndyke's neck of the woods—the supercomputer basin of the Midwest known as the Twin Cities—SDI is guaranteed to have a significant impact. If the scheme gets off the ground, supercomputers will fly it. You're not going to fire a rail gun with a Commodore 64.

"Our niche hasn't faced a slump," says Bob Gaertner, vice president for human resources and communications at Cray Research in Minneapolis, which, like ETA, has no SDI contracts. "Business has been very solid in 1985 and 1986. SDI does represent an opportunity to sell supercomputers. Given the heavy R&D

content, those people bidding on contracts are almost certainly going to need supercomputers for battle management."

That's not all they're going to need supercomputers for. Battle Management has been further refined into Battle Management/Command, Control and Communications or BM/C3 to its friends (and enemies, for that matter). Just because the BM/C3 requirements are the most complicated and massive in the entire project doesn't mean someone can sit down and draw a weapon on a scratch pad. That's still going to require computers to play their traditional role in numerical modeling.

"We're using mostly Cray X-MPs, which are two-dimensional machines," says a Department of Energy (DOE) national labs staffer. "SDI problems are three-dimensional. I think Seymour [Cray, the company founder] saw ahead to both academic and SDI problems, because the Cray 2 is the first three-dimensional machine. It has the necessary access to an additional 256K to increase its memory, whereas the X-MP only has a 128K solid-state disk to add to its memory. I think the Cray 2 and 3 are going to get significant play here and at the other national labs."

Cray play may indeed be very significant. Capitol Hill sources have hinted that battle management software will be developed on the Cray 3, which the company has said will be released in late 1987.

"There will be some trickle down from this," says the DOE source. "People will mimic it and try to get into the market. Don't forget there is a significant Crayette world out there."

SDIO is not about to forget any piece of the computer industry. There are enough BM/C3 issues to keep many companies busy for a decade or so. According to the report to Congress on SDI, BM/C3 is further broken down into a technology project, an experimental systems project, and a national test bed with a dedicated central national test facility.

The experimental systems project is to define and develop experimental versions of BM/C3 architectures that will lead to systems that coordinate and control the satellites, tracking systems, and lasers—all the elements of SDI, SDIO wants you to know that the experimental versions of these architectures "must demonstrate the ability to survive and operate reliably even in the presence of failures caused by nuclear effects, severe electromagnetic threat or direct enemy threats." Don't you feel better already?

The national test bed project will define, develop, build, and integrate a number of geographically distributed facilities that are "interoperable."

But neither of these projects will get off the paper on which they're printed without the BM/C3 technology project. That also comes in five parts: battle management algorithms, network concepts, processors, communications, and software engineering.

In the 12 pages SDIO spends describing BM/C3, only one sentence really matters: "The battle management software to be developed for the SDI may be the most complex ever attempted."

After that, the details. There's extensive discussion of the need for algorithms performing such functions as situation and damage assessment, defensive firing strategies, and network management. It admits that the need "for highly efficient computing algorithms in this environment presents a new and very strenuous challenge to the field of distributed computing." Reliable fault-tolerant, high-performance processing is called "essential" for battle management of a future system based on SDI technologies. Just to make sure no one misses the point, software for a multilayered ballistic missile defense will be "very complex, not only due to the amount of software required, but also due to the functions to be carried out by software."

That assessment has caused major controversy in the scientific community. In the summer of 1985, SDIO appointed the Eastport Study Group, a panel of eminent scientists chaired by Danny Cohen of the Information Sciences Institute at the University of Southern California. The panel's job was "to devise an appropriate computational/communication response to the battle management computing problem and make recommendations for a research and technology development program to implement the response."

The panel concluded that computing resources and battle management software for a strategic defense system are within the capabilities of the hardware and software technologies that could be developed within the next several years. But the complexity of the battle management software and the necessity to test, simulate, modify, and evolve the system make BM/C3 the paramount strategic defense problem.

That conclusion led SDIO to move up software on the priority list and consider changing SDI's emphasis from systems hardware to battle management computing. That would be a major realignment in SDIO's mental set, since the Defensive Technology Study Team (the Fletcher Panel, named after chairman James Fletcher)—established after President Reagan's SDI proposal in March 1983 to define a long-term R&D program aimed at eliminating the threat posed by ballistic missiles—had recommended in its report an "appliqué approach" of designing the system first and then writing the software to control it.

The Eastport Group said that was the "wrong approach for SDI" and that system architecture and BM/C3 must be developed together. A Senate staff report last March noted that if that shift in emphasis were required, "current systems architectures [developed prior to the Eastport study] might be reversed." Calls to the SDIO office seeking further elaboration were not returned.

The Eastport recommendation led to a major rift in the scientific community over the feasibility of SDI. Eastport member David Parnas, a professor of computer science at the University of Victoria in British Columbia and consultant to the U.S. Naval Research laboratory in Washington, resigned from the panel in protest. He wrote in the May–June issue of *Common Cause* magazine that "taking money [panel members received $1,000 per day] for developing a shield against nuclear missiles—while knowing that such a shield is impossible—felt like fraud." He also said that SDI discussions "often ignore computers, focusing on new developments in sensors and weapons."

Parnas's action sparked a revolution in the scientific ranks. University of Illinois physicist Mike Weissman has organized a petition drive in which more than 3,800 faculty members and 2,800 graduate students have pledged "neither to solicit nor accept SDI funds." Weissman claims that at least 56% of the total faculty of the nation's top 14 physics departments have signed on despite what he calls "risking their careers."

An open letter to the Congress, originally signed by five Nobel laureates and computer pioneer John Backus, gathered 1,600 signatures from current and former government and industrial laboratories personnel before being presented to Congress last May. The signers expressed their "serious concerns" that "recent statements from the [Reagan] administration give the erroneous impression that there is virtually unanimous support for this initiative from the scientific and technical community. In fact, the SDI has grown into a major program without the technical and policy scrutiny appropriate to an undertaking of this magnitude."

They've got that right. SDI hasn't just grown. It's exploded. From the program's modest $900 million birth in FY '84, its budget has more than tripled. At press time, the House had appropriated $3.4 billion for DOD's piece of SDI and $308 million for DOE's slice for FY '87. The Senate bill gave DOD $3.65 billion and DOE $300 million. That represents substantially less than SDIO's FY '87 budget request of $4.8 billion, a 77% increase over its FY '86 budget. How much padding was built into that $4.8 billion only SDIO knows for sure, and you can bet a space-based weapon it isn't telling. The House was scheduled to vote in late July on an amendment to hold for FY '87 the FY '86 SDIO budget line of $2.75 billion.

But even $2.75 billion ain't chopped liver. "My impression is that these guys are so busy spending they can't write checks fast enough," says the DOE national labs staff member.

Meanwhile, the big question is still unanswered: if SDI gets up in the sky, will it work? Does anybody in the computer industry really care?

"For our kind of product, if SDI shut down in the 1990s, I don't know that the world would be a whole lot different," says Cray's Gaertner.

"If you're CCA, whether SDI works is almost incidental," Draeger says. "We're assigned a job, we do the specs, and when we finish we get paid. In the meantime, we learn a hell of a lot about software engineering workstations we otherwise wouldn't."

A source close to the military research establishment thinks the computer industry would be better off if SDI is eventually grounded. "If the government says, 'This was a great idea, but we still have to wait for the technology base to work', then the people working at the cutting edge of technology would turn to something else.

"If SDI's a go, you're going to spend an awful lot of money on guys in hard hats pouring concrete." The attention paid to SDI will shift from the technology to the nitty-gritty of building the hardware, the source believes. Where does that leave the computer industry? With many questions, few answers, but a couple of extra bucks in its collective pocket. ∎

Mergers: A Raw Deal for MIS?

Nine months ago, the biggest problem on Gerry Cornish's mind was whether he should sell a VAX 11/780 and get another HP 3000 for his dp shop.

Other relatively mundane matters occupied the MIS director as his working year seemed to stretch predictably before him. Then, suddenly, his New York–based employer, John Blair & Co., a broadcast media firm, became the victim of a hostile takeover attempt and the fabric of Cornish's well-ordered world was ripped apart. All his plans—his whole future—were put on hold.

The ensuing tussle between John Blair and the "predator," MacFadden Holdings, publisher of *True Confessions* and *Teen Beat* magazines, made for juicy copy in the business press. But in Cornish's shop, with each day came anxiety.

"My plans, budget, everything, was frozen. Pet projects had to be put on the back burner," says Cornish. "My staff found it increasingly difficult to live with the uncertainty, and began to leave."

Cornish says he has lost more than 30% of his staff over the past three to six months. "With everything on hold I can't attract new staff," he says.

Now, like many others before him, Gerry Cornish is learning firsthand that mergers made in some corporate heaven can be hell in the computer room.

Not all mergers go badly, though sometimes it seems that way. The experts tell us that 70% fail to live up to expectations, but only half are outright failures.

"I've worked on seven corporate mergers—all of them traumatic—and I can tell you that the hardest things to marry are people and old programs," says Bob Patrick, a dp consultant in Rosamond, Calif., and a DATAMATION adviser. "Neither of them travel well, and both resist change."

Bill Synott, senior vp of information services at First National Bank, Boston, adds, "It's much easier to marry numbers on paper and get a match. Financials fuel mergers; ill-fitting technologies and people break them."

Mergers have been on the upswing since 1981, according to W.T. Grimm & Co., a Chicago-based research firm specializing in tracking mergers. "There were some 3,001 mergers, consolidations, and acquisitions across the nation last year, with a total price tag of almost $180 billion," says the company's president, James J. Kelly.

Deregulation's catalytic power is reshaping banking, transportation, and communications. Banks (including holding companies) struck the largest number of deals in 1985, according to Grimm. Protection from bad markets and safety from competitors were major factors that affected industries such as computers and oil.

"In banking it's either grow or die," First National's Synott explains. "Some banks have found themselves leapfrogged by the acquisitions of competitors and are anxious to regain parity," he says.

Even IBM, indirectly at least, is helping to fuel the current merger fever and is as much a beneficiary as the deal-making lawyers, investment bankers, and Wall Street brokers. "IBM is everywhere, and the number of software environments is shrinking. Such de facto standardization makes it easier for corporations to merge their technologies, if not their people," says Ted Withington, a vice president at research firm Arthur D. Little Inc., Cambridge, Mass., and a DATAMATION adviser.

A recent example is the GE-RCA megamerge, one of the largest merger deals outside the oil business. NBC, now a GE subsidiary, is converting from Sperry to IBM. And now GE itself is "beginning to pick its spots," as one of its dp executives puts it, and convert from Honeywell to IBM. The former RCA facility at Cherry Hill, New Jersey, an IBM center, is beginning to absorb the people and activities of GE's large Corporate Operating Services data center in Schenectady, New York, a longtime Honeywell bastion. "There's no policy to convert the whole of GE to IBM," says Mick CoFone, manager of Computer Services for the new conglomerate, and formerly vp in charge of all RCA's computer operations. "When a productivity increase can be demonstrated with the IBM approach, we'll consider it, but there's still a lot of Honeywell left in GE."

One could cite many other reasons for the seemingly endless shuffling of corporate ownership—including cash-rich utilities with wandering eyes. Overall, however, the biggest factor seems to be the failure of previous mergers, consolidations, and acquisitions.

"Corporations aren't so much anxious to acquire as to divest," claims Grimm's Kelly. "Programs haven't worked out, and they are intent on redeploying assets." Divestitures accounted for 41% of the 3,001 deals last year—up 5% from the year before, he says.

When two companies merge, particularly within the same industry, consolidation of the two MIS operations is usually a top priority. Yet time after time the marriage of the two computer cultures fails to achieve the synergy desired. Why?

"It's personalities and old-fashioned ways of organizing data that don't mesh in mergers," says George P. Dinardo, senior vp of information management and research at the Mellon Bank, Pittsburgh, and a veteran of five mergers and hundreds of other smaller acquisitions and conversions.

"Data has traditionally been organized around individual applications rather than in shared, corporate databases," he explains. Dinardo warns that such data structures become rigid and don't lend themselves to new uses when companies merge or are acquired. "They're also wickedly difficult to maintain," he adds.

The Mellon executive stresses that the disposition of computer systems in a merger situation is largely a matter of common sense and sound planning. "But people—particularly dp people—are another matter," he says, "and require special handling."

"It's important to remember that all mergers, even 'friendly' ones, take place in an atmosphere of fear and uncertainty. If you're not careful," he says ruefully, "you can lose good people at any stage in the process."

Two years ago, after digesting four banks

"relatively painlessly," Dinardo faced his biggest challenge. He was asked to absorb the $5-billion Gerard Trust Bank in Philadelphia. Critics said that this larger-than-life and autocratic executive would "stub his toe," and sure enough, he did.

A total of 15 systems in Philadelphia had to be converted over to the Mellon integrated data structure that Dinardo has carefully built up over the past 17 years. "Core" teams from Mellon Bank were put in charge of the conversions with "shadow" teams from Gerard in support; Dinardo, as was his style, began cracking the whip.

"I kept hitting my schedules and angered a lot of people," remembers Dinardo. "After the third conversion, things started to go wrong. Gerard people started to leave and complained vociferously to the press, who had a field day."

Dinardo was tagged General George for his authoritarian ways, and was given a Prussian helmet that is still on his desk. "I have to be honest," he says, "the whole world told me I couldn't do a bank that size, and I was determined to prove them wrong." General George won his war, but with heavy casualties.

"You tend to forget that the other side has its pride too. Gerard had been a losing concern, and was very labor intensive, but it still had its pride. One thing I learned," Dinardo reflects, "was that I should have put them in charge of the conversions and given them more responsibilities."

The colorful MIS executive completed his conversions in one year, and clipped $10 million a year, 33%, off Gerard's $30 million dp budget. "But I could have done it at a more leisurely pace—say 18 months—and avoided a lot of bad feeling."

Today, Dinardo's hard-earned knowledge is eagerly tapped by other banks looking to merge. "What I tell them is to be firm—after all, your goal is always to merge and control two entities—but be a little more caring about the psyches of the other side."

Arrogance aside, one of the greatest dangers in a merger situation is a lack of dialogue between corporate chiefs and the dp department. "MIS people can make or break a merger," says John Arnold, president of ExecuTrak Inc., a Waltham, Mass., consulting firm that acts as a counselor and catalyst for mergers and acquisitions. "Management should make every effort to boost their morale and keep them informed about the merger."

"All too often, a friendly merger opportunity can die on the vine because of the insensitive handling of MIS personnel," says Arnold, whose company has consulted on more than 85 mergers, consolidations, and acquisitions. Arnold cites the recent case of two banks, which he declined to identify. Bank A, cash starved and desperate, sold an option to buy its stock to bank B in another state as soon as interstate regulations would allow. To prepare for the eventual merger, the potential acquirer asked for a meeting with an MIS task force from bank A to discuss the future shape of the combined dp operation. "In the one-sided discussion that followed, B laid its game plan on the MIS group —a plan that called for almost total obsolescence of A's computers and dp procedures," Arnold explains. "The visiting MIS group wasn't asked for its judgment and advice, and left the meeting shocked and demoralized."

Bank A had originally called in Arnold to help keep its people motivated during the long merger process. "After MIS had told its tale, A's new cry was 'Help us regain our freedom!'" says Arnold. Witness the power of MIS in banking, where it often *is* the business: bank A created new preferred stock that it sold overseas, and proceeded to buy its first option back. MIS, in this case, was instrumental in breaking the merger off.

Consultant Patrick has witnessed similar situations. "Management tends to forget that MIS is a subculture that exists in isolation from the rest of the corporation," he observes. "For this reason it's the focal point for tensions that build up during the merger process."

Patrick warns management not to place

A Dry Run

One clear lesson that can be learned from past merger failures is that a corporation must first get a unified view of its own data before it can hope to successfully merge with another.

The technology is emerging to help companies do this, and well-integrated operations will soon be able to simulate the effects of a merger without actually merging.

As might be expected, IBM is playing a leading role in all this. Using input from its huge GUIDE user group, the computer giant is designing a new data dictionary—or repository—that it hopes will allow its customers to have a more integrated view of data and the applications that process them.

"The evolution of IBM's System/38 database architecture is also a significant step in this process," claims Ted Withington, a vp at Arthur D. Little Inc., Cambridge, Mass., and a DATAMATION advisor.

New tools to assist in the design of shared corporate databases are beginning to reach the market. Jack Crawford, president of HI-TECH, Hartford, Conn., claims that his firm's new dictionary and CAD/CAM tools—now in beta test at four corporate sites—permit customers to create and model data and processes at a high level, meaning that nontechnical people can do it.

"One thing they can do," Crawford says, "is simulate the effects of a merger of two data structures." This is because, with the exception of its people, a corporation is essentially one vast data structure. "The possibilities are exciting," Crawford declares.

This trend hasn't escaped the notice of IBM's superelite salesmen, the IBM account executives. "Some 168 of these salespeople account for $10 billion of IBM sales," says Withington, who was recently on a consultants' panel with some of them. "The only thing they all agreed on was that customers want to move with all speed to an integrated resource management system [IRM]. This is the Holy Grail of computing, but no one has managed to find it yet."

Mergermania makes it even more vital that a solution is found. Banks, for example, need to present to the customer an image of a unified system. First, because they can't serve their clients without it, and second, because the more integrated their data structure is, the easier it is for them to acquire other companies.

"The first companies to reach IRM will have the edge over the others. They'll be able to acquire more, merge more, and sell more," states Crawford. "The impact on the future shape of the industry could be enormous."

special demands on the dp shop early in a merger. "The board of directors of the new combination is usually out to achieve something from day one to show how clever it was in making the marriage. What happens is that they immediately place additional demands on the dp guys in addition to their regular work."

Adds Patrick, "The board starts screaming for a consolidated balance sheet for the new corporation. It wants to get the financials together and the production numbers together, but the board forgets that the marriage partners chart these processes in different ways. New translation programs have to be written by dp. It all takes time.

"It's best not to do anything on the first day. Take a two-martini lunch and soberly assess the work to be done," quips Patrick. "Put together a realistic timetable that dp can live with."

Most agree that the key to a successful merger is good planning. "But there's usually little time to do any before the partners agree to the merge," adds Dinardo. Merger discussions are often conducted at lightning speeds and in complete secrecy. MIS is rarely considered for any length of time before a deal is struck, let alone planned for.

"Usually I'll get a call," Dinardo explains, "someone on the board will tell me we're going to merge and ask me to figure out a plan in five minutes. The board's biggest concern," he laughs, "is that my department doesn't have body odor!"

Generally, it's not possible for the acquirer to get an in-depth view of the dp operation he is attempting to digest. "MIS departments tend to get nervous or hostile when task forces or auditors appear in their domain," says Arnold. As John Blair's Cornish learned, even the hint of a merger can decimate a dp operation.

Arnold says that discreet interviews with the managers, customers, and dealers of the organization to be acquired are helpful in determining its attitudes toward the merge. "But dp is a closed world. To find out how they operate, it's probably best to send out dp consultants on scouting missions."

What dp consultants generally discover on these sorties is that the MIS department is not ready to be crunched together with its equivalent somewhere else. "Most dp shops have neither the time or the people for much more than maintenance of old code and rigid data structures," claims Patrick. "They are not ready to do major systems planning overnight. Often it can take 60 days or more to free available talent."

If, after these warnings, the merger is still on, there are costs that can and can't be computed, the experts say. The heaviest costs will be accrued by those attempting to convert aging and poorly documented software, as well as both retrain and relocate staffs. In contrast, it's relatively easy to consolidate the two hardware and communications environments, and this is the one area where considerable savings can be achieved.

What can't be estimated is the cost of lowered staff morale and high turnover. Take for example the case of two industrial companies, the larger in Chicago and the smaller in Los Angeles, whose dp departments were "crunched" together, as one insider put it, over a two-year period. Many of the dp people in L.A. didn't want to relocate and refused to cooperate in the merger. "When the good people left, so did their documentation and files," remembers the insider. "The whole thing was a shambles." This conglomerate is now attempting to "unmerge" and its stock is climbing once more.

Bonuses and other incentives can sometimes help in these situations. Often it's vital to leave some of the very best people in the dp shop that is being wound down—to hold the pass, as it were. This shop has to go on producing until it completely atrophies. The people left behind to hold down the fort are worth their weight in gold and should be handsomely rewarded, say experts.

"You'll always lose people who can't deal with uncertainty," GE's CoFone explains. "The key to keeping the rest is lots of communication and an open door policy. I keep telling my [former RCA] people that GE didn't buy us for our buildings and our machines. They bought the skills of our organization.

"In the final analysis," he concludes, "it's more an issue of people getting merged, not technology."

While conversions can't be avoided in a merger—programs get old and unadaptable—the time-honored practice of converting applications to existing systems, either "ours" or "theirs," must end, according to First National's Synott.

Synott describes trying to choose the best applications as a nightmare. "I don't see how you can do it without conflict," he says. "And when you've done it, you still don't have integrated applications.

"The only sensible approach," he advises, "is to create a common database that meets the business needs of the new combine and rewrite your applications to work with that."

Carl Steiner, the director of planning for Baxter Travenol's Information Services Organization, agrees, but adds, "The technology to do this is only just beginning to emerge. Until it does, you have to choose your merger partner very carefully."

Steiner believes that the best possible merger situation is one that involves two growth-oriented companies that are compatible, or complementary, in terms of their product lines or services. "The merged company provides a larger environment for talented people to grow," he explains.

It helps if both organizations are IBM shops with the same operating system, and if they're both in the same geographic location. A case in point is the recent merging of Steiner's employer, a $4-billion drugs conglomerate based in Chicago, and American Hospital Supply, based in Deerfield, within 15 miles of each other. The only fly in the ointment is that AHS, once a Burroughs user, is still converting some of its programs to IBM. "This process is almost complete," says Steiner.

ADL's Withington describes Baxter Travenol's recent merger with AHS as one of the best fits in recent years. "Real synergy," he declares.

Steiner says that the two companies were heading in the same direction in the medical services area. "Their distribution capability complemented our manufacturing capability. There's plenty of talent in both organizations and both sets of files were well structured," he adds.

If Steiner is right, AHS, at least, is one company that won't return to the board of America's favorite high stakes game: asset juggling. Something precious will have been salvaged: a whole, which, for once, is greater than its parts. ∎

Emergency Handbook '86

Lucy H. Labson
EXECUTIVE EDITOR

Clayton Raker Hasser
EDITOR

Robert L. Edsall
DEPUTY EDITOR

Judith A. Cash
MANAGING EDITOR

Elizabeth R. Pollack
ART DIRECTOR

Diann Peterson
SENIOR COPY EDITOR

The possibility of medical emergency is a stressful reality for all physicians; in some ways the stress is greater for those who do not spend all day in emergency rooms, because they are less prepared. These articles resulted from a survey to identify the emergencies doctors think about the most. They contain the best available advice in a format designed for fast access to information.

Patient Care serves primary-care physicians, particularly those specializing in family practice or internal medicine. "Emergency Handbook '86" first appeared in the September 15, 1986, issue of *Patient Care,* published by Medical Economics Company, Inc. © 1986. Reprinted with permission.

Emergency Handbook 1: General Medicine

INITIAL ASSESSMENT

1. The Conscious Patient

- If you suspect an overdose of a tricyclic antidepressant, cocaine ("crack"), or another agent that can cause cardiac arrest, the patient requires immediate transport to the hospital emergency department (ED), with transmission of cardiac rhythm via ECG telemetry from the ambulance if possible. IV administration of 5% dextrose in water should be started as soon as possible.
- If you suspect an overdose of another drug or drugs, however, proceed to initial evaluation of the patient's condition.

(a) Observe vital signs

Regardless of the drug or drugs taken, your first priority is to determine the stability of respiratory and cardiovascular function.

- Monitor vital signs every 15 minutes.
- If the patient is in your office and initial signs are stable, plan to initiate resuscitation or provide immediate transportation to the EL if his or her condition deteriorates. Sudden cardiac arrest is not uncommon, particularly with overdoses of cocaine or tricyclic antidepressants, despite initial stability.

(b) Obtain the history

- Obtain as much information as possible from the patient (if he is sufficiently awake and the vital signs are normal) and from the patient's companions about the drugs involved, if any.

Equipment

Nondrug
EG monitor
Endotracheal tubes
Equipment for hemodialysis or peritoneal dialysis
Equipment for measuring arterial blood gases
Hypothermia and hyperthermia blankets
Infusion pump or similar device
IV equipment
No. 36 French Ewald or large-bore orogastric tube (Lavacuator)
Oxygen and related equipment
Sample collection equipment for blood and urine
Swan-Ganz catheter
Thermometer capable of registering hypothermia and hyperthermia

Drug
Acetylcysteine (Mucomyst)
Activated charcoal (CharcolantiDote, Liquid-Antidose)
5% dextrose in water
Diazepam (Valium)
Dopamine HCl (Dopastat, Intropin)
50% glucose solution
Hydralazine HCl (Apresoline)
Ipecac syrup
Magnesium citrate
Magnesium sulfate (Epsom salt)
Naloxone HCl (Narcan)
Norepinephrine bitartrate (Levophed)
Phenytoin sodium (Dilantin)
Physostigmine salicylate (Antilirium)
Potassium chloride
Propranolol HCl (Inderal)
Saline: normal, one-half normal, and one-quarter normal
Sodium bicarbonate
Sodium nitroprusside (Nipride, Nitropress)
Sodium sulfate
Sorbitol
Thiamine HCl (Biamine)
Vitamin K_1 (AquaMEPHYTON, Konakion)

Intoxication Syndromes of Commonly Abused Drugs

ACETAMINOPHEN
Abdominal pain
Nausea
Tender liver edge
Vomiting

DEPRESSANTS
Decreased blood pressure
Depressed respiration
Depressed tendon reflexes
Variable pupils (Exception: In glutethimide [Doriden] poisoning, pupils are dilated.)

EXCITATORY DRUGS
Agitation
In cocaine or "crack" use:
   Arrhythmias
   Horizontal and Vertical Nystagmus
   Seizures
Dilated pupils
Hyperactive tendon reflexes
Hyperpyrexia
Increased blood pressure
Increased heart rate
Paranoia, nervousness
Shallow respiration

HALLUCINOGENS
Dilated pupils
Disorientation
Hyperactive tendon reflexes
Hyperpyrexia
Increased blood pressure
Increased heart rate
In phencyclidine (PCP) use:
   Constricted or normal pupils
   Extreme hypertension
   Nystagmus
   Sensory anesthesia
   Violent behavior

NARCOTICS
Constricted pupils
Decreased blood pressure
Diminished or absent reflexes
Low body temperature
Pulmonary edema
Slow or absent respiration
Stupor or coma

SALICYLATES
Confusion
Ecchymosis
Hearing loss
Hematuria
Hyperpyrexia
Hyperventilation
Nausea
Tinnitus
Vomiting

TRICYCLIC ANTIDEPRESSANTS
Agitation
Anticholinergic symptoms:
   Dilated pupils
   Dry mouth
   Flushing
   Hyperpyrexia
Arrhythmias
Confusion
Hallucinations
Hyperactive reflexes
Hypotension

■ If street drugs are involved, the patient, and even the drug dealer, may not really know their composition. Your familiarity with the drugs popular in your area and their street names will be helpful, as will your awareness of the prescribing habits of other local physicians.

■ An impaired mental state or a desire to withhold information may make the personal and medical history less than completely accurate, but they are still important. In particular:

Has the patient had prior episodes of drug abuse?

Does he have diabetes or another chronic disease?

Has he recently experienced an emotional trauma?

Does he have a history of psychiatric illness?

Has he ever attempted suicide?

Does he take any medications?

■ Before diagnosing drug overdose, rule out encephalitis, hypoglycemia, and a psychotic episode on the basis of the patient's history, symptoms, and physical examination.

■ Symptoms of overdose may include lethargy, somnolence, stupor, delusions, or combativeness.

■ Clusters of symptoms associated with certain specific drugs or classes of drugs may provide additional clues to the specific agent or agents involved (see "Intoxication syndromes of commonly abused drugs").

NOTE: Polydrug abuse is more the rule than the exception. For example, patients who use methadone HCl (Dolophine) often take diazepam (Valium) as well.

2. The Unconscious Patient

(a) Assess vital signs

Quickly evaluate respiratory and cardiovascular function in the unconscious patient and initiate cardiopulmonary resuscitation or other supportive measures as appropriate.

- If the patient is in your office, arrange for immediate transport to the ED.
- Defer consideration of what drug or drugs are involved in a suspected overdose until vital signs are stable.

(b) Obtain the history

Obtain historical details from the patient's companions or from the emergency medical crew (see **1b**). Look for medical information tags.

3. Laboratory Tests

(a) Tests for drugs

- Obtain blood and urine samples for drug screening.
- Flag suspected causative drugs when requesting a drug screen, even if you're aware of what is normally included in your laboratory's analysis.
- If the laboratory findings come back negative, a drug may still be involved; the patient may have taken a substance not included in the screen, or there could be a problem with the laboratory procedure.

(b) Other tests

- *For all patients* order:
An evaluation of electrolytes.
Hepatic and renal function tests and a CBC. These allow you to document any progressive damage that might occur in the aftermath of drug overdose. This is particularly important for acetaminophen poisoning because associated liver damage only becomes apparent several days later.

- *For selected patients* order arterial blood gases. These are indicated if the patient is comatose or in respiratory distress, or if the drug involved—a salicylate, for instance—causes acidosis.

INITIAL TREATMENT

Once respiratory and cardiovascular signs are stable in the patient with a suspected drug overdose, consider the need for other supportive and aggressive measures. Provide oxygenation, monitoring it where appropriate with repeated blood gas determinations, and maintain appropriate acid-base, fluid, and electrolyte balances.

1. Naloxone HCL

(a) Indications

- Naloxone HCl (Narcan), which is virtually never contraindicated, is given almost routinely when a drug overdose is suspected. A good response is diagnostic for narcotic intoxication as well as lifesaving.
- Initial impressions may be misleading, however, if the patient is a polydrug abuser. For example, the patient who has taken methadone HCl (Dolophine) and diazepam (Valium) will improve as naloxone blocks the effects of the methadone. But a clinical deterioration will occur in spite of naloxone administration when the diazepam takes effect. The findings of a well-targeted drug screen are invaluable in this situation.

(b) Administration

- The initial naloxone dose is 0.4-2.0 mg IV. If the overdose is severe or if a new, potent designer drug was involved, consider giving a larger dose.
- Whatever the dose, repeat it if the patient does not respond within two minutes. Continue repeating the dose, to a maximum of 10 mg.

- If an unconscious patient fails to respond to several injections of naloxone, the possibilities are massive narcotic overdose, overdose of a nonnarcotic drug, and a medical condition.
- Even the patient who responds initially to naloxone can relapse into unconsciousness. For example, since methadone is a long-acting drug, the salutory effects of the initial doses of naloxone may wear off while the methadone is still potent.

2. Fluids and Antihypotensives

(a) *Fluid replacement*

IV fluids are indicated routinely in drug overdose but only to replace losses at a maintenance rate. Indiscriminate administration of IV fluids may produce pulmonary edema, particularly in tricyclic antidepressant overdose.

- In general, administer one-half or one-quarter normal saline, except when the patient is hypotensive. Administer a 500-mL bolus of normal saline for hypotension.

(b) *Antihypotensive therapy*

- If the patient's blood pressure does not increase in response to the saline, correcting metabolic acidosis with a bolus of sodium bicarbonate, 0.5-2.0 mEq/kg, is necessary, especially in tricyclic antidepressant overdose.
- If the patient's hypotension persists, add a 200-mg ampule of dopamine HCl (Dopastat, Intropin) to a 250- or 500-mL bottle of saline or 5% dextrose in water and titrate the dose as outlined by the advanced cardiac life support (ACLS) standards of the American Heart Association.* Instill the dopamine at a rate of 2–5 µg/kg/min, adjusting upward as necessary; use an infusion pump or another metered device to control the rate of flow.
- Alternatively, norepinephrine bitartrate (Levophed) can be used to treat hypotension.

*Adult advanced cardiac life support. *JAMA* 1986; 255:2933–54.

Add 4 mL of norepinephrine bitartrate solution to 1 L of a 5% dextrose in saline or 5% dextrose in water solution and administer the solution IV. Depending on the patient's response to the initial 2-3 mL, adjust the rate of flow to approximately 0.5-1.0 mL/min to maintain a low normal blood pressure.

3. Other Agents

(a) *Glucose*

- Assume that the patient is hypoglycemic.
- Administer 50 mL of a 50% glucose solution IV. Repeat as clinically indicated.

(b) *Thiamine HCl*

- Administration of glucose to a nutritionally deficient individual may precipitate Wernicke's encephalopathy.
- Administer thiamine HCl (Biamine) 100 mg IM.

(c) *Thermal control blankets*

- If the body temperature is severely elevated as a result of an overdose of excitatory drugs, hallucinogens, or salicylates, the use of a hypothermia blanket may be necessary to decrease body tempertaure.
- If the body temperature is severely decreased, as it might be in narcotic overdose, the use of a hyperthermia blanket may be necessary to increase body temperature.

(d) *Sodium bicarbonate*

For tricyclic antidepressant poisoning, alkalinize the blood with a sodium bicarbonate drip. Add 2 ampules containing 44.6 mEq sodium bicarbonate per ampule to 1 L of 5% dextrose in water. Adjust the rate to maintain a blood pH of 7.5. If the patient is in critical condition, infuse the sodium bicarbonate drip for 24 hours after his or her condition stabilizes.

4. Gastric Emptying

(a) General considerations

■ Consider inducing emesis or initiating gastric lavage to empty the stomach fully and prevent further absorption if the overdose occurred via oral administration.

■ Gastric emptying is contraindicated if:
The drug or drugs were taken intravenously.
The patient ingested a caustic substance or a petroleum distillate in addition to the drug or drugs.
Seizures are present (see **7**, page 251).

(b) Induction of emesis

■ The patient must be alert enough to protect the airway for 20–30 minutes after administration of an emetic. Seizures, unconsciousness, semiconsciousness, and any other threats to airway patency are indications for proceeding instead with gastric lavage.

■ Ipecac syrup is the preferred emetic agent, especially in children. The use of soap solutions or apomorphine HCl is no longer recommended. Copper sulfate solutions can cause hepatic and renal failure; saline solutions can induce hypernatremia and convulsions.

■ The dose of ipecac syrup in adults is 30 mL, followed by 350-475 mL (12-16 fl oz) of water; in children, give 15 mL ipecac syrup and then 175-240 mL (6-8 fl ox) water; in infants, give 10 mL ipecac syrup and then 60-120 mL (2-4 fl oz) water. Repeat in 30 minutes if necessary.

■ Examine the gastric contents for clues to the offending drug, including broken capsules and pieces of tablets, and send the samples to the laboratory for analysis.

■ Ipecac usually is not administered more than two times.

(c) Indications for gastric lavage

■ Gastric lavage is still considered by many authorities to be the most thorough method of gastric emptying, especially in adults, and is the only method that can be used in unconscious patients.

■ The procedure can be effective hours after ingestion if gastric emptying has been slowed —as occurs, for example, in salicylate intoxication.

■ In conscious patients, gastric lavage is the preferred approach for those who have taken an overdose of tricyclic antidepressants.

■ Contraindications for gastric lavage are the same as those for gastric emptying in general (see **4a**, above).

CAUTION: Aspiration pneumonia is a common complication of an improperly conducted gastric lavage.

(d) Procedure for gastric lavage

If one isn't already in place, insert an endotracheal tube to protect the airway, using anesthesia if necessary.

■ Use the largest bore lavage tube available, preferably a No. 36 French Ewald tube or a large-bore orogastric tube (Lavacuator); the large bore enhances the removal of capsules and tablets.

■ Place the patient on his left side, head down.

■ Aspirate the contents of the stomach without lavage fluid initially to obtain an uncontaminated sample for laboratory testing.

■ Install 150-250 mL of warm tap water; use saline in children to reduce the risk of inducing electrolyte imbalance. Do not use excessive force. Too much pressure forces the stomach contents and lavage fluid into the small intestine, increasing absorption of the drug.

■ Allow the stomach to be emptied by gravity, or, alternatively, apply suction.

■ Continue lavaging, 150-200 mL at a time, until the output from the stomach is the same color and clarity as the water or saline. Then instill and remove an additional liter of lavage fluid.

NOTE: Glutethimide (Doriden) and meprobamate (Equanil, Meprospan, Miltown, etc.) have a tendency to cake in the stomach. Gentle stomach massage may be necessary to remove all of the drug.

5. Drug Adsorption and Catharsis

(a) General considerations

Once the patient can take fluids, administer activated charcoal (CharcolantiDote, Liquid-Antidose) and a cathartic to remove any drug or drugs in the gastrointestinal (GI) tract that might remain after induced emesis or gastric lavage. Cathartic agents include sorbitol, magnesium sulfate (Epsom salt), sodium sulfate, and magnesium citrate. Sorbitol can be mixed with the charcoal, giving it a sweet flavor; this solution produces the most rapid onset of catharisis.

(b) Cautions and contraindications

- Do not use activated charcoal in acetaminophen poisoning. The charcoal adsorbs the antidote, acetylcysteine (Mucomyst) (see also "Further Management," **2,** page 253).
- Do not use cathartics if the patient has an ileus or shows evidence of GI bleeding.
- If the patient is in renal failure, either avoid using magnesium sulfate and magnesium citrate or use them cautiously.

(c) Procedure

- For an adult, combine 50-100 g activated charcoal with 240 mL (8 fl oz) water; in children, add 30 to 50 g to 120 mL (4 fl oz) water. Pass the liquid into the lavage tube if one is already in place or have the patient drink it .
- Have the adult patient drink one of the following:

1-3 g/kg of sorbitol in a 35-70% solution, to a maximum of 240 mL of a 70% solution; or

30 g of magnesium sulfate or sodium sulfate in a 25% solution; or

300 mL of a commercial magnesium citrate solution

- For the child, give:

1.0-1.5 g/kg of sorbitol in a 35% solution, to a maximum of 50 g/dose; or

250 mg/kg of magnesium sulfate or sodium sulfate in a 25% solution; or

4 mL/kg of a magnesium citrate solution, to a maximum of 300 mL

- For the patient who has taken an overdose of a tricyclic antidepressant, readminister activated charcoal q6h until the patient is stable. This facilitates removal of the drug as it recycles through the digestive tract.

6. Anticholinergic Symptoms

(a) General considerations

- For patients who have taken an overdose of an anticholinergic drug or another atropine-like agent, treatment with physostigmine salicylate (Antilirium) may be indicated.
- Physostigmine is contraindicated if the ECG demonstrates a QRS interval of 100 ms or more.
- Any evidence of an intraventricular condition defect or heart block precludes the use of physostigmine.

CAUTION: The use of physostigmine in any patient suspected of taking a tricyclic antidepressant overdose is considered by most authorities to be contraindicated and is used only in the most severe, life-threatening circumstances when all other available therapeutic measures have failed.

(b) Administration and cardiac monitoring

For the patient who has had an overdose of an anticholinergic drug, or for the rare patient who has had an overdose of a tricyclic antidepressant that has caused life-threatening anticholinergic symptoms:

- Administer 2 mg of physostigmine IM or IV, delivered no faster than 1 mg/min. Repeat every 15-30 minutes for 3-4 doses.
- Physostigmine may cause bradycardia and, in patients who have taken overdoses of tricyclic antidepressants, other cardiac abnormalities. It should be administered in conjunction with cardiac monitoring and constant observation.

7. Seizures

For those patients who develop seizures secondary to drug overdose, one of the following treatments may be indicated:

(a) Diazepam

- Administer diazepam, titrating the dose up to 5 to 10 mg IV over 2-5 minutes.
- Repeat in 5-mg increments every 5-15 minutes until the seizures abate.
- Respiratory depression or hypotension is an indication to stop administration of the drug.

(b) Other agents

- Consider using anesthesia if the patient experiences continued seizures, as often occurs with cocaine overdoses and massive overdoses of amphetamines; consult with an anesthesiologist in order to obtain an appropriate protocol.

8. Hypertension

The management of hypertension produced by cocaine, amphetamines, or phencyclidine (PCP) is controversial. Some experts recommend treating hypertension prophylactically, while others do not treat patients unless hypertension becomes life-threatening. Observation may suffice in patients with mild hypertension, while antihypertensive agents may be necessary when the hypertension is moderate or severe.

(a) Mild hypertension

- Mild hypertension produced by amphetamines, cocaine, or PCP may be managed for frequent blood pressure monitoring and careful observation of the patient's vital signs and neurologic symptoms.
- Alternatively, treat with propranolol HCl (Inderal), up to 40 mg po. If the clinical condition warrants it, repeat in doses of 20-40 mg q4-6h, as needed to bring the blood pressure under control.

(b) Moderate and severe hypertension

Any one of several antihypertensives can be used to treat moderate or severe hypertension:

- A 1-mg bolus of propranolol may bring the hypertension under control.

CAUTION: When using propranolol in a cocaine or amphetamine overdose, be prepared to add sodium nitroprusside (Nipride, Nitropress). Hypertension associated with an amphetamine or cocaine overdose is produced by peripheral vasoconstriction and increased cardiac output and heart rate. Propranolol will lower the heart rate but may increase vasoconstriction, causing the blood pressure to go even higher.

- If the hypertension worsens, dissolve 50 mg of sodium nitroprusside in 2 to 3 mL of 5% dextrose in water. Then dilute this in 250 to 1,000 mL of 5% dextrose in water. Do not use any other diluent. Administer the drug initially at 0.5 μg/kg/min by infusion pump or another device that permits precise measurement of the rate of flow. Adjust the rate of infusion upwards if necessary, but do not exceed 10 μg/kg/min.
- If the diastolic pressure rises above 120 mmHg, give hydralazine HCl (Apresoline), 25 mg IM or IV. Monitor the blood pressure and repeat the initial dose every hour if necessary.

9. Arrhythmias

An ECG is particularly important when the drug involved is a cardiotoxic agent such as cocaine, a tricyclic antidepressant, or an amphetamine. These drugs may cause runs of ventricular premature beats, ventricular tachycardia, and sudden cardiac death.

(a) Tricyclic antidepressant overdose

Ventricular arrhythmias in this setting impose grave risk, as does hypotension (also see **2,** page 248).

- Insert a Swan-Ganz catheter.
- Administer a bolus of sodium bicarbonate, 0.5-2.0 mEq/kg. If the bolus results in correction of the arrhythmia, add 2 ampules of sodium bicarbonate, each containing 44.6 mEq, to 1 L of 5% dextrose in water. Administer this solution by IV drip; run it in slowly to maintain an arterial blood pH of 7.5.
- If sodium bicarbonate fails to resolve the ventricular arrhythmias, administer phenytoin sodium (Dilantin) IV, 100 mg over three minutes.
- If phenytoin sodium fails, administer physostigmine*, 2 mg IV, delivering not more than 1 mg/min. Use this drug with extreme caution: Physostigmine itself can cause bradycardia and cardiac abnormalities in patients who have taken tricyclic antidepressants and is the drug of last resort in this setting.

(b) Cocaine overdose

Arrhythmias occur frequently in patients who have sustained cocaine overdoses. The agent of choice in this situation is IV propranolol HCl because it corrects ventricular arrhythmias and ventricular tachycardia. Administer IV propranolol with cardiac and blood pressure monitoring.

- Administer a 1-mg bolus of propranolol IV if the patient develops runs of ventricular tachycardia or ventricular fibrillation. Repeat the bolus every minute if necessary for a maximum of five doses.**
- If the patient becomes hypertensive while taking propranolol, add sodium nitroprusside (see **8b,** page 251).
- Lidocaine HCl (Xylocaine) and dopamine should be used cautiously in cocaine overdose.

FURTHER EVALUATION

1. Associated Conditions

Conditions common in intravenous drug users include:

- Acquired immunodeficiency syndrome
- Aspiration pneumonia
- Heart valve infections
- Hepatitis
- Phlebitis
- Pneumococcal pneumonia
- Pulmonary edema
- Pulmonary and renal emboli
- Subacute bacterial endocarditis

2. Criteria for Hospitalization

Following emergency care for drug overdose, the decision to release the patient or admit him or her to the hospital is generally based on the need for continued observation and treatment and the facilities in the ED for long-term observation.

(a) Releasing the patient from the emergency department

- Release is generally appropriate after observation if:
   The patient never lost consciousness.
   His condition is stable.

---

*This is not an FDA-recognized indication for physostigmine salicylate.

**This exceeds the manufacturer's recommended dosage for propranolol HCl.

The agent is known.

The agent is nonlethal and has no major systemic toxicity.

The patient may need psychiatric assistance, however.

CAUTION: The victim of a methadone HCl (Dolophine) overdose must be admitted for at least 24 hours.

(b) Special considerations

■ The disposition of patients who have taken overdoses of tricyclic antidepressants is a source of considerable controversy. Some authorities maintain that the patient who is completely asymptomatic for six hours after the overdose be discharged. For medicolegal reasons, others admit all such patients regardless of their clinical condition.

■ The patient who has taken a hallucinogen other than phencyclidine may be observed in the ED, reassured, and given 5 to 10 mg of diazepam (Valium). This dose of diazepam may be repeated three or four times over the next 24 hours if the patient is still agitated or anxious. Higher doses may be indicated. The patient may be discharged if no other symptoms appear during this period, and if psychiatric admission is not warranted.

(c) Admitting the patient for hospitalization

■ Criteria for admission to the intensive care unit include:

The need for respiratory or cardiovascular support or the presence of serious complications.

Any symptoms associated with an overdose of a tricyclic antidepressant, even if they appear mild in the first six hours after the drug was taken.

Seizures or arrhythmias.

■ Criteria for general hospital admission include:

Overdose of an agent with potentially lethal effects, complications, or delayed effects. Acetaminophen is an example of the latter; associated liver damage may not be evident for three days. If such damage becomes evident, keep the patient in the hospital until liver function tests return to normal, which may take several weeks.

Unconsciousness at any time in the aftermath of a drug overdose; the patient needs hospitalization for 24 hours after becoming asymptomatic.

Overdose of an unknown drug.

An attempted suicide.

FURTHER MANAGEMENT

1. Methadone HCl Overdose

After admitting the patient to the hospital, start a naloxone HCl (Narcan) drip of a 4 mg/L solution at a rate of 75 to 100 mL/h. Continue the naloxone drip for 24-48 hours or until the effects of the methadone have worn off. The administration of naloxone should not be considered a substitute for careful monitoring of the patient.

2. Acetaminophen Overdose

(a) Overview

■ The potentially significant hepatic toxicity of an acetaminophen overdose may not be apparent for up to three days.

■ Acetylcysteine (Mucomyst) inhibits liver damage, even when given several hours after the overdose.

■ Baseline liver function tests become a helpful guide as the patient's condition evolves.

(b) Assessment

■ Use the Rumack-Matthew nomogram to determine the potential lethality of an acetominophen overdose and the need for administering acetylcysteine.

■ If you are unsure precisely how long ago

the overdose occurred, err on the side of exaggerating the time lapse when you read the nomogram. For instance, if the overdose might have taken place anytime in the last four to eight hours, use eight hours. This makes the red flag value 100 µg/mL rather than 200 µg/mL and ensures conservative treatment.

(c) Acetylcysteine

- Acetylcysteine should be started within 16-24 hours after the overdose.
- Even if only one plasma reading indicated toxicity, the patient must complete the course of acetylcysteine therapy.
- Have the antidote mixed with juice or a soft drink to make it more palatable.
- The initial dose is 140 mg/kg.
- Follow up with 70 mg/kg q4h for a total of 17 doses.

3. Salicylate Overdose

As a preliminary step in follow-up care for the patient with salicylate intoxication, obtain arterial blood gas readings and an evaluation of blood salicylate level, blood sugar, electrolytes, and BUN.

(a) Assessment

- Use a nomogram to interpret the serum salicylate level.
- Serum levels of >120 mg/dL may be fatal unless treated immediately and appropriately.
- Consultation with a nephrologist is usually warranted for any patient whose salicylate level is greater than 80 mg/dL.
- The serum salicylate level may not always correspond to the clinical condition, which may warrant more aggressive therapy than the blood level suggests.

(b) Vitamin K

For severe salicylate poisoning administer a single 25-mg dose of vitamin K_1 (AquaMEPHYTON, Konakion); do not give more than 1 mg/min. If the prothrombin time has not decreased within 6-8 hours, give the same dose again.

(c) Forced alkaline diuresis

Forced alkaline diuresis with sodium bicarbonate may be indicated, especially in the face of metabolic acidosis. This procedure is contraindicated in the elderly. Pulmonary edema is a real danger during the diuresis; consultation with a cardiologist is advised.*

- Insert a Swan-Ganz catheter in order to facilitate immediate treatment if pulmonary edema develops.
- Prepare an IV solution composed of 1 L of 5% dextrose in water, 1 L of one-half normal saline, 3 g of potassium chloride, and 75 mL of 8% sodium bicarbonate solution.**
- Administer this solution to the patient at a rate of 2 L/h for three hours.
- Determine the serum salicylate level q4-6h to confirm that it is falling towards the nontoxic range. Urinary pH should be 7 or greater. Evaluate the patient's overall clinical condition in order to confirm the abatement of symptoms.

(d) Hemodialysis

Hemodialysis or peritoneal dialysis is indicated for:

- The elderly patient who develops metabolic acidosis as a consequence of severe salicylate poisoning.
- The patient who develops pulmonary edema during forced alkaline diuresis.
- The patient whose salicylate level does not fall within 4-6 hours, or is greater than 100 mg/dL.

---

*See "Cardiogenic pulmonary edema," pages 255–57.
**Some authorities recommend varying the composition of the solution based on the needs of the individual patient, as determined by monitoring of arterial blood gases, electrolytes, and urine output.

- The patient whose clinical condition worsens. ∎

Emergency Handbook 2: Cardiology

INITIAL ASSESSMENT

1. Presentation

A presumptive diagnosis of acute pulomonary edema can usually be made from the patient's appearance and the circumstances of presentation.

(a) Overview

- Unless the patient has inhaled toxic fumes or developed some other problem that *clearly* points to damage to the alveolocapillary membrane, suspect that the pulmonary edema is cardiogenic until proved otherwise. Although you may have to consider adult respiratory distress syndrome (ARDS) and other causes after the patient is stabilized, they are far less common than pulmonary edema of cardiac origin.
- Since cardiogenic pulmonary edema and chronic obstructive pulmonary disease (COPD) tend to occur in the same patient population, suspect that COPD may be an underlying problem.
- The patient who develops acute pulmonary edema after hospital admission for trauma or for another noncardiac problem probably has ARDS.*

---

*This article will focus on evaluation and management of the patient who presents at the hospital or physician's office with acute respiratory distress. It will not attempt to cover evaluation and management of the patient who develops acute respiratory distress as an inpatient or whose presenting history indicates that acute respiratory distress is a result of damage to the alveolocapillary membrane.

(b) Immediately recognizable symptoms and signs

- Severe dyspnea.
- Production of frothy sputum.
- Extensive diaphoresis.
- Terrified appearance.
- Extreme restlessness.
- Preference for sitting bolt upright.

The last three symptoms and signs will be absent if the patient is in cardiogenic shock.

Your experience in treating patients with various types of dyspnea helps in making the differential diagnosis: The degree of desperation associated with dyspnea due to pneumonia or bronchitis would usually rank 5 or 6 on a scale of 1 to 10 while that due to acute pulmonary edema would usually rate a 9 or 10.

2. History

The patient's condition will limit history taking to questions with brief replies. Direct as many of your questions as possible to the patient's spouse or to another person who brought the patient in.

(a) Cardiovascular clues

- A positive history in this area is highly likely. Ask quickly about heart attacks, chest discomfort, shortness of breath, hypertension, and palpitations. Also ask about increasing peripheral edema and difficulty sleeping flat.
- If the cardiovascular history is negative, wait for the results of an ECG before ruling out cardiogenic pulmonary edema.

(b) Pulmonary clues

- Determine whether the patient has a history of asthma or COPD; ask about the use of oxygen at home.
- Although differentiating between pulmonary embolus and acute myocardial infarction

Equipment

Emergency Department
Nondrug
Arterial blood gas analyzer
Arterial line
Central venous pressure cannula
Continuous positive airway pressure (CPAP) equipment
Defibrillator
ECG machine
ECG monitor
Foley catheter
Infusion pump
IV lines and fluids
Mechanical ventilator
Nasal cannula
Nasotracheal or endotracheal tube
Oxygen and related equipment
Positive end-expiratory pressure (PEEP) equipment
Rotating tourniquet machine (or three blood pressure cuffs or rubber tubing)
Sphygmomanometer
Swan-Ganz catheter
X-ray equipment

Drug
Aminophylline
Bumetanide (Bumex)
Digoxin (Lanoxin)
Dopamine HCl (Dopastat, Intropin)
Ethacrynic acid (Edecrin)
Furosemide (Lasix), IV
Meperidine HCl (Demerol)
Morphine sulfate
Naloxone HCl (Narcan)
Nifedipine (Procardia)
Nitroglycerin — IV, sublingual, and spray (Nitro-Bid IV, Nitrostat IV, Tridil, etc., Nitrostat, Nitrolingual)
Potassium supplements, oral and IV
Sodium nitroprusside (Nipride, Nitropress)

Office
Blood pressure cuffs or rubber-tubing tourniquets (three)
ECG machine
Furosemide (Lasix), injectable and oral
Hydralazine HCl (Apresoline)
Lidocaine HCl (Xylocaine), IM
Morphine sulfate, injectable
Nifedipine (Procardia)
Nitroglycerin, spray and sublingual (Nitrolingual and Nitrostat)

(MI) can be difficult, the differential diagnosis of pulmonary embolus and acute pulmonary edema is usually straightforward. Nevertheless, you may want to inquire whether the patient has recently been in a cast or has been sitting for a prolonged period.

(c) Medication history

Determining which medications the patient takes regularly may help differentiate asthma/COPD from acute pulmonary edema.

3. Physical Examination

A complete physical exam is impractical due to the severity of the patient's condition.

(a) General appearance

- If the patient has acute pulmonary edema, intense vasoconstriction will cause pallor and cyanosis. The skin may be mottled, and the eyes may protrude. Look for signs of heart failure such as bulging neck veins and peripheral edema.

- The patient with underlying COPD is likely to have an enlarged anteroposterior chest diameter (barrel chest) and a tendency to use accessory muscles for breathing. He or she may appear to be breathing in practiced fashion, as though used to being short of breath: The patient may purse the lips and try to breathe slowly.

- Rarely, a patient may present in the emergency department (ED) or in your office with acute pulmonary edema due to viral pneumonia or some other septic process. If so he may look toxic and have a fever.

- If diffuse intravascular coagulation is the cause of ARDS, you'll probably find ecchymoses and other evidence of coagulopathy.

(b) Auscultation

- Breathing in acute pulmonary edema is rapid, usually 30-50 breaths/min, and labored.
- A classic sign is bubbling rales to the

Quick Guide to Blood Gas Values in Acute Pulmonary Edema

This table may be useful as a rough guide to the severity of acute pulmonary edema. It is not meant to be used out of context of the patient's clinical condition, nor is it intended to be a primer in the interpretation of blood gases.

Condition	P_{O_2} (mmHg)	P_{CO_2} (mmHg)	pH	HCO_3- (mEq/L)	Comment
Normal	70–100	35–42	7.35–7.45	24–26	
Respiratory alkalosis	<70	20–30	>7.45	15–20	An early response to acute pulmonary edema. Low P_{CO_2} indicates hyperventilation.
Respiratory acidosis	<70	>45	<7.35	>27 or normal	A later response $P_{CO_2} > 45$ suggests lungs are stiff and respiratory muscles fatigued. Normal pH suggests severe underlying COPD.
Combined metabolic and respiratory acidosis	<50	>60	<7.25	<15	Potentially a preterminal phase as suggested by $P_{CO_2} > 50$.

apices, usually posteriorly but possibly anteriorly as well.

■ Wheezing and expiratory prolongation with no bubbling rales suggest an acute asthma attack. A patient with cardiogenic pulmonary edema may sometimes wheeze, however, not because of COPD but possibly in response to localized hypoxemia.

(c) Blood pressure

Blood pressure measurements are helpful in management but not in making the differential diagnosis of acute respiratory distress. Typically, the patient with acute pulmonary edema or another form of acute respiratory distress has markedly elevated blood pressure, in the range of 160-200 mmHg systolic and 90-100 mmHg diastolic. In the late stage of acute respiratory distress, cardiogenic shock may cause hypotension.

(d) Other findings

Percussion usually reveals no abnormalities in acute pulmonary edema or other forms of acute respiratory distress. If acute pulmonary edema is caused by hemorrhagic pancreatitis, the patient exhibits signs of acute abdomen; an inability to lie flat, however, normally precludes an adequate exam of the abdomen.

4. Laboratory Tests

Administering oxygen and starting IV morphine sulfate and furosemide (Lasix) take precedence over ordering laboratory tests when auscultatory and other clinical findings strongly suggest acute pulmonary edema (see "Initial Treatment," **1a, 1b, 1c,** and **1d,** pages 258–59). Once you've taken those steps, obtain a baseline ECG and a portable chest X-ray, and draw an arterial blood sample. Initiate continuous ECG monitoring as soon as feasible.

(a) Portable chest X-ray

Have the patient in a sitting position for the chest X-ray.

■ The pathognomonic radiographic sign of acute pulmonary edema is diffuse bilateral haziness of the lungs.

■ Prominent upper pulmonary vessels, an

early sign of left ventricular failure, may also appear on the chest X-ray in acute pulmonary edema.

- Fluffy, perihilar infiltrates may be present in the early stages of acute pulmonary edema as the alveolar spaces just begin to fill.
- Cardiogenic pulmonary edema is almost always associated with cardiac enlargement; in noncardiogenic pulmonary edema, the heart is usually normal in size.

EXCEPTION: If acute pulmonary edema is due to an acute MI, the heart may be normal in size, but the ECG will probably show evidence of the MI.

- Radiographic evidence of COPD includes a flat diaphragm and bilaterally hyperaerated lung fields. If COPD is the cause of acute respiratory distress, the vascular changes of acute pulmonary edema may be absent. In addition, you may identify an infiltrate of pneumonia that provoked the attack.

(b) Arterial blood gases

Although blood gas values are not helpful for diagnosing acute pulmonary edema, they provide insight into the severity of the problem and are useful for management (see "Quick guide to blood gas values in acute pulmonary edema," page 257).

- If COPD is minimal or absent, initial blood gas determinations will probably reveal acute respiratory alkalosis—perhaps a P_{O_2} of 50 mmHg, P_{CO_2} of 20 to 30 mmHg, and pH of 7.5. If CO_2 is retained, the patient may develop respiratory acidosis—perhaps a P_{O_2} of 50 mmHg, P_{CO_2} >45 mmHg, and pH of 7.2; eventually metabolic acidosis may occur, which may be confirmed by a decrease in measured CO_2 on an SMA-6.
- If the patient has severe COPD, his system has adjusted to excess CO_2. Initial blood gas determinations will probably reveal compensated respiratory acidosis—for instance, a P_{O_2} of 50 mmHg, P_{CO_2} of 45 mmHg, and a normal pH.

(c) Other studies

Specimens for CBC, SMA-6, blood sugar, cardiac enzymes, urinalysis, and other studies can be obtained at any time, but obtaining them should not delay immediate treatment.

INITIAL TREATMENT

The goal of initial treatment is to stabilize the patient and gain time to perform a more thorough workup. Therefore, you may need to begin treatment for presumed cardiogenic pulmonary edema even if you're not sure of the etiology. Or you may have to treat in favor of heart failure even though some measures may exacerbate COPD.

1. In the ED

(a) Delivering oxygen

- Administer oxygen, 5 to 10 L/min by nasal cannula; the patient is unlikely to tolerate a mask. With known COPD, give 4-5 L/min and follow closely for slower respiration, sleepiness, and increasing P_{CO_2}.
- When clinical evidence and blood gases suggest improved condition and the patient is sufficiently sedated, consider initiating continuous positive airway pressure (CPAP) without intubation to further improve oxygenation. Since CPAP requires the use of a tight-fitting mask, a nurse must monitor the patient closely to prevent him or her from pulling it off.

(b) Inserting an IV line

Starting an IV line and keeping one in place may be difficult if the patient is particularly restless but is necessary to administer IV morphine sulfate. Without IV morphine your ability to obtain blood pressure readings, an ECG, and chest X-ray may be seriously hampered.

(c) Giving morphine sulfate

Use morphine sulfate to provide mild vasodilation and to allay anxiety. Start with 4 mg IV and give additional 2-4 mg doses, q5min, to a total of 12-16 mg or until the patient's restlessness decreases.

CAUTION: Give morphine or other narcotics with extreme care if the patient has COPD. Use 2-4 mg doses of morphine and check the blood pressure 2-5 minutes after each dose. If morphine depresses ventilation, give naloxone HCl (Narcan), 0.1-0.4 mg IV q5min until respiratory depression disappears. Repeat if the problem recurs.

■ Allergy to morphine is exceedingly rare. Adverse reactions are usually due to excessive dosing or use when the drug is contraindicated, as in acute bronchial asthma. If the patient or a family member reports an allergy to the drug, give meperidine HCl (Demrerol), 25 mg IV, instead.* Repeat if needed.

(d) Effecting diuresis

■ Give furosemide (Lasix), 40 mg IV over 1-2 minutes; if the patient already takes furosemide, consider doubling the usual dose for IV administration.

■ Insert a Foley catheter to verify diuretic response, and check the blood pressure 15 minutes after giving the initial dose. Expect furosemide to cause tremendous diuresis— approximately 100-200 mL of urine every 10 minutes. As diuresis occurs, the patient should begin to breathe less rapidly, struggle less, and say he's feeling better.

■ If the response is inadequate, double the dose q20-30 min until urine output improves or the dose is 200-400 mg.

■ If the response is still not adequate, add bumetanide (Bumex), 0.5-1.0 mg IV over 1-2 minutes or ethacrynic acid (Edecrin), 5-10 mg IV.

■ When the blood pressure is ≥100 mmHg

―――――――――
*This is not an FDA-recognized indication for meperidine HCl.

systolic, administering IV dopamine HCl (Dopastat, Intropin), 5-10 µg/kg/min, may be resorted to as an extreme measure that induces diuresis by dilating the renal arterioles.*

(e) Controlling hypertension

■ Before the IV line is started, give one or two 0.4-mg tablets of sublingual nitroglycerin (Nitrostat) or 1–2 doses of nitroglycerin spray (Nitrolingual). Alternatively, use a hypodermic needle to punch holes in a 10-mg nifedipine (Procardia) capsule and administer sublingually.**

■ If the blood pressure is not within normal range by the time an IV line is started, give sodium nitroprusside (Nipride, Nitropress), 0.5-10.0 µg/kg/min IV, using an infusion pump or another metered device to control the rate of flow. IV nitroglycerin (Nitro-Bid IV, Nitrostat IV, Tridil, etc.), 5-10 µg/min, is an alternative when the patient has chest pain or when the maximal dosage of nitroprusside is ineffective.

CAUTION: This dosage assumes that nonabsorbent IV tubing is used. If polyvinyl chloride tubing is used, a great amount of nitroglycerin will be absorbed, and a starting dosage of 25 µg/min may be needed.

■ Whatever drug you use, titrate until the blood pressure is in normal range. Since time is too tight in the first 5-10 minutes for inserting a Swan-Ganz catheter or starting an arterial line, have a nurse check the blood pressure q5min. If the systolic pressure falls below 90–100 mmHg, slow or stop the infusion.

(f) Controlling hypotension

■ Give dopamine, 2-5 µg/kg/min by an infusion pump or another metered device to control the rate of flow. Titrate to a maximum of 10-30 µg/kg/min until the systolic blood pressure exceeds 100 mmHg. Continue for 1-2 hours. Avoid nitroglycerin, rotating tourni-

―――――――――
*This is not an FDA-recognized indication for dopamine HCl.
**This is not an FDA-recognized indication for nifedipine.

quets, phlebotomy, and other measures that would exacerbate the hypotension.

NOTE: Dopamine may not be necessary if the blood pressure is 85-90 mmHg, the patient is stable and alert, urine output is satisfactory, and acute MI is a distinct possibility.

(g) Controlling atrial fibrillation

If atrial fibrillation is present, consider cardioverting at 50 to 100 J delivered energy. As a secondary measure, consider giving digoxin (Lanoxin).

- Although digoxin is slightly slower in onset of action than short-acting digitalis preparations, its availability in both IV and oral forms allows an easier transition to the oral form in the following days.
- If the patient has been or may be taking a digitalis preparation, administer 0.10-0.25 mg IV over two minutes. If you're certain the patient is not taking digitalis, administer 0.50-0.75 mg IV over two minutes.
- Repeat the drug in 30-60 minutes if necessary.

Digoxin is preferred over a β-blocker, since β-blockers have a negative inotropic effect. Digoxin is *not* indicated when the patient is not in atrial fibrillation: The drug's positive inotropic effect is rather weak.

EXCEPTION: Digoxin may be worth trying for the desperatelly ill patient once you've given the maximum amount of morphine, gotten the blood pressure under control, and effected rapid diuresis.

(h) Rotating tourniquets

Although once a mainstay of therapy, rotating tourniquets are now indicated only when the patient is so agitated that it's virtually impossible to get an IV started. If the rotating tourniquets can sequester enough blood in the arms and legs, you may gain additional time for injecting the diuretic and having it take effect.

- If a rotating tourniquet machine is unavailable, use three blood pressure cuffs or rubber tubing.
- Inflate the cuffs to a point higher than the venous pressure to trap venous blood in the arms and legs, but lower than the arterial pressure to avoid impeding the flow of arterial blood. A pressure of about 40 mmHg usually suffices.
- Set the machine to rotate inflation of the cuffs every five minutes, or rotate one of the cuffs to another extremity every five minutes.

(i) Assessing the need for phlebotomy

Consider phlebotomy as a last-ditch measure when the patient is still frothing and has severe rales even though you've given maximum medication and applied rotating tourniquets.

- To rid the patient of 200-500 mL of blood in the shortest possible time, use a central venous pressure cannula in a subclavian vein. An advantage of this approach is that the cannula can be used later on to insert a Swan-Ganz catheter.
- Alternatively, insert a 16-gauge needle into a large antecubital or femoral vein.

(j) Assisting bronchodilation

Aminophylline may be indicated when significant wheezing or a prolonged expiration phase accompanies acute pulmonary edema. Some authorities, however, consider bronchodilation indicated only when acute asthma is the cause of respiratory distress.

- Since aminophylline accelerates the heart rate, it is contraindicated if the patient has tachycardia or multifocal ventricular premature beats.
- If you choose to give aminophylline, administer 5-6 mg/kg over 10 minutes, followed by a maintenance dosage of 0.2-0.5 mg/kg/h.

(k) Intubating

Ventilatory assistance will help push fluid out of the lungs, and, by maintaining positive airway pressure, may help prevent further accumulation of fluid in the alveolar spaces.

- *Clinical indications.* The candidate for intubation looks extremely ill, regardless of blood gas values. Breathing has become exceptionally rapid and the patient is hypoventilatory. He is also sluggish, confused, or unresponsive. A patient who needs intubation will usually let you perform the procedure with little resistance; a "chronic lunger" may ask to be intubated.
- *Blood gas indications.* In general, a $CO_2 > 50\text{-}60$ mmHg is an indication to intubate: The patient is then in a preterminal phase, and time is short for allowing medical measures to take effect. Also consider intubation if you can't get the P_{O_2} above 60 mmHg and blood gas levels suggest CO_2 retention.

2. In Your Office or in the Patient's Home

In the rare instances when you see a patient with acute pulmonary edema in your office or at the patient's home, the basic treatment protocol is the same as in the ED, but your options are more limited. While waiting for the paramedics, employ as many of the following substitute measures as necessary:

(a) Control hypertension

- Give sublingual nitroglycerin or nitroglycerin spray, 0.4 mg q5min, to a total of 3-5 doses or for as long as the blood pressure is elevated. Alternatively, use a hypodermic needle to punch holes in a 10-mg nifedipine capsule and administer sublingually.* Avoid use of nitroglycerin ointment (Nitro-Bid, Nitrol,

*This is not an FDA-recognized indication for nifedipine.

Nitrostat, etc.); absorption is unpredictable due to poor peripheral circulation.

- If the blood pressure does not respond and an IV cannot be started soon, try hydralazine HCl (Apresoline), 5-40mg IM.
- *Do not* give sodium nitroprusside except in the hospital, since the careful blood pressure monitoring needed is impractical in other settings. (For other cautions, see "Don'ts in acute pulmonary edema," page 262.)

(b) Take an electrocardiogram

If a monitor is unavailable, follow the pulse and obtain an ECG rhythm strip if you feel an irregularity.

(c) Initiate diuresis

Give furosemide, 40 mg IV or IM, with a needle and syringe if an IV line is unavailable. An oral dose of 40-80 mg may not work but could be worth trying.

(d) Apply rotating tourniquets

Use rubber tubing or belts if an insufficient number of blood pressure cuffs are available (see **1h,** page 260).

(e) Evaluate vasodilation/sedation

In general, avoid using subcutaneous or IM morphine, since poor peripheral circulation makes absorption unpredictable. Morphine may be indicated, however, for the patient who is highly agitated and won't arrive at a hospital for some time: Give 4-10 mg SC or IM.

(f) Manage arrhythmia

If the patient won't be at the hospital within a half hour or if you detect multifocal premature ventricular beats or ventricular tachycardia, consider giving 10% lidocaine HCl (Xylocaine), 200-300 mg IM.

Don'ts in Acute Pulmonary Edema

1. Don't inadvertently overload the patient with fluid. Prepare IV agents in 2:1 or 4:1 concentrations to limit fluid intake.

2. Don't use topical, subcutaneous (SC), or IM preparations because the circulation is so poor and vasoconstriction so intense that these agents won't work quickly enough. In addition, IM injections will confuse interpretation of creatine kinase (CK) unless you have access to CK isoenzymes on a stat basis.
EXCEPTION: IM hydralazine HCl (Apresoline), lidocaine HCl (Xylocaine), or SC or IM morphine sulfate may be indicated in the office or home when arrival at a hospital is anticipated to be 30 minutes or more away.

3. Don't raise the cuff pressure above the level of arterial pressure when using rotating tourniquets, since this will impede the flow of arterial blood to the arms and legs and increase afterload.

4. Don't give a β-blocker for atrial fibrillation because of negative inotropic effects.

5. Don't use digoxin (Lanoxin) in acute pulmonary edema except when indicated for atrial fibrillation. The drug's positive inotropic effect is rather weak.

6. Don't routinely use echocardiography in the early stages. The procedure requires the patient's cooperation, and a fluid-filled lung is a significant barrier to sound waves.

7. Don't use the central venous pressure (CVP) as a guide to therapy. Unless the CVP is quite low, suggesting severe hypovolemia or shock, interpretation can be difficult: Changes in the superior vena cava may not reflect changes in the left side of the heart.

8. Don't leave the Swan-Ganz catheter in the wedge position; a significant pulmonary infarct may result.

FURTHER EVALUATION

1. Clinical Status

Since the metabolic and hemodynamic changes that occur in acute pulomarny edema may resolve somewhat slowly, clinical factors are generally more reliable than laboratory values in assessing the patient's response.

(a) Appearance/symptomatology

The responsive patient feels and looks better within 10-60 minutes after the initiation of therapy. Ideally, the patient is alert, cooperative, and able to give a more detailed history. He or she also appears warm and adequately perfused. Fright and diaphoresis have diminished.

(b) Physical examination

- Signs of good response within the first 10-60 minutes of therapy include a stable blood pressure within normal range and a decreased heart rate of about 100-110 beats/min. Respiration is less labored, although rales may not clear for some time.

- Once you've achieved stabilization, the patient's condition is likely to hold, at least for the short term. Transfer to an intensive care or coronary care unit is now indicated.

- A third heart sound (S_3) is likely in acute cardiogenic pulmonary edema and may be discernible 2-3 hours after stabilization. If respiratory distress is primarily due to COPD, S_3 is absent and rales are minimal.

- Failure to respond to initial therapy may mean that the cause of the patient's acute pulmonary edema is noncardiogenic (see "Clues to the Cause," page 263).

(c) Routine follow-up

- Check the blood pressure every 15-30 minutes until stable. If the patient is receiving sodium nitroprusside (Nipride, Nitropress), check the blood pressure every five minutes until an arterial line is established.
- Follow blood gases and electrolytes as the clinical situation dictates.
- Order an ECG later in the day and 2-3 more during the course of hospitalization to assess the possibility of acute MI or other cardiac disease.
- Follow the MB fraction of creatine kinase every 6 hours for approximately 36 hours or until acute MI is documented.
- To ascertain whether the lungs are clearing, order 1-2 additional chest X-rays during the course of hospitalization.

2. Swan-Ganz Catheterization

(a) Indications

If the patient responded well to initial treatment, a Swan-Ganz catheter can be helpful but is not essential. On the other hand, the catheter may be crucial if:

- Stabilization was difficult to achieve, or
- The patient is doing poorly after an hour of emergency treatment, or
- A massive MI is the probable cause of the patient's acute pulmonary edema.

The Swan-Ganz catheter also provides useful guidance for fluid replacement when an underlying condition, such as bleeding ulcer, has caused hypovolemia.

(b) Diagnostic interpretation

- Swan-Ganz data usually settle any remaining question about a cardiac cause: In cardiogenic pulmonary edema, the pulmonary capillary wedge pressure is high (>20 mmHg); in noncardiogenic pulmonary edema, the wedge pressure is usually normal or low (4-12 mmHg or less).
- If a pulmonary embolus is present, the pulmonary artery end-diastolic pressure (PAEDP) is high (>25 mmHg), and the wedge pressure is low. Order a lung scan or pulmonary angiogram.
- With cardiac tamponade, the right- and left-side filling pressures are the same. Order two-dimensional echocardiography.
- Rarely, a tall *v* wave may be present, which suggests that the cause is acute mitral regurgitation. Don't rely on Swan-Ganz pressure readings as a guide to fluid administration when a *v* wave is present, since they will be artifically elevated. Instead, rely on urine output, blood pressure, heart rate, arterial blood gas values, and the severity of rales.

(c) Management information

- PAEDP below 15 mmHg often signals dehydration and the need to reduce the diuretic or morphine sulfate dosage or adjust the ventilator pressure.
- PAEDP above 25 mmHg usually prompts providing additional diuresis in response to the elevation in pulmonary venous pressure.
- A PAEDP of 18-24 mmHg is optional, but readings of 15-25 mmHg probably require no hemodynamic adjustments.

3. Clues to the Cause

(a) Cardiogenic

When evidence points to a cardiogenic cause of acute pulmonary edema, consider the following specific problems:

- An acute MI can provoke or be the sequela of acute pulmonary edema.
- Of the arrhythmias, ventricular techycardia is the most likely to be associated with acute pulmonary edema. Significant ventricular ectopy following stabilization is the tip-off.
- Cardiomyopathy may be part of the clinical picture.
- Chronic congestive heart failure with fluid

retention is often associated with an episode of acute pulmonary edema.

■ In the hypertensive patient, acute pulmonary edema may have occurred as a result of fluid or sodium overload.

■ Valvular disease may be the underlying problem. Consider ordering echocardiography to assess ventricular performance and to detect possible valvular disease, such as aortic stenosis or mitral stenosis. Both may be difficult to hear with a stethoscope in the context of acute pulmonary edema.

As a general measure, radionuclide ventriculography or two-dimensional echocardiography will reveal the status of the left ventricle; consult with a cardiologist as necessary.

(b) Noncardiogenic

■ Consider adult respiratory distress syndrome when further evaluation yields no evidence of a cardiac problem and the patient hasn't responded to initial treatment according to your expectation for pulmonary edema of cardiac origin—for instance, if diuresis and nitrates didn't seem to help.

■ Reevaluate the possibility of aspiration of gastric contents, disseminated intravascular coagulation, pancreatitis, pneumonia, pulmonary embolus, and other causes. Swan-Ganz data should be helpful in this task.

FURTHER TREATMENT

In addition to treating the underlying cause of pulmonary edema as appropriate, consider the following general measures:

1. Oxygenation

If mechanical ventilation has not been effective against hypoxemia, or if toxic levels of oxygen may be necessary for a prolonged time, consider instituting positive end-expiratory pressure (PEEP) to stop fluid inflow. Start at 5 cm H_2O and adjust according to the level of arterial oxygen.

■ Since PEEP can increase the total level of fluid in the lungs and reduce cardiac output, don't leave the patient on it for more than 12-24 hours; 4-6 hours is preferable.

■ Extubate and wean the patient from oxygen as soon as feasible.

2. β-Blocker Withdrawal

Discontinue any β-blocker the patient may have been taking.

■ If pulmonary edema clears readily, discontinue the drug abruptly or wean the patient by halving the dose at each dosing interval.

■ If the patient remains in pulmonary edema, withdraw the drug abruptly. Although abrupt withdrawal might precipitate an MI, that possibility does not significantly increase the risk the patient already has for such an event. Use a nitrate or calcium channel blocker if angina subsequently develops.

3. Hypokalemia

Consider treating hypokalemia empirically if you know the patient has a low serum potassium level and he or she is acidotic, has an irritable heart, and is receiving a potent diuretic.

■ Give potassium by mouth at a concentration of 20-40 mEq/L; the amount may depend on the palatability of the preparation.

■ The IV route is preferable when the patient has a malignant arrhythmia, he has been taking digitalis, and you suspect a severely depressed serum potassium level. Since the patient is probably acidotic and infusion of potassium could lead to asystole, give no more than 10-15 mEq/L/h and follow the ECG closely during the infusion.

■ Adjust therapy as appropriate when exact serum levels of potassium become available. ■